Evolution and Institutions

To Paul Dale Bush, Geoffrey Harcourt, Warren Samuels and Marc Tool –
and to the memory of Edith Penrose

Evolution and Institutions

On Evolutionary Economics and the Evolution of Economics

Geoffrey M. Hodgson

Research Professor at the University of Hertfordshire Business School

formerly

Reader in Institutional and Evolutionary Economics, University of Cambridge

Edward Elgar

Cheltenham, UK • Northampton, MA, USA

Published by
Edward Elgar Publishing Limited
Glensanda House
Montpellier Parade
Cheltenham
Glos GL50 1UA
UK

Edward Elgar Publishing, Inc.
136 West Street
Suite 202
Northampton
Massachusetts 01060
USA

Paperback edition 2000
Paperback edition reprinted 2001

A catalogue record for this book
is available from the British Library

Library of Congress Cataloguing in Publication Data
Hodgson, Geoffrey Martin, 1946–
    Evolution and institutions : on evolutionary economics and the
evolution of economics / Geoffrey M. Hodgson
    Revised, updated, and synthesized essays originally drafted
between 1991–1995.
    Includes bibliographical references and index.
    1. Evolutionary economics.   I. Title.
HB97.3.H633   1999
330.1—dc21   98–50848
                                                               CIP

ISBN 1 85898 813 6 (cased)
       1 85898 824 1 (paperback)

Printed and bound in Great Britain by MPG Books Ltd, Bodmin, Cornwall

Contents

Figures

Figures

Preface and Acknowledgements

This book is about the future of economics as a viable discipline. It synthesizes several essays, all originally drafted in the years 1991–95, around this broad theme. The essays have all been updated and revised, some extensively. This work follows an earlier collection of articles by the author in *After Marx and Sraffa* (1991). However, it is not essentially a second instalment of collected works. An aim has been to recast the essays so that they form a relatively integrated narrative and reveal a common set of motifs. By keeping within the early 1990s time frame, and excluding some other publications in that period, it has been possible to give the volume some degree of unity and cohesion.

My own views are continuously evolving. Accordingly some changes have been made, as well as elaborations and corrections, to the works reprinted here. These alterations are too numerous to mention, but generally they concern detail rather than overall thrust.

A prominent theme in these essays is the evolution of what is now often described as 'evolutionary economics'. A growing body of innovative thinking in economics is now grouped around the 'evolutionary' label. Links are also made here between the evolutionary themes in the 'old' institutionalism of Thorstein Veblen and John Commons, on the one hand, and the modern evolutionary economics of Richard Nelson and Sidney Winter, on the other.

The title and content of this present book also in part reflect my long-standing belief that, while ideas are extremely important, ideas alone do not change the world. Some of the historical and case studies included here support this point. If social scientists are to engage with society then there must be some engineering of (learning and evolving) institutions as well as the manufacturing of ideas.

This book does not represent all the themes that have been present in my research output in the 1990s. Another volume, *Economics and Evolution,* appeared in 1993. In addition I have published elsewhere on the existence and analysis of varieties of capitalism, leading to a consideration of possible scenarios for a post-capitalist future (Hodgson, 1996a, 1998e). Other studies have been concerned with the constructive development of institutionalist theory (Hodgson, 1997d, 1998b).

I wish to thank, among others, Esben Sloth Andersen, Philip Arestis, Stephen Batstone, Stephan Boehm, Royall Brandis, Guido Bünstorf, Dale Bush, Ronald Coase, Richard H. Day, Michael Dietrich, Kurt Dopfer, Nicolai Foss, John Foster, Frederick Fourie, Elizabeth Garnsey, Horst Hanusch, Geoff Harcourt, Alan Hughes, Bruna Ingrao, Neil Kay, Christian Knudsen, John Laurent, Tony Lawson, Uskali Mäki, Scott Masten, Anne Mayhew, Stanley Metcalfe, Jonathan Michie, Philip Mirowski, Joel Mokyr, Mario Morroni, Richard Nelson, John Nightingale, Bart Nooteboom, George Norman, Joanne Oxley, Pavel Pelikan, Edith Penrose, Christos Pitelis, Jochen Runde, Malcolm Rutherford, Warren Samuels, Malcolm Sawyer, Ernesto Screpanti, Colin Shaper, Gerry Silverberg, Peter Skott, Ian Steedman, Roger Tarling, Paul Twomey, Andrew Tylecote, Robert Wade, Roy Weintraub, Karel van Wolferen, Yuval Yonay and several anonymous referees for helpful discussions or comments.

The following publishers and journals are thanked for permission to use material from previously published articles: the Association for Evolutionary Economics (publisher of the *Journal of Economic Issues*), Basil Blackwell, the *Cambridge Journal of Economics*, Cambridge University Press, Edward Elgar Publishing, the *Journal of Economic Studies*, Kluwer Academic Publishers, and Routledge.

I am also very grateful to Tokyo International University for the support of a research grant and to Musashi University, Tokyo for the use of its facilities for work on the final revisions to the text.

1. Introduction:
The Century of Lost Opportunity

1.1. WHERE IS ECONOMICS GOING?

As its subtitle suggests, this book is not only about developments in evolutionary economics (a type of economic analysis) but also about the evolution of economics itself as a discipline. At the start of the twentieth century, the term 'economics' was just beginning to be widely used in Britain, America and elsewhere. It was gradually replacing the earlier term 'political economy'. For Alfred Marshall in his *Principles* – first published in 1890 – 'economics' seemed to connote 'a science pure and applied, rather than a science and an art' (Marshall, 1949, p. 36). The aim, therefore, was to make the subject more 'scientific'. However, the intention was not to make economics more narrow. On the contrary, Marshall saw economics as a 'broad term', in contrast to the 'narrower' political economy. Marshall was concerned to understand the nature and development of economic transactions, processes and systems. He would not have approved of the subsequent extent of mathematical formalization and narrowing of the subject that has been carried out in the name of 'scientific rigour'. Unlike many 'economic theorists' today, Marshall regarded mathematics as a subsidiary instrument, rather than the essence, of the subject.[1]

---

[1] Marshall proposed the following rules in 1906: '(1) Use mathematics as a shorthand language, rather than as an engine of enquiry. (2) Keep to them till you have done. (3) Translate into English. (4) Then illustrate by examples that are important in real life. (5) Burn the mathematics' (Pigou, 1925, p. 427). If

1

After Marshall's *Principles,* the subsequent hundred years has witnessed a dramatic narrowing and formalization of economics as a discipline. In the last thirty years of the twentieth century, the subject has been overrun by mathematical formalists, seemingly concerned more to convert discourse into equations than to understand or explain real economic structures and processes. Leading journals that have existed for most or all of the century, such as the *American Economic Review,* the *Economic Journal,* the *Journal of Political Economy* and the *Quarterly Journal of Economics,* show this change. Before the 1920s, verbal expositions dominated more than 90 per cent of the published articles. By the early 1990s, over 90 per cent of the articles in the leading and enduring journals were dominated by algebra, calculus and econometrics (Stigler *et al,* 1995, p. 342).

1.1.1. The Limits of Formalism in Economics

Advocates of mathematical formalism in economics will claim that it has brought rigour and precision to the subject. But, as Thomas Mayer (1993) pointed out, there is some kind of a trade-off between truth and precision in economics. Modellers will claim that realism or descriptive accuracy are impossible in a theory, because simplification and abstraction are always necessary. There is more than a grain of truth in this. But it does not justify the abandonment of reality for the model. Instead the theoretical endeavour should lead to a methodological enquiry concerning the criteria by which we assess the theoretical costs and benefits of chosen assumptions and abstractions. As Alfred Whitehead (1926) insisted, it is necessary for a science to be constantly vigilant and critical concerning its own assumptions. This does not mean that we can take a naive empiricist view that theory can be discovered simply from the facts. Neither should it allow us to play the obverse, deductivist game of exploring their logical consequences of assumptions chosen arbitrarily at will, with disregard for the facts.

At least two Nobel Laureates have expressed misgivings about the way in which mathematics now dominates economics. Wassily Leontief (1982, p. 104) questioned the empirical basis of many of the assumptions and mathematical theorems:

---

mainstream economists had followed Marshall's laws then the subject would be better for it.

Page after page of professional economic journals are filled with mathematical formulas leading the reader from sets of more or less plausible but entirely arbitrary assumptions to precisely stated but irrelevant theoretical conclusions.

Milton Friedman (1991, p. 36) argued, with characteristic clarity, that mathematics was of limited use and had often got in the way of the analytical message:

Again and again, I have read articles written primarily in mathematics, in which the central conclusions and reasoning could readily be restated in English, and the mathematics relegated to an appendix, making the article far more accessible to the reader.

We may open the pages of any leading mainstream economics journal to confirm the modern predilection is for the exploration of the characteristics of a model rather than the characteristics of reality. The implicit research procedure is roughly as follows. Because the world is messy and complicated, it is first necessary to develop a simplified model of it. Assume such a model. Then discuss that instead, possibly without any further reference to the real world. If any such reference is required, make some guarded claim of predictive accuracy or explanatory power, typically without reference to rival explanations or models. After all, it is easier to demonstrate mathematical prowess on the basis of assumptions of your own choosing. You can thus gain a reputation as an economist without too much involvement with the messy disorder of reality. The outcome, however, is that this may mean that economics becomes rigorously irrelevant and precisely wrong. Formalism becomes a means to escape from reality rather than a tool to help understand it. This does not mean that mathematics is useless in economics, it simply means that it is not a substitute for understanding how real economies are structured and how they work.

A training in formalistic theory at the expense of real-world investigation deprives economists of the intuitive powers of judgement and understanding of practical problems and complexities. In practice, the inward-looking obsession with technicalities at the expense of the understanding of reality has made economics ill-equipped to deal with major economic transformations and crises, such as the oil price hikes of the 1970s and the dramatic developments in the Eastern Bloc in 1989 and after (Murrell, 1991; Ormerod, 1994). Likewise, mathematical economic models told us little of the East Asian financial crises of the late 1990s.

This is not to say that there is an absence of theoretical advance, of a kind. Some of this formal work is of significant heuristic value. Overall, the rate of theoretical change in economics in the last third of the twentieth century has been considerable. Much has been published, many new theorems proved, countless regressions run. It is not being suggested here that there is no value whatsoever in this mathematical effort. The point being made is that the dominant preoccupations of mainstream university economics departments often do not encompass the pressing issues of the day; they do not generally foster the study of real economic processes, systems and institutions. The intellectual resources have not been wasted in their entirety. But they have been grievously misallocated.

Even when the standard postulates of neoclassical theory are challenged by the modellers – with the occasional formal articles on interdependent preferences, sticky prices, imperfect information, and so on – it is often in the form of an intellectual puzzle rather than an investigation into real phenomena. The theorists

> typically assume the rest of the mathematical apparatus of the neoclassical model: it is as if the established theory challenges the model-builder to a game of 'what can you explain if you accept all of the standard assumptions except one?' . . . But each round of the game begins anew; the results never accumulate into a comprehensive alternative framework. (Ackerman, 1997, p. 656)

The reason for this failure of cumulative advance is that little, if anything, is 'explained' by such formalistic procedures. Reality is not part of the game. All we are asked to consider are propositions in the form: assume X and then Y logically follows. The formalistic defence is that if X were true then clearly the particular syllogism would in fact be relevant to the real world. Perhaps. But the perennially confounding problem is that the model is always a closed system, whereas real economies are open systems, subject to unrelenting exogenous forces or shocks. Economic reality is neither homogeneous nor inert. It is neither mechanistic nor rigorously predictable. As George Shackle (1967, p. 292) expressed it:

> The mathematicians incline to regard economics as the study of mechanism, and with mechanism we are able, sometimes in practice, always in abstract argument, to abolish the distinction between past and future, to design a system where 'ignorance' can no more affect outcomes than it can affect the operation of gravity, to treat all as determinate, fateful and calculable.

In particular, as Shackle (1972, p. 26) insisted elsewhere, mathematical models have difficulty incorporating learning and novelty:

Mathematics can explore the meaning of what is already implicitly stated, of what is already *given*. A mathematical model of society in its economic affairs can treat the members of that society as gaining access steadily or step-by-step to items in a bank of knowledge which the model in some sense specifies . . . Such a model has no place for what we are calling *novelty*.

Models, therefore, are never enough. They can never replace the open-ended character and flexibility of other forms of academic discourse concerning reality (Lawson, 1997). As the philosopher of science Mary Hesse (1955, p. 88) explained:

A formal, symbolic language can never be a substitute for thought, because the application of a symbolic method to any empirical matter presupposes very careful analysis of the subject matter . . . that the essentials have been grasped and properly expressed in language. In other words, it presupposes that the work of clarification has already been done . . . some necessary overtones of meaning are lost when a word is precisely and uniquely symbolized. The vagueness of living languages as compared with mathematics is the price they pay for their applicability to the world and their capacity for growth.

The process of formalization of economics is now so complete that it has also managed to protect itself from any perception or accusation of a disciplinary 'crisis'. Publications with phrases like 'the crisis of economics' in their title or subtitle were prominent in the 1970s and early 1980s.[2] By the 1990s, however, such talk of 'crisis' seemed stale. Today, the majority of economists perceive no crisis in their subject. In response to such downcast statements, they will point to the substantial changes and adaptations in the theoretical corpus of the discipline since the 1960s.

Yet, despite all the changes and new developments, the crisis is still there. General equilibrium theory has run into the sand (Hahn, 1980, 1991). The project to base macroeconomics upon 'sound microfoundations' is in ruins (Kirman, 1989, 1992; Rizvi, 1994a). Chaos theory challenges the possibility of using economic models for predicting the future: non-linear models can display extreme sensitivity to initial conditions, making meaningful prediction impossible (Grandmont, 1986). Game theory faces

---

[2] Robinson's 1971 Richard Ely Lecture, delivered to the American Economic Association, was titled 'The Second Crisis in Economic Theory' (Robinson, 1973b, pp. 92–105). See also, for example, Bell and Kristol (1981). Significantly, Ormerod (1994) chose for the sombre 1990s the perhaps more appropriate title: *The Death of Economics*.

serious questions concerning its meaning and applicability (Rizvi, 1994b). Indeed, game theory has raised more questions – including about the core assumptions of economics – than it has answered (Bicchieri, 1994; Binmore, 1987; 1988; Hargreaves Heap and Varoufakis, 1995; Mirowski, 1986; Sugden, 1991; Varoufakis, 1990).

The gravity of this crisis is not widely appreciated, however. The means by which this crisis has been evaded and concealed has been to turn economics more and more into a branch of applied mathematics, where the aim is not to explain real processes and outcomes in the economic world, but to explore problems of mathematical technique for their own sake. By this gambit, the failure of mainstream economics to provide a coherent theoretical apparatus to explain real phenomena is obscured. Seemingly, explanation no longer is the goal, and reality is no longer the object of reference. Economics thus is becoming a mathematical game to be played in its own terms, with arbitrary rules chosen by the leading players themselves, unconstrained by questions of descriptive adequacy or references to reality.

1.1.2. The Institutionalization of Formalism

The evaluation of discursive and conceptual work in economics requires a broad and deep knowledge of multiple connotations and precedents. It must be carried out by people with a rich, accumulated knowledge of the subject, gained through extensive conversation with other experts, wide reading and broad intellectual exploration. It requires scholars with years of learning and experience. For these reasons the evaluation of non-formalistic research work by academic assessors is often difficult and controversial.

The evaluation of formalistic economics is more straightforward, and requires much less background knowledge. Hence there are functional as well as fashionable reasons for the triumph of formalism. Bruno Frey and Reiner Eichenberger (1993, p. 186) noted that top American economics 'journals take an author's capacity to treat issues in a formalized way within the existing paradigm as a low cost screening procedure that restricts an otherwise potentially huge supply of papers.' If mathematics is seen as a symptom of scientific rigour then a crude measure of scientific content becomes its propensity. Once mathematical formalism becomes established as the standard, its manifest proclivity becomes a ready-made criterion for the evaluation of articles for publication, or the research output of an individual for peer review.

The practice of formalism requires neither knowledge of the history of economics, nor even of the history of real economies. A mathematical article can be assessed largely in its own terms. Hence the history of economic thought, and even economic history, has largely disappeared from the curricula. Formalism can thrive even in a culture of philosophical and methodological naiveté. Crucially, formalism requires only limited mastery of English or any other major language. It will thus be encouraged outside the anglophone world in departments keen to emulate perceived global norms. It grows cumulatively and feeds upon itself, just as bad money drives out the good.

It is difficult to avoid the conclusion that the growth of formalism has diverted attention away from studies giving attention to theoretical context and development and involving conceptual sophistication and insight. Apart perhaps from the mathematics itself, the predilection with formalism may even have stifled originality and conceptual flair. Robert Clower, a former editor of the highly prestigious *American Economic Review*, commented on his time as editor: 'What was remarkable was the absolute dullness, the lack of any kind of new idea, that predominated in the selection of papers' (Colander and Coats, 1989, p. 27).

As mathematics has swamped the curricula in leading universities and graduate schools, student economists have become no longer equipped nor encouraged to analyse real world economies and institutions. Arjo Klamer and David Colander (1990, p. 18) reported a survey which showed that only 3 per cent of graduate students on top US economics programmes perceived 'having a thorough knowledge of the economy' to be 'very important' for professional success, while 65 per cent thought that 'being smart in the sense of problem-solving' is what matters and 57 per cent believed that 'excellence in mathematics' was very important. Frey and Eichenberger (1993, p. 190) likewise remarked that postgraduates are taught 'in a theory-oriented, abstract way and to pay little attention to institutional facts.'

In 1988 the American Economic Association set up a Commission on the state of graduate education in economics in the US. In a crushing indictment, the Commission expressed its fear that 'graduate programs may be turning out a generation with too many *idiot savants* skilled in technique but innocent of real economic issues' (Krueger *et al*, 1991, pp. 1044–5). Alan Blinder (1990, p. 445), a member of the Commission, commented:

> Both students and faculty find economics obsessed with technique over substance . . . the many macro and micro theory exams the Commission examined . . . tested mathematical puzzle-solving ability, not substantive knowledge about economics . . . Only 14 percent of the students report that their core courses put substantial emphasis on 'applying economic theory to real-world problems.'

Donald McCloskey (1991, pp. 10–14) wrote at about the same time:

To put it rigorously, the procedure of modern economics is too much a search through the hyperspace of conceivable assumptions. . . . One economics department after another has been seized by the formalists and marched off to the Gulag of hyperspace searching. Few graduate programs in economics teach economics, especially to first-year students. They teach 'tools,' tools which become obsolete every five years or so.

Yet these warnings have been unheeded. Subsequently the situation has got worse, rather than better, and has been replicated on an international scale.

Remarkably, many of the leading and living theorists who have advanced our understanding of economic behaviour and systems are currently not located in departments of economics. Prominent and seminal names such as W. Brian Arthur, Christopher Freeman, Richard Nelson, Herbert Simon and Sidney Winter have prospered elsewhere. Much of their work is cited less in the most prestigious economics journals and more in publications of schools of business, technology policy, public policy and international relations. The economics department has become the haven of the applied mathematician rather than the student of the real world economy. Regrettably, it now nurtures symbol rather than substance and formula rather than fact.

In contrast, at the beginning of the twentieth century, almost all the academics who were trying to understand and explain the workings of real world socio-economic systems and processes were located in university departments of economics. Such departments accommodated William Stanley Jevons, Alfred Marshall, Thorstein Veblen, John Maynard Keynes and Joseph Schumpeter. By the end of that century this was no longer the case. Many leading economists of the early twentieth century would have difficulty gaining tenure in a major university, judged by the predominant mathematical standards of today. By the end of this century, much of the study of real-world economies was being pursued outside of departments of economics.

Looking today at many economics departments, particularly in Britain and America, we see preoccupations that are remote from the concerns of leading economists at the end of the nineteenth century. In such departments the manner of work and discourse, and the criteria of professional evaluation, bear little resemblance to the situation in 1900. The type of economics department which harboured the broad and worldly concerns of Jevons, Marshall, Veblen, Keynes and Schumpeter is no more. Visit the economics departments in, for example, Cambridge and Manchester in Britain, and Chicago and Harvard in the United States, and the pre-eminent concern will be found to be mathematical rigour, rather than relevance and realism. The mathematicians will control student recruitment, the curriculum, the recruitment and promotion of faculty and the gateways to publication in most prestigious journals (Hodgson and Rothman, 1999). They will sit on the committees that appoint chairs, distribute resources and evaluate national or institutional applications for research funding. They will downgrade the non-mathematician and the dissident questioner of core assumptions. If a heterodox economist can be found there at all, he or she will complain of being deprived of power, and any remaining influence will be subject to the goodwill and dominant norms of the formalists. Many such economists have simply given in, and adopted the techniques, methods and assumptions of the majority.[3] Perhaps there is no longer a 'crisis of economics': merely the whinging of the small and recalcitrant minority.

In such departments – and regrettably there are now many of them – economics as a broad and vital subject, as in the Marshallian era, is indeed no longer in crisis. It is dying, if not dead. Whether lingering or deceased, there is little hope of recuperation within the prevailing departmental structures. Outside, in the business, government and other non-academic communities, the perception is widespread and growing of economics as a technical and rarefied discipline, of questionable relevance and limited practical use. This widespread opinion is manifest in the declining student enrolments on economics degree courses and in a shift towards close substitutes such as business studies.[4]

Yet this public dissent has not – so far – helped those who would like economics to change its course. On the contrary, declining enrolments and shrinking budgets in economics departments have led to a narrowing of the economics curriculum, the virtual disappearance of job opportunities for non-mathematical, non-neoclassical, historical, institutional, Post Keynesian or methodologically-inclined economists, and ever-more tenacious attempts to defend the virility of orthodoxy against its critics.

---

[3] To prevent their possible embarrassment, I will not list the names of several prominent colleagues who have in conversation defended their adoption of formalistic approaches, not in terms of the intrinsic value of formalism itself, but largely or wholly on the grounds that that is the only way their research will be valued by their peers. I wonder if the reader has had similar experiences.

[4] Neoclassical economics is perhaps less at home in this arena. Teece and Winter (1984) argued convincingly that most real-world management problems are dynamic, complex and often difficult to structure analytically. They suggested that in these circumstances the neoclassical assumption of transparently rational decision-making in a world of known outcomes or probabilities is of relatively little use.

1.1.3. Institutions, Evolution and Variety in Economics

These processes are global. They are largely driven by developments within the United States, whose dominance of the research, publications and leading journals in the subject has become overwhelming, especially in the last quarter of the twentieth century.[5] The move towards English as the international language of academia has helped to reinforce this American dominance. Economics research in Britain is now too inadequate, underfunded and underpaid to take advantage of the global anglophone shift. As recently as 1980, Britain had Sir John Hicks, Nicholas Kaldor, Edith Penrose, Joan Robinson, George Shackle and Piero Sraffa. Today they are all gone, and the country has very few prominent economists of international standing. Elsewhere in Europe, research in economics is also weaker than in the United States.[6] Compare this again with the situation a century ago, when, by a wide margin, the two countries with the most prestigious economists were Germany and Britain. Germany was the stronger, with its thriving historical school and the rising group of dissident Austrians within its linguistic sphere. Accordingly, before the First World War, many American economists went to Germany to receive their graduate training (Herbst, 1965). The state and prestige of economics research in Britain and Germany is very different today.[7]

Furthermore, the plight of economics is likely to get even worse before it gets better. The processes of formalization are locked-in to the institutional structures and gathering increasing momentum. As in the case of economic globalization, the international process of formalization of academic

---

[5] According to numbers of citations in the Social Science Citations Index for 1972–83, the US and Canada provided 72 per cent of all eminent living economists and Europe provided just 25 per cent (Blaug, 1986).

[6] For comparative discussions of the state of European economics see Frey and Eichenberger (1993), Baumol (1995) and Kirman (1994).

[7] This experiment is suggested to the reader: ask a knowledgeable American economist to list the internationally prominent and living (a) British economists, and (b) German economists. The respondent will typically have difficulty counting beyond the fingers of one hand in each case. How are two nations – once mighty in economics – fallen! By contrast, any knowledgeable economist outside the United States will have little difficulty in listing a dozen prominent American economists. The loss of Britain's prominence in economics is manifest even its leading university departments. The global and domestic neglect of the rich legacy of the German historical school is a failure of immense and scandalous proportions.

economics is largely driven by the United States. This American dominance is likely to persist for some time.

However, the rate of change in other countries varies significantly. National institutions and other local circumstances dominate the extent and pace of formalization and Americanization. Of primary importance is the extent of usage of English language and the existence and strength of a countervailing academic literature in a language other than English. An economics discourse in a non-English language may help to protect separate intellectual traditions for a while. On the other hand, the global pressures to publish in leading, English language, economic journals, gives the advantage to the mathematician. If your first language is not English then it is difficult to write it at the level required for an academic journal. The mathematician can gain access to leading journals by publishing in mathematics.

Also of major significance are the extent of national centralization of professorial appointments and the degree of concentration of research-grant-awarding institutions. In some countries – but not Britain or the United States – professorial appointments are made by government agencies, at the national or regional level. Research grants are centralized in some cases, as in Britain. However, national committees appointing economics chairs or distributing research grants are vulnerable to national take-over by formalists concerned to upgrade the 'scientific' credentials of their national research.

These linguistic and institutional factors help to explain the relative rates of formalistic degeneration in the last few years. Consider the situation in some selected countries. In the United States, the lack of a centralized professorial appointment process and the existence of multiple research-grant-awarding institutions has allowed a tiny minority of heterodox economists to survive at the less-influential fringes of academia. But they are rapidly decreasing in number, with fewer heterodox recruits in the next generation to replace them. In Britain, the centralization implicit in the nationally-funded Research Assessment Exercise has greatly accelerated the process, to the extent that non-mainstream economists have great difficulty in getting appointed to a faculty position in all but a handful of departments of economics (Lee and Harley, 1997). In Sweden, as an extreme case, general fluency in English combined with a national centralization of research grant and professorial appointment agencies has meant that heterodoxy has been completely eliminated within departments of economics, but survives in business schools and elsewhere. France, Germany, Italy, Netherlands and Austria retain dwindling minorities of heterodox economists. These endure largely because of the receding strength of the French *régulation* school, 'Austrian' economics, Marxism, Post Keynesianism and other weakened heterodoxies. Yet, at the same time, in these Continental European countries, a rapid process of formalistic take-over is visible.

In the countries of the former Eastern Bloc, from Russia to the Czech Republic, orthodoxy has been tainted with the disastrous policy of economic 'shock therapy' in the early 1990s. Yet the level of university education is inadequate, library resources are impoverished, and the quality of heterodoxy is accordingly low by international standards of scholarship. The brighter and more influential scholars travel to the United States to study, and many return as enthusiastic envoys of American economic formalism.

Of all the OECD nations, heterodox economics remains the strongest by far in Japan. In that country there is a relatively decentralized and pluralistic academic structure and an accepted academic propensity to publish in Japanese. But even in this exceptional case, the global processes of academic Americanization and the growing formalization of economics are there to observe.

Even for the mainstream, this predicament is hardly a healthy one. Creative advance depends on criticism. Notably, many of the developments in modern mainstream economics have been prompted by its critics.[8] For example, the critics used to complain that mainstream economists used to ignore institutions and treat the firm as a 'black box'. Largely in response, since the 1970s there has been a sustained attempt to remedy the defect. We refer to the spectacular growth of the 'new institutionalism' of Douglass North (1981, 1990), Mancur Olson (1965, 1982), Richard Posner (1973), Andrew Schotter (1981), Oliver Williamson (1975, 1985) and others. As another example, mainstream economists used to assume 'perfect information' in most of their models. Yet work in the 'economics of information' – while being limited in its treatment of information and knowledge – has explored the dramatic implications of relaxing the assumption of perfect information (Lamberton, 1996; Stiglitz, 1987, 1994). Again, mainstream models of macroeconomic growth used to exhibit decreasing returns. No longer (Lucas, 1988; Romer, 1986). Last but not least, the endogenous preference function of neoclassical theory has been strongly criticized for excluding the influence of culture on the formation of

---

8 The word 'mainstream' here means what it says. (The term 'neoclassical' is defined in Chapter 2 below.) For instance, the (non-neoclassical) historical school was the *main stream* of German economics from the 1830s to the 1930s. In contradistinction, neoclassical approaches formed the *main stream* of British economics from the 1890s and of American economics from the 1940s.

preferences. Yet Nobel Laureate Gary Becker (1996) has made an heroic attempt to remedy this defect, which in appearance – if not in essence – seems to remedy the flaw.[9]

What happens, however, when all critics are removed from the vicinity of the department of economics? The danger is that the subject will lose the stimulation that is provided by controversy and dissent. The denial of pluralism within departments of economics deprives the mainstream of a major source of intellectual drive. In ideas, as in nature, *variety is the evolutionary fuel*. When pluralism and variety disappear, innovation and progress may slow to a halt. The current policy of intellectual intolerance within economics is ultimately self-defeating. The cries of heresy against the works of the heterodox – 'that's not economics!' – betray a weakness within mainstream economics itself. Pluralism is necessary for innovation and scientific advance. A science that denies pluralism may enjoy a brief and absolutist hegemony but will eventually suffer a dull death.[10]

What else can we glean from this rather pessimistic picture? First, the evolution of economics as a discipline is in part the product of its institutional integument. Some of the essays in this book develop this point in more detail. Those that wish to improve matters must learn from the past. Second, the advanced state of degeneration of economic science means that it will take some time for the processes of narrowing and formalization to be reversed. This reversal may even involve an alternative choice of name for the subject, just as 'economics' replaced 'political economy' at the end of the nineteenth century. However, the new subject will have at its centre the study of real socio-economic systems, and so the term 'economics' should not be abandoned lightly. 'Institutional economics' or even 'institutional and evolutionary economics' are possible, maybe temporary, expedients. Another is to attempt to find academic space for the subdiscipline of 'economic sociology'.[11]

---

[9] For brief critiques of Becker's approach see Hodgson (1998b, 1998e).

[10] The International Confederation of Associations for the Reform of Economics (ICARE), a growing network of many heterodox associations and groups, formed in 1993 – with the author as current President and John Adams as its more active Secretary – has the promotion of pluralism in economics as its main objective.

[11] Friends such as Mark Granovetter, Neil Smelser and Richard Swedberg are engaged in this project (Smelser and Swedberg, 1994; Swedberg, 1993, 1996). However, there are problems with the term 'economic sociology'. First, the term could suggest the application of mainstream economic techniques to sociology, as in the case of Coleman (1990), rather than the study of the economy *per se*.

Maybe these labels are temporary expedients because scholars of real socio-economic systems must envisage a total realignment and redivision of the social sciences. Other social sciences, such as sociology, also face severe internal problems of lack of direction and self-definition. Actual theoretical and empirical research into the workings of real socio-economic systems is now fragmented and dispersed through business schools, departments of sociology, departments of geography, departments of technology policy, and elsewhere. A realignment of the disciplinary frameworks and departmental boundaries throughout the social sciences is both pressing and necessary (Gulbenkian Commission, 1996). But, at least for reasons of institutional inertia, it will take some considerable time to achieve.

Overall, a reversal of the degeneration of the science of socio-economic systems is possible, even if it may take a long time to come about. To accomplish this, mere criticism of the prevailing orthodoxy is not enough. The most central and urgent task is to build an alternative theory. But it must be a theory that is lasting and well-grounded. It is all too easy, as we can observe in economics, to build yet another 'model' upon slightly different assumptions. It is all too easy, as can be seen in the sister science of sociology, to invent new terminologies and categories, only to see most of these well-intended innovations escape enduring attention and rapidly expire. The shelves of the libraries of the social sciences are groaning with the detritus of forgotten theories.

With some justice, the orthodox criticize the dissenters for their slow progress in forging an established and accepted alternative. But to condemn too easily is to forget the history of orthodoxy itself. Neoclassical economics took the compounded efforts of more than a dozen exceptionally gifted minds. It took more than ninety years – from the 1860s to the 1950s – to emerge in its modern form. Likewise, the construction of a new economics is a massive task: it will take decades and it will involve many scholars. The new conceptual framework will have to be grounded in the past literature of the subject, with appropriate comparisons and delineations. It will have to be forged in the knowledge of both methodology and key developments in other

---

Perhaps 'sociology of the economy' would be better, but that also concedes claim of the title 'economics' to the mainstream, and wrongly suggests that sociology itself provides the means to understand economic phenomena. 'Sociology' is not an ideal refugee camp because it lacks a clear or adequately defined object of analysis and is itself in a deep theoretical crisis. Furthermore, 'economic sociology' has no obvious defences against the ubiquitous assumptions of rational choice and the formalist methods that are arguably the problems with mainstream economics. Perhaps for these reasons it will offer no more than a temporary hideout for the economic heretic.

sciences. The construction of a new and lasting theory may best be built using the history of thought as a quarry, hewing out and shaping material with tools taken from the modern philosophy of the social and natural sciences. The use of methodology and the history of ideas in this way is unfashionable, but in this manner we may produce a solid building that will endure the real and conceptual weathers and earthquakes of the future.

It will be many years before the situation improves. But progress is nevertheless possible. After all, the processes of producing and distributing wealth are central to all our lives, and to the human life process itself. There should be a science devoted above all to the study of such phenomena. And eventually the realization that mainstream economics is lost up a formalistic cul-de-sac will dawn upon the relevant university and government authorities, as many people in academia and business have recognized already. They will address the problem that, at least in Europe and North America, the study of real economies is fragmented and largely carried on outside departments of economics. Action may then be taken, and the study of real socio-economic systems may be put in its proper place. In the meantime, those commitment to a more relevant and meaningful science of economics must face, often in difficult, underfunded and isolated circumstances, the urgent task of building something new.

In addressing evolutionary economics, in its later chapters, this book focuses on a direction of enquiry that has already provided a rich body of both theoretical and policy-oriented material. To explore and develop this further is one of the best chances we have for reforming economics in the twenty-first century.

1.2. SOME THEMES OF THIS BOOK

The essays in this volume reflect both on the origins and on the consequences of the narrowing and increasing irrelevance of mainstream economics in the twentieth century. They also address some of the attempts to redirect theoretical economics towards worldly issues during those years, in the hope that something enduring can be learned from them. Much attention is given to the promise that evolutionary economics may provide a way of the future.

A predominant concern of this book is that economics should escape from its narrowness and exclusivity, not only to tolerate different approaches and paradigms within itself but also to learn genuinely from the insights and contributions of other sciences. This is not to suggest, however, that other social sciences are free of their own problems. Indeed, as noted above, economics with the rest of social science is approaching a crisis of identity concerning its core precepts, which is likely to lead to a re-examination both of the boundaries and of the content of these disciplines.

Strangely, elements of this crisis were already apparent at the end of nineteenth century, only to be evaded and ignored. They had to await the next *fin de siècle* to re-emerge. In part, these problems concerned the relationship between the social and the biological sciences, and the conception of the human agent. Leading pragmatist philosophers of the 1890s, such as William James and Charles Sanders Peirce, addressed these problems and their work influenced Veblen and other economists. But this inspiration did not last. It was swept aside by other movements in the social sciences. Pragmatist philosophy and instinct psychology were in severe decline by the 1920s, as all the social sciences broke their links with biology and embraced positivism and behaviourism (Degler, 1991). The rise of formalism in economics was a slightly later result of the triumph of positivism and the search for technocratic solutions to the real-world economic crisis of the 1930s.

Today, however, both positivist philosophy and behaviourist psychology are discredited. Furthermore, the rise of chaos and complexity theory has challenged the possibility of accurate prediction and reductionist formalization in complex systems (Gleick, 1988; Lewin, 1993; Stewart, 1989; Waldrop, 1992). Biology is challenging the foundations of social science (Hirst and Woolley, 1982; Pinker, 1994; Plotkin, 1994; Weingart *et al* 1997). Yet modern economics has shown only a minimal cognisance of these developments. While other social sciences attempt – hitherto inadequately – to cope with these issues, economics has become even more stranded and isolated, advancing the metaphors and methods of an earlier epoch in an inadequate attempt to cope with the complex ideas of the new millennium. The relationship between economics and biology is another theme of this book.

This volume also addresses the fact that economics does not change through the force of argument alone, being affected by shifts in ideology and its own institutional structures. The study of the interaction of a science with its institutional and cultural environment is usually described as the 'sociology of science': it would be the 'sociology of economic science' in this case. Yet the use of the term 'sociology of' here would wrongly suggest that sociology should be a method or agenda of analysis, rather than itself being defined in terms of an object of analysis in the real world. A similar mistake is made by those who see economics as defined by a set of core (neoclassical) assumptions and methods, and not by the scientific study of the real-world object known as the economy. For these reasons, Uskali Mäki and I proposed in 1994 the alternative title 'the institutions of economics' to describe the subdiscipline concerned with the study of the institutional and cultural context of economic science, and the interaction of this context with its content and development. Techniques such as citation analysis can be used in this endeavour. It is hoped that existing and further research into 'the institutions of economics' will be useful for those that are concerned with the reform of economics as a discipline.[12]

1.2.1. A Brief Overview

This has been rather a pessimistic chapter. But this book as a whole shifts progressively and cautiously to a more optimistic mood. It examines several past and present trends in non-neoclassical economic thought, finding some promise in recent developments. But there are some difficult lessons to learn on the way. The following chapter discusses some misguided criticisms of neoclassical theory alongside more conciliatory attempts to reform or augment neoclassical doctrine is some manner, including the 'socio-economics' of Amitai Etzioni. Another scrutinizes the fate of the 'Cambridge' critique of neoclassical capital theory, which during the 1960s and 1970s seemed to threaten the theoretical foundations of neoclassical economics, but is now almost completely forgotten or ignored. After discussion of these challenges to orthodoxy, there is a discussion of the constitutive role of metaphor in economics, and of how the subject may have become either trapped or liberated by its own metaphors. A general case for pluralism in economics is developed, on the basis that pluralism is necessary for economics itself to evolve.

The book then turns to the evolution of what has been described as 'evolutionary economics', in the belief that these strands of thinking are the most useful for future theoretical advance. In 1898 Thorstein Veblen called for the building of economics as an 'evolutionary science' along 'post-Darwinian' lines. The 'old' institutionalism thus has legitimate but not exclusive, title to the word 'evolutionary'. The historical rise and fall of the 'old' institutionalism is discussed at length.

Later chapters turn to more recent developments in evolutionary economics. They address the development of the Nelson–Winter brand of

---

[12] The 'institutions of economics' has been adopted as one of the research areas of the European Association for Evolutionary Political Economy, the second largest association of economists in Europe.

'evolutionary economics' that has emerged as perhaps the major challenger to mainstream economic theory in the 1990s. The work of Nelson and Winter is considered as a major, still vigorous and highly promising challenge to mainstream theory. Three final chapters consider at some length the application of related 'evolutionary' and 'competence-based' ideas to the theory of the firm. It is in this area where evolutionary economists and other non-mainstream thinkers have made a major theoretical and empirical contribution that has endured at least to the end of the twentieth century. It is hoped that this book will contribute to their development and enhancement after the year 2000.

1.2.2. The Sextuple Entendre

In short, this book discusses a number of challenges to the mainstream position but above all it addresses the limits and potential of institutional and evolutionary economics as its major rival for the future. This leads us to the choice of the words *evolution* and *institutions* in the title. A *sextuple entendre* is invoked. The six intertwined themes stemming from these two words are as follows:

(1) This book is concerned with the processes of economic *evolution* and economic *institutions,* as real phenomena to be investigated by economic science. In other words, this book addresses evolutionary processes and institutions in socio-economic systems. Evolutionary processes considered include the alleged evolutionary selection of rational behaviour. Particular institutions discussed include the firm.

(2) The evolution *of* institutions is a related theme and is touched upon in some chapters of this book. How do institutions evolve, and in what sense? The work of Thorstein Veblen, Richard Nelson, Sidney Winter and others is considered in this context, including discussions of the evolution of institutions such as the firm.

(3) This book also promotes the terms *evolutionary* and *institutional* as interchangeable or complementary terms to describe a broad but distinctive stream of economic thought: 'evolutionary economics' and 'institutional economics' are treated as synonyms; they are both broadly descriptive of the approach adopted here. Veblen (1898a) asked 'why is economics not an evolutionary science?' and his work inspired what was later called 'institutional economics'. At the end of the twentieth century, and in various ways, both 'evolutionary economics' and 'institutional economics' have enjoyed a revival.

(4) More particularly, this book discusses the relationship between *biological* evolution and the study of economic institutions. This involves

discussion of the use and influence of biological metaphors in economic science, and their merits and limitations.

(5) This book also addresses the problem of the *evolution* of economics as a discipline. How can we understand the past *evolution* of the academic and other *institutions* which harbour and promote the prevailing economic doctrines? Why is mainstream economics in some respects so resistant to change? Under what *institutional* circumstances could economics itself *evolve* in the future? Accordingly, a major theme of this work is the 'institutions of economics' as defined above.

(6) Last but not least, and following from the last point, it is contended here that the *evolution* of academic *institutions* devoted to the study of real world economies requires a policy of academic pluralism. From an *evolutionary* stance, the *institutional* policy conclusion concerning the development of economics itself is the maintenance and replenishment of variety within academia. Only through extensive pluralism and critical conversation can economics innovate and progress.

Appendix: The Increasing Volume of Citations

This book makes some use of citation analysis. In particular, the citation rates of three twentieth century classics are analysed, namely Edith Penrose's *The Theory of the Growth of the Firm* (1959), Piero Sraffa's *Production of Commodities by Means of Commodities* (1960) and Richard Nelson and Sidney Winter's *An Evolutionary Theory of Economic Change* (1982).

Since 1956, citations have been recorded by the Institute of Scientific Information (ISI) in the United States. Over the years, the ISI have kept a list of several hundred prominent journals in the social and other sciences. The regularly published Social Science Citation Index records the occasions when any work has been cited in any one of these prominent journals.

In the last 30 years the overall number of citations in social science has increased more than tenfold, as shown in Figure 1.1.[13] The explosion in the volume of citations has to be taken into account in time-series citation analysis. The way this is done in this book is to divide the actual number of citations for the work in question for a given year by the total volume of

---

[13] These data are published annually by the ISI. Data for the individual years 1966–68 are not available and have been estimated here by interpolation.

citations in the social sciences, as given in the graph below. This gives the 'citation share' (per million) in Figures 3.1, 7.1 and 11.2.

Figure 1.1: Total Citations (in Millions) to All Authored Journal and Monograph Items in the Social Sciences

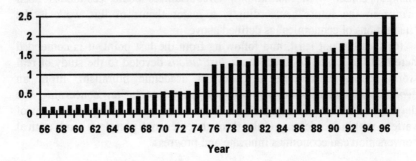

This explosion in the amount of scientific information will have dramatic implications for the progress of science itself. One danger, clearly, is that academia will be drowned in a sea of published mediocrity. Another is that relatively superficial 'scientific' criteria – notably the degree of mathematical formalism – will dominate the evaluative process.

For the gem of wisdom to be discovered, much more than wisdom itself will be required. Sheer perseverance will not be enough to tackle the scale of the problem. We shall have to rely increasingly on the facilities of institutions that filter and accredit the growing mass of information. This raises the perplexing problem of judging – on the basis of limited information – the judgement of others, raised by Frank Knight long ago (Knight, 1921, p. 311; Hodgson, 1998e, pp. 191–2).

PART ONE

Rival Paradigms in Economics

2. False Antagonisms and Doomed Reconciliations

This chapter is concerned with a set of criticisms of neoclassical economics, particularly concerning its alleged normative stance and its attitude to the market.[1] The problematic relationship between positive and normative judgements in economics is discussed here. A widespread allegation that neoclassical or mainstream economics are inherently 'pro-market' is criticized. The more fundamental question is raised as to the extent to which neoclassical theory addresses markets at all. Also briefly examined is the prominent and related attempt of Amitai Etzioni (1988) to develop an alternative 'socio-economic' approach in which alleged neoclassical defects are rectified.

Section 2.1 opens with a discussion of the fact–value distinction. It also defines neoclassical economics and addresses a number of criticisms of it. These include a position that is quite common among heterodox economists: it is widely suggested that neoclassical economics should be judged (and condemned) largely for its normative and policy outcomes. We then go on to discuss in more detail the particular, *pro-market* normative stance that is often associated with neoclassical economics.

In Section 2.2 it is argued that neoclassical theory has theoretical limitations when dealing with markets in the real world. It is thus not only wrong but *over-generous* to describe neoclassical theory as 'pro-market'. The reason being that neoclassical economics is actually blind to essential market features and processes. In theoretical terms, the failure to identify or

---

[1] Alongside text written specially for this volume, this chapter uses material from Hodgson (1992b, 1993e).

encompass its key features incapacitates any pro-market sympathies. Section 2.3 concludes the chapter.

2.1. NEOCLASSICAL ECONOMICS AND ITS CRITICS

2.1.1. The Problem of the Fact–Value Distinction

Do we judge a theory simply or mainly by its normative stance or policy outcomes? It is popular among heterodox economists to suggest that one should. This suggestion is often bolstered by arguments that, contrary to the 'positive economics' proposed in the neoclassical textbooks, it is impossible to separate (positive) judgements of fact from (normative) judgements of value, at least in the social sciences.

Clearly, many orthodox economists have played ideological havoc with their ideas – consider the pro-market uses of monetarism, Laffer curves, rational expectations, and the like – while simultaneously and deceptively entertaining the dubious proposition of a value-free social science. But there is a dangerous, obverse error, committed by many on the heterodox fringes: that is to evaluate theories mainly or wholly in terms of their normative, rather than their analytical, content.

Many examples of this error may be found. For instance, several heterodox economists have entirely dismissed the brilliant insights of Friedrich Hayek – one of the greatest economists of the twentieth century – simply because of his unpalatable policy conclusions. Another case is the frequent dismissal of neoclassical economics not because of its analytical limitations but because of the supposed conclusion that it supports a free-market policy. Other instances can be detected in frequent heterodox attempts to classify economic theories primarily in terms of ideological categories – such as the vague, political trichotomy of 'conservative', 'liberal' and 'radical' – rather than in terms of their core assumptions and theories. Instances of such errors are legion in the history of heterodox economic theory.

The relationship between fact and value in social science is complicated and has been widely discussed and debated. We cannot go into the debate in detail here. Instead, the main concern is to identify some unacceptable stances that have emerged among the critics of economic orthodoxy. These involve the evaluation of a theory in social science from the point of view of its normative outcomes: a theory is accepted or rejected largely on that basis.

An extreme way of supporting this view is to argue that positive and normative positions are *equivalent*. A less extreme version of this is simply not to worry too much if our criticism switches from positive to normative mode. Another version is to argue that normative values are 'always with us' and thereby to judge a theory primarily by its normative values. Such standpoints are common, especially among economists and other social scientists who are critical of mainstream economics. I contend here that they are both dangerous and ineffective, even in their own terms.

These standpoints are not criticized here from the point of view of an outdated and positivist view of social science. The view is emphatically endorsed here that judgements of fact are difficult or even impossible to disentangle from judgements of value. But that does not mean that they are the same thing, nor that we should disregard the difference. Recognition of our entry into a 'post-positivist' era does not mean that 'anything goes'.

In contrast, Paul Dale Bush (1993) took the argument from Richard Rorty that 'there is no epistemological difference between truth about what ought to be and truth about what is'. Rorty and Bush thus upheld, quite literally, that there is no difference between knowing an *is* and knowing an *ought*. On the contrary, it is argued here that this position is manifestly unacceptable, and it means abandoning any distinction whatsoever between science and ideology.[2]

For example, knowing that many people in the world today are poor is not the same thing as saying that they should remain impoverished. A statement about what *is* is not equivalent to a statement about what *ought* to be. Far from it being radical, the reckless confusion of the positive with the normative leads to extremely conservative outcomes. If there is no epistemological difference between positive and normative statements then we are led into a conservative cul-de-sac. Any statement we may make concerning what *is*, becomes equivalent, according to this precept, to a statement that it ought to be there: any statement about the world as it is becomes equivalent to a moral sanction of that existing state of affairs.

It is well known that David Hume argued that we can never derive an *ought* from an *is*. Much subsequent philosophical discussion has shown that Hume's statement, while having a realm of validity, is not strictly or universally true (Roy, 1989; Proctor, 1991). For example, faced with a

---

[2] I apologise for singling out my friend Dale Bush for criticism here. The suggestion that the distinction between the normative and the positive can be entirely abandoned is so widespread among heterodox economists that other cases are too plentiful to list. I hope that Dale will forgive me for taking advantage of his evident personal warmth and good humour.

decision between an untried and uncertain option, on the one hand, and one which is well-tried and traditional, on the other, it is often reasonable to opt for that with which we are familiar, and to reject change. In fact, even the most radical thinkers do this all the time. In an uncertain world we are always relying on the safety of habit or precedent (Dewey, 1939). Mere existence may thus carry a normative weight. In that sense, people do often elicit an *ought* from an *is* and in some circumstances it is understandable that they should do so.

Emphatically, however, this does not mean that we can generally and logically derive an *ought* from an *is*. The fact that people, in following custom, sometimes educe an *ought* from an *is* does not mean that the social scientist should necessarily do so as well. Indeed such a position would preclude scientific advance because it would reduce explanation to normative preference. Scientists are obliged to distinguish, as much as is possible, between positive and normative statements. Rejecting Hume's epistemology does not draw us to an inevitable conclusion that the distinction is meaningless or unsound.

Positivism as a philosophy is untenable (Quine, 1953; Bhaskar, 1975; Caldwell, 1982). But in this post-positivist age there is a danger of falling into a normative morass. To accept a complex interrelationship between the positive and the normative does not mean that we abandon all aspects of the distinction. Regrettably, many social scientists have gone so far. Consider another example. In a heterodox economics journal Clive Beed (1991, p. 470) asserted the 'anti-positivist' proposition that: 'The distinction between positive and normative science is untenable.' However, this particular statement is highly ambiguous, depending on different possible meanings of 'distinction between'. For instance, if all positive statements are contaminated by values then 'distinction between', in the sense of a complete, hermetic division, is clearly untenable. But this does not mean that we cannot classify statements between those which are broadly (although not wholly) positive, on the one hand, and those which are broadly (although not wholly) normative, on the other. It is like saying 'the distinction between the firm and the market is untenable' on the grounds that firms and markets are entangled and inseparable. This is a *non sequitur*. We may reject exclusive dualisms while maintaining distinct criteria of classification. Furthermore, it would be no improvement and a serious mistake to replace a positivistic dualism by a homogenising monism where all statements have the same epistemological status.

Consider the following, often repeated, arguments that judgements of value cannot be entirely separated from judgements of fact:

(a) Factual propositions are contaminated with values because of the unavoidable value biases of the researcher or her audience. This is especially the case in the social sciences where the phenomena under investigation themselves involve the values of human agents and where factual statements may have stronger emotive force.

(b) Factual propositions are contaminated with values because the researcher must make a value judgement about what is important or valuable in order to do the research in the first place.

(c) Factual propositions are contaminated with values because the researcher depends upon resources, and the provision of these is in turn dependent upon the value judgements and vested interests of corporate, political, or other social institutions.

(d) Factual propositions in social science are contaminated with values because the researcher is a human agent and inevitably is part of the social system under investigation.

There are other propositions along these lines, but we need not extend the list any further here. Propositions (a) to (d) are endorsed by the present author. They support the statement that 'values are always with us'. But they do *not* amount to the idea that positive and normative statements are epistemologically equivalent. Judgements of fact and value are always tangled together in the practice of economic analysis, but that does not mean that judgements of fact and value are the same thing.

Gunnar Myrdal is well known for his emphasis on the inevitability of value judgements in social science. He wrote: 'Valuations are present in our problems even if we pretend to expel them. The attempt to eradicate biases by trying to keep out the valuations themselves is a hopeless and misguided venture' (Myrdal, 1958, p. 131). So far so good. But does this mean that Myrdal was saying that positive and normative statements are epistemologically indistinguishable? In fact he implied the opposite:

Values do not emerge automatically from the attempt to establish and collect the facts. Neither can we allow the individual investigator to choose his value premises arbitrarily. *The value premises should be selected by the criterion of relevance and significance to the culture under study.* (Myrdal, 1958, p. 134).

This passage clearly indicates that, for Myrdal, facts and values were not the same thing. Values do not 'emerge automatically' from facts, neither is the choice of value premises an arbitrary matter. In short, Myrdal believed that 'values are always with us', but he did not make the mistake of treating them as epistemologically equivalent to facts.[3]

It is not being argued here that it is possible or desirable to cleanse theoretical economics of value judgements. What is being suggested is that the normative cart should not pull the positive horse. To put the cart before the horse, or to fail to see any distinction between vehicle and animal, is to disable any attempt to move economic theory along a different track. Any such attempt would be rightly dismissed as mere political rhetoric.

These brief remarks have not done justice to the complex question of the relationship between facts and values. Nevertheless, for the scientist, theories should not be evaluated through primarily ideological lenses. Above all, to see the essential difference between orthodoxy and heterodoxy as being largely a matter of policy outcomes is to neglect the essential task of criticizing and replacing core philosophical and theoretical ideas.

In sum, in social science, statements about fact are always contaminated with values. But this does not mean that factual statements and judgements of value are epistemologically equivalent. If they are, then we might as well pack our scientific bags and become political agitators instead. Nothing will endanger the current revival of institutional and evolutionary economics more than the adoption of such a course of action by its leading protagonists.

Those that define neoclassical economics by its normative outputs disable their criticism of that school. To take this stance is to regard normative evaluation as more important than understanding and explaining what is going on in the real world. Rival views are rejected not on the basis of the lack or otherwise of analytic insight, but on the perceived ideological outcomes of the theory. The whole process of scientific criticism and endeavour degenerates into ideological propaganda and posturing.

This does not mean that, as scientists, we can or should abandon any commitment to appropriate values. Normative issues are important. They

---

[3] However, Roy (1989, p. 109) went so far as to allege that: 'Where the valid and useful line between the positive and the normative is exaggerated by the humean to be one which is impenetrable and ineradicable, Myrdal and [his editor and translator] Streeten over-react to erase it completely.' This is an exaggeration, because a clear and explicit attempt to eradicate the distinction is absent from the Myrdal–Streeten text. Nevertheless, Myrdal did not erect sufficient defences against any attempt to collapse science into ideology. Note that Roy himself, in a careful and forceful critique of Humean epistemology in economics, still rightly maintained that the 'line between the positive and the normative' is 'valid and useful'. In fact, it is *essential* to any non-arbitrary, scientific or analytic discourse about the world.

should not and cannot be ignored. Nevertheless, the explanation of economic phenomena must be the foremost priority for the scientist. Any alternative approach to the mainstream must first stake its claim to be an identifiable approach to economics on the basis of its incisive *analysis of what is*, rather than on its judgements of what *ought* to be. In addition, mainstream economics should be analysed in terms of its core propositions and methodology, and not exclusively by its ideology. After all, if we wish to change the world, and especially in a constructive and consensual manner, then it is first of all necessary to understand it.

2.1.2. Defining Neoclassical Economics

Let us attempt to identify the key characteristics of neoclassical economics; the type of economics that has dominated the twentieth century. One of its exponents, Gary Becker (1976a, p. 5) identified its essence when he described 'the combined assumptions of maximizing behavior, market equilibrium, and stable preferences, used relentlessly and unflinchingly'. Accordingly, neoclassical economics may be conveniently defined as an approach which:

(1) assumes rational, maximizing behaviour by agents with given and stable preference functions,
(2) focuses on attained, or movements towards, equilibrium states, and
(3) is marked by an absence of chronic information problems.[4]

Point (3) requires some brief elaboration. In neoclassical economics, even if information is imperfect, information problems are typically overcome by using the concept of probabilistic risk. Excluded are phenomena such as severe ignorance and divergent perceptions by different individuals of a given reality. It is typically assumed that all individuals will interpret the same information in the same way, ignoring possible variations in the cognitive frameworks that are necessary to make sense of all data. Also excluded is uncertainty, of the radical type explored by Frank Knight (1921) and John Maynard Keynes (1936).

---

[4] This definition of neoclassical economics clearly excludes members of the Austrian school, such as von Mises and Hayek, particularly because of their explicit critique of attributes (2) and (3), and because of their rejection of typical conceptualizations of rationality under (1). If 'neoclassical' is used in this precise sense then the Austrian school is essentially non-neoclassical, despite it sharing some common features with neoclassicism.

Notably, these three attributes are inter-connected. For instance, the attainment of a stable optimum under (1) suggests an equilibrium (2); and rationality under (1) connotes the absence of severe information problems alluded to in (3). It can be freely admitted that some recent developments in modern economic theory – such as in game theory – reach to or even lie outside the boundaries of this definition. Their precise placement will depend on close inspection and refinement of the boundary conditions in the above clauses. But that does not undermine the usefulness of this rough and ready definition.[5]

Although neoclassical economics has dominated the twentieth century, it has changed radically in tone and presentation, as well as in content. Until the 1930s, much neoclassical analysis was in Marshallian, partial equilibrium mode. The following years saw the revival of Walrasian general equilibrium analysis, an approach originally developed in the 1870s. Another transformation during this century has been the increasing use of mathematics, as noted in the preceding chapter. Neoclassical assumptions have proved attractive because of their apparent tractability. To the mathematically inclined economist the assumption that agents are maximizing an exogenously given and well defined preference function seems preferable to any alternative or more complex model of human behaviour. In its reductionist assumptions, neoclassical economics has contained within itself from its inception an overly formalistic potential, even if this took some time to become fully realized and dominant. Gradually, less and less reliance has been placed on the empirical or other grounding of basic assumptions, and more on the process of deduction from premises that are there simply because they are assumed.

Nevertheless, characteristics (1) to (3) above have remained prominent in mainstream economics from the 1870s to the 1980s. They define an approach that still remains ubiquitous in the economics textbooks and is taught to economics undergraduates throughout the world. In this chapter we focus primarily on the core assumptions of this approach, and the manner in which they have been tackled by their critics.

---

[5] Modern 'rational choice' approaches in political science and sociology (for exemplars and critics see: Coleman, 1990; Coleman and Fararo, 1990; J. Friedman, 1995; Green and Shapiro, 1994; Hirsch, 1990; Orchard and Stretton 1997; Udéhn, 1996) also involve the adoption of similar assumptions.

2.1.3. Is Neoclassical Theory Pro-Market?

Neoclassical theory has often been used to serve free market policies. Many of its developers and practitioners have had pro-market inclinations. In all its versions, it is based on an ontological individualism that fits in well with the individualistic ethos of many free market ideas. However, it is important not to go much further, and suggest, for example, that neoclassical theory is necessarily and inherently pro-market, or that the domain of neoclassical theory coincides with the domain of pro-market policy. It is wrong to presume that 'neoclassical economics' and 'pro-market policies' are one single package.

Neoclassical economics is not necessarily pro-market, for the following reasons. First, it has to be recognized that many of the pioneers of neoclassical economic theory, including Léon Walras, Alfred Marshall and Philip Wicksteed, were sympathetic to socialist or social-democratic ideas. By today's standards, some of them would be leftist radicals. Walras called himself a 'scientific socialist'. His theoretical efforts in economics were motivated by a desire to demonstrate the economic advantages of price regulation and the public ownership of natural monopolies, including land. Marshall was concerned about the problems of poverty in Victorian Britain, and was sympathetic to worker co-operatives. Wicksteed also advocated land nationalization and had sympathetic and personal links with the socialist and radical movement.

Similar alignments have persisted well into the twentieth century. For example, Irving Fisher – the neoclassical economist who led in America the drift into mathematical formalism and general equilibrium theory – vigorously advocated reflationary measures during the Great Depression. Another group of neoclassical economists in the 1930s, led by Oskar Lange, used neoclassical economic tools to argue for the superiority of a version of socialist planning. Neoclassical theory was thus the weapon of the socialists *against* pro-market critics of planning such as Ludwig von Mises and Friedrich Hayek.

Still later, after 1945, leading neoclassical general equilibrium theorists Kenneth Arrow and Frank Hahn declared their sympathies for various interventionist and social-democratic economic policies. Indeed, Hahn and others have justified the whole general equilibrium theoretical project as an attempt to demonstrate the *limits* of the market mechanism. Even more recently, alleged 'Marxists' such as Jon Elster and John Roemer explicitly embraced neoclassical tools of economic analysis, while retaining leftist political credentials. True, there are many conservative and pro-market neoclassical economists. But neoclassical theory spans the conventional political spectrum – from the extreme pro-planning left to the extreme pro-market right – and is not definable in terms of the policy stances of its adherents. Whatever its defects, neoclassical theory is a relatively adaptable and politically flexible creature.

Second, the fact that neoclassical theory can readily be packaged as either pro-market or anti-market suggests that this theoretical approach does get to the essence of the phenomenon. Indeed, its doctrinal plasticity is a symptom of its failure to provide an adequate explanation of how markets work. It really concedes too much to neoclassical theory to suggest that it has an adequate theoretical foundation upon which to build any pro- (or anti-) market policy. Neoclassical theory is essentially neither pro-market nor anti-market. This is because, as explained below, it has no adequate theory of markets at all. It would be more accurate to say that neoclassical theory was blind to the real market, and consequently to its real virtues or its vices.

2.1.4. A Taxonomy of Economists

Having defined neoclassical economics, and established that some of its adherents are generally pro-market, while others take a stance favouring significant public intervention in the economy, it is possible to divide the set of neoclassical economists itself roughly into two camps. The precise dividing line between the pro-marketeers and the others need not concern us at this stage. It is also important to recognize that most, if not all, pro-marketeers favour some (limited) public intervention in the economy. The key point being emphasized here is that neoclassical economics can be, and has been, used to support a variety of policy stances, including on the question of the market.

The same is true of non-neoclassical economics: a variety of policy positions are possible from a non-neoclassical standpoint. For example, both Karl Marx and Friedrich Hayek were non-neoclassical economists, but their positions were almost diametrically opposed on the question of the market.

A third criterion is the extent to which an economist used mathematics. Again, the precise dividing line between the mathematical and the non-mathematical economist need not concern us at this stage. No more than a rough-and-ready dividing line is necessary to establish that some academic economists are inclined to make extensive use of mathematical techniques while others are not.

These three criteria give us no less than eight types of economist, as shown in Figure 2.1 below. One or two illustrative examples of each type of economist are given in each box.

Figure 2.1: An Illustrative Taxonomy of Economists

		Supporting some degree of planning or other substantial public intervention in the economy	Inclined to favour or defer to free-market policies
Neoclassical	Substantial use of mathematics	Kenneth Arrow Paul Samuelson	Gary Becker Robert Lucas
	Limited or no use of mathematics	Léon Walras Philip Wicksteed	Milton Friedman Lionel Robbins
Non-neoclassical	Substantial use of mathematics	Wassily Leontief Piero Sraffa	John von Neumann
	Limited or no use of mathematics	Karl Marx Thorstein Veblen	Friedrich Hayek Joseph Schumpeter

A point being emphasized here is that it is a mistake to see the economics profession as divided principally into just two camps. Figure 2.1 suggests that there are not one but at least three major dimensions separating modern economists. Normative attitudes to the market constitute one dimension. The nature of the core assumptions to the economic theory give another. Finally, there is the degree to which mathematics is used in the development and presentation of economic analysis.

Positions on each dimension are rarely chosen in isolation. For example, methodological individualism is sometimes adopted because of sympathy for an individualistic ideology. But that does not mean that methodological individualism and political individualism are the same; it is possible to separate them both analytically and doctrinally.

What is striking is that it is possible, on the basis of a binary classification in each dimension, to find examples of each of eight types of economist. This means that critics of mainstream economics have to fight on at least three fronts. Concentration of the forces of battle on one of them will not ensure victory in the others.

2.1.5. Is There a Place for Neoclassical Theory?

Let us shift the emphasis from matters of criticism of orthodoxy towards the construction of alternatives. Although neoclassical theory has met with an abundance of critiques, there is still disagreement over the outlines of a viable new or alternative economics. In what direction should we explore for new ideas and frameworks?

This question raises yet another: Assuming it is possible to build a superior framework for economic theory, would it subsume neoclassical theory within itself as a special or limiting case? In other words, would the superior framework be broader, richer, and multi-dimensioned, but preserve the neoclassical construction internally as a subset? Or would we reach a different result with the clash of two quite different theoretical structures or paradigms, one being incompatible with the other?

These broad questions are usefully approached from the starting point of Etzioni's (1988) major attempt to lay down the foundations of a 'new economics'. Is it possible to augment the underlying, mechanistic metaphor of neoclassical theory with 'a moral dimension', as Etzioni suggests?

It is contended below that neoclassical economics is deficient not simply because of the moral and other limitations of its utilitarian philosophy, but also because of its general treatment of time and its analysis of economic processes. For instance, in neoclassical theory, as in classical physics, time is reversible. Consequently, there are no real and irreversible choices for individuals, and the nature and significance of economic changes are undermined. These problems are illustrated by reference to the limitations of neoclassical theory in regard to the analysis of the market.

There is no disagreement with Etzioni's general case that moral issues and norms are important in economic theory and policy. Nevertheless, some points of theoretical disagreement emerge. These are instructive for any attempt to develop an alternative approach to the study of socio-economic systems, and for that reason they are elaborated here.

2.2. MARKETS AND NEOCLASSICAL THEORY DON'T MIX

Etzioni's complaint concerned in part the limited moral salience of neoclassical economics. He argued that all human choices have a moral or ethical component: 'All items have at least two valuations: their ability to generate pleasure and their moral standing' (Etzioni, 1988, p. 254). He thus saw neoclassical economics as a *subset* of an adequate 'socio-economic' theory. Neoclassical economics was seen as valid and appropriate for the analysis of a *subsystem* of the whole society:

> rather than abandon neoclassical concepts and findings, they are viewed here as dealing with subsystems within society (markets) and personality (in which rational decision-making is circumscribed, substituted *and*, on occasion, supported by emotions and values). (Etzioni, 1988, p. 3)

There are a number of problems with this statement. It assumes that neoclassical economics is acceptable as a theory in some limited sense and it applies to a subsystem of the real economy. In other words, neoclassical economics is seen as appropriate for the analysis of some components of the socio-economic system.

However, this contradicts the prevailing conception of 'economics' developed by neoclassical economists themselves. Is economics defined by its methods, or by its object of study? Since Lionel Robbins's (1932) famous book, most neoclassical theorists have defined economics in terms of a set of theoretical assumptions and tools, not in terms of the study of the economy, or of any subsystem of it. Hence neoclassical economists would not define their subject as the analysis of a particular set of phenomena, neither is it seen as essentially being related to specific 'subsystems' such as markets. Instead, neoclassical economists often see themselves as general evangelists of 'the economic approach' applied to all sorts of varied domains. They define their discipline in terms of its core assumptions and ideas, not any real world object of study.

Defining economics as a particular approach to the analysis of many varied phenomena creates the impetus for the self-proclaimed 'economic imperialism' of modern neoclassical theory; it is assumed that these assumptions and tools can be applied to an apparently limitless number of social phenomena, including decisions to have children, to marry, or to commit suicide (Becker, 1981; Hammermesh and Soss, 1974). As Jack Hirshleifer (1982, p. 52) explained, 'economic imperialism' involves 'the use of economic analytical models to study all forms of social relations rather than only the market interactions of "rational" decision makers . . . All aspects of life are ultimately governed by the scarcity of resources.'

In contrast, heterodox theoretical traditions often define economics as the science that attempts to explain the workings of the real world economy. Just as psychology is about the psyche, and biology about the biotic world, economics is seen as the study of the economy. Hence institutional, Post Keynesian and Marxian economists define their subject in terms of an object of analysis rather than a method of study. Contrary to Etzioni's conciliatory tone, any attempt to consign neoclassical economists to the study of a subset of the real socio-economic system has to challenge the prevailing definition of economics by neoclassical economists themselves. Any attempt to construct a new economics has to face up to this problem.

2.2.1. Neoclassical Theory is Market-Blind

There is an even more serious problem with Etzioni's suggestion that neoclassical theory can be retained in a limited sense because it 'deals with' the market subsystem. The fact is that neoclassical economics does not adequately 'deal with' such central phenomena as markets. Even if we put aside the highly important theoretical deficiency of neoclassical theory identified by Etzioni (1988, pp. 77–83) – that real-world markets are normally infused with moral norms as well as cost-based decisions – there are still major intrinsic flaws in the neoclassical model, making a reconciliation between neoclassical and 'socio-economic' theory highly problematic.

The central focus of neoclassical economics is not on the market but on the outcomes of given individual preferences between ranked alternatives.[6] Neoclassical theory is a tapestry woven principally from assumptions concerning individual preferences. It is not essentially about markets. Nevertheless, many sociologists, anthropologists and dissident economists endlessly and mistakenly repeat the neoclassical-market mantra. This does too much credit for neoclassicism. Take it from the horses' mouths. Neoclassical mentors Gary Becker and Richard Posner (1993, p. 422) wrote:

> economics is still mistakenly identified with monetary transactions in explicit markets, selfish behavior, and short-term relations. It is true that economists assume that the behavior they are trying to explain is a product of rational choice . . . It is not an assumption that people maximize pecuniary income or are selfish all or most of the time or are materialistic but only that they are sufficiently forward-looking to select apt means to ends, which might include the welfare of others, such as offspring.

---

[6] Note that the word 'choice' is avoided here. The fact that neoclassical economics lacks a genuine concept of choice is discussed in Hodgson (1988, 1993b) and raised again in Chapter 6 below.

For neoclassical economists, their subject is all about consistent choices and their outcomes. It is not essentially about markets, at least in a rich, institutional sense. Adequate concepts of property, contract, exchange and market are absent from neoclassical theory. When attempts are made to discuss exchanges and markets in neoclassical economics then the main element of the narrative is the increases of utility received by the individuals involved, not the transfer of property rights within a framework of legal institutions (Commons, 1924; Ellerman, 1982, 1992; Hodgson, 1982b; Levine, 1977, 1978). When institutions appear they are discussed primarily in terms of the incentives, information and constraints that they provide for utility-maximizing individuals. The ontology is of atomistic individuals, rather than of structures. A sign of the institutional weakness of neoclassical analysis on this score is the fact that adequate definitions of the market are rare in its texts (Hodgson, 1988). Far from being market-centred, neoclassical analysis is market-blind.

The fact that neoclassical economists frequently use the word 'market' does not mean that they are employing the concepts of property, exchange and market in an adequate or precise way. This is illustrated by neoclassical theorist Becker (1976a, p. 206) when he wrote that 'a *market* for marriages can be presumed to exist' (emphasis in original). Note that, for Becker, markets are little more than a means by which agents can transact in some vague manner, to increase their mutual utility. Accordingly, Becker showed an inability to make an adequate distinction between (a) sex traded intentionally for money or commodities, and (b) sex based on mutual agreement or desire rather than pecuniary or commodity exchange. Yet modern cultural (and religious) norms make a very strong differentiation between these two types of sexual relationship. Because he deploys no adequate notion of property, commodity exchange or market, these differences are elided in Becker's analysis of the family. By reducing all transactions to the mutual enhancement of 'utility', neoclassical theory is generally heedless to the moral, cultural and institutional distinctions that are involved. It cannot understand the phenomenon of the commodification of human relations, let alone explore its consequences.

The failure to associate rigorously and consistently the concepts of 'market' and 'exchange' with such factors as the legal transfer of property rights has created havoc in the neoclassical theory of the firm. For example, some firms may use price indicators for internal accounting, and products may be 'exchanged' by one internal department with another. It may be concluded that this is evidence of an 'internal market'. But typically these exchanges do not involve the exchange of property rights. The firm as a whole, unlike its departments, is a 'legal person', entitled to hold and exchange property. The objects of 'exchange' between departments remain the property of the firm. What are involved are accounting transfers, rather than genuine commodity exchanges. Even if a subdivision of the firm is delegated the power to enter into contracts with outside bodies, typically and legally it is the firm as a whole that is party to the contract. Normally the subdivision is merely exercising delegated powers: it acts 'in the name' of the corporation, and the corporation as a whole is legally responsible for its liabilities under the agreed contract.

There is also a widespread neoclassical supposition that 'internal labour markets' exist inside the firm. However, even the pioneers of the concept, Peter Doeringer and Michael Piore (1971, pp. 1–2) admitted that 'internal labor markets' are not governed primarily by the price mechanism but by 'a set of administrative rules and procedures'. David Marsden (1986, p. 162) went further: 'internal labour markets offer quite different transaction arrangements, and there is some doubt as to whether they fulfil the role of markets'. Much of the loose talk about 'internal markets' within firms derives from a sloppy use of the term 'market' which, unfortunately, pervades mainstream economics today. In terms of devolved and defined property rights, and genuine exchanges of those rights, 'markets' are rarely, if ever, found *within* the firm.[7]

Confusion over the nature of markets and exchange allows neoclassical economists to ignore the reality of non-market organization in capitalist firms and to understand everything in 'market' terms. In fact, the neoclassical conception and analysis of exchange and markets is extraordinarily weak. The problem arises because neoclassical economics cannot distinguish adequately between market and non-market forms. Yet the mistaken conception by its critics of neoclassical economics as a market-based doctrine is so widespread that one hesitates to give examples. But two examples of such misunderstandings we shall give.

Robert Lane (1991) was typical of many critics when he repeatedly described mainstream economics as 'market economics'. Likewise, the leading feminist economist Julie Nelson (1996, p. 20) wrote: 'Clearly the central concept in mainstream economics is that of "the market".' The grain of truth in these statements is that most mainstream economists have tended to favour pro-market policies for some time. However, these statements

---

[7] Would a competition between employees for an advertised post within the firm be an 'internal labour market'? Although this is closer than many other cases to a true market, a one-off competition for a post would nevertheless lack the regular and repeated exchanges that characterize true markets. On the nature of the market see Hodgson (1988).

mislead insofar as they suggest that mainstream *theory* is centred on markets, defines markets clearly, or has an adequate conception of them.

Bernard Barber (1977) was much more accurate when he bemoaned the lack of attention to the concept of the market *throughout* economics and social science. In fact, key concepts, such as markets and money, are treated inadequately by both sociologists and economists (Ingham, 1996a, 1996b). Sociologists often ignore these 'economic' concepts because they wrongly believe that economics has them well analysed and understood. Other sociologists have taken the view that their role is to add 'social' and 'cultural' context to 'economic' phenomena. Yet this suggests that the 'economic' and the social or cultural are conceptually separable, and allows economics to define the central terms of the discourse. In truth, neither sociologists nor economists have adequately analysed the market.[8]

2.2.2. Neoclassical Theory Excludes Real Time

The modern neoclassical analysis of markets is mainly based on the type of general equilibrium analysis pioneered by Léon Walras in the 1870s, and formalized during the postwar period by theorists such as Kenneth Arrow, Gerard Debreu, and Frank Hahn, two of whom won Nobel Prizes for their efforts.[9] Within its own terms, neoclassical economics has no extensive or rigorous alternative to this Walrasian theory. This kind of analysis assumes that tastes and preferences, along with technology, are given.[10] With the aid of an entirely fictitious auctioneer, the economy 'gropes' towards an equilibrium position in all markets and towards the determination of a complete final vector of prices. This theoretical construction has been subject to decades of criticism, and it is impossible to survey it all here. We shall confine our discussion to some relevant highlights.

Attempts to encompass time and change in the Walrasian model have followed the pioneering work of Arrow and Debreu. The basic idea is to incorporate all future products and developments with the assumption of a

---

[8] Rare exceptions include Baker (1984), White (1981) and Zelizer (1993).

[9] Arrow and Hahn (1971), Debreu (1959), Walras (1954).

[10] In at least one passage Walras (1954, pp. 380–81) himself considered the possibility of changing tastes and preferences. For this and other reasons a distinction should be drawn between Walras's theory and the narrower 'Walrasian' theory that infuses modern neoclassicism. See also Currie and Steedman (1990), Jolink (1996) and Walker (1996) on the more 'dynamic' or 'evolutionist' aspects of Walras's own theory.

complete set of futures markets. In addition, there are markets for each possible 'state of the world.' To make the problem tractable, however, trading in futures markets has to be integrated into a 'single gigantic once-for-all "higgle-haggle"' (Meade, 1971, p. 166). All present and future trades in all markets take place in one period of time. As Hahn (1980, p. 132) remarked: '*The assumption that all intertemporal and all contingent markets exist has the effect of collapsing the future into the present*'.[11]

Not only does this approach deny the flux of time by collapsing the future into a single instant. There are other problems. The Arrow–Debreu approach creates 'too many' markets. It is impossible to envisage a full list of futures markets, partly because of the escalating complexity and the information problems involved. Arrow (1986, p. S393) himself summed it up: 'A complete general equilibrium system . . . requires markets for all contingencies in all future periods. Such a system could not exist.'

In a brilliant paper, Roy Radner (1968) showed that the informational demands on the auctioneer would be excessive in such a completely specified Walrasian system. For instance, with only a thousand commodities, a thousand possible states of the world, and a thousand present and future dates, there will have to be a billion different markets. Agents are supposed to observe prices in all these markets and make appropriate bids. Clearly this is absurd. In line with Herbert Simon's (1957, 1959) arguments concerning 'bounded rationality', Radner argued that the number of markets and the amount of information each agent is supposed to process has to be drastically reduced in anything approaching a feasible model. One means of doing this, he asserts, is to introduce something corresponding to money. However, it will be shown below that this has not yet been done successfully in a Walrasian model.

2.2.3. Neoclassical Theory Excludes Money and Uncertainty

According to John Maynard Keynes, money is a means of dealing with an uncertain future, i.e. a future of events to which we can attribute no calculable probability. Uncertainty in this sense is excluded from Walrasian theory. There may be risk, but it is made tractable by the probabilistic

---

[11] In addition, there are attempts in neoclassical general equilibrium theory to overcome the constraints of one-off trading in the Arrow–Debreu model, by various forms of 'search' or 'conjecture' theory. However, these have not provided neoclassical theory with a full, operational system. Indeed they have created still more unsolved problems of mathematical tractability. For brevity the remarks here are confined to the Arrow–Debreu type of model that has dominated the literature.

calculus. For this reason and others, money has yet to be successfully accommodated in such a general equilibrium framework.

This failure has been admitted by leading general equilibrium theorist Hahn (1988, p. 972): 'monetary theory cannot simply be grafted on to Walrasian theory with minor modifications. Money is an outward sign that the economy is not adequately described by the pristine construction of Arrow and Debreu.' Hahn may not agree with Keynesians or others in their proposed theoretical solution to this problem, but his observations concerning the endemic failings of Walrasian theory are valid.

Consider a world of either perfect knowledge, or one in which the probabilities of all possible events are well described and known. Given that money is not a direct source of utility for consumers, why would people hold onto money in such a world? Money would be used merely as a means of exchange, and as a means of obtaining desired commodities. In Karl Marx's terms we would have $C - M - C$ and not $M - C - M'$. But it is the $M - C - M'$ form that represents the situation under capitalism, where money (and its enlargement, from M to M') becomes not simply a means, but an end.

In the real world, an important reason for holding money is that it helps us deal with real uncertainty. However, in such a situation we do not necessarily know what the expected benefits or losses may be, particularly as we do not know nor can we estimate the appropriate probabilities. If we could adequately estimate all the appropriate probabilities then we would have less reason to hold on to money as a reserve asset. In other words, the incorporation of money proper must involve the introduction of an asset, but not one possessed according to any complete, utilitarian calculus. As Stephen Horwitz (1992, p. 15) rightly remarked: 'the properties of real-world moneys throw a monkey wrench into the neoclassical theory of economic exchange.' In sum, neoclassical theory does not and cannot adequately represent a monetary economy.

2.2.4. The Walrasian Model Represents a Centralized System

The Walrasian auctioneer has to gather, process and communicate huge amounts of information. All the information relevant to the formation of prices has to be in the auctioneer's hands. Knowledge, in short, has to be centralized. Clearly, this is against the spirit of a market system.

The statement that the Walrasian model represents a centralized system rather than the decentralization associated with the market may be surprising for those who learn their economics simply from the orthodox textbooks. It will be even more surprising for those who learn their economics with good lacings of free-market ideology. But the statement is supported by a number of knowledgeable economic theorists. Discussing the Walrasian foundations of orthodox macroeconomics, Fabrizio Coricelli and Giovanni Dosi (1988, p. 130) wrote: 'It is not far from the truth to say that the current neo-classical approach to the microfoundation of macroeconomics is based on the representation of the economy as a *centralized* system.' Also, in a discussion of the Walrasian model, Claude Ménard (1990, p. 110) presented a 'cruel dilemma' for orthodoxy:

> either the *tatonnement* is coupled with an auctioneer, and we have a market economy whose consistency is guaranteed by the most powerful central agent one could imagine; or there is no such thing as an auctioneer, but the model is largely an empty set, since there is no indication at all how prices would be adjusted.

However, it is even worse than this. All economic agents rely on 'tacit knowledge' (Polanyi, 1958, 1967) upon which all skills and judgements depend. Tacit knowledge, typically embodied in habits and routines, cannot be readily codified or communicated. As Friedrich Hayek (1948, 1982) and others have argued, such knowledge is not only vital, it is also highly dispersed in a market economy. It is simply impossible for this dispersed and decentralized knowledge to be gathered together, either by a central planning authority or by a Walrasian auctioneer.[12]

In contrast, in the fantasy world of Walrasian theory, the auctioneer knows all, and what he or she does not know is eliminated from the model. Consequently, the Walrasian model of neoclassical theory does not correspond to a real market system where much information and knowledge is decentralized, and is not even amenable to centralization. It corresponds more closely to a mythical, centralized, non-market economy where the central authorities know everything; all other knowledge that cannot be fitted into the plans and conceptions of the centre is systematically disregarded, destroyed, or rendered useless. To drive the point home: the Walrasian 'market' model conjures up the idea of a totalitarian and repressive police state rather than a liberal market system, despite common rhetoric to the contrary. A similar point was made long ago by the perceptive institutional economist Morris Copeland (1931, p. 18):

---

[12] The endorsement of Hayek on this and some other points by no means implies acceptance of his largely non-interventionist and free-market policy stance. Indeed, Hayek's core arguments in the planning debate (see below) are accepted by theorists such as Nove (1983) and myself (Hodgson, 1984, 1988), who are more sympathetic to socialism. For some criticisms of Hayek see Hodgson (1998e).

A vigorous government policy directed toward realizing the neo-classical cost-accounting Utopia would probably resemble Russian communism more than it would laissez faire.

2.2.5. Lessons from the Great Planning Debate

In Retrospect, the true nature of neoclassical economics is illuminated by the Great Planning Debate. In this controversy, von Mises (1920) argued that complete central planning would be ineffective and irrational, partly because all relevant knowledge cannot be gathered together by a central authority. Socialists such as Oskar Lange and Frederick Taylor (1938) and others responded to von Mises by constructing an allegedly plausible model of 'market socialism' in which the coordinating actions of the market, including the setting of prices, were simulated by central planners.

Contrary to popular and textbook myth, it has now been shown that this debate was not won by the proponents of planning.[13] Ironically, the socialist reply to von Mises in the 1930s made extensive use of a Walrasian theoretical model. Their quasi-market solution simply replaced the Walrasian auctioneer with a central planning authority. Contrary to its frequent description as 'market socialism', the Lange-type model did not include markets in any true or adequate sense. In the Lange thought experiment the workings of the market were merely simulated, and to a limited degree. In fact, the models developed by Lange and his collaborators involved a high degree of centralized co-ordination and knowledge that excluded any real-world market.

Notably, the Lange-type 'solution' assumed away important features of the real world such as decentralized knowledge, true uncertainty and historical time. The related problems for centralized planning were summarily ignored. The Lange-type solution was not a solution at all. The debate was 'won' largely by ignoring the arguments of the opposition and the realities of the issue. Persuasive power emanated from the technocratic rhetoric of the neoclassical model, rather than its capability to represent the essence of the planning problem.

The opposing argument, as developed by Hayek, was that the Walrasian model used by Lange *et al* did not give an adequate representation of real-world market systems. Attention to relevant features of real markets,

---

[13] For a selection of these re-examinations, see Lavoie (1985), Murrell (1983), Vaughn (1980), Keizer (1989). The debate is also discussed in Hodgson (1998e).

particularly those concerning decentralized knowledge and the processes of coordination and change, excludes the Walrasian construction. It is both an inadequate theorisation of the market and an unsuitable basis for a comparative evaluation of planning and market systems.

2.3. CONCLUSION

As noted in the first chapter, the development of general equilibrium theory has reached an impasse. Quite early on, it was realized that the potential diversity among individuals threatened the feasibility of the project. Consequently, many types of interaction between individuals have to be ignored. Even with the restrictive psychological assumptions of rational behaviour, severe difficulties are faced when the behaviour of a number of actors are brought together (Arrow, 1986; Kirman, 1989, 1992; Rizvi, 1994a). A fundamental consequence is the breakdown of the individualistic or atomistic type of economic analysis, such as that of a Walrasian type.

This means that it is difficult to simply graft on to neoclassical analysis the 'social', 'cultural' or 'moral' elements that are seen to be absent. The problem is of irredeemable defects at the theoretical core. It is thus not a question of adding 'context' or additional 'dimensions' to neoclassical economic theory. A theoretical revolution is required at the core of economics itself. The Walrasian and mechanistic assumptions at the hub of orthodox economics have to be replaced.

This does not mean that nothing has been learned from neoclassical theory. Furthermore, it may be possible to make use of the insights of great neoclassical theorists, such as Marshall. Some formal models are at least of heuristic value.[14] But neoclassical economics is inadequate for the analysis of institutional structures such as markets. For this and other reasons a new theoretical paradigm is required.

Such a negative verdict does not help to make friends in mainstream economics departments. In the existing climate it is likely to damage a professional career. But – especially for the scientist – personal popularity

---

[14] For example, in a formal model, Schelling (1978) showed that racial segregation can result from the cumulative effect of weak causes. This does not necessarily reveal the processes of segregation in the real world but it does lead us to become more sensitive to the actual possibility that weak forces might cumulatively lead to strong effects. Other theoretical work of equally strong heuristic value includes the models developed by Arthur (1989) and Axelrod (1984).

and professional self-interest must never be ranked above truth. Would anyone deny this maxim? Heresy is bad for the career; but conformism stunts the enquiring mind and professional cowardice is bad for the soul.

After all, the times may change. It is significant that an orthodox theorist of the stature of Hahn (1991, pp. 48–50) has noted the rise of evolutionary theories in economics and predicted that in the next hundred years 'the subject will return to its Marshallian affinities to biology.' His successors, he concluded, will not be so preoccupied with 'grand unifying theory' or so immersed in 'the pleasures of theorems and proof.' They will succumb instead to 'the uncertain embrace of history and sociology and biology.' His collaborator Arrow (1995, p. 1618) remarked along similar lines: 'the very notion of what constitutes an economic theory will have to change. For a century, some economists have maintained that the biological is a more appropriate paradigm for economics than equilibrium models analogous to mechanics. . . . economic theory may well take an analogous course.'

Such a development would be a return to the theoretical tradition of the 'old' institutionalism of Thorstein Veblen and John Commons, perhaps in everything but name. Notwithstanding the castigations of the mainstream, later chapters of this book show how the 'old' institutionalism remains on the agenda. In the following chapter, we shall turn to another assault on neoclassical theory. However, despite its logical rigour it failed to have a lasting impact or provide an adequate basis for an alternative theory. It is thus another important object lesson for the critic of mainstream economics.

3. A Case Study: The Fate of the Cambridge Capital Controversy

In the 1960s and 1970s, economics was in a much more pluralistic state than in the 1990s.[1] For a few years, Marxian economics attracted a significant following, in both Europe and America. In addition, a substantial theoretical attack, originating from the University of Cambridge in England, seemed to undermine the foundations of mainstream economic theory. In retrospect, however, the assault was a failure. Although the critics had logic on their side, mainstream economics was largely unaffected by the debate. This was also despite the fact that the origin of the critical assault was widely known as one of the most prestigious universities in the world – the faculty of economics of Alfred Marshall and John Maynard Keynes. This chapter is a contribution to the analysis of this failure, in the hope from it some crucial lessons may be learned.

In 1960, the Cambridge economist Piero Sraffa published a slim volume of only 96 pages that was over thirty years in the preparation. The central proposition of the work is that there is no measure of capital independent of distribution and prices. *Production of Commodities by Means of Commodities* constituted a devastating logical attack on the aggregate production function of neoclassical theory and theories of supply, distribution and growth based upon it.

A few years earlier, Sraffa's friend and colleague Joan Robinson (1953) had asked the forbidden question: how is capital to be measured? Sraffa drove home the argument that there was no independent measure. A physical measure is useless unless capital consists of a single good, or

---

[1] This chapter is a slightly revised version of Hodgson (1997b).

uniform bundles of goods. A price measure is impossible unless there is a prior set of relative prices. But, in a capitalist system, such prices depend on the rate of profits. If the production function is a function of 'capital' and this is measured in price terms, then the view that this function leads to a determination of the rate of profits involves circular reasoning.

In such terms, Sraffa's work was a highly destructive *internal* critique of the type of neoclassical theory which made extensive use of aggregate production functions, in application to theories of supply, growth and distribution in particular. It showed that such aggregate production functions with 'capital' as a single factor were unfounded on any general theory in which there were heterogeneous capital goods, including fixed capital. They could represent no more than an imaginary world where there were no machines or raw materials, other than a mythical, single and ubiquitous common substance – the fabled 'Ricardian corn'.

More than a third of a century later, however, aggregate production functions are still common both in the textbooks and core journals of mainstream economics. Why is this so? This chapter was written with this question in mind and may help contribute to a full answer. A full explanation must involve not only the internal logic of the theories and debates but also the culture and institutions of the economics profession itself.

Clearly, we can do no more than to touch upon these issues here. Neither is it possible to enter into all the technical controversies that took place, particularly over the nature and measurement of capital (Harcourt, 1972, 1994; Ahmad, 1991) and the Marxian labour theory of value (Steedman, 1975, 1977; Steedman *et al*, 1981). Instead, the purpose of this chapter is to place the Sraffian opus in the wider context of the theoretical development of economics and of the evolution of the economics profession itself. Perhaps in this way some new lessons can be learned.

Notably, the survival of the aggregate production function after the Sraffian attack is not a simple story of deafness and inertia on the part of orthodoxy. Leading American neoclassical economists such as Paul Samuelson (1966, 1989) were involved in the capital theory debates and eventually conceded much ground to the Sraffians.

The technique adopted here is to consider the fate of Sraffa's *Production of Commodities* in the light of its recorded citations in the academic journals. Section 3.1 of this chapter considers the slow take-off of the *Production of Commodities* and the capital theory debates of the 1960s. Section 3.2 addresses the heyday of that work, from the early 1970s to the mid-1980s. In Section 3.3 notable attempts to synthesize Sraffa with Keynes are addressed. Section 3.4 concludes this chapter by considering the subsequent decline in attention to Sraffa and his legacy.

3.1. THE PRODUCTION OF CITATIONS BY MEANS OF CITATIONS

With all its faults and shortcomings, the use of the data in the Social Science Citations Index (SSCI) has become established as one of the best methods of assessing the impact or visibility of a scholarly work. A large number of the more well-established academic journals are regularly analysed for the number of times the articles within them cite particular works. Currently, in the subject area of economics alone, well over one hundred journals used to obtain these data. In the other social sciences there are many more. All the 'core' economics journals are present on this list, along with a number of publications specialising in heterodox approaches.

The citation data for Sraffa's *Production of Commodities by Means of Commodities* are presented in Figure 3.1. A citation count of 15 indicates that the *Production of Commodities* has been cited 15 times in that year, by all the journals on the SSCI list, including both economics and non-economics journals.

Figure 3.1: Citations to Sraffa's *Production of Commodities*
(All editions, including translations)

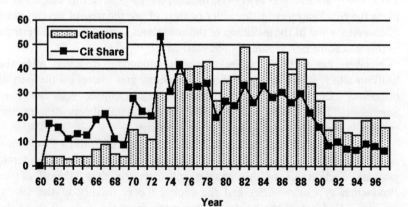

Several points are worthy of note. First, it was not until ten years after its appearance that annual citations to *Production of Commodities* reached double figures. This is a remarkably poor start, given the theoretical significance of the work. The 'incredibly long gestation period' (Harcourt, 1972, p. 14) of this volume prior to publication was followed, after birth, by an equally incredible decade of neglect.

Second, it is in the 1970s and 1980s that citations to the work reach their higher levels. However, the highest citation level of 49, achieved in 1982, is itself relatively low for a work of this stature and importance. The highest 'citation share' (the number of citations for the work divided by total number of citations in the social sciences, in millions) was achieved in 1973. This year may represent the peak of popularity for Sraffa's volume. However, this reputation did not endure.

Finally, there has been a precipitous fall in citations to the work after 1988, reaching low levels after 1990. The fall in citation share is even more severe. In sum, there has been a decade of delayed recognition, followed by two decades of moderate attention, followed by dereliction in the 1990s.

What can be the explanations of the delayed ascent, moderate rise and serious fall of the impact of Sraffa's classic, as measured by citations? Part of an answer can be obtained by considering the publications associated with the debates around Sraffa's work. Shortly after it was published it received two lengthy and positive reviews, by Meek (1961) and Robinson (1961). However, none of these reviews was in a top-ranking economics journal.[2]

In 1961 two notable followers of Sraffa – Joan Robinson from Cambridge and Piero Garegnani from Italy – visited the Massachusetts Institute of Technology and engaged in controversy with Samuelson. One result was the famous attempt by Samuelson (1962) to rescue orthodoxy with the 'surrogate production function'. His article was published in the UK-based *Review of Economic Studies*, which is generally regarded as one of the core mainstream economics journals.[3] In it Samuelson made a brief reference to Sraffa. However, even this mention by a future Nobel Laureate did not immediately improve the flow of citations to Sraffa's book.

Indeed, Sraffa was not always the main character in the early capital theory debates. Much of the early controversy was over the use of aggregate

---

[2] See also Harcourt and Massaro (1964).

[3] The most famous and widely-used definition of a core journal in economics is in Diamond (1989). However, Diamond's list is out of date and uses imperfectly specified criteria. A recent and more rigorous alternative is provided by Burton and Phimister (1995).

production functions in T. W. Swan's (1956) and Robert Solow's (1956) neoclassical models of growth and distribution (Ahmad, 1991, ch. 4; Harcourt, 1972, chs. 2–3).

The mid-point of the 1960s had passed before the debates over capital-reversing and reswitching began in earnest and drew more attention to Sraffa's book. Notably, a number of anti-neoclassical articles on these themes appeared in a symposium in the prestigious (and US-based) *Quarterly Journal of Economics*. They included essays by Piero Garegnani (1966), Michio Morishima (1966) and Luigi Pasinetti (1966). They were followed by an article by Joan Robinson and Khaleeq Naqvi (1967) in the same journal. The publication of these articles in the *QJE* was of enormous significance for the capital controversy. In 1966–67 the issues were discussed at length in a top American journal. One wonders how different the story might have been if an American core journal had not opened its pages to these strange and controversial imports from Europe.

Furthermore, in the *QJE* symposium Samuelson conceded much of the argument with a co-authored recantation (Levhari and Samuelson, 1966) and his milestone 'summing up' article (Samuelson, 1966). The possibility of capital-reversing and reswitching had been established, undermining the general notion of a 'well-behaved' production function. On this critical point, Samuelson admitted defeat, and essentially acknowledged the victory of Cambridge, England in the debate.

Even then, citations to *Production of Commodities* remained at a very low level for another five years. It is impossible to be sure, but it is likely that two journal publications are largely responsible for raising the profile of Sraffa's book in the early 1970s.[4] The first, and probably most important, was the survey of the capital controversies by Geoffrey Harcourt (1969) in the *Journal of Economic Literature*. This extended the Cambridge (UK) attack from the *QJE* bridgehead across the Atlantic and reached another strategically significant core journal – published by the American Economic Association – which has consistently scored highest in terms of citation impact.[5] Harcourt (1972) followed this with the definitive monograph on the capital theory debates of the 1960s, which must have added to the impact of his *JEL* article.

---

[4] The brevity of this list may be questioned. Note also Pasinetti (1969). Bhaduri's (1969) important critique of Samuelson's surrogate production function made no reference to Sraffa and did not use a Sraffian framework of analysis.

[5] For an explanation of 'citation impact' and specific citation impact figures see the regularly published SSCI *Journal Citations Reports*.

The second crucial journal article was Garegnani's (1970) *coup de grace* against the aggregate production function. This appeared in the *Review of Economic Studies*, reportedly despite the earlier wishes of its editors to reject it. Garegnani showed that the typical textbook picture of a 'well behaved' production function was based on highly restrictive and implausible assumptions. Garegnani's article was quickly reprinted in a widely-circulated reader produced by Penguin and edited by Hunt and Schwartz (1972). Along with the publication of related Penguin readers by Harcourt and Laing (1971) and Sen (1970), all this helped the capital theory debates to reach a wider audience.

Accordingly, and probably as a consequence of these publications in the 1969–1972 period, the number of citations received by *Production of Commodities* jumped from an annual average of 4.9 in the years 1961–69 to 15 in 1970 and 30 in 1973.

3.2. REVOLTING CITES

The mood of the times should not be forgotten: 1968 and all that. Protest and political turmoil in many developed Western countries spilled over into academia with an intensified questioning of established assumptions and approaches. In particular, there was a massive growth in interest in Marxism in general and Marxian economics in particular.

Sraffa had been an intimate friend of Antonio Gramsci and had Marxian sympathies. The *Production of Commodities* was widely viewed as rehabilitating both classical economics and the economics of Marx. Nevertheless, Sraffa's editorship of the collected works of Ricardo brought suspicion upon him as a 'neo-Ricardian' from the more 'fundamentalist' adherents of Marx.

In 1975 Ian Steedman published a demonstration of the possibility of 'positive profits with negative surplus value' in the *Economic Journal*. Using a Sraffian framework, Steedman undermined the labour theory of value. Steedman (1977) extended this argument and critique in an influential book. In the contemporary context of high academic interest in Marxism an enormous controversy erupted (Harcourt, 1982a; 1982b, ch. 14; Hodgson, 1982a, 1982b).

This may have done a great deal to improve the citation rate of the *Production of Commodities*, but – as Steedman was the first to acknowledge – it did little to repulse neoclassical orthodoxy or to build a positive theoretical alternative. Indeed, Steedman's main object had been to purge the heterodox critics of 'obscurantism'. This was seen as a necessary ablution before a rigorous theoretical alternative could be developed.

Critical and open-minded heterodox economists were faced with a dilemma concerning the theoretical status of the Sraffian system itself. Two very different points of view emerged. One group saw the work of Sraffa and his followers as primarily an internal critique of neoclassical theory that had exposed logical inconsistencies and faulty foundations. In this view the significance of Sraffa's work was still important but primarily destructive of orthodoxy. A second group saw Sraffa as providing much more: a common foundation for a new heterodox economic theory embracing the insights of Marx, Keynes, Kalecki and others. The Sraffian approach was seen as providing an appropriate foundation for the analysis of the essential workings of the capitalist mode of production. This latter group are dubbed here the 'constructivist' Sraffians.[6]

3.3. BUILDING CITES FOR A NEW HETERODOXY

The leading 'constructivist' Sraffians were John Eatwell, Piero Garegnani and Murray Milgate.[7] In a number of publications in the late 1970s and early 1980s they argued that the Sraffian framework was a secure foundation for the Keynesian theory of effective demand (Garegnani, 1978, 1979a; Eatwell and Milgate, 1983). However, this meant interpreting Keynes in 'long-period' rather than 'short-period' terms. It also involved the downplaying of the key concepts of uncertainty and expectation in Keynesian analysis.

This was in great contrast to other Keynesians that had emphasized problems of uncertainty and had argued that the economy cannot be captured by a static analysis. While Garegnani (1979b, p. 183) echoed by Eatwell (1979, 1983) denied a 'central role to uncertainty and expectations',

---

[6] According to Roncaglia (1991), there are three constructivist approaches within Sraffian economics, the 'Smithian' (Sylos-Labini), the 'Ricardian' (Pasinetti), and the 'Marxian' (Garegnani). Attention here is concentrated on the latter category, which is arguably the closest to, and the most reliant upon, Sraffa's work.

[7] This section draws from material published in Hodgson (1989). Earlier, Hodgson (1982b) had written in a 'constructivist' spirit, in the sense that that word is used here. But it is a transitional work, and by the time of its appearance its author abandoned the constructivist Sraffian project for an institutionalism that was later developed in Hodgson (1988).

they did this in opposition to others such as Paul Davidson (1972), Brian Loasby (1976), Hyman Minsky (1976) and George Shackle (1974) who saw uncertainty and expectations as being central both to the work of Keynes and to positive developments based upon it.

The fact that Sraffa's long-period analysis represents a major amendment to Keynes's theory was admitted by Sraffian theorists themselves. For instance, Garegnani (1979b, p. 183) insisted that the 'short-period character of Keynes theory' is a weakness. Following this, Eatwell (1983) stated that there are 'many parts of *The General Theory* which either do not address or . . . directly contradict the notion of long-period theory . . . it frequently appears that Keynes is simply presenting a theory of . . . short-period positions' (pp. 271–2).

As early as 1973, Robinson expressed some misgivings about the exclusive focus of the Sraffian constructivists on the long-period: 'In reality', she wrote, 'all the interesting and important questions lie in the gap between pure short-period and long-period analysis', (Robinson, 1973a, p. 60). By 1980 her differences with the constructivists had become even more clear, as Harcourt (1985) related in an incisive account of this episode: 'in her debates with Garegnani, and with Eatwell and Milgate, Joan Robinson used her views on the inadmissibility of long-period comparisons for describing processes, which she developed in her critique of neoclassical theory, to criticize the central stress by these authors on the notion of centres of gravitation or long-period positions' (p. 106). Sraffian 'values' or 'prices of production' were rejected because they could not be incorporated in a theory which was set in historical time (Robinson, 1974, 1979b, 1980; Bhaduri and Robinson, 1980).

Robinson (1979b) also asked what was the meaning of the normal rate of profits in long-period analysis: does it mean 'what the rate of profit on capital will be in the future or what it has been in the past or does it float above historical time as a Platonic Idea?' (p. 180). Garegnani (1979b) replied that the normal rate of profits is located in the present: 'It corresponds to the rate which is being realized *on an average* (as between firms and over time) by the entrepreneurs who use the dominant technique . . . it is also the rate of profits which that present experience will lead entrepreneurs in general to expect *in the future* from their current investment' (p. 185).

This response suggests that long-period analysis is a short-period one as well, for the long-period average is seen to bear upon short-period decisions. But how do entrepreneurs *know* what the average rate of profits is, or if the rate of profits in their own enterprise is above or below it? How can entrepreneurs form expectations of a future rate of profits on the basis of this present average rate of profits which is unperceived and unknown? Even if it were known, why should entrepreneurs assume that it would remain the same in the future? These questions are neither raised nor answered in the Garegnani–Eatwell–Milgate extension of Sraffian theory.

It is also questionable that a Sraffian world of fixed coefficients can represent the long-period if this is meant to include capital accumulation and technological change. Sraffian theorists have suggested that these phenomena can be encompassed by the comparative-static analysis of the switching of techniques. But as Robinson (1980) put it: 'It is a mistake in methodology to compare two technical systems . . . and then to switch from one to the other. A switch is an event in historical time which has to be accounted for by introducing historical causation in the story. This is where Sraffa leaves us and hands us over to Keynes' (p. 134). Technological change is a process, through time, with future consequences which are rarely known with any precision in the present. It involves, for instance, investment in research and development where the payoffs are essentially uncertain, and changes in the social relations of production resulting from industrial struggles or the reorganization of work. A static matrix of Sraffian input–output coefficients cannot represent these processes.

Furthermore, it was not simply key Keynesian concepts such as uncertainty and expectations that were the casualties of this attempt to build a theory upon Sraffian foundations. The very emphasis on *physical* inputs and outputs in the Sraffa system neglected questions of learning and knowledge which had been given little attention by orthodoxy and heterodoxy alike. Robinson (1975, p. vii; 1979a, pp. 37–40, 94–5, 116) hinted at them after she belatedly stumbled in about 1970 across Veblen's (1919a, pp. 185–200) critique of neoclassical capital theory.[8] In any adequate sense, it is difficult to relate knowledge and learning to the physical coefficients of the Sraffa system, just as the personal

---

[8] Robinson (1979a, p. 95) concluded that Veblen was 'the most original economist born and bred in the USA'. She noted in particular Veblen's critique of John Bates Clark's conflation of 'capital goods' with 'capital'. It is not clear if she was aware that Veblen was one of the first to point out the 'amount of capital' can be derived only through a process of valuation: 'The value involved is, like all value, a matter of imputation' (Veblen, 1919a, p. 371; See also pp. 196–7). He thus hints at the problem of circular argumentation much later identified by Robinson and Sraffa. Veblen rejected the 'factors of production' approach in its entirety, seeing production as much to do with 'the accumulated, habitual knowledge of the ways and means involved . . . the outcome of long experience and experimentation' (Veblen, 1919a, pp. 185–6). See also Hodgson (1994b).

transformations involved in the learning, cognitive and innovative processes fit uneasily with the agent driven mechanistically to maximize utility with given preference functions.[9]

Finally, the Sraffian approach does not offer a theory of human agency and interaction. It simply suggests that the long-period positions will somehow reflect and affect the expectations and actions of agents, without explaining how the average rate of profits and long-period prices are attained. Whatever the strengths of Sraffian analysis, particularly its destructive critique of neoclassical and Marxian theories of value and capital, this lack is a serious weakness. In consequence it cannot be claimed that Sraffian analysis provides an adequate or entirely appropriate foundation for heterodox theory.[10]

Sraffian theory was also criticized in an article by Frank Hahn in the *Cambridge Journal of Economics*. Against 'the followers of Sraffa', Hahn (1982) argued that 'there is no correct neo-Ricardian proposition which is not contained in the set of propositions which can be generated by orthodoxy . . . the neo-Ricardian attack *via* logic is easily beaten off' (p. 353). If true, this would much diminish both the destructive and constructive versions of Sraffian theory.

In fact, the more careful Sraffians had always made it clear that their attack was effective against the *aggregate* neoclassical production function only. Other, disaggregated versions of neoclassical theory, such as general equilibrium theory of the genre of Arrow and Hahn (1971), were not vulnerable to such a critique. In these models, capital could be treated as heterogeneous and disaggregated. Formally, Hahn was right in suggesting that his version of general equilibrium theory could also generate 'badly behaved' aggregate production functions, reswitching and other curiosa. But the Arrow–Hahn type of theory had not been the foundation of Solovian and other models in which capital as a single factor of production entered as an input. Instead, aggregate production functions abound.

Further, the possibility that general equilibrium theory could generate similarly 'perverse' results did not imply that Sraffian theory was of lesser

---

[9] Instead, it has been the evolutionary and institutional frameworks of Nelson and Winter (1982), Dosi *et al* (1988), Lundvall (1992) and Morroni (1992) that have brought the issues of knowledge, learning and innovation to the fore.

[10] Duménil and Lévy (1987) attempted to construct a more dynamic model based on Sraffian foundations. However, objections still remain: crucial problems of information and knowledge are assumed away. For more on the limitations of the Sraffa–Keynes synthesis see Harcourt and O'Shaughnessy (1985).

importance. In fact, if Hahn is right then general equilibrium theory is a special case of Sraffian analysis, rather than the other way round. General equilibrium theory involves *additional* assumptions, such as individual utility maximization, which are not present in Sraffian analysis and thus confer upon it a more general status.

The Sraffian constructivists hinted that they held to a different model of human behaviour, based on habits and rules rather than the utility-maximizer of neoclassical theory. Such an approach was begun in the institutionalism of Thorstein Veblen and John Commons. But neither the links to institutionalism, nor a specific theory of human action along these lines, were developed by the constructivists. If they had been, things might have been different. The behavioural core of constructivist Sraffian theory remained empty.

In a significant and related development, Steedman (1984) showed that deviations of market prices from 'prices of production' would not necessarily have the same sign as the corresponding deviations of market profit rates from the equivalent norm. This suggested that the 'classical' idea that prices tend to move towards 'centres of gravitation' is open to question (Boggio, 1985; Duménil and Lévy, 1987). With the vulnerability of such a core proposition, it would be understandable that confidence in the 'constructivist' Sraffian project would be undermined.

In the mid 1980s the constructivist project had hardly started. However, rather than rising to the challenge, its protagonists left it in its unfinished state. This virtual abandonment of the project needs to be explained. Did the criticisms of Robinson and others make their mark? Or was it the shadow of doubt over the 'centre of gravitation' idea that was more significant? Gary Mongiovi (1992), a younger member of the constructivist group, declared almost a decade later that the theoretical research programme engendered by Sraffa's work 'is still in the early stages of development' (p. 544). Indeed, despite the expenditure of much ink and paper, it has remained more or less in that state for well over a decade, and faith has been lost in the constructivist promise.

3.4. OUT OF CITE – OUT OF MIND

Ironically, for mainstream economists, general equilibrium theory was soon to become a falling star. However, Sraffian theory was not a major force behind this shift. Part of the motivation behind the development of postwar general equilibrium theory had been to develop the microfoundations for economics as a whole. Key developments in the 1970s thwarted this project. Although they were not given due attention at the time, they eventually played a role in transforming mainstream microeconomic theory and bringing general equilibrium theory down from its pedestal.

In the 1970s, Hugo Sonnenschein (1972, 1973a, 1973b), Rolf Mantel (1974) and Gerard Debreu (1974) showed that, starting from the assumption of individual utility maximization, the excess demand functions in an exchange economy can take almost any form. There is thus no basis for the assumption that they are generally downward sloping. This problem is essentially one of aggregation when individual demand functions are combined. The consequences for neoclassical general equilibrium theory are devastating (Kirman, 1989). As S. Abu Turab Rizvi (1994a) put it, the work of Sonnenschein, Mantel and Debreu is quite general and is not restricted to counter-examples:

> Its chief implication . . . is that the hypothesis of individual rationality, and other assumptions made at the micro level, gives no guidance to an analysis of macro-level phenomena: the assumption of rationality or utility maximization is not enough to talk about social regularities. This is a significant conclusion and brings the microfoundations project in [general equilibrium theory] to an end (p. 363).

Hahn (1975) immediately accepted the consequences, and compared the impact of the Sonnenschein *et al* results with the Sraffian critique:

> The neo-Ricardians   . . . have demonstrated that capital aggregation is theoretically unsound. Fine . . . The result has no bearing on the mainstream of neoclassical theory simply because it does not use aggregates. It has a bearing on the vulgar theories of the textbooks . . . Results most damaging to neoclassical theory have recently been proved by Debreu, Sonnenschein and Mas-Collel (p. 363).

On the whole, however, the problems raised by Sonnenschein *et al* were not given sufficient attention by either orthodox or heterodox theorists at the time.

Rizvi (1994a, p. 361) saw the later appearance of Shafer and Sonnenschein's (1982) review of the Sonnenschein-type aggregation problems as crucial in bringing the issue to the notice of the profession.[11]

---

[11] See also Duffie and Sonnenschien (1989).

Notably, the issues were previously ignored in two books which had addressed the microfoundations project: Geoffrey Harcourt (1977) and Roy Weintraub (1979). Quickly after 1982, however, the pursuit of general equilibrium theory and the neoclassical microfoundations project were abandoned by many in the mainstream avant-garde.

Notably, the Sraffian critique contributed little to this development. Nor did it influence the new alternative mainstream paradigm: game theory. Rizvi (1994b, pp. 3–4) argued that the rise of game theory in the 1980s was due primarily to the 'decreasing returns' of Arrow–Debreu–McKenzie general equilibrium analysis and the arbitrariness and existence problems exposed by Sonnenschein and others. Game theory filled the vacuum.

The Sraffian critique was not only bypassed, it became irrelevant for the new mainstream core theory. Sraffian results have no apparent critical effect on game theory. Losing their status even as internal criticisms of the mainstream core, they became less and less relevant.

This is not to suggest that all mainstream theorists were as rigorous as Sonnenschein or as agile as Hahn. The great majority simply ignored both the capital theory debates and even the Sonnenschein results. Versions of aggregate production functions abound and are central to recent and fashionable developments such as real business cycle theory and endogenous growth theory. For many, it is as if the capital controversy had never happened.

What morals can be drawn from this tale? In lieu of a conclusion a few shall be suggested:

1) The fate of theory is not a matter of cold logic alone. The slow reception and relatively weak impact of the Sraffian critique of neoclassical theory was due in part to its origin outside the top American universities that have dominated post-1945 economics research. Even its Cambridge pedigree was not good enough. The *Production of Commodities* became prominent only after the appearance of key contributions in core economics journals, notably the *Quarterly Journal of Economics* and *Journal of Economic Literature*, and after it had been given attention by leading American economists, notably by Samuelson.

2) There was more to the increase of interest in the 1970s in Sraffa's works than their intrinsic logic. They became tied up with the wave of political radicalism that swept Western universities and the associated debates around Marxian economics.

3) The Sraffian constructivists never developed a widely-accepted theoretical system to rival the neoclassical one. Attempts to do this by Eatwell, Garegnani and others faltered, largely in controversy over the

interpretation of Keynes' legacy. In particular, because no alternative theory of human agency was proposed to replace the idea of individual utility maximization, the centre of the neoclassical system remained unchallenged. The Sraffian assault on neoclassical theory was directed largely at aggregate production functions and left the ontological and behavioural foundations of the citadel intact.

4) Ironically, neoclassical general equilibrium did eventually suffer devastating blows in the 1980s, when Sonnenschein and others demonstrated key problems of aggregation starting from individual utility maximization. Cold logic did then have an effect, but only when it was directed at core propositions and the central microfoundations project of mainstream theory. The Sraffian critique had failed to do this.

5) From the outset, whether conceived as an internal critique of neoclassical economics or the foundation of an alternative paradigm, Sraffian economics had no theory of individual human action and no story concerning the actions of agents and their consequences. It thus had nothing to say about these key causal relations with a socio-economic system. This defect always left it vulnerable by comparison with mainstream theory, which does embody a theory of human action, whatever its faults.

6) Further, the identification of the stationary-state parameters governing distribution in a socio-economic system (namely the technological coefficients and the real wage) is not itself an exploration into causal relations and processes. Sraffian analysis replicates the formalistic and deductivist methodology that dominates mainstream economic theory. As a critique of orthodoxy, the Sraffian approach is thus disabled.

7) The fate of the Cambridge capital controversy is also a poignant case study for those that believe that mainstream economic theory will not change unless there is a ready-made and viable alternative. Essentially, this adage remains true. However, after being largely unshaken by the Cambridge assault – and unattracted by its 'Post Keynesian' alternative theories – mainstream economics quite quickly shifted the focus of its attention from general equilibrium to game theory, despite the latter being relatively underdeveloped and of uncertain outcome.

The fate of Sraffian theory and the capital controversy is both a tragedy and an object lesson for all those committed to a better and more humane economics and a basis for economic policies that may contribute to the building of a better world.

4. Metaphor and Pluralism in Economics

'Complexity' is a word of the moment. Books about a new 'emerging science' centred on complexity have now made their way into the best-seller lists (Lewin, 1993; Waldrop, 1992).[1] Such populist outcomes should make us cautious. Nevertheless, there is some substance in the claims made by those who see an emergent paradigm in the making. There are several methodological implications of this shift. One of central importance is the breakdown of the reductionist project, especially in those sciences addressing complex systems, such as economics and biology.[2] Two further implications follow immediately: first, the necessity for a much more self-conscious and open use of metaphor in the analysis of complex systems, and second, the recognition that there can be no complete and final explanation and that we shall always be faced by a plurality of competing theories.

The first section of this chapter discusses the breakdown of reductionism, with particular attention to economics and biology. The second section asserts the need for the self-conscious use of metaphor in science and argues that metaphor has always, in fact, been constitutive for science and has a

---

[1] This chapter – with the exception of its appendix – is a revised version of Hodgson (1997a).

[2] While central to the argument here, the concept of complexity has proved notoriously difficult to define. Stent (1985, pp. 215–6) made a useful stab at the problem, arguing that 'the complexity of a phenomenon is not to be measured by the number of component events of which it is constituted, but rather by the diversity of the interactions among its component events.' See Lloyd (1990) for a review of definitions of complexity.

subterranean presence in economic theory. The third section discusses the implications for theoretical pluralism and concludes the chapter.

4.1. THE LIMITS TO REDUCTIONISM

Inspired in particular by classical physics and its apparent analytical and practical successes, orthodox economists have long been labouring under a reductionist research programme. The complexities of socio-economic systems have been addressed by attempting to build up a composite picture from atomistic, individual units, just as the particle forms the elemental unit in Newtonian mechanics. Accordingly, reductionism typically involves attempts to explain the whole through its analytical reduction to its presumed microfoundations and component parts.

Many economists pay lip service to methodological individualism and the view that social wholes should be explained solely in terms of the individuals comprising them (Hodgson, 1988, 1993b). However, the complexity of social phenomena means that this methodological practice has never been successfully applied, except in trivial cases, and is bound to be unsuccessful in any complex social system (Udéhn, 1987).

While mainstream economic theory has long been engaged in an attempt to place economics on secure and individualistic microfoundations, it was quickly realized that the potential diversity among individuals threatened the feasibility of this project. Many types of interaction between the individuals have to be ignored to make the analysis tractable. Indeed, it was not easy to develop a composite picture from a diversity of types of individual agent.

Even with the standard assumptions of rational behaviour, and its drastic psychological and epistemological limitations, severe difficulties are faced. As Arrow (1986, p. S388) has been led to declare: 'In the aggregate, the hypothesis of rational behaviour has in general no implications.' Consequently, it is widely assumed that all individuals have the same utility function. Among other things this denies the possibility of 'gains from trade arising from individual differences' (p. S390).

Fabrizio Coricelli and Giovanni Dosi (1988, p. 126) argue that 'the project of building dynamic models with economic content and descriptive power by relying solely on the basic principles of rationality and perfect competition through the market process has generally failed.' Attempts to base macroeconomics on neoclassical microfoundations involve faith in the 'invisible hand' and in the substantive capabilities of individuals to calculate endlessly and make supremely rational choices. Yet the results of this theoretical endeavour show no more than a very crippled hand, incapable of orderly systemic co-ordination even in relatively simple models:

> Moreover, note that these results are obtained despite an increasing attribution of rational competence and information processing power to individual agents. Certainly . . . the attempt to 'explain' macroeconomics solely on the basis of some kind of 'hyper-rationality' of the agents . . . and the (pre-analytical) fundamentals of the economy (i.e. given technology and tastes) has failed. (Coricelli and Dosi, 1988, p. 136)

Hence it is no exaggeration to say that in economics the microfoundations enterprise has effectively collapsed, and for reasons well known to and understood by the leading theorists of the genre.[3] The gravity of the present crisis for mainstream economics can be illustrated by considering a few selected topics.[4]

First, theoretical work in game theory and elsewhere has raised questions about the very meaning of 'hard core' notions such as rationality. Yanis Varoufakis (1990) surveyed some of the recent results concerning the problems of rational decision making in the circumstances where a limited number of other actors are believed to be capable of 'irrational' acts. Such 'irrationality' need not stem from stupidity; it is sufficient to consider the possibilities that rational actors may have incomplete information, limited computational capacities, slight misperceptions of reality, or doubts concerning the attributes of their adversaries. Agents do not have to be substantially irrational for irrationality to matter. Irrational behaviour may emerge simply where some people are uncertain that everybody else is rational.

Second, the intrusion of chaos theory into economics has put paid to the general idea that economics can proceed simply on the criterion of 'correct predictions'. With non-linear models, outcomes can be oversensitive to initial conditions and thereby reliable predictions are impossible to make concerning any extended period. In particular, chaos theory has confounded the rational expectations theorists by showing that even where most agents know the basic structure of the economic model, in general they cannot

---

[3] See also Kirman (1989, 1992), Lavoie (1992, pp. 36–41), Rizvi (1994a), Screpanti and Zamagni (1993, pp. 344–53) and the discussion in Chapter 6 below.

[4] The crisis in economic theory afflicts heterodox as well as orthodox traditions. However, for reasons of brevity the other topics and schools of thought are not discussed in detail here.

derive reliable predictions of outcomes and thereby form any meaningful 'rational expectations' of the future (Grandmont, 1986).

Third, recent research into the problems of the uniqueness and stability of general equilibria have shown that they may be indeterminate and unstable unless very strong assumptions are made, such as the supposition that society as a whole behaves as if it were a single individual. Essentially, this demolishes the entire microfoundations project. Facing such profound problems, Alan Kirman (1992, p. 118) wrote: 'there is no plausible formal justification for the assumption that the aggregate of individuals, even maximizers, acts itself like an individual maximizer.' He concluded: 'If we are to progress further we may well be forced to theorize in terms of groups who have collectively coherent behaviour. . . . The idea that we should start at the level of the isolated individual is one which we may well have to abandon' (Kirman 1989, p. 138). The theoretical implications of these uniqueness and stability results for general equilibrium theory are devastating. The indeterminacy and instability results produced by contemporary theory lead to the conclusion that an economy made up simply of self-contained individual agents has not structure enough to survive.

Typically, the textbook macroeconomics that is spun out of neoclassical theory goes well beyond the rigours of general equilibrium theory, to make bold and general claims concerning the relationship between wages and unemployment, and inflation and the money supply. Only the more honest and careful neoclassical theorists have questioned such macroeconomic derivations from microeconomic assumptions. For instance, Arrow (1986, p. S386) states that he knows 'of no serious derivation of the demand for money from a rational optimization'.

4.1.1. The Ubiquitous Problem of Analytical Intractability

As in other sciences, a strong reductionist tradition still survives in biology. In the nineteenth century, after the publication of Charles Darwin's *Origin of Species*, there was a prominent tendency on behalf of his followers to assume that explanations of social phenomena were reducible to biological terms. In the latter part of the twentieth century, sociobiologists such as Edward Wilson (1975) started a project to explain as much as possible of the social behaviour of animals and humans in terms of their constituent genes. Likewise, Richard Dawkins (1976) seemed to maintain that the behaviours of organisms, groups and whole species can be largely explained in terms of their genes. It may well be the case that biology is of relevance for the study of social phenomena (Hirst and Woolley, 1982; Pinker, 1994; Plotkin, 1994;

Weingart *et al* 1997) but the extreme view that they can be understood wholly or largely in biological terms has been rightly challenged.

Yet biological reductionism has unmanageable computational problems. Consider the prediction of evolution with multiple loci or alleles: 'even the simplest multi-locus case of two alleles at each of two loci is analytically intractable. This should not be surprising: the problem of dimensionality nine (there are nine possible genotypes, with independently specifiable fitness parameters) is already more complicated than the three-body problem of classical mechanics' (Wimsatt, 1980, p. 223). Like the three-body problem, this biological computation has been solved for a variety of special cases (Roughgarden, 1979, pp. 111–33) but has not been solved in general. Similar problems of intractability arise from the Schrödinger equations for subatomic particles.

Consider the apparently simple case of the three-body problem in mechanics. While this problem has been solved for two bodies, the differential equations that result from applying these laws to three bodies are so complicated that a general solution has not been found. Instead, partial solutions have been achieved by resorting to approximations or constraints of various kinds, such as the assumption that one body has negligible mass (Stewart, 1989, pp. 66–72). Hence mathematical solutions cannot be found to configurations of this very first level of complexity, involving just three bodies. This indicates the operational limits of reductionism, even in mechanics. The hope that predictions can be made with such a simple three-body system is in vain. There is here no consolation for the biological or economic reductionist who aims to predict by breaking down all complex phenomena to the interactive behaviour of atomistic or individual parts.

Chaos theorists have shown that in non-linear systems, tiny changes in crucial parameters can lead to dramatic consequences (Gleick, 1988; Stewart, 1989). The result is not simply to make prediction difficult or impossible; there are serious implications for the notion of reductive explanation in science. We cannot with absolute confidence associate a given outcome with a given set of initial conditions, because we can never be sure that the computations traced out from those initial conditions are precise enough, and that the initial conditions themselves have been defined with sufficient precision. Hence in chaos theory the very notion of explanation of a phenomenon by reference to a system and its initial conditions is challenged.

As leading mathematicians of chaos have themselves proclaimed, chaos theory 'brings a new challenge to the reductionist view that a system can be understood by breaking it down and studying each piece' (Crutchfield *et al.*, 1986, p. 48). The impact of chaos theory for science as a whole is likely to be profound. Not only is the common obsession with precise prediction confounded; the whole atomistic tradition in science of attempting to reduce each phenomenon to its component parts is placed into question.

However, this does not mean that such non-linear equations relating to a lower level of analysis are worthless. Although they may be of limited computational or predictive use, they retain some explanatory power. Furthermore, as noted later below, chaotic systems do exhibit some kind of order about which deductions may be drawn.

4.1.2. The Limitations and Biases of the Counter-Strategies

Strategies have been devised to attempt to deal with the general analytical problems associated with complex systems. For instance, Herbert Simon (1968) has examined 'the hypothesis of near decomposability' through which it is assumed that a complex system can be decomposed into a set of subsystems. For this to be feasible, all strong interactions must be contained within the boundaries of subsystems, and interactions between variables or entities in different subsystems must be appreciably weaker than those relating variables or entities in the same subsystem. If this is the case then a short-run approximation to the behaviour of the system can be made by ignoring the interactions between subsystems, and analysing each one as if it were isolated.

However, the general applicability of this principle is in doubt. Apart from the remaining problem of long-term interactions, biologists have shown that under feasible conditions there can be permanent and substantial linkage disequilibrium between subsystems (Maynard Smith, 1978; ch. 5; Roughgarden, 1979). This suggests that systems can be treated as being nearly decomposable only in a limited number of special cases.

In a seminal work of genetic reductionism in biology, George C. Williams (1966) claimed that reductive problems can be solved one locus at a time and then extended to a global solution by 'iterating over all loci'. This is now recognized by critics as invalid. Williams wrongly presumed that gene frequency alone is an adequate basis for a deterministic theory of evolutionary change, and ignores context dependence. This referred to a situation where the fitness or behaviour of an organism may be significantly dependent on its environmental context, often leading to two-way interactions between a unit and its environment. As William Wimsatt (1980, p. 240) argued: 'Illegitimate assumptions of context-independence are a frequent error in reductionist analyses.'

In the course of his argument, Wimsatt (1980, p. 241) highlighted 'the practical impossibility of generating an exhaustive, quasi-algorithmic, or exact analysis of the behaviour of the system and its environment'. In response to this complexity 'the reductionist must start simplifying. In general, simplifying assumptions will have to be made everywhere, but given his interest in studying relations *internal* to the system, he will tend to order his list of economic priorities so as to simplify, first and more extremely, in his description, observation, control, and analysis of the environment than in the system he is studying. After all, simplifications internal to the system face the danger of simplifying out of existence the very phenomena and mechanisms he wishes to study.' However, there are clear pitfalls in ignoring the complexities of the environment and some of its interactions with the system in question. Therefore the reductionist research strategy, Wimsatt rightly concluded, has an inbuilt bias towards the inclusion of certain types of relations and the exclusion of others.

It should be pointed out that the general idea of a reduction to parts is not being overturned here. Some degree of reduction to elemental units is inevitable. Even measurement or classification are acts of reduction. Science cannot proceed without some dissection and some analysis of parts. However, although some reduction is inevitable and desirable, complete reductionism is both impossible and a philosophically dogmatic diversion. What is important to stress is that the process of analysis cannot be extended to the most elementary sub-atomic particles presently known to science, or even to individuals in economics or genes in biology. Complete reductionism would be hopeless and interminable. In practice it is never achieved. Reduction is necessary to some extent, but it can never be complete. What is contentious, is not reduction *per se*, but its chosen scope and extent, and the ultimate reliance placed on it in comparison with, or to the exclusion of, other general methodological procedures.

4.2. THE ROLE OF METAPHOR

Faced with this problem of complexity and the failure of complete reductionism, some other methodological approach is required. As W. Brian Arthur has explained:

> If you have a truly complex system, then the exact patterns are not repeatable. And yet there are themes that are recognizable. In history, for example, you can talk about 'revolutions', even though one revolution might be quite different from another. So we assign metaphors. (Quoted in Waldrop, 1992, p. 334)

Among the preliminary tasks of scientific analysis are taxonomy and classification, involving the assignment of sameness and difference. Classification, by bringing together entities in discrete groups, must refer to common qualities. To peer into the complex reality and make some sense of it we are guided inevitably by frameworks and habits of thought that we inherit from our past. We construct 'ideal types' (Dyke, 1985). We use metaphor. As Arjo Klamer and Thomas Leonard (1994, p. 31) put it: 'Science needs metaphor since it provides the cognitive means to chart the unknown.'

In contrast, scientists often regard metaphors as mere literary ornaments. It is sometimes suggested that they should be removed to reveal the essential theory below. For instance, in economics, Joseph Schumpeter (1954, pp. 17–18, 30, 119, 211, 537, 788–90) persistently alleged that analogies with physics or biology were at best an irrelevant diversion and at worst completely misleading. He wrote at a time when positivistic views of science were at their apogee, and metaphor and analogy were thus regarded as an obstruction on some hypothetico-deductive road to truth.

Typically, in economics and elsewhere, recourse to mathematical modes of expression is motivated in part by a desire to remove all such metaphorical 'literary frills'. However, modern philosophers of science take a very different view. Mary Hesse (1980, p. 111) complained that: 'It is still unfortunately necessary to argue that metaphor is more than a decorative literary device, and that it has cognitive implications whose nature is a proper subject of philosophic discussion.' Similarly, Max Black (1962, p. 237) concluded in prominent study of metaphor and analogy in science: 'Metaphorical thought is a distinctive mode of achieving insight, not to be construed as an ornamental substitute for plain thought.'

Clearly, for a positivist, a formalist or a nominalist the use of metaphor is a superficial matter, even a distraction: a confusing renaming of entities that can have nothing to do with their essence. But this kind of response is challenged by modern philosophers who argue that metaphor is constitutive and perhaps even indispensable for science. Now we are 'beyond positivism' (Caldwell, 1982) in the methodology – if not the perceived practice – of economics and other sciences. We cannot found theory simply on facts; the facts do not 'speak for themselves', and can neither verify nor strictly falsify our theories. Metaphor is not an ornament: it is an unavoidable means of constituting and ordering our thoughts. As Friedrich Nietzsche wrote in the nineteenth century:

What, then, is truth? A mobile army of metaphors, metonyms, and anthropomorphisms – in short, a sum of human relations, which have been enhanced, transposed, and embellished poetically and rhetorically, and which after long use seem firm, canonical, and obligatory to all people (Kaufman, 1982).

Metaphors may lead or mislead. By their nature, they are never complete, precise, or literal mappings. If they were precise representations they would not be metaphors, and the juxtaposition of similar but different conceptual frameworks would be lost. This juxtaposition, involving a degree of similarity and dissimilarity, can have both creative and damaging effects. In this sense, metaphors are always imprecise or 'wrong'. We are always faced with an unavoidable and tangled choice of imperfect metaphors.

Metaphors are more than similes. For example, to describe the economy as 'evolving' is not simply to state that the economy develops like an organism or a species in the natural world. It also may prompt the investigator to consider the many meanings and ambiguities in the term 'evolve' and the many extensions and facets of the implicit analogy between the natural and the social world. As Paul Lewis (1996, p. 498) argues: 'Metaphor is *prior* to analogy, describing similarities and analogies that were unknown before their existence was pointed out by metaphor. Metaphor uses the known to express the unknown'.

In economics the triumph of formalism has done nothing to limit the extensive use of metaphor, with terms such as 'human capital', 'market forces', 'consumer sovereignty' and 'natural rates of unemployment'. The use of metaphor affects not merely the phrasing, but the structure and substance of the discipline (Samuels, 1990). Yet the metaphorical references may be partially obscured by the progress of formalism in economics. As mathematical symbols replace words, the analogies may seem to disappear. This is an illusion. As Donald McCloskey (1985, p. 74) put it: 'Noneconomists find it easier to see the metaphors than do economists, habituated as the economists are by daily use to the idea that of course production comes from a "function" and of course business moves in "cycles".'

4.2.1. The Role of the Mechanistic Metaphor in Economics

The use of metaphor in economics has sometimes been acknowledged. Even at the foundation of modern economic science, Adam Smith appealed specifically to metaphor and Newtonian mechanics in his essay on *The Principles which Lead and Direct Philosophical Enquiries: Illustrated by the History of Astronomy* (A. Smith, 1980). As Brian Loasby pointed out, Smith used Newtonian astronomy as primarily a set of 'connecting principles' (Loasby, 1989, pp. 1–5; 1991, pp. 6–8). For Smith, these made sense of his experience and fitted in with his theoretical work. Indeed, Smith was remarkably candid about the role of metaphor and 'imagination' in science. In the tradition of Descartes and Newton, the aim must be to simplify, to reduce to elemental laws, to render 'nature a coherent spectacle' made up of a few 'primary and elementary objects' (A. Smith, 1869, p. 386).

It has been argued extensively, by Philip Mirowski (1989b) and others, that modern economics is still dominated by the metaphor of a mechanistic system. Many commentators typify the kind of mechanistic ideas that permeate economics as essentially Newtonian, although Mirowski saw as crucial the additional influence of the energetics movement in physics in the latter half of the nineteenth century. Whatever the precise details of the account, the consensus is that modern economics is still heavily influenced by the kind of mechanistic thinking that dominated physics around the middle of the nineteenth century. In particular, the evidence for the substantial influence of physics on the architects of the 'marginal revolution' is substantial. As Mirowski has shown, the founders of modern mainstream economic theory all made explicit reference to the mechanistic metaphor, and indicated that their work was guided by such a vision of constitution and structure.

However, the precise details of the transfer of metaphor need to be examined. Here some questions can be raised about Mirowski's account in his *More Heat Than Light*. He argued that the transfer was overt and generally self-conscious, supposing that the economists involved were continually aping physics and its every twist and theoretical turn.

There are at least two flaws in this version of the story. First, it underestimates the subtlety of the process of metaphorical transfer. While there are cases of the direct appropriation of concepts and mathematical formalisms – amply documented by Mirowski – the constitutive transfers are at a deeper and less conscious level, affecting the ontology, epistemology and methodology of the subject. With such 'deep level' transfers the contamination of economics by mechanistic thinking is even more profound than Mirowski has suggested.

The second flaw is that Mirowski disregards the 'institutions of economics' (or the sociology of the economics profession). We may illustrate this by considering later developments in physics in the twentieth century and their influence on economics. For instance, Mirowski made a case that quantum theory has had an effect on econometric practice from the 1930s (Mirowski, 1989a). Apart from this, however, the general effect of post-quantum physics on economics since 1930 has not been crucial.

If economics has been driven by physics in the direct and overt manner suggested by Mirowski then he would have to account for the fact that the deeper implications of modern quantum theory have not been incorporated. Indeed, the organicist and indeterminist aspects of modern quantum theory are in profound contradiction to the Cartesianism, reductionism and atomism at the root of both the earlier physics and of modern economics (Bohm, 1980).

Consideration of these points suggests a slightly different story, although it cannot be discussed in detail here. Walras, Jevons, Edgeworth and Pareto did ape the physics of their time. The reigning belief in the latter decades of the nineteenth century was that an integrated science was possible, spanning both the physical and the social worlds. The principles of physics were thus borrowed by the economists. Subsequently, the professionalization and institutionalization of economics eventually locked the subject into that particular genre. Once the new norms of scientific activity became established in the emergent economic journals and economics departments of the late nineteenth and early twentieth century then they set down the self-reinforcing standards for subsequent research. Scholars seeking publication or promotion had a better chance of success if they conformed to these norms. The canon of mathematical formalization was endowed with particular prestige. In the twentieth century, the natural and social sciences have ostensibly parted and gone their separate ways. The evolution of economics as a discipline gives us one more example of the phenomenon of locked-in behaviour depending very much on initial circumstances.

Accordingly, the initial role of physics was crucial – in contributing greatly to the initial intellectual environment and in legitimating the allegedly scientific credentials of the subject – but since the early decades of the twentieth century economics has been driven less by physics than by its own momentum. It is institutional practice, including a very outdated view of science and an over-obsession with mathematical formalism, that drives economics along its present groove – not an overt and unabating desire to replicate everything going on in modern physics or other natural sciences.[5]

---

[5] As Peter Allen and M. Lesser (1991, p. 166) have wittily suggested, the evolution of economics as an academic profession is a case of lock-in comparable to the evolution of the peacock's tail. Although the male's beautiful tail makes it more successful in mating and producing offspring, there is no useful function or enhancement of fitness in terms of finding food or escaping predators. Just as the beautiful tail evolves with the peacock, economics has evolved an ever more intricate and beautiful mathematical formalism, similarly with little or no functional advantage for the development of economic policy. The developers of abstract theorems and proofs are awarded with prestige and resources, although

This does not mean that the role of the mechanistic metaphor in economics is diminished. Far from it: it is subtle and ubiquitous.

Although no other social science has used mathematical techniques as extensively as economics, the cache of mathematical tools employed has typically been rather limited. Nineteenth century physics did not only offer 'scientific' credentials: it provided an armoury of formal techniques, with differential calculus in pride of place. It is only recently that the kind of mathematics bestowed in the last third of the nineteenth century is beginning to be overshadowed by other formal developments, particularly game theory.

In overt terms, however, modern economics has almost forgotten the source of the crucial metaphor from which it gained so much formal and theoretical inspiration during the eighteenth and nineteenth centuries. Both the methodology and the history of economic thought, now generally and almost completely disregarded by economists, are noticeably absent from undergraduate syllabi and academic job descriptions. With the ever sharper focus on mathematical form rather than conceptual substance, attention has been shifted away from the nature and origin of core assumptions in economics.

This is one reason why the exposure of the role of metaphor is so important. It can reveal deeply embedded structures of thought, and provide a clue to why the subject develops along one path rather than another. The reforming theoretician can then identify, and attempt to remove or alter, the malign features at the theoretical core. If we ignore metaphor, or regard it like Schumpeter as a useless diversion, we are impelled to place all our faith in facts and *a priori* arguments. By this neglect we are condemned to remain with current orthodoxy. The facts themselves are structured by the dominant theories, and orthodoxy offers us a highly restricted choice of axioms upon which theory may be built.

While Mirowski claimed that mainstream economics has continued consciously to ape physics, his ironic thrust was to suggest that they often got the physics wrong. Yet the intellectual aptitudes of economic theorists in a foreign discipline are of little relevance. The whole point of metaphor, as the history of science reveals, is that ideas from elsewhere do not have to be perfectly understood or entirely appropriate in order to inspire novelty. It has been remarked above that metaphor is always 'wrong' so the fact that the

---

there is an increasing suspicion by those on the outside that economics has less and less to do with real economies.

economists 'got their physics wrong' is no great revelation nor apt source of mockery.[6]

Our revised version of Mirowski's story has a better and deeper irony. In the 1870s neoclassical economics attempted to gain the accolade of a science by adopting a thoroughly reductionist research programme, based on the tenet of methodological individualism. In Newtonian spirit, the idea was to found economics on allegedly 'self-evident' axioms about atomistic human behaviour, and to develop the formal theoretical apparatus from there. Such a view of science contrasted with the self-conscious application of metaphors to complex systems, the intuitive insight, or the *gestalt*. The deeper irony was that precisely at the moment of foundation of the neoclassical system its architects were forced to make extensive use of metaphor from another domain of study. On reflection, this is a deep embarrassment to the Cartesian or Newtonian way of doing things. It is no accident that, far from chasing every turn in physics, subsequent neoclassical economists quickly forgot this source of original inspiration.

Contrary to Mirowski, the more serious problem for economics is not the general appropriation of metaphor from the natural sciences but more fundamentally the adoption of a positivist conception of science in which the role of metaphor is specifically denied. In this manner the source of the constitutive assumptions of modern economics has been ignored, despite their continuous transmission through the orthodox mathematical formalisms and their reinforcement through the social structure of the economics profession. For this reason, the ingrained mechanistic metaphor in economics is even more difficult to remove and to replace.

The argument that metaphors are indispensable to scientific discourse counters the mistaken and positivist view of a metaphor-free science. In addition, and concerning particular subjects such as economics, it would lead us to the self-conscious evaluation of metaphor, rather than the futile

---

[6] Examples of error in metaphorical transfer are legion in both the physical and the social sciences. The unconvinced should read Koestler (1959) and take – as one of several examples in that brilliant book – Kepler's obsessive belief in the false idea that everything in the universe is built around some basic geometrical symmetries and the way in which it led to the birth of modern cosmology. Likewise, in economics, Marx adopted from the classical economists the untenable notion of 'value' as a substance generated by labour alone: with it he constructed the wonderful theoretical edifice of *Capital*. Yet essentially this theoretical structure survives and prospers without any labour (or substance) theory of value (Hodgson, 1982a), and still provides some of the best insights into the workings of modern capitalism.

attempt to remove it entirely, as found in the work of Schumpeter and many others.[7]

Neither should we commit the opposite error of assuming that science is *all* about texts and metaphors, and not about reality at all. The recognition of the importance of metaphor does not necessarily involve a surrender to some kind of post-modernist, anti-realism. Lewis (1996) showed convincingly that a constitutive understanding of metaphor is perfectly compatible with the realist view that there is a reality outside the words and text of the theory, or the mind of the theorist.

An opposite danger is to react against post-modernism or anti-realism by shunning the role of metaphor. Hence Mathieu Carlson (1997) wrongly played down the constitutive role of metaphor in science for fear of letting the post-modernist barbarians enter the gates. In disagreement with Carlson, a criticism here of Mirowski's account is partly that he could go *further* in recognising the role of metaphor and – contra post-modernism – adopt a more open stance towards some (pragmatist or other) version of philosophical realism.

4.2.2. From the Mechanistic to the Biological Metaphor in Economics

The deficiencies of the metaphor taken from classical mechanics have been discussed by a number of authors (Georgescu-Roegen, 1971; Gowdy, 1985; Hodgson, 1993b; Norgaard, 1989; Sebba, 1953; Thoben, 1982; Veblen, 1919a). There are a number of perennial problems involved, all relating to the limitations of Cartesian philosophy and Newtonian principles. For instance, movement is reversible in the 'conserved system' of Newtonian mechanics; there is no arrow of time. 'Classical mechanics only knows motion, whereas at the same time the processes of motion are completely reversible and in no way give rise to any qualitative changes' (Thoben, 1982, pp. 292–306, 293). Although in some non-conserved, mechanistic theoretical systems the possibility of irreversibility emerges – such as with the addition of friction – the reasons are quite different from those in more complex systems. Above all, with mechanistic presuppositions, cause and

---

[7] Mayntz (1992, p. 53) notes that in the past sociologists used the metaphor of natural selection, but because 'no attempt at conscious theory transfer was made . . . the question of how biological and sociocultual evolution might differ was not explicitly raised.' This is surely an object lesson for all those who want to keep their metaphors at arm's length.

effect can be mirrored by logical syllogism, and logical replaces historical time (Robinson, 1974).

It is relatively easy to trace the derivation of the ideas of rationality and equilibria, the core concepts of neoclassical economics, from the inheritance of mechanistic thought: 'Classical mechanics considers a system of material points upon which directional forces operate at a distance according to calculable laws of motion. The choice of paths is governed by the principle of least action, which may be termed the economic principle if we take the term in its widest sense as denoting a maximum-minimum principle' (Sebba, 1953). Hence, subject to a combination of forces, economic agents optimize to the point of equilibrium as if they were mere particles obeying mechanical laws.

In addition, there is a general difficulty of incorporating information, learning and knowledge in a mechanistic scheme. In classical mechanics there is no place for thoughts and ideas: all is mere matter, subject to Newtonian laws. As Norbert Weiner (1954, p. 29) remarked: 'In nineteenth-century physics it seemed to cost nothing to get information'.

It is not proposed here that the use of mechanistic thinking in economics has been entirely without value. Nevertheless, the limitations are severe. In sum, the mechanistic metaphor excludes knowledge, qualitative change, and irreversibility through time. It entraps economics in equilibrium schema where there are no systematic errors and no cumulative development. Clearly much is missing here. The strength of the alternative, biological, metaphor is that a place can be found for these important features of economic life.

Another extremely important reason why ideas from biology are of relevance to economics is that both economic and biotic systems are highly complex. They both encompass tangled structures and causalities, involve continuous change and embrace huge variety. Partly for this reason, there is the problem of levels of abstraction and appropriate units of analysis. This has been faced up to and debated by a number of prominent biologists, but far less attention has been given to this vital issue in economics. The adoption of biological metaphors may help to redress the balance.

Taking recourse to biology is not simply a tactic. It is held that real world economic phenomena have much more in common with biological organisms and processes than with the mechanistic world of billiard balls and planets. After all, the economy involves living human beings, not merely particles, forces and energy. Nevertheless, there are risks involved in this trade; biology has been often abused by social scientists in the past, sometimes with horrendous social and political consequences.

It is still widely assumed that evolutionary thinking leads to the rejection of any kind of state subsidy or intervention, and the support for *laissez-faire* on the basis of the idea of 'survival of the fittest'. However, it is wrong to assume that evolutionary theorising always points to the optimality of competitive outcomes, or to laws of evolutionary 'progress', or to the sagacity of *laissez-faire*. According to modern theory, evolutionary processes do not necessarily lead to – by any reasonable definition – optimal consequences. Similar arguments apply in the economic as well as the biotic context (Dupré, 1987; Gould, 1978, 1980, 1989; Gould and Lewontin, 1979; Hodgson, 1993b, ch. 13; Oster and Wilson, 1978, ch. 8; and Sober, 1981).

Moreover, it should be emphasized that biology has internal problems of its own; it is no panacea. Indeed, biology is not itself free of mechanistic metaphor and reductionist methods. A large number of biologists are committed to reductionism, even concerned to explained biological phenomena in physical terms. Within its boundaries, however, there are also pronounced attempts to transcend such strains of thought.

Furthermore, the explicit recognition of the underlying metaphor can perhaps help the theorist to develop 'auto-immune systems' against a rejected strain of thought. For instance, attention to the problem of excessive formalism would lead to the consideration and development of appropriately descriptive and historical approaches to counter an emerging infatuation with the tools and techniques of mathematical biology. While the adoption of a biological metaphor rather than a mechanical one does not itself cure the problem of excessive formalism, the recognition of the complexity and irreducibility of socio-economic reality should warn against this addiction.

It is important to emphasize that all metaphors create difficulties as well as solutions. Accordingly a precise transfer of ideas is neither possible nor desirable. As noted above, metaphorical transfer is *always* 'inaccurate' or 'false'. The use of metaphor is more to do with the stimulation of new ways of thinking or lines of enquiry, rather than the transfer of precise models or analogies. As Renate Mayntz (1992, pp. 68–9) put it:

> What we do . . . is not to use the natural science theory to explain social phenomena, but the natural science theory stimulates a new way of viewing the social phenomena that, guided by some rather abstract notions, triggers a process of social science theory building. Strictly speaking, the potentially most productive mode of borrowing is therefore one where transfer in a direct way does not take place at all.

Accordingly, use of the biological metaphor raises questions about its limitations as well as its potential. But the recognition of problems with the metaphor does not necessarily mean that we have to dispense with it entirely. Indeed, we cannot dispense with the metaphor unless we have another to put in its place.

In particular, there is a serious problem involved in the use of both biological and mechanical metaphors. This concerns the conceptualization of the human agent. It has been argued by several critical economists that – despite the rhetoric – orthodox and mechanistic economics provides no room for real individual choice (Buchanan, 1969; Lachmann, 1977; Loasby, 1976; Shackle, 1955). These economists argue that deterministic systems – as in classical mechanics – offer no space for real choice, because individual actions are predetermined. The same problem applies to modern biology. Darwinian natural selection invokes genetic replication and random variation or mutation, but seemingly affords no role for intentionality, purposefulness or choice.

Unlike classical mechanics, however, biology has addressed this and related problems in the past. The concept of 'vitalism', involving choice, will and purpose, has been persistent within biology. Although 'vitalism' is now out of fashion, it raises real issues of importance, even if the notion is shunned by biologists who confine themselves to causal rather than intentional explanations. Dissenters to strict Darwinism, including Arthur Koestler, have tried to instate concepts of will and purpose in the science, but with limited effect. This whole problem should not be ignored or underestimated: It is addressed at length elsewhere.[8]

Despite all the problems and dangers, it is suggested here that modern biology provides a rich source of ideas and approaches from which a revitalised economics may draw. In all, the application of an evolutionary approach to economics seems to involve a number of advantages and improvements over the orthodox and mechanistic paradigm. For instance, it enhances a concern with irreversible and ongoing processes in time,[9] with long-run development rather than short-run marginal adjustments, with qualitative as well as quantitative change, with variation and diversity, with non-equilibrium as well as equilibrium situations, and with the possibility of persistent and systematic error-making and thereby non-optimizing behaviour.

---

[8] See Koestler (1967), Hodgson (1993b, ch. 14) and Chapter 6 below.

[9] It should not be assumed, however, that all evolutionary processes in biology are irreversible: see Mani (1991). An extended discussion of irreversibility in economics is given by Dosi and Metcalfe (1991).

In short, an evolutionary paradigm provides an alternative to the neoclassical 'hard core' idea of mechanistic maximization under static constraints. The theory of rational choice at the core of mainstream economics relies on static assumptions, the notion of an eventually constant decision environment, and the idea of global rationality, which are all challenged by evolutionary theory (Cooper, 1989; Goldberg, 1975).[10]

Finally, connecting economics with biology may also result from a recognition that as human beings we are part of the natural world. Although the levels and modes of analysis in the two disciplines are quite different, reflecting the emergent properties in each sphere, the provision of conceptual and theoretical links pays respect to the common reality (Bhaskar, 1979; Hirst and Woolley, 1982; Pinker, 1994; Plotkin, 1994; Weingart *et al* 1997). The social sciences have become dangerously disconnected from the biotic world and it is necessary once again to explore the connections, but without reducing the discourse all to one single level of analysis.

4.3. IN CONCLUSION: THEORETICAL PLURALISM

The Latin word *cogito* comes from *coagitare*, to shake together. Much creativity in science comes from the integration of hitherto unrelated ideas or frames of thought. Examples are plentiful (Koestler, 1964). Pythagoras observed a blacksmith at work and noticed that iron bars of different lengths gave out sounds of different pitch under the strokes of the hammer: conceptions of sound and length, of music and measure, were amalgamated. In 1820 Hans Christian Oersted saw that an electric current flowing through a wire deflected a nearby compass. He thus discovered the hitherto unrecognized link between magnetism and electricity, created the concept of

---

[10] See also ch. 8 of the present volume. As Foss (1994a) has argued, there is a key ontological difference between neoclassical and the kind of 'evolutionary' economics exemplified by Nelson and Winter (1982) and Witt (1987). Whereas evolutionary economics theorises on the basis of a universe that is open, with novelties and emergent properties, neoclassical economics suppresses novelty. The importance of such open systems and emergent properties is stressed by philosophical realists such as Bhaskar (1979) and Lawson (1989a, 1997). See also Dyke (1985) who also discussed the problem of closure in complex phenomena. The existence of open systems and emergent properties is incidentally another major reason why the reductionist project in science is confounded.

electromagnetism and inspired the development of the electric motor. Michael Faraday set himself the problem of finding the connections between light, heat, magnetism, and electricity and developed a unified theory of electromagnetic radiation. Energy and matter became later unified in Albert Einstein's theory of relativity.

The founder of pragmatism, Charles Sanders Peirce (1958, pp. 123–5) argued that an important source of creativity in science was the 'abductive' transfer of metaphor from one scientific discourse to another. 'Abduction' was Peirce's addition to the traditional dichotomy of induction and deduction. It concerned the creative process of forming an explanatory hypothesis. According to Peirce (1934, p. 90), induction 'never can originate any idea whatever. No more can deduction. All the ideas of science come to it by the way of abduction.' Hence abduction alone could account for creativity and progress in science. By abduction, Peirce seems to have in mind the spark of intellectual creativity or intuition, kindled in the tinder of assimilated facts. He wrote:

> The abductive suggestion comes to us like a flash. It is an act of *insight*, although of extremely fallible insight. It is true that the different elements of the hypothesis were in our minds before; but it is the idea of putting together what we had never before dreamed of putting together which flashes the new suggestion before our contemplation (Peirce, 1934, p. 113).

For Peirce, the 'abduction' via metaphor of ideas from another context enables us to put together 'what we had never before dreamed of putting together'.[11] As long ago as 1882, Peirce (1958, p. 46) wrote:

> But the higher places in science in the coming years are for those who succeed in adapting the methods of one science to the investigation of another. That is what the greatest progress of the passing generation has consisted in. Darwin adapted biology to the methods of Malthus and the economists; Maxwell adapted to the theory of gases the methods of the doctrines of chances, and to electricity the methods of hydrodynamics. Wundt adapts to psychology the methods of physiology; Galton adapts to the same study the methods of the theory of errors; Morgan adapted to history a method from biology; Cournot adapted to political economy the calculus of variations.

---

[11] For elucidations of the notion of abduction, in a realist philosophical framework related to economics, see Lawson (1989a; 1997).

Ultimately, the clashes and tensions between different approaches in a subject provide the sources of creativity and novelty. A possible source of creativity in science is through the juxtaposition of two different frames of reference, so that already existing but previously separate ideas can cross-fertilise. Accordingly, Larry Laudan (1977, p. 103) argued that the amalgamation of different research traditions may produce a sum greater than the constituent parts. Arthur Koestler (1964) coined the term 'bisociation' to describe the kind of adjoining of different ideas that occurs in the act of scientific creation. Providing such a bridge between different discourses and contexts, metaphor can thus be both creative and constitutive.

However, there is no guarantee that metaphor can play a creative role. Conceivably, in any given context there is a large set of metaphors that would be employed to no positive benefit. Nevertheless, the inspired choice of metaphor seems to be a major source of theoretical innovation in science.

Compare the degree of theoretical pluralism inside modern economics with that in modern biology. Although both disciplines are still strongly affected by a reductionist imperative in the culture of modern science, in biology there are debates concerning methodology and core propositions. For instance, in biology there is a debate about the nature and boundaries of the subject, embracing a discourse concerning reductionism and the appropriate units of evolutionary selection and also over the viability of further reduction from genetics down to molecular biology, and even below to chemistry and physics (Sober, 1984a). In contrast, confident in the Newtonian metaphor of the indivisible, 'individual' particle, mainstream economics traditionally proscribes discussion of the psychological or social foundations of individual purposes and preferences as being beyond the bounds of the discipline.

The internal lack of consensus within biology is itself refreshing. A variety of forces and tensions within that subject point to an organicist ontology, a less rigid methodology, and the transcendence of mechanistic thinking. These indicators are discussed in the work of leading mainstream biologists such as Theodosius Dobzhansky and Ernst Mayr, as well as more heterodox scientists such as Niles Eldredge and Stephen Jay Gould, along with historians of biology such as Edward Manier (Dobzhansky, 1968; Eldredge, 1985; Gould, 1982; Manier, 1978; Mayr, 1985a).

Partly because of the acknowledged complexity of the phenomena that it attempts to analyse, biological science exhibits a theoretical pluralism (Gould and Lewontin, 1979; Mayr, 1985b). Substantially, this involves a break from the Newtonian practice of single explanations that are supposed to displace all superfluity. Characteristically, Darwin himself placed great stress on his argument that natural selection was not the only possible element in evolution. In the final edition of the *Origin of Species* he wrote:

As my conclusions have lately been much misrepresented, and it has been stated that I attribute the modification of species exclusively to natural selection, I may be permitted to remark that in the first edition of this work, and subsequently, I placed in a most conspicuous position – namely at the close of the Introduction – the following words: 'I am convinced that natural selection has been the main, but not the exclusive means of modification.' (Darwin, 1872, p. 395)

Hence Darwin accommodated the possibility of a plurality of different but complementary theories. Note that this kind of pluralism is that of 'theory complements', rather than of 'theory substitutes' where different and incompatible theories are involved.[12] Furthermore, as David Hull (1973, pp. 3–36) pointed out, Darwin's methodology was not rigidly axiomatic. There is a rigorous deductive core, but it is deemed to prove little on its own and it is thus placed in the context of a mass of empirical material. Again this contrasts with the Cartesian–Newtonian tradition in science.

Hence in biology there are deductive arguments combined with contingent empirical premises and conclusions. Typically, in biology a number of theories and explanations compete in their claims to identify the main, rather than the exclusive, cause in given real circumstances. Fortunately, biology does not present the near-monopoly of methods and approaches that threatens to stifle economics today.

Faced with these problems there is no instant solution. Neither is there an adequate and well-formed heterodoxy waiting in the wings. Austrian economics, Post Keynesian economics, Marxian economics, institutional economics: they are all afflicted with deep internal theoretical problems of their own. We have to be candid about the limitations of even our most favoured approach in economics, whatever it may be.

An obvious but crucial argument for theoretical pluralism in science can be derived from biology itself. Darwinian evolution depends on variety, and variety is the evolutionary fuel. Without the maintenance and regeneration of a variety of forms evolution would come to a stop. The evolution of scientific ideas requires diversity and pluralism as does evolution in nature. Let a thousand flowers bloom.[13]

---

[12] A useful taxonomy of types of pluralism is offered by Uskali Mäki (1997). The kind of pluralism advocated in the present chapter is further qualified below.

[13] Samuels (1997) suggested that the advocacy of methodological pluralism implies the non-existence of a given reality. A contrasting point is made here. A theoretical analysis can neither completely represent nor mirror reality in all its complexity. Consequently, in principle we cannot rule out other viable and

The argument for pluralism applies to economics as well as other sciences. In this regard we can do little better than follow the example of the neoclassical economist Frank Hahn (1984, pp. 7–8):

> The most strongly held of my views . . . is that neither is there a single best way for understanding in economics nor is it possible to hold any conclusions, other than purely logical deductions, with certainty. I have since my earliest days in the subject been astonished that this view is not widely shared. Indeed, we are encompassed by passionately held beliefs. . . . In fact all these 'certainties' and all the 'schools' which they spawn are a sure sign of our ignorance . . . we do not possess much certain knowledge about the economic world and . . . our best chance of gaining more is to try in all sorts of directions and by all sorts of means. This will not be furthered by strident commitments of faith.

Hahn's welcome comment seems to endorse a theoretical pluralism, embracing both neoclassical and non-neoclassical approaches. This pluralism contrasts with the prevailing view that economics is defined in terms of a single, and neoclassical, method or approach. Particularly since the famous essay by Lionel Robbins (1932), among economists the prevailing practice has been to regard this subject as being defined by a single type of method or analysis, with an associated set of core assumptions. If the subject is defined in this way then not much theoretical pluralism within economics is possible; we are stuck with a single type of theory or approach.

Robert Solow was one of the many who seemed to accept this singular outlook when he wrote, with more than a dash of cynicism, on his choice of theoretical approach in economics: 'I know the wheel is crooked, but it's the only game in town' (Solow, 1965, p. 68). Yet if we are stuck with only one, corrupt game then surely the urgent policy prescription must be to develop rival, and perhaps more acceptable, games as alternatives. This option did not seem to occur to this eventual Nobel Laureate.

The danger of 'professional tyranny', stemming from a lack of institutional and theoretical pluralism, was recognized by John Pencavel, a former editor of the prestigious and highly-cited *Journal of Economic Literature*. Pencavel (1991, p. 87) prescribed an appropriate remedy:

---

complementary analyses of that reality. Philosophical realism and the assertion of a given reality 'out there' are perfectly compatible with such a (pluralistic) proposition.

Professional tyranny is less likely where the institutional form of the discipline is pluralistic – where there are many associations of scientists, many journals for the dissemination of ideas, many alternative sources of employment, many ways to acquire the status of a member of the discipline, and, in short, where the discipline's institutions take on a competitive form.

Regrettably, however, these sentiments seem to be confined to a minority. Economists often advocate competition but not in the practice of economics itself. In economics today there is increasing standardisation of thought and core assumptions and methods are defended with renewed zeal. Perhaps the most optimistic interpretation possible of this widespread phenomenon is suggested by Hahn (1991, p. 49) who wrote: 'After all in other spheres, say religion, one often encounters increased orthodoxy amongst some just when religion is on the decline.' Yet even this statement hints at a less optimistic outcome: a religion under threat can lead to an Inquisition rather than a Renaissance. Yet unless renewed variety is generated within the discipline its degeneration into a narrow, over-abstract, and practically non-operational formalism will continue apace.

Strictly speaking, however, this pluralism concerns the policy of institutions toward the funding and nurturing of science. It is 'pluralism of the academy' and it does not concern the *individual practices* of science itself. There is much to be said for tolerance of many different and even antagonistic scientific research programmes within a department, university or nation. But we should not tolerate the existence of inconsistent ideas within our own heads. The role of diversity is not to sanctify or foster contradiction. Tolerance of the right of a scientist to practise, even when we may disagree with his or her views, does not imply tolerance of any method and proposition. The policy toward science must be pluralistic and tolerant, but science itself cannot be so. As Sheila Dow (1997) elaborated, pluralism does not mean that 'anything goes'.

Methodological anarchism means the tyranny of the strong, and the strongest are those currently in power. Hence, despite anarchistic appearances, the precept of 'anything goes' is ultimately conservative. In contrast, the policy of academic pluralism provides a relentless challenge to orthodoxy and heterodoxy alike. We have to recognize the immense and enduring value of pluralism within the discipline without abandoning precision and rigour in our own work.

Appendix: A Plea for a Pluralistic and Rigorous Economics

The following 'plea' was drafted and circulated among prominent members of the economics profession by Uskali Mäki, Donald McCloskey and the present author. It was signed by 44 leading economists – including four Nobel Laureates – and published as a paid advertisement in the May 1992 edition of the *American Economic Review*.

'We the undersigned are concerned with the threat to economic science posed by intellectual monopoly. Economists today enforce a monopoly of method or core assumptions, often defended on no better ground than it constitutes the "mainstream." Economists will advocate free competition, but will not practice it in the marketplace of ideas.'

'Consequently, we call for a new spirit of pluralism in economics, involving critical conversation and tolerant communication between different approaches. Such pluralism should not undermine the standards of rigor; an economics that requires itself to face all the arguments will be a more, not a less, rigorous science.'

'We believe that the new pluralism should be reflected in the character of scientific debate, in the range of contributions in its journals, and in the training and hiring of economists.'

The above text was signed by the following:

Abramovitz, Moses	Galbraith, John Kenneth	Modigliani, Franco*
Arthur, W. Brian	Georgescu-Roegen, N.[+]	Nelson, Richard
Axelrod, Robert	Goodwin, Richard[+]	Olson, Mancur[+]
Blaug, Mark	Granger, Clive W. J.	Pasinetti, Luigi
Boulding, Kenneth[+]	Grandmont, Jean-Michel	Perlman, Mark
Cowling, Keith	Harcourt, Geoffrey	Rothschild, Kurt
Cyert, Richard M.	Heilbroner, Robert	Samuelson, Paul*
Day, Richard H.	Hirschman, Albert	Shubik, Martin
Davidson, Paul	Kindleberger, Charles	Simon, Herbert*
Deane, Phyllis	Kornai, Janos	Spanos, Aris
Denison, Edward	Laidler, David	Tinbergen, Jan*[+]
Desai, Meghnad	Leibenstein, Harvey[+]	Tsuru, Shigeto
Freeman, Christopher	Matthews, Robin C. O.	Vickers, Douglas
Frey, Bruno	Mayer, Thomas	Weintraub, Roy
Furubotn, Eirik	Minsky, Hyman[+]	

* Nobel Laureate   [+] Since deceased

PART TWO

The Evolution of Evolutionary Economics

5. Biological Metaphors in Economics from the 1880s to the 1980s

In economics, the word 'evolutionary' is currently in fashion.[1] Since the 1980s, the number of economics books and articles with 'evolution' in their title has increased rapidly. This revolution is not confined to heterodoxy. Leading neoclassical economists such as Kenneth Arrow and Frank Hahn have turned away from mechanics, seeing biology as the possible inspiration for the economics of the future (Anderson, 1995; Arrow 1995; Hahn, 1991).

The relationship between biology and economics has waxed and waned over the centuries and has worked in both directions. The influence of the economists Adam Smith and Thomas Robert Malthus on Charles Darwin is widely known, even if some of the details remain controversial (Hodgson, 1993b, 1995a). Ideas of competition and struggle in the writings of Smith and Malthus simultaneously inspired economics and biology. Accordingly, to some degree, biological metaphors have always been present in the foreground or background of modern economic theory. What is striking, however, is the temporal variation in the degree of their explicit popularity and use.

Less than a dozen years after the publication of *The Origin of Species* in 1859 the influence of biology on economics had slightly subsided in some quarters. With the emergence of neoclassical economics in the 1870s, its principal inspiration was not biology but physics (Mirowski, 1989b; Ingrao and Israel, 1990).

However, in the 1880s and 1890s – to use a mechanical metaphor – the pendulum swung back. Biology came back into fashion in the social

---

[1] This chapter is a revised and extended version of Hodgson (forthcoming).

sciences. Alfred Marshall had a strong view that 'the Mecca of the economist lies in economic biology' (Marshall, 1949, p. xii). Furthermore, leading heterodox economists such as Thorstein Veblen enthusiastically embraced biology. Overall, the biological metaphor was widely invoked in economics and in social science as a whole in the 1890–1914 period.[2]

Yet this fashion did not last. On the contrary, biological ideas faced an extreme reaction in the social sciences. By the end of the 1920s the use of biological and evolutionary analogies had fallen out of favour in economics and elsewhere. From then on, evolutionary ideas from biology remained largely unexplored in economics until the publication of a famous article by Armen Alchian in 1950. Given the recent resurgence of 'evolutionary' ideas – especially since the publication of Richard Nelson and Sidney Winter's (1982) classic work – the neglect of the biological metaphor for much of the middle of the twentieth century requires an explanation.

There is an important subplot here. By focusing on the interwar decay of the biological metaphor in American economic thought, further reasons are given for the precipitous decline of institutional economics in the United States. It was the dominant paradigm in American economics in the 1920s, but by 1940 it had been marginalised by the rising neoclassical theory. Furthermore, institutional economics was never prominent in Britain, but the turn away from biology had enormous effects on the development of Marshall's legacy.

It is the purpose of this chapter to address these issues, particularly through an examination of the scientific and ideological context in the period. The main focus is on Anglo-American economics, but other significant influences – particularly from Germany – will also be considered.

Clearly, the typical use of the biological metaphor by modern economists such as Nelson and Winter is a far cry from the biological determinism and even racism and sexism of many late nineteenth century writers. Using a biological metaphor in a socio-economic context is very different from believing that our behaviour is largely or wholly determined by our genes.

Nevertheless, studies of the 1880–1990 period strongly suggest that the degree of acceptance of biological metaphors and analogies in social science is closely correlated both with the general prestige accorded to the biological sciences and with the degree of academic acceptance of a biotic foundation for human nature. Accordingly, the popularity of organic and biological analogies throughout the Western World at the end of the nineteenth century

---

[2] See the more detailed discussions of Marshall, Veblen, Spencer, Schumpeter, Menger, Hayek and others in Hodgson (1992a, 1993a, 1993b).

was intimately related to the prominence of what is misleadingly described as 'social Darwinism'.[3] Carl Degler (1991) showed that the idea of a biological root to human nature was widely accepted by social scientists by the end of the Victorian era.

Further, as social scientists began to reject biological explanations of human attributes and behaviour in the early decades of the twentieth century, their revulsion against biological thinking was such that biological and evolutionary metaphors were likewise rejected. This revulsion lasted for several decades and still persists in some quarters today. What has helped to open up more space for a more progressive use of biological metaphors in social science since the 1970s has been the emergence of more pluralistic, multi-causal or non-reductionist discourses in biology and anthropology. Accordingly, biological metaphors have again become legitimate in economics and other social sciences. The adoption of such metaphors is not necessarily interpreted as a return to biological reductionism.

However, it must be emphasized that with metaphor in science much more is at stake than the choice of analogy or mode of literary expression. It was argued in the preceding chapter that metaphor plays a constitutive role in science. Accordingly, the development of economic theory is likely to be affected profoundly by the nature of its chosen metaphor and by the character of the field of discourse to which it is thus connected. The close parallels between the history of modern biology and of modern economics suggest that metaphor works at a deep level in science, affecting its progress in ways that its practitioners are not always aware of.

The question of the use of biological metaphors relates to three key philosophical issues that are touched upon here. The first concerns ontology. For some, like John A. Hobson and most American institutionalists, the use of the metaphor of an *organism* was tied up with the incorporation of an *organicist* ontology. In an organicist ontology, relations between entities were seen as internal rather than external: the essential characteristics of an element are regarded as the outcomes of relations with other entities (Winslow, 1989). Accordingly, in the context of social science, the individual is seen as being moulded by relations with other individuals. In contrast, in an atomist ontology – as pictured by the Greek atomists or in Newtonian physics – entities possess qualities independently of their

---

[3] As Bowler (1983) showed, Darwin's ideas were actually out of vogue in the 1880–1914 period. They were to be revived in the post-1930 synthesis with genetics. It is now widely recognized that most of the proponents of so-called 'social Darwinism' were much closer in their ideas to Spencer or Sumner than to Darwin himself.

relations with other entities. Thereby the individual is taken as given, as in neoclassical economics and classic liberal political thought. Organicism rejects the atomistic starting point of the given individual, and sometimes chooses the cell or organism interacting with its environment as its metaphor.

Second, there is the methodological problem of reductionism. Reductionism is defined as the idea that all aspects of a complex phenomenon must be explained in terms of one level, or type of unit. In social science in the past, reductionism has taken a biological form. Accordingly, attempts were made to explain the behaviour of individuals and groups in terms of their alleged biological characteristics. Reductionism is still prevalent in social science but it typically takes the form of methodological individualism, by which it is asserted that explanations of social structures and institutions must be couched entirely in terms of individuals. Related to this is the reductionist attempt since the 1960s to found macroeconomics on 'sound microfoundations'. Reductionism is countered by the fact that complex systems display emergent properties at different levels that cannot be completely reduced to or explained wholly in terms of another level.[4]

Third, there is the question of the use and prestige of mathematical models in economics and social science. Since the late 1930s there has been a dramatic rise in the status accorded to mathematical modelling in economics. Yet sixty years of effort by thousands of economists in many countries has yielded patchy results. Even with fixed preference functions, theoretical models become extremely complicated. The modellers sometimes resent those who would seemingly make things even more complicated by challenging such fundamental and established assumptions. Accordingly, one reason why individuals are treated as social atoms with given preference functions is to increase the possibility of mathematical tractability. Although biology has engendered its own practices of formal and mathematical modelling, the wider acceptance of the openness and complexity of biological systems has protected the more discursive approaches.

Organic and evolutionary metaphors in social science have a very long history. Our period of concern, however, begins in the closing years of the nineteenth century. The century-long story is complex and multi-faceted; the

---

[4] The concept of emergent property is discussed in more detail in Chapter 6 below and in Archer (1995), Bhaskar (1975, 1979), Kontopoulos (1993), Lane (1993) and Lawson (1997). On the questions of methodological individualism, reductionism, and the failure of the microfoundations project, see Chapters 4 and 6 of the present volume.

sketchiest of accounts must be given here. What may absolve this rudimentary overview of a complex tale is that this is the very first work to address specifically the question of the decline of evolutionary and biological analogies in economics in the 1920s and their post-1945 rebirth.[5]

5.1. THE BIOLOGICAL METAPHOR IN GERMAN SOCIAL SCIENCE BEFORE 1914

Prior to the rise of Charles Darwin and Herbert Spencer in England, organic analogies were prominent in social science in the German-speaking world. Michael Hutter (1994) showed that the German roots of such organic metaphors go back to the eighteenth century and earlier. A number of German social scientists made extensive comparisons between biological and social organisms. With the rise of the German historical school, a strong dependence on the organic metaphor was manifest. It was particularly evident in the works of writers such as Karl Knies (1853), Wilhelm Roscher (1854), Paul von Lilienfeld (1873–81) and Albert Schäffle (1875–81).

In the German-speaking world the organic analogy took a number of forms and linked up with a variety of propositions, from the assertion of an organicist ontology, to the recognition of social influences on individuals, to the assertion of the systemic interdependence of the whole socio-economic system, to a 'stages' theory of history compared explicitly with the growth of an organism. It was also widely associated with the proposition that the socio-economic system could be analysed as if it had a will and mind of its own: surmounting those of the individuals comprising it, just as the brain and nervous system of an organism transcend its individual organs and cells.[6]

The historical school was at its high point of influence in Germany and Austria when in 1883 Carl Menger fired the opening shots of the

---

[5] Partial exceptions are Degler (1991) and Persons (1950). But both devoted relatively little space to economics.

[6] Notably, while Lilienfeld (1873–81) had argued that society is *actually* an organism, Schäffle (1875–81) differed, seeing the organism analogy as appropriate but not literal. For Schäffle, society was not an organism in a biological or physiological sense, but its symbolic and technological unity gave it organism-like qualities. On this basis Schäffle applied quasi-Darwinian principles to the socio-economic system, and, like others, saw collectivities rather than individuals as the units of selection.

Methodenstreit with the publication of his *Untersuchungen*. We need not go into the details of this famous intellectual battle here. It is sufficient to note that Menger did not target the use of the organic or biological analogy as such, but the idea that independent will or purpose could be attributed to the 'social organism'. This idea attracted Menger's devastatingly critical pen. Although the biological analogy was not Menger's main focus, the effect of his critique was to diminish greatly its usage in German social science.

Menger pointed out that some institutions were deliberately created by individuals, but many others were not. He emphasized that social institutions often evolve unintentionally out of the purposeful actions of many interacting individuals. What had to be discarded were explanations of the emergence of social institutions that relied on a 'social will' that could not in turn itself be explained in terms of the purposeful behaviour of individuals. Menger is thus remembered as a critic of 'holism' and as an early architect of methodological individualism.

The two decades of the *Methodenstreit* were so devastating that the use of the organic analogy had become unpopular in Germany and Austria by the beginning of the twentieth century. Instead, there was the ascendancy of methodological individualists such as Joseph Schumpeter. The historical school itself survived the trauma but its use of biological analogies – as in the post-1914 works of Othmar Spann and Werner Sombart – became more qualified. More formalistic and mechanistic models triumphed. As Hutter (1994, p. 306) observes, in Germany and Austria after World War I 'the mechanistic paradigm prevailed in economic thought.' The tide of opinion against evolutionary ideas in German-speaking countries was such that even Schumpeter (1934, p. 57) accepted in 1911 that 'the evolutionary idea is now discredited in our field'.[7]

---

[7] Schumpeter did not embrace biological metaphors. He wrote: 'no appeal to biology would be of the slightest use' (Schumpeter, 1954, p. 789). Nevertheless, Schumpeter's work remains rich in insight and has had a major influence on modern evolutionary economists such as Nelson and Winter. For discussions of Schumpeter's so-called 'evolutionary economics' see Hodgson (1993b, 1997c) and the debate with Kelm (1997).

5.2. HERBERT SPENCER, ALFRED MARSHALL, JOHN HOBSON AND THE BIOLOGICAL METAPHOR IN BRITAIN

In Britain in the 1870–1920 period, biological reductionism was commonplace. It was widely believed that social progress ultimately depended on the human genetic legacy. Such ideas were common amongst both liberals and reactionaries. The first International Congress of Eugenics was held in London in 1912 and English liberal thinkers such as John Maynard Keynes, Harold Laski and Sydney and Beatrice Webb counted themselves as followers of the eugenic movement. Eugenics also had a wide following amongst American social scientists in the second and third decades of the twentieth century.

The towering influence over both the social and the biological sciences in the last three decades of the nineteenth century was Herbert Spencer. He attempted to build a complete system of thought that would embrace both the natural and social sciences. His popular and intellectual influence was enormous. At least in the last decade of the nineteenth century his prestige was probably even greater than that of Darwin.

Spencer developed a theory of social evolution that was strongly influenced by the German theorists. In turn he had a strong influence upon some of them, notably Schäffle (Bellomy, 1984, p. 41). The details of Spencer's view of socio-economic evolution cannot concern us here. It is sufficient to note that it was in key respects different from Darwin's theory of natural selection (La Vergata, 1995). Spencer was much closer to Lamarck than Darwin, stressing the organism's adaptation to the environment rather that the environmental selection of the organism.

Spencer frequently compared society to a living organism. Strictly, however, his ontology was not organicist. The use of an analogy between society and a living thing is not sufficient to qualify as organicism. An individualistic and atomist outlook does not necessarily involve the rejection of the concept of society or the denial of significant human interaction. Spencer started from the individual and drew individualistic conclusions. He saw in society only a limited kind of unity. Society was still addressed in mechanistic terms. It was regarded as no more than the interplay of self-contained individuals pursuing their own ends, plus the social arrangements connecting them.[8]

In sum, Spencer's view of socio-economic evolution was individualistic, deterministic and reductionist (Burrow, 1966; La Vergata, 1995). There is no discussion of emergent properties, or higher and irreducible levels of analysis. His work belongs to the nineteenth century and Victorian industrialization, where scientific prestige belonged to the mechanistic kind of thought and, as Alfred North Whitehead (1926, p. 128) put it, even biology aped 'the manners of physics'.

Marshall was influenced by a number of theorists, but first and foremost was Spencer (Hodgson, 1993a, 1993b; Thomas, 1991).[9] Also Marshall visited Germany several times and the general influence of German-speaking economists upon him was extensive (Streissler, 1990). Influences from Germany included Georg Hegel, the biologist Ernst Haeckel and the aforementioned Schäffle. In front of this acquired intellectual tapestry Marshall built his own version of neoclassical economics.

The first edition of Marshall's *Principles* was published in 1890, at the height of Spencer's prestige. Marshall saw the relevance of biological analogies for economics, yet he was unable to develop them to the full. As Thomas (1991, p. 11) regretfully concluded, for Marshall economic biology 'remained promise rather than substance.'

Marshall repeated his famous sentence on 'the Mecca of the economist' in every preface to the *Principles* from the fifth edition on. However, he delayed and procrastinated over the planned second volume on economic dynamics. Spencer died in 1903 and in a few years his ideas had fallen out of favour. Marshall lost a guiding star. In fact the Spencerian influence had thwarted the development of an adequate evolutionary analysis. The Spencerian character of Marshall's biology meant that after his death his followers were able, with relative ease, to replace these elements by notions more akin to Newtonian mechanics. Most of his disciples did not share his reservations concerning mechanistic modelling, or his concern to journey to the biological Mecca for inspiration and guidance.

---

[8] It was this aspect of his thinking that prompted Durkheim's classic critique of Spencer in 1893 in *The Division of Labour in Society*. On Durkheim's use of the organic analogy see Hejl (1995).

[9] In a 1924 letter in the King's College Keynes Papers in Cambridge (Cox Catalogue no. EJ/6/4/177–82), the mathematician J. R. Mozley explained to Keynes how he had introduced Marshall to Spencer's writings as early as about 1865 (Laurent, 1997).

Far from instigating an interdisciplinary research programme on economic dynamics, Marshall's insights from biology were subsequently ignored. As Nicolai Foss (1991, 1994b) and Neil Niman (1991, p. 32) have pointed out, later Marshallians neglected the biological aspects of Marshall's thinking, and abandoned any attempt to recast economics along such lines. Hence Marshall's influential successor Arthur Pigou (1922) turned instead to physics for inspiration, and in his hands the representative firm became the firm in mechanical equilibrium (Pigou, 1928). As Scott Moss (1984) showed, equilibrium concepts were developed that were inconsistent with the existence of heterogeneous economic agents. The ease with which biology was later purged from the Marshallian system, to be replaced by a fortified metaphor from mechanics, suggests the limited extent and deficient nature of the biological ideas that had been implanted by Marshall in his *Principles.*

John Laurent (1997) has pointed out that Keynes followed the pre-1920s fashion and described society as an organism in his earlier writings. He referred to the 'economic organism' (Keynes, 1913, p. 10) and saw nations as 'vast organic units' (Keynes, 1922, p. 10). However, like most other social scientists, such biological metaphors are less frequent in works appearing at a later date.

Unlike Marshall and Keynes, John A. Hobson was banished from the glittering spires of British academia: he never held a university post. Like Marshall, Hobson was strongly influenced by German economists and their use of the organic analogy. But Hobson's organicism is stronger and more sustained than that found in Marshall's work. Unlike Marshall, he was also influenced by Veblen and he proposed an organicist ontology. He drew strong methodological and anti-reductionist conclusions from his own version of organicism, writing: 'An organized unity, or whole, cannot be explained adequately by an analysis of its constituent parts: its wholeness is a new product, with attributes not ascertainable in its parts, though in a sense derived from them' (Hobson, 1929, p. 32). Hobson thus expressed the idea of emergent properties and higher, irreducible levels of analysis.

Hobson forcefully rejected mechanical metaphors, seeing them as 'squeezing out humanity' and denying human novelty and creativity (Freeden, 1988, pp. 89, 173). Recklessly ignoring Menger's arguments in the *Methodenstreit*, he regarded institutions such as the state as analogous to organisms. Hobson explicitly defended the notion that such institutions could be depicted like organisms, with wills of their own. Apart from a belated and extensive recognition by Keynes (1936, pp. 19, 364–71) of Hobson's importance, he has since been largely ignored by economists.

By the time of Marshall's death in 1924 the dialogue between economics and biology had virtually ceased, at least within the portals of British universities. In his famous article on Marshall on the centenary of his birth, Gerald Shove (1942, p. 323) noted 'a return to the mechanical as against the biological approach' in mainstream economics. As elaborated below, the Keynesian theoretical revolution did not reverse this trend.

The cause of the decline in use of biological metaphors did not lie within Marshall's work alone. Crucial developments in social science in the first three decades of the twentieth century, particularly in America, have to be considered to provide an adequate explanation.

5.3. THE BIOLOGICAL ANALOGY AND THE RISE OF AMERICAN INSTITUTIONALISM

The influence of the German universities upon American academia prior to 1914 should not be underestimated (Dorfman, 1955; Herbst, 1965). Around the turn of the century 'most of the younger American economists went to Germany for their postgraduate education, where they were taught by members of the German historical school' (Morgan, 1995, p. 315). American economists who had studied in Germany included Henry Carter Adams, John Bates Clark, Richard T. Ely and Edwin R. A. Seligman.

From England, Spencer's influence in America was also enormous, and explicitly recognized by the founding fathers of American economics such as Ely (1903, pp. 6–7).

In addition, rising American social scientists such as William Graham Sumner, Lester Frank Ward and Franz Boas had a strong influence on this generation. Sumner, Ward and Boas all embraced evolutionism and organic analogies, despite the differences in their theories and policy conclusions. The American neoclassical economist John Bates Clark followed the fashion and laced his *Philosophy of Wealth* (1885) with organic metaphors and images taken from Spencerian biology. As in Britain and Germany, organic analogies were widely adopted. Like Hobson, leading American social theorists such as Ward (1893), Franklin Giddings (1896) and Henry Jones Ford (1915) conceived of the state or society as an organism, sometimes even capable of a will of its own.

Pragmatist philosophers such as Charles Sanders Peirce and William James were also influenced by developments in biology (Scheffler, 1974). James (1890) published his influential *Principles of Psychology* which argued that much of human behaviour was dependent upon inherited instincts. For several crucial years, instinct theory was prominent in both Britain and the United States. Spencer's *Principles of Psychology*, published in 1894, replicated elements of such an approach. Instinct psychology was further developed by William McDougall (1908).[10]

It was in this context that Veblen published in 1898 his evolutionary manifesto in the *Quarterly Journal of Economics*, asking: 'Why is economics not an evolutionary science?' This essay embraced Darwinism and founded American institutionalism.[11] Along with his subsequent *Theory of the Leisure Class* (1899) it represents a revolution in economic thought. Veblen favoured a complete reconstruction of economics in which mechanistic analogies would be replaced by Darwinian evolutionary methods and metaphors. As Richard Hofstadter (1959, pp. 152–5) remarked:

> Where other economists had found in Darwinian science merely a source of plausible analogies or a fresh rhetoric to substantiate traditional postulates and precepts, Veblen saw it as a loom upon which the whole fabric of economic thinking could be rewoven.

It is not widely realized that Veblen was the first theorist to apply Darwinian ideas to economics. Darwinian natural selection works on the basis of three principles. First, there must be sustained variation among the members of a species or population. Variations may be blind, random or purposive, but without them natural selection cannot operate. Second, there must be some principle of heredity or continuity through which offspring have to resemble their parents more than they resemble other members of their species. In other words, there has to be some mechanism through which individual characteristics are passed on through the generations. Third, natural selection itself operates either because better-adapted organisms leave increased numbers of offspring, or because the variations or gene combinations that are preserved are those bestowing advantage in struggling to survive.

Veblen's adoption of these principles is clear from the following extracts. First, we can find the notion of the relative durability of habits or routines and their role as heritable traits in the following passage:

---

[10] McDougall taught at Cambridge and Oxford and subsequently became a professor at Harvard.

[11] The nature and origins of the Veblenian intellectual revolution of 1896–1899 are discussed in more detail in Hodgson (1998d).

men's present habits of thought tend to persist indefinitely, except as circumstances enforce a change. These institutions which have so been handed down, these habits of thought, points of view, mental attitudes and aptitudes, or what not, are therefore themselves a conservative factor. This is the factor of social inertia, psychological inertia, conservatism. (Veblen, 1899, pp. 190–91)

Second, Veblen (1914, pp. 86–9) recognized the role of creativity and novelty with his concept of 'idle curiosity'. He also repeatedly used the metaphor of 'mutation' to describe changes in habits and institutions (Veblen, 1919b, pp. 5, 40, 57). Third, Veblen, without drawing Panglossian or laissez-faire conclusions, subscribed to a notion of evolutionary selection in the socio-economic sphere:

> The life of man in society, just as the life of other species, is a struggle for existence, and therefore it is a process of selective adaptation. The evolution of social structure has been a process of natural selection of institutions. (Veblen, 1899, p. 188)[12]

Notably, and in contrast to many of his contemporaries, Veblen's approach was both interactionist and anti-reductionist.[13] His interactionist perspective stressed the notion of 'both the agent and his environment being at any point

---

[12] Veblen repeatedly used the metaphor of evolutionary selection. Although the full term 'natural selection' makes a sparse appearance (Veblen, 1899, pp. 188, 207; 1934, p. 79; 1919a, pp. 170, 416). He used 'selection' in an evolutionary sense very often. In the *Theory of the Leisure Class* alone we find it on the following pages: pp. 13, 44, 69, 190, 191, 208, 212, 213–4, 217, 225, 229, 233, 235–9, 241, 246, 319. This reluctance to use the world 'natural' in the social context almost certainly stems from Veblen's opposition to biological reductionism and to his forceful rejection of apologetic notions that social or economic arrangements could be described as 'natural'. It by no means undermines Veblen's affinity to the evolutionary metaphor.

[13] Two versions of interactionism are addressed in the present chapter. The first suggests that actor and structure interact and mutually condition each other to the degree that explanations based on either actor or structure alone are unwarranted (Archer, 1995; Bhaskar, 1979; Giddens, 1984; Lawson, 1997). The second proposes that socio-economic systems interact with their biotic foundation to the degree that (a) explanations based on biology alone are unsuitable and that (b) full explanations of some socio-economic phenomena may involve biological factors (Hirst and Woolley, 1982; Pinker, 1994; Plotkin, 1994; Weingart *et al* 1997). These two versions of interactionism are mutually consistent and jointly opposed to reductionism.

the outcome of the last process' (Veblen, 1898a, p. 391). Although Veblen acknowledged the biotic foundations of social life, he resisted the view that human behaviour could be explained purely and simply in terms of genetic inheritance:

> If . . . men universally acted not on the conventional grounds and values afforded by the fabric of institutions, but solely and directly on the grounds and values afforded by the unconventionalised propensities and aptitudes of hereditary human nature, then there would be no institutions and no culture (Veblen [1909] 1934, p. 143)

This and other passages suggest that Veblen acknowledged different and irreducible levels of analysis and rejected biological reductionism. For Veblen, socio-economic evolution works primarily as the 'natural selection of institutions': it operates at a higher level than the human biotic material.

Although Veblen inspired a new school of economic thought, his theoretical research programme to build an evolutionary economics was advanced only slightly by his followers. John Commons (1934) toyed with the metaphors of quantum physics as well as evolution but saw only a limited role for such analogies. Commons (1897, p. 96; 1934, p. 120) rebutted the analogy with natural selection on the grounds that 'artificial selection' was a more appropriate notion for economic evolution. Also for Commons (1934, pp. 99, 119), the comparison of society with an organism was a 'false analogy'. A difficulty for Commons and other institutionalists was the limited development of evolutionary biology at the time. Biology was going through a crisis. Darwin had failed to explain the mechanisms of heredity and the source of variation in organisms. This gap was not filled until the triumph of the neo-Darwinian synthesis of Mendelian genetics with Darwinian biology after 1940.

5.4. THE REACTION AGAINST BIOLOGY IN AMERICAN SOCIAL SCIENCE

Internal problems in biology were not the only issue. The ideological abuse of science was also a matter of concern. For instance, the establishment of genetics at the beginning of the twentieth century had given a boost to racist and sexist explanations of human character and behaviour in the US. Variations in aptitude and behaviour were regarded by some scientists and ideologists as rooted largely or wholly in the genes. In reaction against this, liberal American academia became increasing disturbed by the racist and sexist conclusions that were being drawn from a biologically-grounded social science.[14]

Boas, an anthropologist and a Jewish immigrant from Germany, was motivated by liberal views and a strong anti-racism. He saw culture and social environment as the major influence on human character and intelligence, and nutritional and other conditions as having a significant effect on some physical characteristics. Notably, Boas was one of the first to use the word 'culture' in its modern academic and anthropological sense.[15]

Largely under the influence of Boas's research, a number of leading American sociologists converted from the view of the primacy of nature over nurture to the reverse. During the 1900–1914 period, leading sociologists such as Charles Ellwood, Carl Kelsey and Howard Odum moved away from the opinion that innate biological factors accounted for human behaviour, to the notion that human characteristics were malleable and that the environment was the most important influence. By the end of the First World War, a number of sociological and anthropological textbooks were in circulation promoting Boasian views.

Boas did not deny the influence of biology on both physical and mental characteristics. He just saw social culture as far more important. However, Alfred Kroeber, a student of Boas, went further. In a number of articles published in the *American Anthropologist* between 1910 and 1917 he declared that social science should be separated, in both method and substance, from biology. Kroeber held that heredity cannot be allowed to have any part in the history of humankind. Independence from biology was indispensable for understanding the meaning and use of the concept of culture.

In the 1890s the biologist August Weismann had struck a blow against Lamarckism and Spencerism by giving strong arguments for the non-inheritance of acquired characteristics. In 1916 Kroeber made use of

---

[14] Much of the information and arguments in this section are derived from Degler (1991).

[15] Earlier the concept had been developed, in particular, by Edward Tylor (1871) and Lewis Morgan (1877). However, for both these authors the word 'culture' was virtually a synonym for 'civilization', and they both embraced a teleological and unilinear notion of its development. While they attempted to erect general theories of cultural development, they failed to produced an adequate causal story of the single-track evolution of civilization. Morgan fell back on psychological and biological explanations of cultural development, and Tylor vaguely hinted at an unfolding or epigenetic dynamic within culture itself.

Weismann's assertion to defend his concept of culture. Weismann's idea of a barrier between the organism and its genetic inheritance suggested to Kroeber that biology could not explain social and cultural achievements.

However, Lamarckism did not necessarily lead to racist conclusions. For nineteenth-century thinkers such as Lester Ward, the Lamarckian belief in the possibility of the inheritance of acquired characters had earlier been the basis for anti-racism (Degler, 1991, p. 22). The Lamarckian view of the plasticity of organisms suggested that human nature was moulded by the environment. In contrast, Kroeber used the *refutation* of Lamarckism as an argument against racism and for the malleability of mankind. Ironically, the validity or otherwise of Lamarckism thus made no difference to this ideological dispute.

The underlying theoretical change was nevertheless dramatic. For Ward both the human organism and human society could change. But with Kroeber it was culture, not the human organism, that was malleable. This conclusion was reached by the assertion of the primacy of culture over genetic inheritance and – more controversially – by a complete separation of biology from social science. This contention was of enduring significance.

Another of Boas's students, Margaret Mead, continued Kroeber's line of argument. In 1928 she published the classic case for the supremacy of culture over biology in her *Coming of Age in Samoa*. By the 1920s, the views of Boas's intellectual progeny had become widely accepted by American social scientists. Ruth Benedict, also a former student of Boas, later consolidated the victory with the publication in 1934 of the equally influential work *Patterns of Culture* (Degler, 1991, p. 206).

Biology and social science had parted company. The effects of this intellectual shift were felt through the Western academic world. Those that continued to assert that biology could explain some differences in human behaviour had lost the academic argument and had become tainted by accusations of racism and sexism. With fascism rampant in Europe and in East Asia, such a position became increasingly difficult in liberal Western academia.[16]

---

[16] In the 1930s, Sombart, and some other Nazi sympathisers, argued that the individual is like a cell serving the organism of the nation, and that the welfare of the whole is thereby above that of the individual. Such biological metaphors were thus used explicitly in the service of fascism (Harris, 1942). However, it would be untenable to argue against all biological metaphors simply on the basis that they can be abused. Hobson and Spencer, for example, used very similar metaphors to sustain liberal or individualistic political philosophies.

Related to this, the same period saw important changes in the prevailing conceptions of method and approach in social science. The positivist philosophy founded earlier by Auguste Compte grew in favour. It was increasingly argued that the social sciences had to gain 'scientific' credentials, and that this should be done by imitating the empiricist and deductivist methods that were believed to be in operation in the natural sciences. The ideological abuses of biology in 'social Darwinism' were seen as a grave warning. For many, such as Max Weber, the lesson was that social science should be 'value free' (Hennis, 1988). Comptean positivism was later superseded by the logical positivism of the influential 'Vienna Circle' in the 1920s.

Connected and parallel developments in psychology were also significant. While William James had appealed to Darwinism, and argued in the 1890s that much of human behaviour was dependent upon instinct, the aforementioned movements in anthropology and sociology undermined this notion. The president of the American Psychological Association, Charles H. Judd, attacked the works of James and McDougall and the very idea of instinct as early as 1909. Leading psychologists argued that instinct provided no explanation that could be verified by experiment. In an increasingly positivistic intellectual climate, the flimsiness of the empirical evidence and the manifest difficulties of experimental verification provided seemingly damning accusations against instinct-based theories of human nature (Degler, 1991, p. 157).

By the early 1920s, even the existence of a sexual instinct in humans and other organisms had come under attack. The Berkeley psychologist Zing Yand Kuo asserted that all sexual appetite is the result of social conditioning. In an extreme statement of the environmentalist position, Kuo argued that all behaviour was not a manifestation of heredity factors but a direct result of environmental stimulation (Degler, 1991, pp. 158–9).

John B. Watson established behaviourist psychology in 1913, arguing on the basis of animal experiments that conditioning was primary and instinct a secondary concept. He had a radical belief in the possibilities of environmental influence over behaviour. In addition he attacked allegedly 'unscientific' notions such as consciousness and introspection. Such ideas could not be grounded experimentally and thus they had to be dismissed from science. Considerations of intent, consciousness and cognition were scornfully dismissed as 'metaphysical', to concentrate instead on empirically manifest behaviour: 'Merely to mention these pariah words in scientific discourse is to risk immediate loss of attention and audience' (Matson, 1964, p. 174). This tied in with a growing general adherence to positivism amongst scientists. The reliance upon measurement and experiment in behaviourism gave it an aura of dispassionate objectivity (Lewin, 1996).

The rise of behaviourism did not mean an immediate schism between psychology and biology. Indeed, drawing inspiration from the mental materialism and anti-dualism of Darwin and others, the early behaviourists argued that the difference between the mental capacities of humans and other animals was merely one of degree. This was different from the instinct psychology of James and McDougall, who saw the mind as a collection of functionally specialised faculties and instincts. In contrast, for the behaviourists, the 'doctrine of mental continuity' in evolution encouraged the imputation of human characteristics from experiments on pigeons and rats. Eventually, however, the fissure between psychology and biology widened, when the behaviourist emphasis on environmental conditioning reached the point where the specifically evolved capacities of each organism were disregarded. Learning was treated as a matter solely of environmental stimulation, ignoring those varied mental capacities bestowed by evolution. Biology and psychology went their separate ways.

Lone and ageing voices cried out in protest. McDougall (1921, p. 333) pleaded that if human instincts were successfully removed from psychological theory there would be 'a return to the social philosophy of the mid-nineteenth century, hedonistic utilitarianism'. Whitehead (1926) argued in vain that science had taken the wrong turn by treating the individual as a machine, without genuine purposefulness or creativity. But with the publication by Watson of *Behaviorism* in 1924 a complete break was made with the idea of instinctive behaviour in human beings. Just thirty years after the heyday of William James, the concept of instinct had virtually disappeared from American psychology.

It is again ironic to note that an extreme position on the possibilities for nurture and environmental conditioning was founded on the rejection of concepts such as consciousness and will. Such phenomena were previously alleged to be developed most extensively amongst humans. Hence their abandonment undermined a previously proposed distinction between humans and other animals. Behaviourism swept these conceptual niceties aside. This also helped those who wished to make statements about humanity on the basis of experiments with rats and pigeons in cages.

One thing that had changed substantially in much of Europe and North America from about 1880 to 1920 was the prevailing conception of science. By the 1920s, Watson and his followers were embracing positivism and disregarding everything as unscientific that could not be directly measured and tested by experiment. Science had allegedly eschewed metaphysics and entered a positivistic and technocratic age.

It is impossible here to discuss all the forces behind these shifts in thinking. Former studies have identified a strong ideological element, however. In seeking to explain the triumph of behaviourism in psychology, Lauren Wispé and James Thompson (1976) argued that it was much to do with the ideological commitment of Americans to individualism, democracy and personal liberty. Such values suggest to Americans that they can shape their own individual destiny. On the other hand, Darwinian evolutionary theory suggested that the individual is programmed by genes or instincts over which he or she has no control. Degler, after an extensive review of the evidence, also argued that the shift in the United States was much to do with the individualistic and aspiring ideological context of American society:

> What the available evidence does seem to show is that ideology or a philosophical belief that the world could be a freer and more just place played a large part in the shift from biology to culture. Science, or at least certain scientific principles or innovative scholarship also played a role in the transformation, but only a limited one. The main impetus came from the wish to establish a social order in which innate and immutable forces of biology played no role in accounting for the behavior of social groups. (Degler, 1991, p. viii)

Furthermore, the rejection of biological and evolutionary thinking in social science was often given an impetus by the fear of giving quarter to racism and other reactionary ideas. Thus Donald Campbell (1965, p. 21) suggested that the reason why evolutionary theory was avoided in the social sciences for many years was 'the early contamination of the evolutionary perspective with the reactionary political viewpoints of the privileged classes and racial supremacist apologists for colonialism'.

In the context of racism and growing fascism in the first four decades of the twentieth century, such developments were understandable.[17] It has to be admitted, however, that they were motivated by ideology rather than clear scientific evidence. No-one decisively refuted the idea that genetic inheritance may influence human characteristics and behaviour, and no-one has done so to this day. It can be accepted that the main constraints on our achievements are social rather than genetic, as Steven Rose *et al* (1984) have forcefully argued. But that does not mean that genetic influences on our

---

[17] Biological determinism grated with left and liberal thought in both America and Europe. Repulsion against it in the interwar period explained both the rise of behaviourism in the United States and the rejection by Stalin in the Soviet Union of Darwinism in favour of the Lamarckian theories of Lysenko (Joravsky, 1970; Medvedev, 1969).

nature and behaviour do not exist. It would mean, rather, that biological determinism and *exclusively* biological explanations of human phenomena are unwarranted.

5.5. THE ECLIPSE OF BIOLOGY AND THE DECLINE OF AMERICAN INSTITUTIONALISM

Following the 'golden age' of the late nineteenth century, the twentieth slipped progressively into what Stephen Sanderson (1990, p. 2) has called the 'dark age' for evolutionism in social science:

> During this time evolutionism was severely criticized and came to be regarded as an outmoded approach that self-respecting scholars should no longer take seriously . . . even the word 'evolution' came to be uttered at serious risk to one's intellectual reputation (Sanderson, 1990, p. 2).

Although nineteenth-century evolutionism in the social sciences had not always based itself on biology, it was nevertheless a victim of the times. Another casualty of the broad reaction against biology in social science was Marshall's 'economic biology'. Even more dramatically, within American economics this general move against biology and evolutionism helped the marginalization of institutionalism and the triumph of neoclassicism. It has been noted already that Veblen's project to build an evolutionary economics was hindered by problems in the development of Darwinian biology from 1900 to 1940. Having failed to develop a theoretical system to rival neoclassicism or Marxism, institutionalism was insecure.

Institutionalism was also vulnerable to shifts in the prevailing conception of scientific methodology. From the turn of the century, and in the name of science, strong American voices argued for reductionism and methodological individualism in social analysis. In 1907, the sociologist Albion W. Small was attacked for his 'social forces error'. As Dorothy Ross (1991, p. 347) pointed out, critics such as

> Edward C. Hayes . . . wanted sociology to adopt 'strictly scientific methods' and study observable behavior rather than mental states. To refer to motives as 'social forces' was to resort to a metaphysical explanation, much like resort to 'vital force' in biology. By 1910, when he issued a full-blown attack at the sociological meetings against the 'social forces error,' one commentator thought he was kicking a dead horse . . .

This was an American *Methodenstreit*. The shift in thinking towards reductionism was facilitated by the reduction in popularity of organic analogies. This movement in thinking gathered strength, albeit against the resistance of the so-called 'social interactionists.' Thus in 1927 the sociologist Floyd Allport decreed 'that "the methodology of natural science" required that sociology drop the concepts of "group" and "institution" altogether' (Ross, 1991, p. 433). The response of the social interactionists was that the individual was no more a fixed unit than the group and that intersocial stimulation and social relationships affected social behaviour. Despite this resistance, reductionist notions – claiming the spurious authority of 'scientific methodology' – did much damage to the institutionalists. John Commons seemed especially vulnerable with his concept of 'collective action'.

In America in the 1920s, both the triumph of positivism and the unpopularity of instinct psychology struck at the pragmatist foundations of institutional economics. The pragmatist ideas of Peirce and James were formative for institutionalism. Yet the rise of positivism meant that the Peircian methodological project to transcend both deduction and induction was pushed to one side. Peircian and other metaphysical and ontological speculations became unfashionable, to be replaced by a naive faith in the unaided authority of evidence and experiment. The precipitous decline of instinct psychology also created severe difficulties for institutionalism. Deprived of such psychological foundations the institutionalist critique of the rational actor paradigm was traumatised and arguably weakened. Considering this onslaught against its core ideas it is amazing that the institutionalism of Veblen and Commons survived as long as it did.

Outside institutionalism, the concept of habit followed that of instinct into exile. After occupying pride of place in the writings of Emile Durkheim and Max Weber, and in sociology generally until the First World War, the concept of habit was purposefully excised from the discipline (Camic, 1986). This excision was a defensive response to the conceptual homogenisation of action by the behaviourist psychologists and the general emphasis that was put on environmental conditioning, even to the point of denying any space for human agency. Economics followed sociology by likewise relegating the concept (Waller, 1988). The idea of habit was seen as too closely related to that of instinct. Both were regarded as being part of the earlier and unacceptable biological baggage. The complete separation of the social sciences from biology involved the establishment of concepts of the human agent which were unrooted in physiology and biology. Seemingly alone among social scientists, the institutionalists retained the notion of habit.[18]

Institutionalism survived the interwar period by downplaying part of its legacy. This is best illustrated by considering the later generation of institutionalists, educated in the interwar years and rising to prominence after the Second World War. The leading and by far the most influential American institutionalist in this category is Clarence Ayres.[19] Sufficiently distanced in time from James, McDougall and the early institutionalists, Ayres (1958, p. 25) took with him the rejection of instinct psychology, declaring that the very notion of instincts was 'scientifically obsolete.'

In addition, and largely at Ayres's instigation, the institutionalists shifted their philosophical emphasis from Peirce to John Dewey (Mirowski, 1987). Dewey had greater faith that science in general, and scientific experiment in particular, could serve both as routes to truth and as the bases of social policy. Although Dewey was not a positivist and was a critic of many of the interwar developments in scientific methodology, his reverence for science and his faith in its liberating qualities fitted in well with the times.

The positivistic climate of the 1920s pushed the institutionalists towards empiricism. For a time, they were able to exploit the positivist mood, insisting against rising neoclassicism on the need for an empirical foundation for the postulates of economic theory. One of the most influential living exponents of institutionalism, Wesley Mitchell, became increasingly engrossed in statistical studies. About that time he argued for the statistical salvation of institutionalism in the following terms:

> I want to *prove* things as nearly as may be and proof means usually an appeal to the facts – facts recorded in the best cases in statistical form. To write books of assertion or shrewd observation, won't convince people who have been in the habit of asserting other things or seeing things in a different perspective. . . . I

---

[18] It was retained however, without further significant development of the critique of and alternative to the rational actor paradigm of neoclassical theory. As in the work of Ayres an alternative, institutionalist theory of individual human agency was neglected in favour of a version of cultural determinism (Rutherford, 1994, pp. 40–41). For Ayres (1961, p. 175): 'In a very real sense . . . there is no such thing as an individual'. Habit became simply the corporeal expression and repository of mysterious cultural forces supposedly driving all economic and technological change (Ayres, 1944).

[19] Tool (1994, p. 16) noted: 'Ayres and his students have been among the most significant contributors to the development of institutional economics in the last half-century.'

often find that the only real answer lies in doing a lot of work with statistics. (Quoted in Ross, 1991, p. 321)

The statistical turn was resisted by others but Mitchell was resolute in his support of the primacy of empirical work, emphasising this point in his 1925 presidential address to the American Economic Association. Pressed by Jacob Viner and other critics, Mitchell had some difficulty in promoting a clear and consistent defence of his empiricist view of the development of knowledge (Seckler, 1975, pp. 110–16). In 1927, an American Economic Association roundtable of 'eight eminent economists and statisticians, including Mitchell, debated the role of statistics in economics and all seven of Mitchell's colleagues attacked his position, arguing that statistics offered a useful empirical and analytical tool but could not remake a theory' (Ross, 1991, p. 415). Ross saw this event as a 'turning point' in the fortunes of institutionalism, evincing a gathering impatience of the critics with the failure of that school to develop a systematic theory. Seemingly having gained an initial advantage over the more aprioristic economists by embracing positivism in the new intellectual climate, institutionalism was ultimately to lose out. The positivist turn gave institutionalism no impetus to develop its own theoretical system. The task was in any case more difficult because institutionalism had abandoned much of its philosophical and psychological legacy.[20]

Significantly, institutionalism also adapted to the greater anthropological emphasis on the concept of culture. Such a turn was far from alien to institutionalism, as Veblen himself had pioneered an analysis of culture in his *Theory of the Leisure Class* (1899). Indeed, culture was a crucial concept within institutionalism from the beginning (Mayhew, 1987, 1989). But there is also early evidence of a shift in its explanatory status, as Malcolm Rutherford (1984) elaborated.

Although Veblen never entirely abandoned a genetically transmitted view of instinct, 'his use of instinct theory declined markedly in his later work' (Rutherford, 1984, p. 333).[21] After Veblen, and contrary to the founder's views, leading American institutionalists began to propose that human nature and behaviour was *exclusively* determined by culture. Accordingly,

---

[20] Myrdal (1958, p. 254), himself an institutional economist, saw interwar American institutional economics as marked by a 'naive empiricism'.

[21] In Hodgson (1992a, 1993b) I mistakenly suggested that Veblen moved away from the view that instincts are biologically inherited. I am grateful to Malcolm Rutherford for correcting me on this point.

although Mitchell (1910) had earlier seen instinct as central to the explanation of human behaviour, he later 'concluded that Veblen's instinct of workmanship could not be a single heritable trait, but at most a stable disposition shaped and passed on by cultural experience' (Ross, 1991, p. 384). As the institutional economist Allan Gruchy (1972, p. 43) explained approvingly, and with an apparent genuflection to positivism: 'Mitchell did not follow Veblen in emphasizing the instinctive basis of human behavior, because instincts cannot be objectively analyzed'. In the coming years it became clear that institutionalism had abandoned what had been seen as an embarrassing part of its Veblenian legacy. As early as 1924, the prominent institutionalist Albert Wolfe (1924, p. 472) wrote, in an influential institutionalist collection of essays, that behaviourist psychology offered 'a promise of a scientific basis for an understanding of economic motivations'.

A few years later the rot had reached the top. Mitchell (1937, p. 312) had lost confidence in both Darwinism and instinct psychology as foundations for institutionalism: 'The Darwinian viewpoint is due to be superseded in men's minds: the instinct–habit psychology will yield to some other conception of human nature.' Later on, Ayres (1958, p. 29) expressed a complete break with any notions of a biological determination of human nature: 'It is now quite conclusively established that no such complex behavior patterns are in a literal sense "inborn". We now know that such patterns are wholly cultural.' The human mind was seen as an empty vessel or *tabula rasa*, to be filled by the culture and environment in which it was situated. This removed the question – that had much concerned Veblen among others – of the evolved biological faculties of the mind and their relation to culture and institutions. However, in the circumstances, rather than being compromised by the increasing emphasis on a biologically untainted concept of culture, the institutionalists became its most enthusiastic devotees.[22]

---

[22] In contrast, Veblen held the view that culture could be moulded in part by the genetic inheritance of a group. Ayres (1952, p. 25) went so far as to describe this notion of Veblen's as racism: 'worst of all, perhaps, was his tentative addiction to racism. He was somehow persuaded that "the dolicho-blond race" was possessed of certain peculiar propensities which shaped its culture – an idea which present-day anthropologists most decisively reject.' As Tilman (1992, p. 161) points out, this allegation ignores both the ideological and scientific context of Veblen's own time and, more importantly, the fact that Veblen never expressed animosity towards any race in his writings. The supposition of racial differences in Veblen's writings was never seen by him as grounds for racial discrimination or repression. Indeed, such a deduction would be illegitimate, as normative statements about

While the increasing emphasis on the role of culture did not seem to embarrass or undermine institutionalism, this school of thought was affected by the concomitant separation of biology and social science. Accordingly, the Veblenian research programme of building a 'post-Darwinian' and 'evolutionary' economics was compromised, if not abandoned. Although the general concept of culture was not itself a problem for institutionalism, the intellectual context in which the shift to culture took place made the further development of a systematic institutionalist theory much more difficult.[23]

The crunch came with the Great Depression of the 1930s. The personal recollections of Gunnar Myrdal are particularly apposite. When he came to the US at the end of the twenties, institutional economics was still seen by many as the 'wind of the future'. However, at that time Myrdal was at the

---

human rights are not logically deducible from empirical statements about human differences, nor from theoretical statements about the causes of human attributes or behaviour. Similarly inappropriate accusation of 'racism' against Veblen are made by Blaug (1968, p. 679) and by Samuels in his 1990 introduction to Veblen (1919a, p. ix). These accusations seem to stem from the view that propositions concerning differing attributes of different ethnic groups are racist, and that anti-racism is dependent upon the denial of such differences. On the contrary, an unconditional anti-racism, independent of the denial or assertion of any empirical or theoretical proposition, is stronger than a conditional anti-racist stance.

[23] Despite the shift away from biology, the institutionalists retained the alternative description of themselves as 'evolutionary' as well as 'institutional' economists. However, this was more to do with Ayres's (1944, p. 155) influential view that the term 'institutional economics' was 'singularly unfortunate'. He complained of 'the misnomer of "Institutionalism"' (Ayres, 1935, p. 197) because he saw institutions never as enabling but typically as a negative constraint on progress, as 'a bad thing from which we are bound to try perpetually to redeem ourselves' (Ayres to Dewey, 29 January 1930; quoted in Tilman, 1990, p. 966; see also McFarland, 1985, 1986). For Ayres, it was 'technology', not institutions, that served human progress. Ayres's view of institutions contrasted with that of Veblen and Commons, who saw institutions as both constitutive and enabling of action, and in even some cases as marks of evolving civilization, as well as accepting their possible conservative and constraining effects. The adoption of the alternative 'evolutionary' label stressed dynamic notions of economic change, in contrast to the equilibrium thinking of neoclassical economics. As in the case of Schumpeter, it did not necessarily connote any reference to biology. Uneasiness with both alternate labels persisted within American Institutionalism. Royall Brandis has remarked to the author that when the institutionalist 'Association for Evolutionary Economics' came to establish its journal in the late 1960s, deadlock between adherents of the 'institutional' versus 'evolutionary' labels led to the adoption of the very prosaic *Journal of Economic Issues* title.

'theoretical' stage of his own development and he was 'utterly critical' of this orientation in economics. He 'even had something to do with the initiation of the Econometric Society, which was planned as a defense organization against the advancing institutionalists' (Myrdal, 1972, p. 6). Myrdal went on to explain a key event in the decline of the popularity of institutionalism in the United States:

> What I believe nipped it in the bud was the world-wide economic depression. Faced with this great calamity, we economists of the 'theoretical' school, accustomed to reason in terms of simplified macro-models, felt we were on the top of the situation, while the institutionalists were left in a muddle. It was at this stage that economists in the stream of the Keynesian revolution adjusted their theoretical models to the needs of the time, which gave victory much more broadly to our 'theoretical' approach (Myrdal, 1972, p. 7)[24]

Notably, without referring to Myrdal, Dorothy Ross (1991, p. 419) corroborates the argument:

> Institutionalism as a movement . . . fell victim to the Great Depression and its Keynesian remedy. For self-proclaimed experts in historical change, their inability to come to any better understanding of the Depression than their neoclassical colleagues was a considerable deficit. Mitchell in particular, who predicted like everyone else that the downturn would right itself within a year or two, was driven deeper into his program of empirical research by this proof of ignorance. Whether a more powerful and genuinely historical institutional economics would have done better is impossible to say. Like the left-liberal economists generally, the institutionalists were drawn into the Keynesian revision of neoclassicism.

---

[24] What makes this personal testimony particularly striking is the fact that years later – in the 1940s – Myrdal converted to institutionalism, and subsequently won the Nobel Prize in Economics. The institutionalist Ayres (1935, p. 173) seems partially to corroborate Myrdal's analysis by his contemporary report that the 'cutting edge of the issue between [the neoclassical economists] and the "Institutionalists" would seem to be the incapacity of the latter to demonstrate the failure of the present economic order which they propose controlling'. A hostile critic of institutionalism took a remarkably similar view when he noted that 'the greatest slump in history finds them sterile and incapable of helpful comment – their trends gone awry and their dispersions distorted' (Robbins, 1932, p. 115).

Frank Knight came to a similar verdict. Knight regarded himself as an institutionalist – albeit a maverick one – and was at the strategic location of Chicago in the 1930s and 1940s. He asserted that institutionalism was 'largely drowned by discussion of the depression, or perhaps boom and depression, and especially by the literature of the Keynesian revolution' (Knight, 1952, p. 45). [25]

However, the process of institutionalist decline outlined by Myrdal, Knight and others, took some time. Even before Keynesianism had become influential in America, institutionalists were active in the early inspiration, planning, inauguration, and implementation of President Franklin Roosevelt's New Deal, which lasted from 1933 to 1940 (W. Barber, 1994, 1996; Stoneman, 1979; Wunderlin, 1992). But the New Deal was not inspired by Keynes, and the institutionalist involvement with Roosevelt's economic policy had no clear theoretical cutting edge. The institutionalists provided no clear overall theoretical justification for their interventionist policies. [26]

Keynesianism was in the ascendancy after the publication of the *General Theory* in 1936 and was helped by a drift of Anglo-American opinion towards state intervention and planning (Colander and Landreth, 1996). It

---

[25] Evidence of Knight's institutionalism includes the following. Like several other leading institutionalists, such as Mitchell, J. M. Clark and A. F. Burns, Knight tried to marry institutionalism with aspects of mainstream theory. Hence Knight (1924, p. 262) wrote: 'deductive theory and "institutional" economics' are both relevant: 'at one extreme we might have a discussion limited to the abstract theory of markets . . . at the other extreme we should have the philosophy of history . . . and that is what institutional economics practically comes to. It should go without saying that all are useful and necessary.' This point of view persisted throughout his life. In a letter dated 16 February 1937 to his friend Clarence Ayres – another leading institutionalist – Knight reported that he was trying to give a course on 'Economics from an Institutional Perspective' at Chicago. Knight's Reading List for Economics 305, Winter 1937, says: 'The task of institutionalism [is] that of accounting historically for the factors treated as *data* in rationalistic, price-theory economics.' (Samuels, 1977, p. 503). Years later Knight (1957, p. 43) remarked: 'I am in fact as "institutionalist" as anyone, in a positive sense.' The subsequent and persistent failure of institutionalists and non-institutionalists alike to acknowledge Knight's evident and avowed institutionalist credentials would itself be an interesting case study in the 'institutions of economics', which regrettably we cannot pursue here.

[26] Biddle (1996, p. 144) notes that citations to works by Mitchell – the leading institutionalist of the time – suffered a substantial decline as early as the mid-1930s.

seems that the institutionalists, while emphasising the complexity of economic phenomena and the need for careful empirical research, were eventually out-theorised by the mathematical Keynesians. This group of young and mathematically-minded converts to Keynesianism developed what now seem in retrospect to be extraordinarily simple macroeconomic models. Influential academic contributions published from about 1938 to 1948 – including from Alvin Hansen and Paul Samuelson in America, and Roy Harrod and John Hicks in England – helped to transform Keynesian ideas and make them mathematically tractable. The attraction of this approach was partly its technocratic lure, and partly because it proposed very simple apparent solutions to the urgent problem of the day. The apparent policy usefulness of the new approach was crucial in its struggle for ascendancy (Yonay, 1997). According to this doctrine, it appeared that the problem of unemployment could be alleviated simply by increasing a variable called G. The 'solution' was plain and transparent, dressed up in mathematical and 'scientific' garb, and given all the reverence customarily accorded to such presentations in a technocratic culture.[27]

In general, institutional economists were not hostile to the Keynesian revolution. Even before the *General Theory* was published, the institutionalist John Maurice Clark (1935) gave a cautious welcome to Keynes's policies. Finding an institutionalist precedent for Keynes's ideas, Rutledge Vining (1939, pp. 692–3) wrote: 'Much of Keynes's theory of employment can be dug from Veblen's intuitions', particularly in the *Theory of Business Enterprise* (1904). Sympathetic economists such as William Jaffé and Richard Ely also perceived similarities between the works of Veblen and Keynes, and their joint parallels in Roosevelt's policies (Tilman, 1992, pp. 111–12). On the theoretical side, institutionalism eventually formed its own synthesis with Keynesianism, interpreting Keynes in terms of an organicist ontology and giving much less emphasis than the American Keynesians to mathematical modelling (Dillard, 1948; Gruchy, 1948).

By the end of the Second World War, Keynesianism dominated the economics profession in both Britain and America. Of course, the ascendant 'Keynesianism' was different in several key respects from the economics of

---

[27] Ironically, this reigning view ignored the fact that any practical implementation of a policy to increase government expenditure depended precisely on a detailed knowledge of the workings of government, financial and other *institutions*. For their concern with such details the institutionalists were much maligned by the mathematical technocrats. Their expert knowledge in this area, however, partly explains the fact that they were in government bodies at the forefront of the implementation of the expansionary economic policies of the Roosevelt era.

Keynes. As noted by Benjamin Ward (1972) and Terence Hutchison (1992), this became as much a 'formalistic revolution' as a Keynesian one. The evidence suggests, however, that Keynes himself was at best sceptical of econometrics and mathematical modelling in economics. What did emerge from 1938 to 1948 were the foundations of the neoclassical-Keynesian synthesis, based on key developments in neoclassical microeconomics and a mechanistic system of macroeconomic modelling with some Keynesian affinities.[28]

Nevertheless, after the decline of biology in social science, modelling in terms of mechanistic, functional relationships became more common in economics. Arguably, these two developments were related. It should not be concluded, however, that the retention of biological metaphors would have stemmed the mathematical tide. Biology is not necessarily an antidote to mechanistic modelling, nor would it have been reliably so in the 1920s and 1930s. As early as 1925 Alfred Lotka attempted 'to reformulate biology as a branch of physics' (Kingsland, 1994, p. 233) with the publication of his *Elements of Physical Biology*.[29] Biology itself has long exhibited internal tensions between formal and discursive analysis, between holism and reductionism, and between atomism and organicism. The decline of biology in social science did not itself directly cause the turn to mechanistic modelling. Rather, the failure of biology to deliver the theoretical goods for institutionalism in the first third of the twentieth century disabled such economists and created a breach into which the voguish econometricians, modellers, and mathematicians could storm.

Even in microeconomic theory the battle was lost. In the early decades of the twentieth century the institutionalists seemed on strong empirical ground, suggesting the neoclassical postulate of maximizing behaviour was incompatible with contemporary psychology. However, Samuelson (1938) and others began to insist that economics could base itself on the claims of 'revealed preference' alone, and did not need to invoke any psychological

---

[28] For discussions of the rise of mathematics and dynamic modelling in economics see Mirowski (1991) and Weintraub (1991). Keynes's own views on mathematical modelling are clear in a letter to Roy Harrod of 16 July 1938: 'In economics . . . to convert a model into a quantitative formula is to destroy its usefulness as an instrument of thought' (Keynes, 1973, p. 299). For more on Keynes's critical views of econometrics and mathematical modelling see Moggridge (1992, pp. 621–3). A good overview of the Keynesian theoretical issues is found in Littleboy (1990).

[29] Samuelson (1947) borrowed a number of mathematical techniques from the mechanistic biology of Lotka (1925).

theory of human behaviour (Lewin, 1996). Sociology had broken with psychology, and mainstream economics rapidly followed suit. The institutionalist objection that the assumption of maximizing behaviour was psychologically unrealistic was thus rendered largely ineffective. Mainstream economics then saw itself as independent of any psychological postulates. The earlier separation between biology and social science had made such a stance possible.

America institutionalism had lost some of the crucial theoretical battles even before all eyes were diverted by Hitler's seizure of power in 1933 and the spread of fascism in Europe. Subsequently, the Nazi holocaust extinguished all varieties of biologistic social science in Anglo-American academia. Eugenic and other ideas that were common amongst liberals as well as conservatives in the pre-1914 period were seen as dangerously allied with fascism and ethnic repression. All references to biology had to be removed from social science. Anyone who argued to the contrary was in severe danger of being labelled as a racist or a fascist. Such cataclysmic political developments finally terminated the long, post-1880 flirtation of social science with biology. In 1940 such ideas were at their nadir in the Anglo-American academic world.

5.7. THE SPORADIC RETURN OF BIOLOGY AND THE RE-INVENTION OF EVOLUTIONARY ECONOMICS

After the Second World War a partial return to biology occurred in the social sciences. The transition was given impetus by two separate developments in the science of life, in the 1940s and the 1970s. Their effects on the social sciences were significant. In economics, two notable episodes of 'biological' thinking occurred immediately after each of these developments in biology, in 1950 and in the 1970s. This is more than mere coincidence. Indeed, in the case of developments in the 1970s, the references to the contemporary developments in biology were direct and explicit.

The first impulse was the emergence of the neo-Darwinian synthesis in biology. The elements of this synthesis had been in place long before, but the new paradigm did not become fully established until the 1940s. A group of Darwinians working in Britain and the United States (principally Theodosius Dobzhansky, Ronald Fisher, John B. S. Haldane, Julian Huxley, Ernst Mayr, George Gaylord Simpson, G. Ledyard Stebbins, Bernhard Rensch and Sewall Wright) accomplished a synthesis between the theory of natural selection and Mendelian genetics. Only then did the Mendelian gene became fully incorporated into the theory of evolution, giving a plausible explanation of the presumed variation of offspring and the selection of species. This had not been achieved by Darwin or any other nineteenth century biologist. As Mayr (1980, pp. 39–40) pointed out: 'What happened between 1937 and 1947 was . . . a synthesis between research traditions that had previously been unable to communicate.' The postwar 'evolutionary synthesis' gave the Darwinian idea of natural selection a renewed vitality which has continued to this day.

The timing of Alchian's famous article of 1950 is therefore apposite. Capitalising on the triumph of a new Darwinian biology, he made an explicit appeal to the metaphor of natural selection. However, he made no reference to the earlier work of Veblen: the memory of the earlier evolutionary foray had been lost. Alchian (1950) proposed that the assumption of maximizing behaviour by business firms is not necessary for the scientific purposes of explanation and prediction. Selective success, Alchian argued, depends on behaviour and results, not motivations. If firms never actually attempted to maximize profits, 'evolutionary' processes of selection would ensure the survival of the more profitable enterprises. Alchian's argument was essentially a mixture of a behaviourist emphasis on the observable, neglecting conscious motivations; a positivist fix on prediction, downplaying explanation; and a half-assimilated biological analogy. It thus captured the intellectual mood of the time.

This evolutionary idea was taken up and modified by Stephen Enke (1951) who argued that with sufficient intensity of competition and 'in the long run', conditions of intense competition would mean that only the optimizers remain viable. Milton Friedman (1953) developed this further, by seeing 'natural selection' as grounds for assuming that agents act 'as if' they maximize, whether or not firms and individuals actually do so. Going further than Alchian, he used 'natural selection' as a defence of the maximization hypothesis for individual firms.

About the same time the inventive heterodox economist Kenneth Boulding published his *Reconstruction of Economics* (1950). In it he borrowed 'population thinking' and associated models from ecology. Capital goods were represented as a population with different vintages that entered the capital fund like births and deaths of organisms in a species.[30] Further,

---

[30] On the nature and relevance of 'population thinking' – taken from Darwinian biology – to economics see Foss (1994a), Hodgson (1993b), Mayr (1985a) and Metcalfe (1988).

in this work Boulding was one of the first to emphasize that the economy was part of, and depended upon, the ecosystem.

It is very likely that this flurry of evolutionary theorising was prompted by the major developments in biology in the 1940s. Compared with that in the 1970s, the first postwar impulse from biology was much more significant from the biological point of view but it had the lesser effect on economics and social science. The much diminished effect on social science of the first and greater impulse from biology is explicable, given its immediacy after the Nazi holocaust, and considering the prior degree of reaction against biological thinking in the social sciences in the 1920s and 1930s.

There were also theoretical reasons for the diminished effect of this first postwar wave of evolutionary thinking on economics. Arguing that biological analogies were inappropriate for economics, Edith Penrose (1952) responded to Alchian and others. She argued that neo-Darwinian theories of evolution excluded the deliberative and calculative behaviour that was characteristic of human action in the economic sphere. 'To treat the growth of the firm as the unfolding of its genetic nature is downright obscurantism. To treat innovations as chance mutations not only obscures their significance but leaves them essentially unexplained' (Penrose, 1952, p. 18). Penrose raised some probing and fundamental questions about the relationship between economics and biology which still remain on the agenda of both sciences. Within three years, Alchian (1953, p. 601) had retreated, when he wrote that in his earlier paper the 'reference to the biological analogy was merely expository'.

For economists, Friedman's intervention in 1953 was especially influential. It became a classic defence of the neoclassical maximization hypothesis. It used the new authority of evolutionary biology to rebut lingering institutionalist and behaviouralist doubts about that core idea. Beyond that, however, the biological analogy was little used in economics for the subsequent twenty years.

Again ironically, Friedman's use of the metaphor of natural selection bolstered a key element in the mechanistic paradigm and rebutted the 'evolutionary' economists in the institutional camp. In an article published in the same fateful year of 1953, Gregor Sebba (1953) traced the derivation of the ideas of rationality and equilibria, the core concepts of neoclassical economics, from the inheritance of Newtonian and mechanistic thought. In fact, Friedman had applied simplistically a half-assimilated idea from Darwinian biology to reinforce the mechanistic paradigm of neoclassical economics. While Darwinian evolution had focused on the origins of diversity and variety, Friedman saw evolutionary processes as producing an evolutionary optimum. Eleven years later, Sidney Winter (1964) showed that

Friedman's argument had a highly limited applicability, even in evolutionary terms.[31]

In other social sciences the postwar re-emergence of biology was more pronounced. Immediately after the end of the Second World War the nature-nurture controversy was renewed in psychology, and in 1948 the anthropologist Clyde Kluckhohn declared that biology as well as culture had a part in the explanation of human behaviour. In the 1950s even Kroeber had shifted his view and was ready to acknowledge biological roots of human nature (Degler, 1991, pp. 218–21).

The concept of instinct also enjoyed a slow rehabilitation. Much of the original impetus behind this development came from Europe. In the 1930s the Austrian ethologist Konrad Lorenz produced scholarly articles on instinctive behaviour. In 1951 the Oxford ethologist Nikolaus Tinbergen published his *Study of Instinct* in which he argued that much of human behaviour is instinctive. By the 1960s the concept of instinct had re-emerged in American psychology. In 1973 Lorenz and Tinbergen were awarded, with Karl von Frisch, the Nobel Prize for their work on instinctive behaviour (Degler, 1991, pp. 223–4).

Furthermore, behaviourist psychology came under attack. In the 1950s Harry Harlow performed a set of famous experiments on rhesus monkeys which suggested there was more to monkey behaviour than stimulus and response. An infant monkey would cling to a soft artificial mother in preference to a wire-framed surrogate which dispensed milk. Some instinctive drive must have accounted for this apparently self-destructive behaviour. Another set of experiments, by J. Garcia and R. A. Koelling in 1966, showed that rats could not be conditioned to avoid flavoured water when deterred by electric shocks, but the animals would readily learn to do so when drinking the water was followed by induced nausea. This suggested a functionally-specific instinct to avoid nausea-inducing substances, and again undermined the notion of a generally conditioned response. Behaviourism was thus hoist with its own experimentalist petard. In addition, the critiques of behaviourism by Noam Chomsky (1959) and Cyril Burt (1962) announced a return of the concept of consciousness to psychology, thus undermining the hegemony of positivism in that subject.[32]

---

[31] See Boyd and Richerson (1980) and ch. 8 of the present work.

[32] More generally, although positivism greatly increased in popularity in American scientific circles in the first half of the twentieth century, the publication in 1951 of Quine's essay 'Two Dogmas of Empiricism' (reprinted in Quine, 1953) helped to check and reverse the movement. Quine effectively undermined the distinction

Leading biologists themselves argued that the social sciences could not ignore the biotic foundations of human life. For instance, Dobzhansky (1955, p. 20) stated: 'Human evolution is wholly intelligible only as an outcome of the interaction of biological and social facts.' A related point was endorsed by the anthropologist Alexander Alland (1967, p. 10):

> Biologists now agree that the argument over the primacy of environment or heredity in the development of organism is a dead issue. It is now generally accepted that the function and form of organisms can be understood only as the result of a highly complicated process of interaction.

By the early 1970s some sociologists such as Bruce Eckland and political scientists such as Albert Somit had argued that the ties between the biology and the social sciences should be re-established. In 1970 the political scientist Thomas Thorson argued that Darwinian evolutionary theory would be useful in developing a theory of social and political change. Human affairs, he argued, would be best understood from the perspective of biology rather than physics. The dialogue between biology and politics was encouraged by an international conference in Paris in 1975 in which a number of American social scientists participated (Degler, 1991, pp. 224–6).

In several key respects, the postwar return to biology took a distinctive form. In particular, the triumph of the neo-Darwinian synthesis in the 1940s and the discovery of the structure of DNA by Crick and Watson in 1953 brought forth a renewed faith in the possibilities of reductionism. It was believed that if the behaviour of organisms could be explained by the genetic code; all sciences should emulate this achievement and explain the whole in terms of the parts. Of course, not all biologists held such views and many saw organisms as outcomes of interactions between genes and environment. Nevertheless, prestige had gone to those who had seemingly broken the whole into its constituent parts.

Thus in 1972, echoing Menger in 1883, Hayes in 1910 and Allport in 1927, anthropologist George Murdock repudiated the idea of 'the social aggregate as the preferable unit for study' instead of the individual. The concept of culture was seriously flawed, he argued. It was the individual who made culture, not the other way round. A focus on the individual as the unit would bring anthropology in line with biology (Degler, 1991, p. 235). For

---

between science and non-science in logical positivism and denied that statements could be judged true or false purely on the basis of sense experience. 'The publication of this essay in 1951 was one of the key events in the collapse of logical positivism' (Hoover, 1995, p. 721).

some, the return to biology became a rejection of culture as a determinant of behaviour, and a celebration of reductionism in science. For them it was as if the clock had been turned back to 1890. Fortunately, this stance was not universal.

It is noted below that the year 1975 marked a turning point in the influence of biology on economics. References by economists to biology were relatively uncommon in the preceding twenty years. There are a few notable exceptions. Coming from the institutionalist tradition, Morris Copeland (1958) attempted to revive interest in Veblen's evolutionary project. Jack Downie (1958) covertly renovated the biological analogy in Marshallian economics by bringing diversity and 'population thinking' into the picture of competition between firms (Nightingale, 1993). Announcing a significant turn in his own thinking, Hayek (1967a) made a number of references to evolutionary biology in an important essay. Michael Farrell (1970) made an isolated mathematical contribution.

In economics in the 1954–1974 period, by far the most important work inspired by biology was by Nicholas Georgescu-Roegen: *The Entropy Law and the Economic Process* (1971). He asserted the value of biological as well as thermodynamic analogies and founded a distinctive version of 'bio-economics'. Subsequently – but apparently quite independently of institutionalism, Hayek and Georgescu-Roegen – the basis of a new theory of economic evolution was outlined by Nelson and Winter (1973, 1974).

The bombshell was *Sociobiology: The New Synthesis*, published in 1975 by Edward Wilson. Even before the appearance of this book the return to biology was well under way. But its appearance stimulated a protracted interest in the alleged biotic foundations of human behaviour. The book was greeted with a great deal of criticism, from both social scientists and biologists. It nevertheless brought biology back onto the social science agenda.

The impact of the new sociobiology on economics was rapid. Gary Becker (1976b) published an article suggesting a genetic determination of a human behaviour modelled along neoclassical lines. Jack Hirshleifer (1977, 1978) and Gordon Tullock (1979) quickly followed with similar calls for the joining of economics with sociobiology.[33] Notably these presentations were

---

[33] These calls did not go unheeded. The biologist Ghiselin (1974) had already imported the mainstream economist's notion of 'methodological individualism', and had echoed the old metaphor of 'nature's economy' in the biotic sphere. The biologists Rapport and Turner (1977) analysed food selection, 'predator switching' and other biological phenomena using indifference curves and other analytical tools taken from economics. Not also that the biologist Maynard Smith (1982)

individualist and reductionist, and emphasized self-interest and individual competition in the biotic as well as the economic world (Gowdy, 1987).

Although their original evolutionary prospectus appeared as early as 1973, Nelson and Winter (1982, pp. 42–3) also recognized the importance of Wilson's work. Although the genesis of their *Evolutionary Theory of Economic Change* had much to do with the growing prestige of biology and the re-introduction of biological metaphors into social science, their work is quite different from that of the Becker–Hirshleifer–Tullock school. Nelson and Winter reject the notion that human behaviour is wholly or largely determined by the genes. Their perspective is complex and interactionist, involving different levels and units of selection, and ongoing interaction between individuals, institutions and their socio-economic environment.

At about this time an evolutionary approach was also developed by Boulding (1978, 1981). This built on his earlier work on biological analogies (Boulding, 1950) but it is significant that his fully fledged evolutionary theory did not emerge in its developed form until the late 1970s. This is later than in other social sciences, particularly anthropology, where the word 'evolution' became quite common in the 1960s.

The author has discovered 17 relevant works (books or academic journal articles) in economics (in English) in the 50 years from 1890 to 1939 inclusive, with 'evolution' or 'evolutionary' in their title or subtitle. Most of these were published before the First World War. This is relatively significant, given the relatively low number of works published at that time. Much of this early usage of the term 'evolutionary' was by institutionalists of the old school.[34]

After 1939 there was a significant gap. No work in economics has been found in the 1940s with 'evolution' or its derivatives in its title or subtitle. It reappears with Alchian in 1950. There was a more dispersed and gradual

---

imported game theory – originally developed in economics by von Neumann and Morgenstern (1953) – into biology. After Maynard Smith had developed the concept of an 'evolutionary stable strategy', this idea was then transferred back to economics by Sugden (1986).

[34] The earliest seven appearances after 1890 are Hobson (1894), Bucher (1901), Ely (1903), Crozier (1906) and Veblen (1898a, 1899, 1908). Five of these have clear links to institutionalism. The subsequent appearances prior to 1960 are MacGregor (1910), Reinheimer (1913), MacDonald (1916), Ashley (1924), Cobb (1926), Bellerby (1927), Harris (1934), Burns (1936), Copeland (1936), Edwards (1938), Alchian (1950), Haavelmo (1954), Reynolds and Taft (1956) and von Mises (1957). The author would be interested to hear of any others that have been omitted.

increase in usage of such terms from 1950 to 1980 and subsequently more rapid growth. The word 'evolutionary' did not become widespread in economics until after 1980. The number of uses in the 1990s is well into three figures.

Notably, the use of the word 'evolution' does not necessarily indicate the adoption of a biological metaphor. Furthermore, the 'evolution-in-the-title-or-subtitle' criterion is very crude. (It allows an important work making explicit use of biology, namely Georgescu-Roegen (1971), to fall through the net.) Nevertheless, the suggestion here is that the changing degree of perceived legitimacy of interdisciplinary discourse between economics and biology has affected the frequency of use of the term 'evolution' by economists.

As in economics in general, references to biology are minimal in Austrian school writings prior to the 1960s.[35] It was Hayek who began to bring evolutionary metaphors into Austrian school economics in the last thirty years of his life. But this writer was restrained by his earlier rejection of 'scientism' in social theory and his denunciation of social theory for a 'slavish imitation of the method and language of science' (Hayek, 1952b, p. 15). Subsequently, however, Hayek (1967b, p. viii) notes a change in 'tone' in his attitude to 'scientism', attributed to the influence of Karl Popper. This is not, needless to say, a matter of mere 'tone', and the door is progressively opened for the entry of the biological analogues.

Although there were earlier hints at what was to come, the first suggestions of a more prominent 'evolutionary' approach in Hayek's work are found in a collection of essays published in the 1960s (Hayek, 1967b, pp. 31–4, 66–81, 103–4, 111, 119).[36] Patchy references to evolutionary theory are also found in a major work produced in the 1970s (Hayek, 1982, vol. 1, pp. 9, 23–4, 152–3, vol. 3, pp. 154–59, 199–202). But we have to wait until the late 1980s to receive the fullest explicit statement of Hayek's evolutionary conception (Hayek, 1988, pp. 9, 11–28). It could not be claimed, therefore, that the Austrian school had consistently embraced the

---

[35] An analysis of Menger's limited notion of 'evolution' is found in Hodgson (1993b). It should be noted that Hayek's (1952a) important critique of behaviourist psychology made reference to biology, although it is not strictly a work in economics.

[36] The 1960s saw also a major change in Hayek's philosophical outlook. He moved away from extreme subjectivism, and gave more emphasis to a conception of human agents as rule-following (Fleetwood, 1995; Lawson, 1994a, 1996, 1997). The philosophical and evolutionary turns in his thought are connected, because rule-following raises the question of the evolutionary origin of those rules

evolutionary metaphor in economics. Hayek's statements of the 1960s in this genre are notable, with other scarce voices of the 1955–1974 period. But they also marked a shift in his own thinking and a reversal of his earlier opposition to 'scientism'. In part, Hayek was being carried by the tide. Overall, the use of the word 'evolution' by Austrian authors did not become common until the late 1980s.[37]

Furthermore, Schumpeter did not use the term 'evolution' in a title of a book or article and the (typically undefined and rather misleading) term 'neo-Schumpeterian' also did not become prominent until the 1980s.

It is too early to judge what kind of 'evolutionary economics' or 'economic biology' will triumph as the influence of biology upon social science becomes even stronger. In general, however, there are important differences with the type of evolutionary theorising which was prevalent in the 1890s. For instance, due to the work of W. Brian Arthur (1989), Paul David (1985) and many others there is now a widespread recognition of the importance of path dependence, undermining the view that evolution generally leads to optimal or even near-optimal outcomes. This parallels a similar stance taken by biologists such as Stephen Jay Gould (1989).

5.8. SUMMARY AND CONCLUSION

It is freely accepted that the present chapter covers a vast canvas and it has not done justice to the details. But it is a largely unseen picture and it needs to be shown first as a whole. A number of general suggestions and observations have been made concerning the relationship between biology and economics. A summary of some of them is appropriate at this stage.

During the twentieth century, biology has influenced economics in a number of quite different ways. A first mode of interaction involves the suggestion that explanations of socio-economic phenomena can be reduced entirely to, and ultimately explained by, phenomena at the biotic level. Before the First World War such a position was accepted by theorists such as Spencer but rejected by others such as Veblen. In the interwar period the influence of biotic phenomena on society was widely denied. The return of biological thinking in economics and the social sciences in the post-1945 period is marked by views which suggest and emphasize a genetic foundation for human behaviour (Becker, Hirshleifer and Tullock) and

---

[37] See the discussion of Hayek's notion of evolution in Hodgson (1993b).

others that, in contrast, eschew biological reductionism (Nelson and Winter).

A second mode of interaction is at the level of metaphor. Ideas were imported from biology to recast economics on a quite different pattern. It was in this sense that Veblen argued for a 'post-Darwinian' economics in 1898, Alchian adopted an evolutionary analogy in 1950, and Nelson and Winter subsequently constructed their theoretical system. This metaphorical mode of interaction is compatible with the view of an autonomous level of socio-economic analysis and a rejection of biological reductionism. It can involve the scrutiny, modification or rejection of particular conceptual transfers from one discipline to another, as well as their acceptance. The open and self-conscious use of metaphor may involve critical comparison rather than slavish imitation.[38]

However, the move away from biological thinking in economics and other social sciences in the interwar period meant the abandonment of *both* modes of analytical interaction: the metaphorical as well as the reductive. In particular, the elaboration of an evolutionary economics inspired by biology became extremely difficult.

Degler (1991) and others have convincingly argued that the declining influence of biology on American social science, in the first four decades of the twentieth century, was largely inspired by ideology rather than scientific evidence. From the nineteenth century, the rise of American economic and political prowess was associated with the rise of a relatively liberal and individualistic ideology. In intellectual circles in the early twentieth century this ideology developed strong anti-racist attributes. It emphasized individual achievement, seeing it as unconstrained by biological inheritance.

Liberal and leftist ideological associations helped to raise the popularity of American institutional economics in such intellectual circles, but also the move away from biology weakened it at a crucial stage of its theoretical development.[39] The Veblenian project to build a post-Darwinian evolutionary economics was thwarted both by the move away from biology

---

[38] See ch. 4 of the present work.

[39] The writings of Copeland (1931, 1958) represent an atypical and consistent attempt to remind fellow American institutionalists of their original links with biology. Thus during the crisis of institutionalism in the early 1930s he wrote: 'economics is a biological science – it studies group relationships among living organisms of the genus *homo sapiens*. As such its generalisations must somehow make peace with the general theory of biological evolution' (Copeland, 1931, p. 68).

in the social sciences and by apparent theoretical difficulties within biology which were not resolved until the emergence of the neo-Darwinian synthesis in the 1940s. By then, American institutionalism had been severely mauled. Neoclassical and 'Keynesian' modelling triumphed.

Furthermore, the failure of institutionalism to develop a systematic theory meant that, by 1929, it seemed muddled and impotent in the face of the Great Crash and the subsequent economic depression. Mathematical modellers offering clear remedies based on relatively simple models with few equations seemed a much more attractive counsel, especially for those concerned to put their economics to practical and humane uses. There is now less faith in the benefits of such modelling (Lawson, 1997; Mayer 1993; Ormerod, 1994) but in a supremely technocratic era they seemed to be the scientific solution to the economic malaise.

So began the cumulative process of increasing formalization in economics. The timings are again apposite, with the late 1930s being the turning point. Up to the 1920s, verbal expositions dominated the subject. In the late 1930s it all began to change. After 1940 the use of mathematics began to rise spectacularly, and gathered pace (Stigler *et al*, 1995, p. 342). The failure of institutionalism was not the only impetus, but the loss of its strategic initiative was crucial.[40]

It has also been suggested that the shifting relationship between economics and biology throughout the twentieth century was closely connected to changing conceptions of science itself. The rise of positivism in the 1920s also helped to marginalise the self-conscious use of metaphor. In addition the growing popularity of reductionism has had varying and complex effects on that relationship.

Several conclusions can be drawn. But two are selected for special mention. The first is to emphasize the dangers of conflating ideology with

---

[40] Some additional factors shifting American economics towards mathematical formalism may be mentioned. First, academic refugees from Continental Europe in the 1930s and 1940s often had a mathematical aptitude of superior quality to their use of English, while American scholars were often deficient in foreign language skills. Mathematical communication was thus advantaged. In addition, after the Second World War, the US National Science Foundation seemingly favoured mathematical economics, deeming it to be more scientific. (The author owes these observations to Royall Brandis.) As the relative prestige of Britain as a world centre of learning in economics declined, it began more and more to ape developments in the United States. Furthermore, Continental Europe was too devastated to regain its academic standing in the crucial years immediately after 1945.

science. The investigation of human nature and the causes of human behaviour – be they biotic or social or an interaction of both – is a matter for science and not for ideology. In general, theories should not be selected on the basis of the ideologies they appear to support. Often the same theory can be used to sustain different ideologies. Just as neoclassical general equilibrium theory was often deployed to support pro-market policies in the 1970s and 1980s, the very same kind of theory was used by Oskar Lange in the 1930s to support a version of socialist central planning. On the other hand, different and even contradictory theories can be used to support the same ideology. For instance, it has been shown above that both Lamarckian and anti-Lamarckian biology have been used to oppose racism.

Ideology and science are inextricably bound together but they are not the same thing. To conflate the two, to judge science in purely ideological terms, is to devalue and to endanger science itself. Scientists cannot avoid ideology. Indeed, they should be committed to a better world. Scientists have ideological responsibilities but they are not simply ideologists. To choose or reject a theory primarily on the basis of its apparent policy outcomes is to neglect the critical and evaluative requirements of science. Dogma is reinforced at both the scientific and the ideological level. The conflation of science with ideology thus degrades them both.

Second, just as science and ideology are related, but operate on different levels, so too should biology and the social sciences. The complete separation of biology and the social sciences is untenable because in reality human beings are not entirely separable from their foundation in nature. The obverse error, to conflate social science and biology so that they become one and the same, also carries many dangers, some of which have been explored above. Neither hermetic separation or complete integration are desirable. A more sophisticated relationship between the disciplines has to be established.[41]

Biology may establish links with, but should not deny the autonomy of, the social sciences. With this conceptualization it is possible to articulate a relationship between economics and biology in which each play their part, but the domination of one by the other is excluded. Such a relationship should provide a rich source of metaphorical inspiration. It remains to be seen that these methodological and ontological insights can be deployed to develop a new evolutionary economics – to continue and consummate the project started by Veblen over a century ago.

---

[41] A foremost example is the 'critical naturalism' discussed in Bhaskar (1979) and Jackson (1995).

6. Meanings of Evolutionary Economics

The term 'evolutionary economics' is currently applied to a confusingly wide variety of approaches within the subject. At least six main groupings using the phrase can be identified:[1]

- Thorstein Veblen (1898a) argued for an 'evolutionary' and 'post-Darwinian' economics. Institutionalists in the tradition of Veblen and John Commons frequently describe their approach as 'evolutionary economics', often using the terms 'institutional' and 'evolutionary' as virtual synonyms, as exemplified in the title of the USA-based and institutionalist Association for Evolutionary Economics.
- Joseph Schumpeter (1976, p. 82) famously described capitalist development as an 'evolutionary process'. Work influenced by Schumpeter is also described as 'evolutionary economics' as evidenced by the title of the *Journal of Evolutionary Economics*, published by the International Joseph Schumpeter Association.
- The approach of the Austrian school of economists is often described as 'evolutionary', as portrayed in Carl Menger's theory of the evolution of money and other institutions, and by the extensive use of an evolutionary metaphor from biology in the later works of Friedrich Hayek, especially in relation to the concept of spontaneous order.

---

[1] This is a revised and substantially extended version of Hodgson (1997e) which in turn makes use of material from Hodgson (1993b, 1995b).

- In addition, the economics of assorted writers such as Adam Smith, Karl Marx, Alfred Marshall and others is also sometimes described as 'evolutionary' in character.
- Evolutionary game theory is a prominent recent development in mathematical economics and has been inspired by related mathematical work in theoretical biology.
- The word 'evolutionary' is sometimes attached to work in what is also described as 'complexity theory', typically that associated with the Santa Fe Institute in the United States, involving applications of chaos theory and various other types of computer simulation. In this and allied simulation work the use of replicator dynamics, genetic algorithms, genetic programming, and so on, can be found.

With such a wide variety of uses, it is unlikely that there is a single, underlying and coherent message. Indeed, the use of the word 'evolutionary' in economics seems very much to be a matter of fashion. Much of the growing use of the term 'evolutionary economics' today can be largely traced to the impact of Richard Nelson and Sidney Winter's classic (1982) work *An Evolutionary Theory of Economic Change*, although other developments in both orthodox and heterodox economics in the 1960s, 1970s and 1980s are also important.

By the late 1980s, work in 'evolutionary economics' had been broadened and accelerated by the growth in both America and Europe of various institutional, Austrian and Schumpeterian approaches to economics.[2] There

---

[2] The European Association for Evolutionary Political Economy and the International Joseph Schumpeter Association were both formed in the late 1980s. Relevant books appearing since 1980 include Andersen (1994), Basalla (1989), Boulding (1981), Blaas and Foster (1992), Clark and Juma (1987), Day and Chen (1993), Delorme and Dopfer (1994), Dosi *et al* (1988), England (1994), Faber and Proops (1990), Foster (1987), Goodwin (1990), Gordon and Adams (1989), Hamilton (1991), Hannan and Freeman (1989), Hanusch, (1988), Hayek (1988), Heertje and Perlman (1990), Hodgson (1988, 1993b, 1995b), Hodgson and Screpanti (1991), Hodgson *et al* (1994), Kay (1982), Kwasnicki (1996), Langlois (1986), Loasby (1991), Louçã (1997), Magnusson (1994), M. McKelvey (1996), W. McKelvey (1982), Metcalfe (1994, 1995, 1998), Mirowski (1994), Mokyr (1990), Van Parijs (1981), Pantzar (1991), Reijnders (1997), Rutherford (1994), Saviotti (1996), Saviotti and Metcalfe (1991), Verspagen (1993), Vromen (1995) and Witt (1987, 1992, 1993a, 1993b). The *Journal of Evolutionary Economics* commenced publication in 1991 and articles on 'evolutionary economics' have also appeared in the *Journal of Economic Issues* (published by the US-based Association for

have been notable and fruitful applications of these ideas, particularly in the sphere of technological change.[3] Evolutionary economics has already established an impressive research programme and has had a major impact on economic policy, particularly in the areas of technology policy, corporate strategy and national systems of innovation. A substantial body of work is now clearly visible, and worthy of reflective evaluation.

Nevertheless, there is still no established consensus on what 'evolutionary economics' should mean. Many economists use the term while wrongly taking it for granted that a common and obvious meaning is implied. As the biologist Jacques Monod is reported to have said in a lecture on biological evolution: 'Another curious aspect of the theory of evolution is that everybody thinks that he understands it!' Likewise, a curious aspect of 'evolutionary economics' is that many people use the term as if it required little further explanation and assume that everyone knows what it means.

Furthermore, 'evolutionary economists' are typically muddled about their own intellectual history. With good reason, Schumpeter is widely associated with something loosely described as 'evolutionary' economics, but it is then wrongly assumed that Schumpeter openly embraced biological – or even Darwinian – analogies in economics (Hodgson, 1993b, 1997c; Kelm, 1997). On the other hand, the explicit advocacy of a 'post-Darwinian' and 'evolutionary' economics by Veblen is widely ignored. Even attempts at a 'history' of evolutionary economics have gone back as far as Adam Smith but downplayed Thomas Robert Malthus and entirely ignored the elusive Veblen (Langlois and Everett, 1994). Regrettably, some scholars of the history of evolutionary economics feel able to invent links that seem attractive and to ignore precedents that would put a disfavoured economist in a more positive light. A false history has thus emerged which attributes too much to some economists and completely ignores others.

These mistaken accounts are sustained by misunderstandings concerning the nature of biological evolution and of evolutionary processes. Nothing is more guaranteed to generate confusion and to stultify intellectual progress than to raise a muddled term to the centrepiece of economic research, while simultaneously suggesting that a clear and well-defined approach to scientific enquiry is implied. It is important both to sort out the different meanings of the term and to consider more carefully its conceptual history.

Evolutionary Economics), the *Journal of Economic Behavior and Organization* and other journals.

[3] Note in particular Dosi (1988b), Dosi *et al* (1988), Freeman (1990), Freeman and Soete (1997).

In an earlier work (Hodgson, 1993b, ch. 3) another taxonomy of relevant meanings of 'evolutionary economics' was attempted. There the principal focus was on the important difference between 'ontogenetic' and 'phylogenetic' conceptions of change. This distinction is useful because it exposes the more limited character of the former type of 'evolution'.[4]

In biology, ontogeny involves the development of a particular organism from a set of given and unchanging genes. Its environment will also affect its development, but nevertheless growth is driven by genetic instructions. Hence the genes represent a given set of (environmentally-dependent) developmental possibilities. In contrast, phylogeny is the complete and ongoing evolution of a population, including changes in its composition and that of the gene-pool. It involves changes in the genetic potentialities of the population, as well as their individual phenotypic development.

By analogy, in economic evolution ontogeny traces institutional and other developments in the context of an environment but with fixed 'genetic material'. If we reject the argument that socio-economic evolution can be explained in terms of the human biotic inheritance then an alternative and analogous supposition is to assume inert individuals with given purposes or preference functions. For example, for the purposes of theoretical explanation, given individuals are assumed in Menger's ([1871] 1981) account of the evolution of money and Hayek's (1982, 1988) discussion of the 'evolution' of spontaneous order. By contrast, Veblen (1899, 1919a) gives more emphasis to changing purposes, preferences, habits and beliefs in his accounts of economic evolution.

However, as in biology, phylogenesis subsumes ontogenesis. The phylogenetic development of a population includes the ontogenetic development of the individuals within it. Hence the objection here to Menger's account of the evolution of money or Hayek's description of the evolution of spontaneous order is not so much that they are wrong, but that they are only part of the story. Indeed, in some other passages in his later works, Hayek (1982, 1988) went some way to broaden the evolutionary picture, considering changes in cultures and individual habits. In fact, the differences between Hayekian and Veblenian economics may not be as wide

---

4 Alternative taxonomies have been attempted elsewhere. In another version (Hodgson, 1997e) the distinction between gradualistic and punctuated – or saltationist – theories of technological evolution in particular (Basalla, 1989; Mokyr, 1990, 1991) and economic evolution in general (Loasby, 1991; Marshall, 1890; Schumpeter, 1976) was incorporated. While these taxonomies are complementary, they do not all focus equally on the most fundamental issues.

as formerly supposed (Boettke, 1989; Leathers, 1990; Rutherford, 1989, 1994; Samuels, 1989; Wynarczyk, 1992).

Accordingly, ontogenetic and phylogenetic conceptions of evolution are not mutually exclusive. These two concepts are useful to distinguish the broader from the narrower notions of 'economic evolution' but they are of only limited use in polarising and patterning the kaleidoscope of methodological approaches and ontological possibilities.

For this reason an alternative and perhaps more fundamental classification is attempted here. This pays particular attention to the varied ontological and methodological foundations of the theories involved. In particular, the incorporation of novelty is essential to phylogenetic evolution and is thus part of its ontological foundation. By contrast, the ontogeny-phylogeny distinction focuses on the mechanisms and processes of evolution.

This chapter then goes on to discuss a core group of evolutionary economists that, although they do not possess exclusive title to the term, give it its most radical and useful meaning.

6.1. VARIETIES OF 'EVOLUTIONARY ECONOMICS': ANOTHER TAXONOMY

Approaches to 'evolutionary economics' are here classified with regard to the following three criteria.

1) **The ontological criterion – novelty:** Whether or not substantial emphasis is given to the assumption that 'evolutionary' processes in economics involve ongoing or periodic novelty and creativity, thus generating and maintaining a variety of institutions, rules, commodities and technologies.

Conceptions of 'economic evolution' that stress novelty typically highlight indeterminacy and the possibility of cumulative divergence, in contrast with convergence and equilibria (Andersen, 1994; Foss, 1994a; Hodgson, 1993b; Witt, 1987). Notably, the Austrian school of economists stress both to the indeterminacy and the potential novelty of human imagination, action and choice (Buchanan, 1969; Lachmann, 1977; Loasby, 1976; Shackle, 1955). Kenneth Boulding (1991, p. 13) wrote: 'One very fundamental principle in evolutionary processes is their profound indeterminacy.' Outside economics, Karl Popper stressed indeterminacy, novelty, and emergent properties (Popper, 1982). However, novelty in at least one sense does not necessarily involve indeterminacy. For instance, chaos theory highlights potential novelty and divergence, and does this using unpredictable but essentially deterministic systems (Gleick, 1988).

2) **The methodological criterion – reductionism:** Whether explanations in 'evolutionary economics' are reductionist or non-reductionist. Reductionism sometimes involves the notion that wholes must be explained entirely in terms of their elemental, constituent parts. More generally, reductionism can be defined as the idea that all aspects of a complex phenomenon must be explained in terms of one level, or type of unit. According to this view there are no autonomous levels of analysis other than this elemental foundation, and no such thing as emergent properties upon which different levels of analysis can be based.

As noted in the preceding chapter, biological reductionism has sometimes been promoted in social science, with attempts to explain the behaviour of individuals and groups in terms of their alleged biological characteristics. Reductionism is still conspicuous in social science today and typically appears as methodological individualism. This is defined as 'the doctrine that all social phenomena (their structure and their change) are in principle explicable only in terms of individuals – their properties, goals, and beliefs' (Elster, 1982, p. 453). It is thus alleged that explanations of socio-economic phenomena must be reduced to properties of constituent individuals and relations between them.[5] Allied to this is the sustained attempt to found

---

[5] Note that the popular term 'methodological individualism' is sometimes used in additional, ambiguous and contradictory ways. Confusingly, Winter (1988) defends 'methodological individualism' while repeatedly invoking concepts such as organizational knowledge and group learning (Winter, 1982). However, what Winter seems to have in mind here by 'methodological individualism' is a rejection of the idea that intentions and interests can be attributed to groups and organizations, rather than individuals. Contrary to Winter, the emphasis in 'methodological' should be on the issue of explanation, not on the attribution or non-attribution of qualities to individuals or groups. The idea that intentions and interests should not be attributed, at least in an unqualified manner, to groups and organizations equally as well as to individuals, is compatible with a rejection of methodological individualism. It is arguable that in the proper, methodological (i.e. explanatory) sense Winter is not a methodological individualist.

Arrow (1994) defined methodological individualism loosely, as the view 'that it is necessary to base all accounts of economic interaction on individual behavior' (p. 1). However, what is meant by 'basing' an account on individuals is not sufficiently clear. If it means that accounts of 'individual behavior' are *sufficient* to explain social or economic phenomena then the existence of emergent properties make such a statement false. On the contrary, if it is means that it is

macroeconomics on 'sound microfoundations'. There are other versions of reductionism however, including versions of 'holism' that suggest that parts should be explained in terms of wholes. Reductionism is countered by the notion that complex systems display emergent properties at different levels that cannot be completely reduced to or explained wholly in terms of another level. By contrast, anti-reductionism generally emphasizes emergent properties at higher levels of analysis that cannot be reduced to constituent elements. The meaning of the term 'emergent property' is elaborated below.

3) **The metaphorical criterion – biology:** Whether extensive use is made of metaphors from biology or not. A motivation for the use of biological metaphors is to replace the mechanistic paradigm which dominates mainstream economics.[6]

It has been frequently argued that economies are closer in their constitution to biotic than to mechanical systems, and that a biological metaphor is thus more appropriate in economics (Georgescu-Roegen, 1971; Hodgson, 1993b; Marshall, 1890; Nelson and Winter, 1982). Others have distanced themselves in varying degrees from biological metaphors (Schumpeter, 1954; Witt, 1992).

---

necessary to recognize that all social or economic phenomena depend on individuals then the statement can be accepted. Arrow further argued that methodological individualism is buttressed by the 'simple fact that all social interactions are after all interactions among individuals' (p. 3). However, the latter proposition is ontological rather than methodological, and does not show that individuals and their interactions are sufficient to explain social or economic phenomena.

Lachmann (1969, p. 94) has asserted that methodological individualism means 'that we shall not be satisfied with any type of explanation of social phenomena which does not lead us ultimately to a human plan.' I have argued elsewhere (Hodgson, 1988, 1993b) that if cultural or institutional influences are always present in the explanation of the behaviour of every individual then we can never reach a stage in the explanation where there are given individuals, free of all such influences. Furthermore, *if* we could reach an explanation of social phenomena in terms of human plans, why should we then be 'satisfied'? Surely we would be obliged as social scientists to consider the terms and conditions under which such plans were conceived and moulded? Contrary to widespread belief, such considerations do not necessarily lead us to a determinist account of human agency.

[6] For discussions of the nature of this paradigm see Georgescu-Roegen (1971) Sebba (1953), Thoben (1982) and Mirowski (1989b).

These three binary criteria give eight possible classifications, portrayed in Figure 6.1. The shaded area in this diagram represents two out of the eight possibilities and is referred to as '*NEAR*' (Novelty-Embracing, Anti-Reductionist) Evolutionary Economics.[7]

Of course, the ordering of the three criteria is arbitrary, in a sense. Nevertheless, it has been suggested that the ontological criterion is the most fundamental (Hodgson, 1993b; Foss, 1994a). Further than this, space does not permit a detailed justification of the classification system. Notably, some of the variants evade precise classification because of ambiguities in the works of the authors involved. An important example here is Hayek, who is placed in two boxes because of some ambiguity of his attachment to reductionism and methodological individualism, and the evolution of his own position. Despite claiming allegiance to this methodological imperative, especially in his later works he has championed group selection and a departure from strict reductionism and methodological individualism has thus been identified (Böhm, 1989; Fleetwood, 1995; Vanberg, 1986).

Taxonomic classifications of authors' theoretical systems are generally problematic. As in many taxonomies, the precise application of the criteria is difficult and in some cases it must be tentative, for example with the criterion of 'extensive use' of the biological metaphor. For this reason this – arguably important – criterion is given the lowest implicit ranking of the four in the above diagram.

As well as a judgement as to what is and is not 'extensive', there is a further judgement required on the nature and degree of the 'use' of the metaphor. Is it explicit or implicit, for instance? For example, although biological metaphors are found in the work of John Commons and Wesley Mitchell, unlike Veblen the use of it is not here deemed to be extensive. Accordingly, there is an important difference on this question within the 'old' institutionalist tradition. Commons is thus put with Ulrich Witt (1992, p. 7), who has criticized the use of the biological metaphor, and with Giovanni Dosi, who like Commons has made no such criticism but does not use such metaphors so openly and extensively as others.

In part the problem here is that the use of metaphor is not admitted, or is even denied, by those who are using it. The metaphorical criterion is the

---

[7] Compared with Hodgson (1997e), I have made some changes to the classification of Hayek, Spencer and Witt in this schema. Here, 'Hayek I' is seen to avoid biological metaphors. Furthermore, Witt (although he acknowledges the role of groups) and Spencer do not seem to have a sufficient notion of emergent properties to sustain a strong anti-reductionist stance.

Figure 6.1: 'Evolutionary Economics' – Another Possible Taxonomy

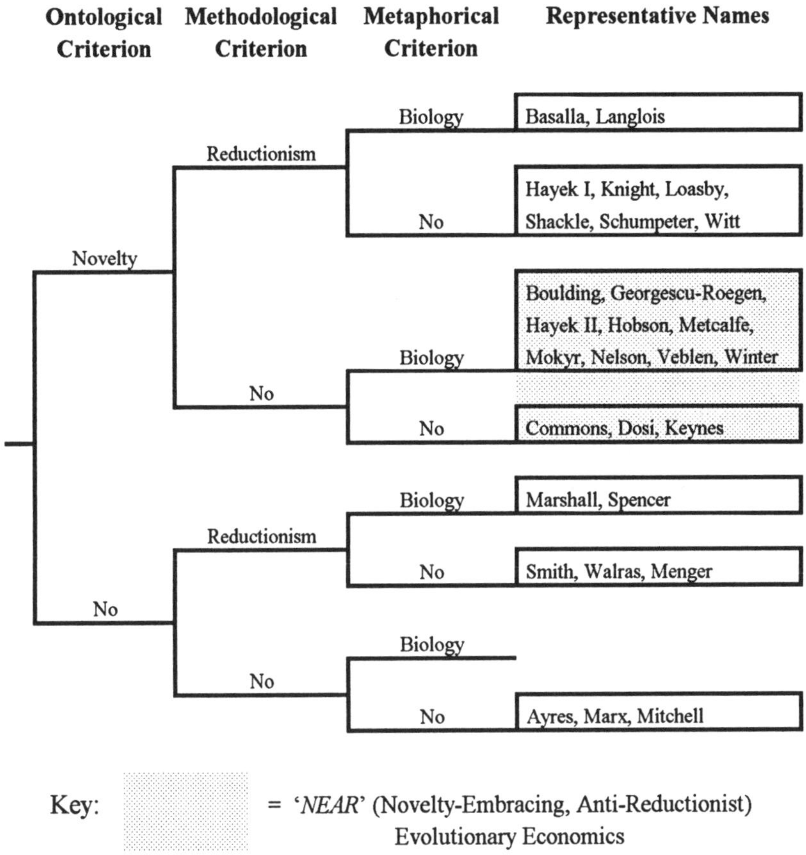

Ontological Criterion	Methodological Criterion	Metaphorical Criterion	Representative Names
		Biology	Basalla, Langlois
	Reductionism		
		No	Hayek I, Knight, Loasby, Shackle, Schumpeter, Witt
Novelty		Biology	Boulding, Georgescu-Roegen, Hayek II, Hobson, Metcalfe, Mokyr, Nelson, Veblen, Winter
	No		
		No	Commons, Dosi, Keynes
		Biology	Marshall, Spencer
	Reductionism		
No		No	Smith, Walras, Menger
		Biology	
	No		
		No	Ayres, Marx, Mitchell

Key: ▨ = '*NEAR*' (Novelty-Embracing, Anti-Reductionist) Evolutionary Economics

lowest ranked for taxonomic purposes primarily because the use of constitutive metaphors is often inadvertent or covert. Elsewhere, it is argued that in economics metaphor plays a deeper role, and is often used less consciously than Philip Mirowski's (1989b) engaging treatise on physics and economics might suggest. As argued in Chapter 4 above, and in accordance with a substantial number of philosophers, metaphor has a deeply constitutive and subterranean presence in science (Black, 1962; Hesse, 1966, 1980; Klamer and Leonard, 1994; Lewis, 1996; Maasen, 1995).

Further problems of taxonomic classification arise with Smith, Marx, Menger, Marshall and Walras. They all recognized invention and innovation in economic processes, but their stress on determinism or unilinear development (Smith), or on a teleological view of history as a progression towards a given end (Marx), or on equilibrium outcomes (Menger, Marshall, Walras), means that they pay less attention than others to novelty and creativity.

A further difference within the 'old' institutionalism arises when we consider Mitchell. He is put with Marx because he put much less emphasis than Commons on the role of human will and purposeful behaviour. Similar to Mitchell in this respect was the American institutionalist Clarence Ayres.

In addition to the lack of unanimity in the 'old' institutionalist camp, there may be several surprises in this classificatory schema. The biggest one might be the placing of Schumpeter. However, the classification can be defended. First, it was Schumpeter himself who coined the term 'methodological individualism' and repeatedly tried to emulate and develop reductionist approaches in economics, particularly Walras's attempt to base explanations of systemic economic phenomena on the 'microfoundations' of individual actors. Second, Schumpeter expressed an uneasiness with the extensive use of metaphors from the natural and physical sciences. He defined the word 'evolution' in broad developmental terms, without involving any reference to biology (Schumpeter, 1954, pp. 789, 964).

The *NEAR* zone of Evolutionary Economics, includes Kenneth Boulding, John Commons, Giovanni Dosi, Nicholas Georgescu-Roegen, the later Friedrich Hayek, John Hobson, John Maynard Keynes, Stanley Metcalfe, Joel Mokyr, Richard Nelson, Thorstein Veblen and Sidney Winter. Again there are some surprises here, particularly the placing of the later Hayek and some 'old' institutionalists in this same zone. The remainder of this chapter is devoted to outlining the *NEAR* approach and arguing for the recognition of its earlier legacy in the writings of Veblen, Commons and Hobson, as well as to some degree in those of Keynes.

6.2. THE MEANING OF *NEAR* EVOLUTIONARY ECONOMICS

6.2.1. The Limits of Reductionism

It is a courageous soul that challenges reductionism in economics. Jon Elster (1983, pp. 20–24) expressed a common view when he wrote:

The basic building block in the social sciences, the elementary unit of explanation, is the individual action guided by some intention. . . . Generally speaking, the scientific practice is to seek an explanation at a lower level than the explandum. . . . The *search for micro-foundations*, to use a fashionable term from recent controversies in economics, is in reality a pervasive and omnipresent feature of science.

In Elster's work, the neo-Aristotelean distinction between 'intentional' and 'causal' explanations becomes a device to use the intentional human individual as the bedrock of explanation in social science. Explanation starts from the individual as the basic 'building block' because the human individual alone can provide 'intentional' impulses to social events. For some reason, we are not required to probe further into the origin of these intentions. Elster's argument has a long pedigree in economics dating back to Carl Menger's work of the 1870s and 1880s (Menger, 1981, 1985) and before.

The particular project to attempt to place macroeconomics on 'sound microfoundations' gathered pace in the 1970s, after the Arrow–Debreu version of general equilibrium theory became established. These days, the idea of explaining wholes in terms of individual parts is often seen as the *sine qua non* of science. Accordingly, theories based on supposed aggregate behaviour are regarded as scientifically unsound and *ad hoc*. Confidence in the necessity of reductionism in science has reached the point that the Nobel Laureate James Tobin (1986, p. 350) wrote that:

This [microfoundations] counter-revolution has swept the profession until now it is scarcely an exaggeration to say that no paper that does not employ the 'microfoundations' methodology can get published in a major professional journal, that no research proposal that is suspect of violating its precepts can survive peer review, that no newly minted Ph.D. who can't show that his hypothesized behavioral relations are properly derived can get a good academic job.

However, several years ago the microfoundations project reached insurmountable difficulties and it has essentially collapsed due to the weight of its internal difficulties. This truth is not widely broadcast but, as noted above in Chapter 3, starting from the assumption of individual utility maximization, the excess demand functions in an exchange economy can take almost any form (Sonnenschein, 1972, 1973a, 1973b; Mantel, 1974; Debreu, 1974). As noted previously, the consequences for neoclassical general equilibrium theory are devastating (Kirman, 1989; Rizvi, 1994a). It ends all prospect of a constructive outcome to the project of building macroeconomics on 'sound microfoundations'. It is as dramatic as that.

Further, recent research into the problems of the uniqueness and stability of general equilibria have shown that they may be indeterminate or unstable unless very strong assumptions are made, such as the supposition that society as a whole behaves as if it were a single individual. Again, this demolishes the entire microfoundations project (Kirman, 1989, 1992; Lavoie, 1992, pp. 36–41; Rizvi (1994a), Screpanti and Zamagni, 1993, pp. 344–53).

Methodological individualism carries similar problems of intractability. Indeed it has never been fully carried out in practice. Lars Udéhn (1987) has argued convincingly that not only is methodological individualism flawed but because of the problems of analytical intractability involved it is inoperable as a methodological approach. The reductionist explanation of all complex socioeconomic phenomena in terms of individuals is over-ambitious, and has never succeeded. Aggregation and simplification are always necessary.

Both the microfoundations project and methodological individualism wave reductionist banners but involve partial reductionism only. As David Sloan Wilson and Elliott Sober (1989) argue, to settle on the individual as the unit of selection involves an inconsistency. Adequate reasons why explanation should be reduced simply to the level of the individual, and stop there, have not been provided. The same arguments concerning explanatory reduction from the macro to the micro, from groups to individuals apply equally to explanatory reduction from individual to gene, gene to molecule, and so on. If we can reduce explanations to individual terms why not further reduce them to the terms of genes? Or molecules? To avoid this 'double standard' one must either accept multiple levels of analysis, each with their own partial autonomy, or reduce everything to the lowest possible level as the biological reductionists attempted in the nineteenth century.

The version of reductionism that suggests that wholes must be explained in terms of parts must take the parts as given. Relaxation of this assumption would lead to the slippery slope of an infinite regress, in which each part has to be explained in terms of its relations with other parts, and so on, without end. Reductionism must assume that we must eventually reach the basic, unperturbable and irreducible parts or individuals where the analysis can come to a stop (Hodgson, 1988, 1993b). A preferable stance is to argue that parts and wholes, individuals and institutions, mutually constitute and condition each other, rejecting single-level theories where explanations of all phenomena are attempted in terms of one type of unit (Archer, 1995;

Bhaskar, 1979; Giddens, 1984; Kontopoulos, 1993; Lawson, 1985, 1997; Nozick, 1977).

It should be pointed out at the outset that the general idea of a reduction to parts is not being overturned here. Some degree of reduction to elemental units is inevitable. Even measurement is an act of reduction. Science cannot proceed without some dissection and some analysis of parts.

However, although some reduction is inevitable and desirable, complete reductionism is both impossible and a philosophically dogmatic diversion. What is important to stress is that the process of analysis cannot be extended to the most elementary sub-atomic particles presently known to science, or even to individuals in economics or genes in biology. Complete reductionism would be hopeless and interminable. As Karl Popper has declared: 'I do not think that there are any examples of a successful reduction' to elemental units in science (Popper and Eccles, 1977, p. 18). Reduction is necessary to some extent, but it can never be complete.

Notably, the adoption of an organicist ontology implies that the reductionist and methodological individualist project to explain all social and economic phenomena in terms of given individuals and the relations between them is confounded. The adoption of an organicist ontology means precisely that the individual is not given (Winslow, 1989). Organicism obstructs the treatment of individuals as elemental or immutable building blocks of analysis. Exponents of organicism argue further that *both* the explanatory reduction of wholes to parts *and* parts to wholes should be rejected. Just as society cannot exist without individuals, the individual does not exist prior to the social reality. Individuals both constitute, and are constituted by, society. Unidirectional modes of explanation, such as from parts to wholes – and vice-versa – or from one level to another are thus thwarted. There is both 'upward' and 'downward' causation (Sperry, 1969; Campbell, 1974).

6.2.2. The Concept of Emergence and the Layered Ontology

The terms 'emergence' and 'emergent property' were first coined and used extensively by the British philosopher of biology C. Lloyd Morgan (1896, 1927, 1933). Morgan defined (1927, pp. 3–4) emergent properties as 'unpredictable' and 'non-additive' results of complex processes. He saw such properties as crucial to evolution in its most meaningful and creative sense, where 'the emphasis is not on the unfolding of something already in being but on the outspringing of something that has hitherto not been in being. It is in this sense only that the noun may carry the adjective "emergent"' (Morgan, 1927, p. 112). For Morgan, evolution creates a hierarchy of increasing richness and complexity in integral systems 'as new kinds of relatedness' successively emerge (Morgan, 1927, p. 203). Also for Morgan, the 'non-additive' character of complex systems must involve a shift from mechanistic to organic metaphors: 'precedence should now be given to organism rather than to mechanism – to organization rather than aggregation' (Morgan, 1933, p. 58).

Crucially, reductionism is also countered by the concept of emergence. Tony Lawson (1997, p. 176) has explained the meaning of this term: 'an entity or aspect is said to be *emergent* if there is a sense in which it has arisen out of some "lower" level, being conditioned by and dependent upon, but not predictable from, the properties found at the lower level.' Furthermore, as Margaret Archer (1995, p. 9) has elucidated: 'What justifies the differentiation of strata and thus use of the terms "micro" and "macro" to characterize their relationship is the existence of *emergent properties* pertaining to the latter but not to the former, even if they were elaborated from it.' (See also Lane, 1993, p. 91 and Kontopoulos, 1993, pp. 22–23.)

Philosophers Roy Bhaskar, Arthur Koestler, Alfred Whitehead and others have proposed that reality consists of multi-levelled hierarchies. The existence of emergent properties at each level means that explanations at that tier cannot be reduced entirely to phenomena at lower levels. Accordingly, notions such as group selection in biology and group knowledge in the social sciences can be sustained (Hodgson, 1988, 1993b; Kontopoulos, 1993; Murphy, 1994). The biologist Ernst Mayr (1985a, p. 58) argued further:

> Systems at each hierarchical level have two characteristics. They act as wholes (as if they were a homogeneous entity), and their characteristics cannot (not even in theory) be deduced from the most complete knowledge of the components, taken separately or in other partial combinations. In other words, when such systems are assembled from their components, new characteristics of the new whole emerge that could not have been predicted from a knowledge of the components. . . . Perhaps the two most interesting characteristics of new wholes are that they can in turn become parts of still higher-level systems, and that they can affect properties of components at lower levels (downward causation) . . . Recognition of the importance of emergence demonstrates, of course, the invalidity of extreme reductionism. By the time we have dissected an organism down to atoms and elementary particles we have lost everything that is characteristic of a living system.

James Murphy (1994, p. 555) has developed a similar argument:

The theory of emergence . . . is a nonreductionist account of complex phenomena. . . . The notion that from complexity emerges new phenomena that cannot be reduced to simpler parts is at the center of modern biology . . . Complex systems very often have a hierarchical structure, and the hierarchical structure of living systems shares some important features with our hierarchy, one being that higher levels can affect properties of components at lower levels.

This again implies 'downward causation'. The fact that structures or elements on one level can profoundly affect those at another level means that no single level provides an explanatory foundation or elemental unit. This confounds reductionism. A layered ontology with emergent properties at each level precludes the possibility of explanatory reduction of one level entirely into the terms of another. Although reductionism is still prominent, both in biology and in the social sciences, in biology strong and influential voices can be found against it.

6.2.3. Embracing Novelty

The importance of novelty is rightly stressed by a number of commentators on evolutionary economics. Notably, Ulrich Witt (1992, p. 3) wrote: 'for a proper notion of socioeconomic evolution, an appreciation of the crucial role of novelty, its emergence, and its dissemination, is indispensable.' Accordingly, Nicolai Foss (1994a) argued forcefully for an ontological characterisation of the divergence between evolutionary and neoclassical thinking in economics. He maintained that the evolutionary economics of the type developed by Dosi, Nelson, Winter, Witt and others is concerned with 'the transformation of already existing structures and the emergence and possible spread of novelties' (p. 21). Indeed, whereas evolutionary economics theorises on the basis of a universe that is open, in the sense that the emergence of novelties is allowed, neoclassical economics addresses closed systems and suppresses novelty. In short, evolutionary and neoclassical economics start from very different ontological assumptions about the social world.

For Esben Sloth Andersen (1994), Metcalfe (1988), Nelson (1991, 1994b), Witt (1987) and others, novelty and creativity are a major source of variety within evolving socio-economic systems. Accordingly, as Metcalfe (1988) in particular has emphasized, a population of entities cannot be represented by a few distinct characteristics which represent their essence. Such 'typological essentialism' is rejected in favour of 'population thinking'. In population thinking, species are described in terms of a distribution of characteristics. Whereas in typological thinking novelty and variation are classificatory nuisances, in population thinking they are of paramount interest because it is precisely the variety of the system that fuels the evolutionary process (Mayr, 1985a).

One way to think about novelty is to regard it as the outcome of a stochastic function. This device is frequently used to mimic novelty in evolutionary modelling. With a large number of parameters the possibilities are huge, and something looking like 'novelty' may be manifest on the basis of random choices of points in mega-dimensional possibility space. However, even with a huge number of dimensions or parameters, this is essentially a closed system. The genuinely novel and creative possibilities of an open system are mimicked by the use of random choices in a huge, closed arena. This stochastic approach is confined to these boundaries; it cannot generate new dimensions or possibilities within which random choices are made. Instead of referring to this as stochastic 'indeterminacy', it is thus more accurate to speak of 'stochastic determination'.

There is another reason why the stochastic approach is limited. A major source of novelty in socio-economic systems is individual creativity and choice. Meaningful human creativity must involve the possibility of creating new frameworks and dimensions, not merely exploring parameter values. So authors go further, and have argued that genuine creativity, real choices and willed changes of purpose mean that human action must contain an element of indeterminacy in the sense of an *uncaused cause*. According to this view, to choose or to create means that our choice or our creation is undetermined: we could have acted otherwise. Hence it has been argued (e.g. Loasby, 1976, p. 9) that the neoclassical idea of behaviour programmed by fixed preference functions does not admit genuine choice. However, the idea of an 'uncaused cause' does not have a widespread appeal, most physical and social scientists assuming that every event must have a prior cause. Even within the Austrian school of economists the notion of an 'uncaused cause' is not ubiquitous and clear statements in its favour are not common. These are confined to a handful of economists.

Let us consider some of them. Frank Knight (1921, p. 221) argued: 'If there is real indeterminateness . . . there is in a sense an opening of the door to a conception of freedom in conduct.' In a similar vein, Nobel Laureate James Buchanan (1969, p. 47) has remarked: 'Choice, by its nature, cannot be predetermined and remain choice.' George Shackle (1972, p. 122) wrote: 'if the world is determinist, then it seems idle to speak of choice'. Shackle (1989, p. 51) further asserted that 'economics is about choice as a *first cause*, that is the coming into being of decisive thoughts not in all respects to be explained by antecedents.' Ludwig Lachmann (1969, p. 93) came from the same intellectual tradition, and argued that spontaneous mental action is 'not a "response" to anything pre-existent' and thus it is wholly spontaneous and undetermined. Brian Loasby (1991, p. 1) has put a similar view: 'the rational choices that economists attribute to economic agents exhibit no signs of purposeful reasoning; they are programmed responses to the circumstances in which those agents are placed.' The common anti-determinism of these authors is here is based on a conception of the essential indeterminacy of human decision-making: of individual choice and decision as a first or uncaused cause.[8]

This is a controversial argument. It revives the old dilemma of determinism versus free will. It can be neither proved nor disproved by evidence. Determinists regard the 'uncaused cause' as a mystical and unsatisfactory escape route, taken because of lack of evidence of a cause; while in fact there may well be a causal process working beneath the surface. On the other hand, we can provide no decisive evidence of a causal process, because we can only observe effects. Mere evidence can confirm the existence of neither a caused nor uncaused cause.

The present author has met many economists and biologists who refuse to admit the possibility of an uncaused cause. To them, it is transparently nonsensical or unscientific. Yet a significant minority of philosophically-inclined social and economic theorists will accept this notion. A preliminary attempt to resolve this conflict – by rising above it, on the basis of the concept of emergence – is hazarded below.

6.2.4. Novelty and Endogeneity

The immediate question here is the locational source of this novelty: is it from within or without the system? This links the issue of novelty with the question of endogeneity or exogeneity. In modern evolutionary economics there is a persistent but questionable emphasis on endogenous change. In his studies of economic development, Schumpeter (1934, p. 63) repeatedly emphasized the sources of change 'from within'.[9]

---

[8] See the discussion and references in Hodgson (1993b, pp. 155, 214–33). A notable philosophical defence of free will on the basis of indeterminism is in Thorp (1980).

[9] However, Schumpeter's own development of this concept of endogenous change was most unsatisfactory. Schumpeter (1934, p. 65) argued that developmental changes in the system 'appear in the sphere of industrial and commercial life, not in the sphere of the wants of the consumers of final products. Where spontaneous and discontinuous changes in consumers' tastes appear, it is a question of a

Likewise, Witt defined evolution as 'the transformation of a system over time through endogenously generated change' (Witt, 1991, p. 87, emphasis removed). Similarly, Andersen (1994, p. 1) regarded an 'evolving' as a 'self-transforming' economic system. We may note in passing that, apart from mere Schumpeterian precedent, it is difficult to find a justification for this stance. In biology, neither individuals nor species nor even ecosystems are entirely 'self-transforming'. Evolution takes place within *open* systems involving *both* exogenous and endogenous change.

It is perhaps no accident that, while misleadingly defining evolution as endogenous change, Andersen, Schumpeter and Witt have put no stress on biological metaphors or analogies. Consideration of biological evolution, necessarily involving open systems, would have perhaps put them on a different tack.

Clearly, part of the reason for the definition of economic evolution in terms of endogenous change is (rightly) to emphasize the creative and entrepreneurial role of the individual in the evolutionary process. However, there are two problems with this justification of endogeneity. The first is that no reason is given why the sources of change must be *exclusively* from individuals. For example, diseases or natural disasters can also affect economic evolution. Also important are clashes of institutions and systems, most dramatically in the case of wars or invasions.

Second, there is a problem reconciling the emphasis on endogenous change with the notions of novelty and creativity. Theorists that stress novelty may either accept or reject the idea that it stems from an uncaused cause. Consider each possibility.

If the possibility of an uncaused cause is admitted then the concepts of exogeneity and endogeneity themselves require refinement. The distinction between exogeneity and endogeneity is typically based on the source of determination. The demarcating criterion is as follows: is the variable

---

sudden change in data with which the businessman must cope'. Accordingly, the industrial entrepreneur is given the exclusive accolade of creativity. Consumer initiative, spontaneity or inventiveness was not regarded as an endogenous source of change, merely as a 'change in data with which the businessman must cope'. Why the producer is given such a privileged status over the consumer is not clear. Schumpeter (1934, p. 66) went on to consider five significant forces of endogenous change, including new goods, new production methods, new markets, new materials, or changes in industrial structure or concentration. It is notable that he fails to mention either changes in consumer tastes or economic institutions as additional sources of endogenous economic development. By implication these are regarded as exogenous, and as mere 'data'. This famous attempt to establish the boundaries of the endogenous zone becomes highly arbitrary and unsatisfactory.

causing change inside or outside the system? But if some events are *uncaused* then is the absence of such a prior cause defined as exogeneity or endogeneity? Clearly the question is absurd in this case.

If the possibility of an uncaused cause is not admitted then the question is raised: is the novelty truly novel when it has been caused by something else? Individual flair and creativity may be illusory, and determined by the circumstances and inherited personality traits of the individual. Without additional philosophical argument there is a danger that the factors allegedly guiding individual decision and action submerge the concept of creative individuality itself.

It is argued below that the concept of individual will and purpose can indeed be rescued by regarding them as emergent properties within the human organism. But again this makes an exclusive stress on endogeneity problematic. If emergent properties are possible, and not capable of full, reductive explanation by a set of other elements, then the same problem of demarcation between endogenous and exogenous sources of determination arises. Emergent properties could be rightly described as endogenous but they are not subject to a complete explanation in terms of endogenous factors.

Whatever route is taken, in each case a definition of economic evolution as endogenous change is problematic.

These arguments suggest that not only is an exclusive stress on endogenous change misleading, but that the dichotomy between endogeneity and exogeneity is problematic. Given the above problems it would be better if the exclusive emphasis on endogeneity was abandoned. The idea of an 'open system' is much more relevant. The distinction between an open and a closed system was first made by Ludwig von Bertalanffy in 1950. The term has been taken up and emphasized by institutional economists such as K. William Kapp (1976) and the realist philosopher Roy Bhaskar (1975, 1979). In particular, Bhaskar discussed the intrinsic and extrinsic conditions of closure. He argued that extrinsic closure is absent in socio-economic systems because such systems interact with their environment. National socio-economic systems export and import, and even the world socio-economic system extrudes waste and is dependent on energy flows from the sun. Intrinsic closure concerns human agents: even if the system was otherwise closed then it would have to be treated as indeterminate because of the potential novelty of human agency. If human beings are more than automata they are not merely programmed responders to external stimuli; their actions cannot always be predicted. For these two crucial reasons socio-economic systems should not be regarded as closed. Accordingly, exclusive emphasis should not be put on endogenous change.[10]

6.2.5. Novelty, Reductionism and the Limits to Formalism

The issue of novelty also raises questions about the use of mathematics in evolutionary economics. These days, much work in this field makes extensive use of mathematics. For example, the *Journal of Evolutionary Economics* has published a high proportion of articles with a degree of mathematical formalism comparable with the most prestigious and formalistic mainstream journals in economic theory.[11] The *Journal of Economic Behavior and Organization* is sympathetic to 'evolutionary economics' but its pages are full of mathematical formalism.

Some contributors are enthusiastic about such mathematical developments, seeing this as a way of making evolutionary economics part of the mainstream (Heertje, 1994, p. 275). This ignores the problem of the extent to which economics is being damaged by an excessive degree of mathematical formalism. In our subject mathematical rigour and elegance are now rated much more highly than empirical richness, explanatory power, conceptual robustness, policy usefulness or even predictive capacity. Arguably, economics suffers as a result.

There are particular reasons why evolutionary economists should be concerned about trends towards over-formalization. Ulrich Witt (1992, pp. 9–10) hinted at this when he wrote:

> Regardless of which mathematical concept seems the most promising, none of them have yet found or, perhaps, even considered an answer to the question of how the emergence of novelty may be adequately represented in a formal treatment of the evolutionary process.

Arguably, mathematical modelling taken to its limits in economics would greatly constrain novelty. Even if chaotic systems can seemingly generate novelty they are limited by their own formal assumptions. In such models

---

[10] Bhaskar's argument has been applied extensively to economics by Lawson (1989a, 1989b, 1994b, 1997).

[11] Current *JEE* editorial policy is to encourage non-mathematical as well as mathematical articles, and the author is personally involved in an attempt to implement this policy. Nevertheless, time-lags and cultural lock-in mean that formalism still, at the time of writing, predominates.

the system needs to be defined by formal assumptions in finite dimensions that limit the possible results. Even a stochastic process constrains the variance and defines a given parametric space of finite dimensions. By its nature, novelty defies the boundaries of formalism. The adoption of formalism inevitably involves the closure of the system (Lawson, 1997). To endogenise the novelty-creating process within a formal framework is always to limit greatly the set of possible novel outcomes (Bonaccorsi *et al*, 1995).

6.2.6. The Link Between Emergence and Novelty

Let us draw some of the above threads together. It would appear that modelling within evolutionary economics founders when it reaches the question of novelty. Genuine novelty can be sustained in one of two ways. One is to postulate the possibility of an 'uncaused cause'. As we have seen, the anti-determinism of Buchanan, Knight, Lachmann, Loasby and Shackle was based on a conception of the essential indeterminacy of human decision-making: of individual decision and action as a first or uncaused cause.

Thinkers in this tradition are essentially replicating the Aristotelian distinction between two types of causality: the 'efficient' or the 'final' cause. Finalistic causality is consistent with the view that individual decision and motivation springs from the human will alone, and has no prior causal determination. Such an idea has a long pedigree in modern philosophy and social science, although it is submerged in both mainstream sociology and mainstream economics. It also has parallels in the now-unpopular notion of 'vitalism' in biology.

There are two major problems with the notion of an uncaused cause. First, it rests uneasily with the attempts of modern science to find causal explanations. The concept of an uncaused cause seems to rule out any further investigation into the causes of a process or event. To most natural sciences it seems magical and mysterious to posit the possibility of an event without a prior cause. Even quantum physics understands the quanta in terms of prior and immanent probabilities. To a modern biologist the idea of an uncaused cause smacks of outdated vitalism or worse. In short, the uncaused cause seems like giving up on science.

Second, the idea that the human will is an uncaused cause seems to privilege humanity above other animals. Humans alone are seen to have independent choice and will. The evolution of humans from animals becomes problematic. An inexplicable line is thus drawn between the biotic and the human world. Social science is detached from biology. Even if some other animals are admitted to have 'free will' then this problem remains.

The question becomes: when in the process of evolution did an organism or species suddenly acquire this attribute? The concept of an uncaused cause is non-evolutionary, at least in the sense that it cannot give the emergence of the uncaused will in higher animals an adequate and scientific evolutionary explanation.

The traditional dichotomy is between free will and determinism. Until recently it has been supposed that if we reject free will then we must become determinists. But perhaps today there is a way out of this dilemma. Maybe we can have the best of both. Briefly, I will try and explain how.

Modern complexity and chaos theory shows that even if the world is deterministic it would behave in an apparently random, even non-probabilistic, and unpredictable way. This does not give victory to determinism in its old fight against indeterminacy. On the contrary, it shows that the concept of free will is operational even on deterministic assumptions. Neither side wins the battle.

In fact, chaos theory suggests that the rules of engagement have changed. To repeat: if the world is deterministic we still have to treat it as if it were indeterministic and unpredictable. Novelty may be caused, but it will often appear as entirely spontaneous and free. Prior causes may exist, but the complexity of the system may prevent adequate prediction or explanation. Thus the very distinction between determinacy and indeterminacy is undermined. We can never know for sure if any event is caused or uncaused, but chaos theory suggests that we have to treat complex systems as if they were indeterministic. Rather than the victory of determinism, and as Philip Mirowski (1990, p. 305) wrote: 'The chaos literature instead reveals the curious symbiosis of randomness and determinism, the blurring of the boundaries between order and chaos.' Chaos theory simultaneously breaks the reductionist bonds and suggests the possibility of emergence, even in a system which is deemed to adhere to deterministic rules.

The concept of emergence makes it possible to have the best of both worlds. As Samuel Alexander (1920), William McDougall (1929), Alfred Whitehead (1926) and others suggested long ago, concepts such as consciousness and purposeful behaviour can be established as emergent properties of highly complex nervous systems in highly evolved organisms. The third alternative, therefore, is to establish the concept of emergence. It is to see consciousness, purposefulness and will as *emergent properties* of a highly developed mental apparatus.

The concept of emergence makes it possible to retain causality, in the sense that human intentions are caused by something, but also to treat them *as if* they were uncaused. The Aristotelian concept of finalism is regarded as an emergent property of mechanical causality. I am suggesting, therefore, that the best route for evolutionary economists to take on this question is to welcome the concept of emergence and its anti-reductionist implications. This makes it possible to reconcile novelty with a causal ontology. It also overcomes the limitations of the 'uncaused cause': the distinctiveness of human will can be recognized without a strict commitment to either indeterminism or determinism.

This brings us to another important result. We have seen that both the embracing of novelty and the rejection of reductionism depend crucially on the concept of emergence. The characteristics of *NEAR* are made both possible and necessary by this idea. The concept of emergence is thus the central characteristic of evolutionary processes in socio-economic systems.

6.3. ANCESTORS OF *NEAR* EVOLUTIONARY ECONOMICS

Our search for precedents for the *NEAR* stance will be confined to economists who have made their major contribution in this genre prior to 1930. The boundaries of *NEAR* exclude many. Consider four so excluded. Menger and Schumpeter are ruled out because of their adherence to methodological individualism. Marshall embraced reductionism and gave little attention to the question of novelty. Although Knight (1921) gave very great emphasis to the reality of indeterminacy and novelty in socio-economic systems, his extreme individualism masked any anti-reductionist feelings.

Some prominent candidates remain, including Hobson, Veblen and Commons. Veblen and Commons are well known as founders of American institutionalism and Hobson is the British economist with the foremost claim to the 'institutionalist' label. Apart from a belated and extensive recognition by Keynes (1936, pp. 19, 364–71) of Hobson's importance, he has since been largely ignored by economists.

6.3.1. Veblen

In the sense that Veblen (1898a, 1899) was the first economist to apply extensively the Darwinian ideas of variety, heredity and selection to economic evolution, he is rightly described as the first evolutionary economist. However, his commitment to *NEAR* principles is not so forthright. A reason for this is that he was hampered by the prevailing, deterministic conception of science. It took the rise of quantum physics after the First World War to break the hold of strict determinism upon scientific thought.

It is sometimes alleged that Veblen 'teeters between free will and determinism' (Seckler, 1975, p. 56), and entertained a conception of science from which purpose and intentionality were excluded (Commons, 1934, p. 654). However, in one of his first articles Veblen (1884) addressed the problem of human freedom and indeterminacy. Furthermore, his subsequent emphasis on human purposefulness is repeated and significant: 'Economic action is teleological, in the sense that men always and everywhere seek to do something' (Veblen, [1898a], 1919a, p. 75). Human beings are 'endowed with a proclivity for purposeful action' (Veblen, [1898b], 1934, p. 80). Veblen's (1914) emphasis on 'idle curiosity', for instance, as well as many of his own explicit statements, would seem to retain a crucial role for human agency in his theory. Veblen (1914, p. 334) also wrote of 'the free movement of the human spirit'. Nevertheless, the nature and definition of what was meant by 'purposeful action' was not always clear, and this is perhaps one source of the controversy over Veblen's line of thought (Seckler, 1975; Langlois, 1989).

On the whole, Veblen favoured causal explanations and he was never able to reconcile this with his belief in human purposeful behaviour. For instance, Veblen (1914, pp. 324 n., 334 n.) rejected the vitalism of Henri Bergson (1911) and others but was unable to develop a systematic picture of his own that was consistent with his predisposition towards explanations in terms of efficient causes. Nevertheless, he did not dispense with the concept of purposeful behaviour. Furthermore, it was a stroke of genius to see that *purpose itself had to be given an evolutionary explanation.* Veblen (1934, p. 80) thus wrote in 1898 of the human animal: 'By selective necessity he is endowed with a proclivity for purposeful action.'

It is suggested above that the solution to this problem involves use of the concept of emergence. Although Veblen was strongly influenced by the original exposition of the concept of emergence by Lloyd Morgan (1896) he failed to make it explicit in his work (Hodgson, 1998d).

Nevertheless, and in contrast to many of his contemporaries, Veblen's approach was interactionist and anti-reductionist. It was interactionist in the sense that actor and structure interact and mutually condition each other to the degree that explanations based on either actor or structure alone are unwarranted. It was also interactionist in the sense that socio-economic systems interact with their biotic foundation to the degree that explanations based on biology alone are unsuitable and that full explanations of some socio-economic phenomena may involve biological factors. Although Veblen ([1909] 1934, p. 143) acknowledged the biotic foundations of social life, he rejected the view that human behaviour could be explained purely and simply in terms of genetic inheritance.

6.3.2. Commons

Commons (1934, p. 55) was aware of the quantum revolution in physics and lived to see the growing arguments for indeterminacy in the human sphere. However, while consistently emphasising the importance of purposeful action, his position on this question was ambiguous. In one passage Commons (1924, p. 82) saw the argument between determinacy and indeterminacy as irrelevant 'for economic purposes'. Despite this, he consistently held to the view that the exercise of human will drastically limited the role of prediction in economics. Nevertheless, the emphasis on purposeful behaviour remained central. Commons (1950, p. 36) went so far as to argue that the 'science of the human will' acting in both 'individuals and all collective organizations' is the 'twentieth century foundation' of economic science.

Despite a degree of vagueness in the specification of his terms, Neil Chamberlain (1963, p. 93) argued that this recognition of the role of individual 'human will' and of the place of 'collective action' comprise Commons's two great achievements. Commons's concepts of 'collective action' and 'collective will' are complex and controversial but they are in part sustained by a belief in units and levels of analysis apart from the atomistic individual.[12] His writings suggest an organicist conception of the human agent, in which people both mould and are moulded by their circumstances.

However, like Veblen, Commons failed to make the concept of emergence explicit in his work. This omission is all the greater than Veblen's, because Commons lived until 1945 (16 years after Veblen) and he was in a better position to appraise the philosophical contributions of Alexander and McDougall. Commons (1934, pp. 17, 96) referred to Alfred Whitehead, but did not make much use of his concept of emergence. The concept of emergence lived on within American institutionalism but only rarely in an explicit form. The crisis of American institutionalism in the 1930s seemed

---

[12] Despite Langlois (1986, p. 4n.; 1989, pp. 285–7), Olson (1965) and Schotter (1981, p. 3), Commons did not take these terms to mean that an organization or collective has a distinct will of its own (Biddle, 1990; C. Lawson, 1996; Ramstad, 1990; Rutherford, 1983; Vanberg, 1989).

to divert it from this central issue. Nevertheless, as we shall see below, the concept of emergence retained a subterranean existence in social science.

6.3.3. Hobson

In a work published in the same year as Veblen's *Instinct of Workmanship*. Hobson (1914, pp. 240–1, 336) saw the role of human error and playful inventiveness as decisive in creating mutations in behavioural patterns, and thereby a source of continuous evolutionary innovation. Interestingly, he gave more stress to the function of the 'freedom of the human will' than Veblen in this context. However, Hobson did not go so far as Veblen to incorporate this idea into an evolutionary theory of the Darwinian and phylogenetic type. There is not a theory of evolutionary change in Hobson's writings that comes close to this.[13]

Hobson drew strong methodological and anti-reductionist conclusions from his own version of organicism, writing: 'An organized unity, or whole, cannot be explained adequately by an analysis of its constituent parts: its wholeness is a new product, with attributes not ascertainable in its parts, though in a sense derived from them' (Hobson, 1929, p. 32). Hobson thus expressed the idea of emergent properties and higher, irreducible levels of analysis.

In his book on *Veblen*, Hobson (1936, pp. 216) approvingly notes an important shift of thinking in the early decades of the twentieth century:

> Emergent evolution brings unpredictable novelties into the processes of history, and disorder, hazard, chance, are brought into the play of energetic action. Intuition is invoked as an independent source of information regarding the higher values, and . . . this line of thought . . . does distinctly contravene the doctrines of mechanical causation in their moulding of modern thought and sentiment. Its emphasis upon novelty in evolutionary processes, and upon elements of chance constitutes a direct challenge to the logic of ordinary thought as well as to the determinist philosophy.

Accordingly, Hobson forcefully rejected mechanical metaphors, seeing them as 'squeezing out humanity' and denying human novelty and creativity (Freeden, 1988, pp. 89, 173). Although Hobson was older than Veblen and

---

[13] This is my excuse for not having a chapter on Hobson in my *Economics and Evolution* (1983b) book. In retrospect, the omission is probably an error of judgement.

Commons, he provided the clearest expression of the essentials of the *NEAR* paradigm.

6.3.4. Enter Mitchell . . . and Keynes

Wesley Mitchell was the third in the founding generation of American institutionalists, and, additionally, one of the fathers of modern macroeconomics. Mitchell's work is not notable for any stress on novelty and creativity but for its anti-reductionist thrust and its consequent contribution to the development of Keynesian macroeconomics. It is for this reason, and for his links with *NEAR* 'old' institutionalists Veblen and Commons, that he is considered here, although his failure to stress novelty places him outside the *NEAR* camp.

Mitchell (1937, pp. 26, 375) argued that economists need not begin with a theory of individual behaviour but with the statistical observation of 'mass phenomena' or 'mass behavior'. Mitchell and his colleagues in the National Bureau for Economic Research in the 1920s and 1930s played a vital role in the development of national income accounting, suggesting that aggregate, macroeconomic phenomena have an ontological and empirical legitimacy.

This was an important incursion against reductionism in economics. It created space for the construction of Keynesianism but the counter-attack from reductionism has been persistent up to the present day. Notably, in defending Mitchell's approach against the reductionist criticisms of Tjalling Koopmans (1947), Rutledge Vining (1949, p. 79) argued that phenomena such as 'trade fluctuations' were not merely aggregates 'of the economizing units of traditional theoretical economics'. Further, 'we need not take for granted that the behaviour and functioning of this entity can be exhaustively explained in terms of the motivated behaviour of individuals who are particles within the whole.' This is a classic rejection of reductionism, implicitly in terms of the existence of emergent properties that cannot be completely explained in terms of the constituent parts.

For Keynesianism, Mitchell's anti-reductionist thrust was crucial. Being traditionally linked with organicist or holistic views, institutionalism developed and sanctioned the conceptualization and measurement of economic aggregates. Through the development of national income accounting the work of Mitchell and his colleagues influenced and inspired the macroeconomics of Keynes (Mirowski, 1989b, p. 307; Colander and Landreth, 1996, p. 141). It was with institutionalism as a midwife that Keynesian macroeconomics was born.

Keynes's own views have been a persistent source of controversy. However, insofar as Keynes is influenced by ideas of the indeterminacy of the human will, of 'animal spirits' and the capacity for creativity and novelty, he fulfils one criterion of the *NEAR* paradigm. Significantly, Keynes was influenced by the philosophy of Whitehead, with its layered ontology, its incorporation of emergence and its emphasis on human creativity. Clearly, in developing an economic theory based on aggregates, Keynes was breaking from reductionism. The second criterion is thus also satisfied. It is thus perhaps no accident that Keynes was so full of praise for Hobson, and even wrote personally to Commons in the following terms: 'Judging from limited evidence and at great distance, there seems to be no other economist with whose general way of thinking I find myself in such genuine accord.'[14]

6.4. CONCLUSION

The challenge provided by evolutionary economics is not only theoretical but ontological, epistemological and methodological. The stress on ontology coincides with a general movement in philosophy back towards matters of ontological grounding that were dismissed as 'metaphysical' in the era of logical positivism.

Arguably, 'evolutionary economics' has now reached a crossroads in its own development, and faces the possibility of both degenerative and regenerative outcomes. Despite the difficulties involved, at least we are now in a position to identify some of the most pressing problems and the philosophical roots of an approach which differs radically from mainstream economics.

The *NEAR* or 'institutional' wing of evolutionary economics legitimates a number of allied endeavours: less in formal modelling and more in economic philosophy, the history of economic thought, economic history, the study of technical and institutional change, empirical enquiry, and the development of economic, industrial and environmental policies.

Clearly, evolutionary economics is at a crucial stage in its history. There is much mutation and variety within this species of economics. It will be very interesting to observe the evolution of the different strains.

---

[14] Keynes to Commons, dated 26 April 1927 (John R. Commons Papers, State Historical Society of Wisconsin, 1982).

PART THREE

The Contributions of Richard Nelson and Sidney Winter

7.   Richard Nelson and Sidney Winter

The names of Richard Nelson and Sidney G. Winter are linked together because of their pathbreaking joint work on economic evolution and their 1982 book *An Evolutionary Theory of Economic Change*.[1] Nelson is known independently for his extensive writing on industry and technical change and Winter has made a number of additional and noted contributions to economic theory. Section 7.1 of this chapter gives some biographical details of both authors. Section 7.2 discusses Winter's important critique of Friedman's often-cited 1953 paper. This leads appropriately to Section 7.3 which evaluates their joint 1982 book. The final section discusses other work in the 1980s and 1990s by both authors.

7.1. BIOGRAPHICAL ESSENTIALS

Richard Nelson was born in 1930 in New York City, USA. He obtained his first degree in 1952 in Oberlin College, and moved on to Yale University where he obtained his PhD in 1956. He returned to Oberlin College as an Assistant Professor but shortly afterwards he was appointed as an economist to RAND corporation. In 1960 he served for a year as an Associate Professor at Carnegie Institute of Technology, followed by a two-year period as a Senior Staff Member on the Council of National Advisors. After returning to the RAND corporation for four more years, in 1968 he became a Professor of Economics at Yale University. He moved to Columbia University, in the city of his birth, in 1986.

---

[1] This chapter is a revised version of Hodgson (1996b).

The underlying theme in Nelson's work is the process of long run economic change, with emphasis on the processes of technological development and the transformation of economic institutions. One of his first major publications was on Harrod-type growth models, in the *Economic Journal* in 1961. A series of subsequent publications on production functions appeared in 1964 and 1965 in the *American Economic Review*, the *Quarterly Journal of Economics* and *The Review of Economics and Statistics*. In the late 1960s Nelson published works on full employment policy, technological diffusion, and productivity growth. This early work established Nelson's reputation as a leading industrial economist by the age of 40, before his joint work on economic evolution with Sidney Winter.

Sidney G. Winter Jr was born in 1935 in Iowa City, USA. He obtained his BA in Economics from Swarthmore College in 1956. At Yale University he received his MA in 1957 and PhD in 1964. From 1959 to 1962 he served alongside Richard Nelson, first as a Research Economist at the RAND corporation and then as a Staff Member on the Council of Economic Advisors. From 1963 to 1966 he taught economics at the University of California at Berkeley. The next two years found him as a Research Economist at the RAND Corporation, crossing paths once more with Nelson. From 1968 he served as a Professor of Economics at the University of Michigan, but in 1976 he joined Nelson as a Professor at Yale University, where he was employed until 1989. Subsequently he took up a post as Chief Economist at the US General Accounting Office in Washington DC. He now works at the Wharton School of the University of Pennsylvania.

In 1964 Winter published his major essay 'Economic "Natural Selection" and the Theory of the Firm'. This was essentially his PhD thesis; it is discussed in the next section and in the following chapter. Some of these early ideas were developed in Winter's 1971 *Quarterly Journal Economics* article and they became an important ingredient in the evolutionary theory of economic change developed jointly with Nelson. Early joint articles announcing the fruits of this collaboration appeared in the *American Economic Review* in 1973 and in the *Economic Journal* in 1974.

7.2. WINTER'S CRITIQUE OF FRIEDMAN

In his 1964 article in *Yale Economic Essays*, Winter made a milestone contribution to the long debate about the objectives of the firm. This debate had started a quarter of a century earlier when the Oxford economists Robert Hall and Charles Hitch (1939) published empirical evidence concerning the behaviour and apparent objectives of the firm. According to their evidence, the firms they studied did not attempt to maximize short-run profits or apply the $MC=MR$ rule. In fact, they did not have sufficient knowledge of their cost curves to find this optimum. Instead, the firms claimed that their aim was long-run profit maximization but they did not attempt to achieve this by finding out about and using the long-run costs curves. In fact they set prices according to the average cost principle. That is, instead of trying to equate marginal revenue and marginal cost, prices were set to cover the average total cost plus a 'normal' profit margin in the order of 10 per cent. Although subsequent empirical studies are not unanimous, they confirm that average-cost pricing is widely used.

Despite this and other corroborative evidence, a major debate followed on the objectives of the firm and the viability and appropriateness of the assumption that the firm is a profit maximizer.[2] On the one hand, economists such as Robert A. Gordon (1948) argued that firms face a large number of complex or uncertain variables. It is implausible that firms could make marginal adjustments to all these variables simultaneously and thereby maximize profits, and they are thus forced to rely on established decision-making routines such as mark-up pricing. In reply, economists such as Fritz Machlup (1946) defended the profit maximization hypotheses. He argued that what matters is the belief of firms as to what their MC and MR values are, not their objective values. If firms are maximizing they are doing so on the basis of their hunches and perceptions – which may or may not correspond to the real situation. The appeal to 'realism of assumptions' is thus misconceived and it is legitimate to assume that firms maximize profits.

In a classic article Armen Alchian (1950) proposed that the assumption of overt maximizing behaviour by business firms is not necessary for the scientific purposes of explanation and prediction. Indeed he went further, arguing that because agents operate in a world of uncertainty and may react in different ways to given stimuli, individual behaviour is not predictable. However, evolutionary processes of selection allegedly ensure that 'optimal' patterns of development can be observed in the aggregate.

Crucially, the use of the biological analogy was severely criticized by Edith Penrose (1952). For several reasons, she argued that the analogy with natural selection in biology was inappropriate for economics. In particular, there was an apparent absence of 'human will' and 'conscious deliberation' in modern biology. Explanations in economics rested crucially on convincing arguments concerning human motivation.

---

[2] See Koutsoyiannis (1979, ch. 11), Vromen (1995) and ch. 8 of the present volume.

Penrose's riposte did not deter Milton Friedman. In his famous 1953 article he took the line that the realism of assumptions is not the key issue, as all theories are inevitably unrealistic. The main criterion for assessing a theory, he asserted, is whether or not it makes correct predictions. On these grounds the profit maximization hypothesis was supported. Following Alchian, Friedman briefly developed the 'evolutionary' line of argument, by seeing 'natural selection' as grounds for assuming that agents act 'as if' they maximize, whether or not firms and individuals actually do so. Friedman argued that competitive 'natural selection' between firms will ensure that the firms which are actually maximizing profits are the ones most likely to survive. Friedman thus argued that empirical evidence on the overt intentions and actions of firms – such as that supplied by Hall and Hitch – was irrelevant.[3]

Friedman's argument was and remains highly influential. Partly as a result of his dismissal of the empirical studies, by the early 1950s this debate had swung in favour of those arguing for the retention of the profit maximization hypothesis. This outcome was of enormous significance for economics in the United States, for it consolidated the supremacy of the rising neoclassical school over the lingering remnants of the formerly influential 'old' institutionalist tradition of Thorstein Veblen, John Commons and Wesley Mitchell. This tradition was pervasive amongst American economists in the 1920s and 1930s. In the 1940s its ideas still infused the works of leading critics of the maximization hypothesis such as Robert Gordon, even if they claimed no more than a loose affiliation with that school.[4]

Nevertheless, although the balance of forces had shifted dramatically, the debate did not end. In the 1950s Herbert Simon launched an attack on the assumption of maximizing behaviour, including profit maximization by firms. In *Models of Man* (1957) and other works he argued that the assumption of 'global rationality' ignores the complexity and uncertainty involved in real-world decision making. Simon rejected the postulate that

---

[3] The differences between Alchian (1950) and Friedman (1953) should not be ignored. Kay (1995) has rightly criticized a passage in Hodgson (1988, pp. 76–7) where I refer to 'the Alchian–Friedman argument'. In fact, Alchian and Friedman differed on the question of whether 'natural selection' leads to profit maximizing behaviour by individual firms. Indeed, Alchian saw such an outcome as meaningless in a situation of uncertainty.

[4] See Keppler (1998) for a discussion of the relationship between Friedman's article and the assault on monopolistic competition theory.

global maximization is possible but retained a qualified notion of 'bounded' rationality. Agents are generally unable to gather and process all the information required for reaching global maximization decisions but they can make a 'rational' decision within a small set of possibilities. It was suggested by Simon and his followers, such as Richard Cyert and James March in their book *A Behavioral Theory of the Firm* (1963) that firms and consumers do not maximize but 'satisfice' instead. 'Satisficing' was defined as attaining an acceptable level of attainment, or 'aspiration level'. Agents make use of given routines or 'rules of thumb' to determine when this aspiration level has been reached. An example of such a 'rule of thumb' is the average-cost pricing principle.

It is no accident that Simon (1979) has acknowledged that he has been influenced by the 'old' institutionalists, particularly Commons. Furthermore, Simon (1979, p. 499) went on to say that 'the principal forerunner of a behavioral theory of the firm is usually called Institutionalism.' (In the context, the 'old' rather than the 'new' institutionalism is implied.) In effect, Simon developed and extended Veblen's (1919a) earlier and radical critique of the maximization hypothesis. The major influence of Simon on their thinking is explicitly acknowledged by Nelson and Winter.

However, Simon did not directly attack Friedman's evolutionary argument, and the first major critique of this was by Winter in his *Yale Economic Papers* article. Winter pointed out that Friedman was vague about the mechanisms of selection and the nature of the evolutionary process. An heritable element was missing from Friedman's account. For selection to work there must be some sustaining feature that ensures that the maximizers or near-maximizers that are 'selected' through competition will continue for some time in that mode of behaviour.

What is required is a degree of inertia in such routines to restrict change so that selection can operate effectively. Although they are not nearly as permanent as the gene, organizations nurture routines and patterns of thought and action which have self-reinforcing and durable qualities. Winter suggested that routines in the firm have a relatively durable quality through time. They may help to retain skills and other forms of knowledge, and to some extent they have the capacity to replicate through imitation, personal mobility, takeovers and so on. For Winter, the fact that firms had routines and decision rules made the analogy with biological evolution viable. Routines had a degree of gene-like stability and the capacity to 'mutate'.

Hence Winter's work was a partial answer to Penrose (1952) as well as a direct attack on Friedman (1953). Winter discovered in the routine an answer to Penrose's complaint that the behavioural mechanisms were not clearly specified in Alchian's presentation of the evolutionary analogy in economics.[5]

Winter's early work is important not only for its penetrating critique of Friedman, but also for its pioneering development of evolutionary theory. Winter laid the basis for the re-application of the evolutionary analogy, but he had done so by asserting the importance of routine-driven rather than maximizing behaviour. Furthermore, Winter had demonstrated that the use of the evolutionary metaphor does not drive analysis inexorably towards the kind of Panglossian and laissez-faire conclusions that Alchian and Friedman had proposed. In a subsequent article, Winter (1971) developed some of the arguments of his earlier paper.

7.3. THE MAKING OF A SCIENTIFIC REVOLUTION

By the late 1960s, Nelson had independently moved towards an evolutionary approach to economic theory. His original work on economic growth was broadly neoclassical, but the difficulties involved in explaining manifest productivity differences within the framework of the neoclassical production function led him to develop a new perspective. Nelson (1994c) wrote: 'In 1964, I was basically a neoclassical growth theorist, albeit of a rather eclectic kind. By 1968 I was almost a full blown evolutionary theorist.' The stage was thus set for one of the most fruitful collaborations in twentieth century economics.

As noted above, some of the basic ideas of *An Evolutionary Theory of Economic Change* (1982) were published jointly be Nelson and Winter in the early 1970s. To their joint venture, Nelson also brought his rich theoretical and empirical knowledge of industrial economics, and Winter carried the important theoretical innovations that he had made to reinstate in economics the evolutionary analogy from biology.

The inspiration provided by this analogy was crucial and explicit. The term 'evolutionary' was addressed by Nelson and Winter in biological terms: 'above all a signal that we have borrowed basic ideas from biology, thus exercising an option to which economists are entitled in perpetuity by virtue of the stimulus our predecessor Malthus provided to Darwin's thinking' (Nelson and Winter, 1982, p. 9). Nelson and Winter were careful to point

---

[5] Routines are implicit, however, in Penrose's (1959) theory of the firm, heralding Nelson and Winter's (1982) later idea of 'routines as genes'. Note also Hirshleifer's (1977) comments on the contributions that followed Alchian (1950).

out the limitations and dangers of this analogy, and the fact that socio-
economic evolution is seemingly more Lamarckian than Darwinian in
character. But this qualification should not divert attention from the crucial
inspirational role of the biological metaphor in their work. This is another
important example of the creative potential of metaphor in the social and
physical sciences.

As evidenced throughout their joint and individual works since the mid-
1960s, both authors have shared a deep anxiety about the theoretical,
empirical and practical limitations of neoclassical economics. This
uneasiness is so profound that it has led to a rejection of the core
assumptions of neoclassical economic theory. The 'reliance on equilibrium
analysis, even in its more flexible forms, still leads the discipline blind to
phenomena associated with historical change'. Furthermore, 'although it is
not literally appropriate to stigmatize orthodoxy as concerned only with
hypothetical situations of perfect information and static equilibrium, the
prevalence of analogous restrictions in advanced work lends a metaphorical
validity to the complaint.' Finally, they rejected 'the assumption that
economic actors are rational in the sense that they optimize' (Nelson and
Winter, 1982, p. 8).

Accordingly, Nelson and Winter developed an alternative theoretical
framework to profit maximization for the analysis of the firm. Instead of
such an optimizing procedure, they proposed an evolutionary model in
which selection operates on the firm's internal routines. Routines include
'characteristics of firms that range from well-specified technical routines for
producing things, through procedures for hiring and firing, ordering new
inventory, or stepping up production of items in high demand, to policies
regarding investment, research and development (R&D), or advertising, and
business strategies about product diversification and overseas investment.' In
their analysis 'these routines play the role that genes play in biological
evolutionary theory' (p. 14).

Routines are not simply widespread and characteristic of much activity
within organizations: they also have functional characteristics. Being
concerned to show how technological skills are acquired and passed on
within the economy, Nelson and Winter argued that habits and routines act
as relatively durable repositories of knowledge and skills. In their words,
routines are the 'organizational memory' (p. 99) of the firm. Furthermore,
routines may have the capacity to replicate through imitation, personal
mobility, and so on. Because of their relatively durable character and their
capacity to replicate, routines act as the economic analogue of the gene in
biology. They transmit information through time in a manner which is

loosely analogous to the conservation and replication of information via the gene.

However, it is freely accepted that innovative activity is possible and much business behaviour is not essentially routine. Such irregular and unpredictable behaviour was accommodated in their evolutionary theory 'by recognizing that there are stochastic elements in the determination of decisions and decision outcomes' (p. 15). Here again there are clear parallels in the biological theory of evolution where stochastic variation is important in many evolutionary models.

Just as the routine is the analogue of the gene, Nelson and Winter borrowed a second key concept directly from evolutionary biology. They developed the concept of 'search' to encompass changes in the routines of firms: 'Our concept of search obviously is the counterpart of that of mutation in biological evolutionary theory' (p. 18). This concept was illustrated by the evolutionary model in Chapter 9 of their book. A threshold level of profitability was assumed. If firms are sufficiently profitable they attempt to maintain their existing routines and do no 'searching' at all. In some cases Nelson and Winter adopted Simon's 'satisficing' idea: agents attempt to gain a given 'aspiration level' rather than to optimize. However, if profitability falls below this level then 'firms are driven to consider alternatives . . . under the pressure of adversity' (p. 211). They invest in R&D and attempt to discover new techniques so that profitability can be restored. In other models, instead of satisficing behaviour, Nelson and Winter consider organizations that are 'always searching' for new and improved techniques.

Third, there is a clear analogue to the idea of economic 'natural selection': 'Market environments provide a definition of success for business firms, and that definition is very closely related to their ability to survive and grow' (p. 9). Clearly, this is the application of the analogy of market competition with the 'struggle for existence' in biology. In this third case, unlike the preceding two, there is much common ground with Alchian, Friedman and many others. However, unlike most of their predecessors, Nelson and Winter were careful not to endow market selection mechanisms or private ownership with the aura of a 'natural' order or the mantle of supreme efficiency (Nelson, 1981b).

The adoption of these three crucial analogues completed the link between the Nelson–Winter concept of economic evolution and the corresponding idea in biology. In biology, evolution requires three essential components. First, there must be sustained variation among the members of a species or population. Variations may be blind, random or purposive in character, but without them, as Darwin insisted, natural selection cannot operate. Second, there must be some principle of heredity or continuity through which offspring have to resemble their parents more than they resemble other members of their species. In other words, there has to be some mechanism through which individual characteristics are passed on through the generations. Third, natural selection itself operates either because better-adapted organisms leave increased numbers of offspring, or because the variations or gene combinations that are preserved are those bestowing advantage in struggling to survive. This is the principle of the struggle for existence. Nelson and Winter explicitly appropriated and amended these ideas from biology to build their evolutionary theory. This triad of ideas demarcates their 'evolutionary' approach from many different and contending uses of the term (Hodgson, 1993b, ch. 3).

However, while the theoretical approach of Nelson and Winter conformed to these three characteristics of evolutionary biology, they make it clear that it does not amount to an exact correspondence. We have already noted that while routines are relatively sturdy in socio-economic terms they are not nearly as durable as the gene in biology. In addition, when routines change their new characteristics can be imitated and directly inherited by imitators or subsidiary firms. For this reason, as several evolutionary theorists have pointed out, in the socio-economic sphere the inheritance of acquired characteristics is possible and thereby socio-economic evolution has apparent 'Lamarckian' characteristics. It could also be classed as Lamarckian because – contrary to the gene-programmed behaviour of Darwinism – there is a place for intentionality and novelty in human behaviour (Hodgson, 1993b, ch. 14). This seemed to overcome an objection to the use of the biological analogy raised by Penrose in 1952. Notably, Nelson and Winter (1982) referred to their own approach as Lamarckian rather than Darwinian.[6]

---

[6] However, Nelson and Winter's declared allegiance to Lamarckism may have given the impression that they believed that this doctrine was viable in biology. This would be misleading. Following Mayr (1960), Waddington (1975) and others, there has indeed been a partial rehabilitation of a modified 'Lamarckism' in modern biology, in which behavioural adaptations are seen as a major driving force in evolutionary change. However, at the genetic level, and contrary to former Lamarckians, the inheritance of acquired characters is still ruled out by most biologists. More recently, in the philosophy of biology, there has also been a reintroduction of teleology and purposefulness into biological discourse (Depew and Weber, 1985). Nevertheless, the enormous differences in durability between the genetic material, on the one hand, and analogous elements in socio-economic evolution (habits, routines, rules, institutions) still have to be emphasised. See

Although Nelson and Winter use formal methods and computer simulations, their work has a strong empirical orientation. 'The approach in much of the book is to lay out what the "stylized" facts seem to be, and then try to develop a theoretical explanation that explains these facts' (Nelson, 1994c). Notably, in making a distinction between 'formal' and 'appreciative' theorising, Nelson and Winter (1982, pp. 45–8) argue that formal modelling should play a significant but not a central role. Instead, as in appreciative theorising, the overriding concern is with empirical grounding and richness. As Nelson (1994a, pp. 154–5) elaborated:

> Appreciative theorizing tends to be close to empirical work and provides both guidance and interpretation. Empirical findings seldom influence formal theorizing directly. Rather, in the first instance, they influence appreciative theory and, in turn, appreciative theory challenges formal theory to encompass these understandings in stylized form. The attempt to do so may identify gaps or inconsistencies in the verbal stories, or modelling may suggest new theoretical storylines to explore. In turn, the empirical research enterprise is reoriented.

Clearly the emphasis here is on the guidance and conceptual framing of empirical study, rather than the development of mathematical formalism itself.

Overall, the joint theoretical work of Nelson and Winter is of enormous significance, being the most extensive and rigorous application of the evolutionary metaphor from biology in economics to date. This creative achievement was in part facilitated by Winter's earlier work, which rigorously examined the conditions under which the evolutionary analogy might apply. Nelson's key contribution was his rich knowledge of industrial organization and technological change. Their *Evolutionary Theory of Economic Change* is not only destined to be a classic of late-twentieth century economics, it also is an archetypal and classical case of the way in which scientific creativity may result from the transfer of metaphor from one discipline to another, but generally only when there is already a rich theoretical and empirical knowledge of the home discipline.

There are additionally instructive aspects of the form, content and context of the work. For instance, although the authors effectively carried out a revolution in our way of thinking about economic change in general and the firm in particular, they sometimes understated their differences with the preceding orthodoxy. For instance, one feature of the Winter (1971) and

---

also the probing discussion of the relationship between neo-Darwinism and neoclassical economics in Khalil (1993).

Nelson and Winter (1982) works is that, despite their dynamic and evolutionary qualities, they are in part attempts to show that the Nelson–Winter type of theory subsumed neoclassical analysis as a special case. Thus they tried to reproduce neoclassical equilibria or production functions by tuning their parameter values, but on the basis of a broader theory which allegedly has greater 'behavioral realism'. Consequently, their work has been seen as occupying an uncomfortable no-man's-land between neoclassical theorists who do not care about empirical realism, on the one hand, and institutionalists and allies who reject neoclassical assumptions, on the other.

As a result, on the one hand, their work has had a limited positive reception amongst heterodox economists. Indeed, Philip Mirowski (1983) has strongly criticized *An Evolutionary Theory of Economic Change* in a review. He pointed out that in seemingly attempting to 'improve' Solow's (1957) production function analysis of growth, Nelson and Winter ignored the theoretical devastation wreaked on Solow's neoclassical theoretical constructions in the Cambridge capital controversy (Harcourt, 1972). This criticism is apposite, for Nelson and Winter paid no attention to the devastating work of Piero Sraffa (1960) and his followers. But at the same time Mirowski underestimated the positive contribution and significance of Nelson and Winter's work.

On the other hand, the impact of their work on orthodoxy has not matched the scale of their own intellectual revolution. Casual inspection of the 1983–1993 citations to *An Evolutionary Theory of Economic Change* in the Social Science Citations Index suggests that this work is cited much more frequently in management and business publications, rather than in the core theoretical journals of mainstream economics. Arguably the impact to date of the book on mainstream economic theory has been detectable but no more than marginal. Nevertheless, the impact of the work has grown steadily. Figure 7.1 gives some indication, using Social Science Citations Index data, of the growing overall impact of Nelson and Winter's 1982 book. Both the annual number of citations and the annual 'citation share' (the number of citations for the work divided by total number of citations in the social sciences, in millions) have shown a clear upward trend.[7]

---

[7] However, Alexander Rosenberg (1994, p. 402) wrote of the Nelson and Winter (1982) volume: 'The capstone of two distinguished careers, few books can have had a more disappointing reception in current economics . . . it has fallen stillborn from the presses'. Yet a growth of annual citation rates to a levels of over 100 in just 10 years after publication is no small achievement. Consider the quite

Figure 7.1: Citations to Nelson and Winter's *Evolutionary Theory of Economic Change*

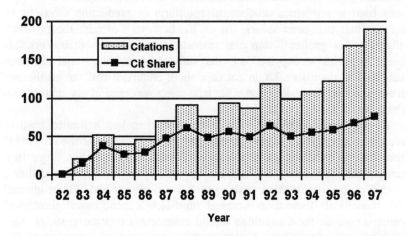

Nelson and Winter have often presented their work less as an intellectual revolution (clearly modesty too has a role here) and more as a result of cumulative development of mainstream thought. In casting their own theory in these terms they have many illustrious predecessors. In his famous study of 'scientific revolutions' Thomas Kuhn (1970, p. 139) noted the 'persistent tendency of science to look linear or cumulative, a tendency that even affects scientists looking back at their own research.' To illustrate, Kuhn (1970, pp. 139–40) explained the way in which Newton reinterpreted Galileo's theory to fit in the story about his own:

> Newton wrote that Galileo had discovered that the constant force of gravity produces a motion proportional to the square of the time. . . . But Galileo said nothing of the sort. His discussion of falling bodies rarely alludes to forces, much less to a uniform gravitational force that causes bodies to fall. By crediting to Galileo the answer to a question that Galileo's paradigms did not permit to be asked, Newton's account hides the effect of a small but revolutionary reformulation in the questions that scientists asked about motion as well as in the answers they felt able to accept.

---

different fate of another heterodox classic, Sraffa's *Production of Commodities by Means of Commodities* (1960), discussed in Chapter 3 above.

In effect, by presenting his own work as merely a cumulative development of Galileo's, Newton ignored the conceptual innovations and paradigm shifts that were implicit in his own theory.

This and many other similar episodes in the history of science leads us to re-examine what Nelson and Winter wrote about their own intellectual antecedents. We are helped by a thoughtful and lengthy (Nelson and Winter, 1982, pp. 33–45) section on this theme. The influence of the works of Simon and the behaviouralists was acknowledged: 'We accept and absorb into our analysis many of the ideas of behavioral theorists' (pp. 35–6). There was apposite recognition of the importance for evolutionary theorising of Armen Alchian's 1950 article, which 'stands out as a direct intellectual antecedent of the present work' (p. 41). And in particular, it was acknowledged that the 'influence of Joseph Schumpeter is so pervasive in our work that it requires particular mention here' (p. 39).

Yet, apart from a brief mention of John Maurice Clark and John Kenneth Galbraith (p. 38), one school is conspicuous by its absence – American institutionalism. There is no mention of Veblen, or of Commons, or of Mitchell, in the entire book. Given the precedence of this school of thought in the United States in the interwar period, such an omission is strange, amounting perhaps to an implicit denial of the significance or relevance of the school to the project in hand.[8]

While not being irrelevant, the invocation of Schumpeter by Nelson and Winter has a deep irony. Schumpeter frequently used the term 'evolution' but what he meant by this was the general idea of economic development, involving technological, structural and institutional change. As noted in a previous chapter, Schumpeter was allergic to analogies with physics or biology, regarding them as irrelevant or misleading. Not only did Schumpeter show no desire to adopt Darwinian ideas in his economics, but also his version of economic evolution contrasted with a Darwinian analogue. In particular, Schumpeter's emphasis on evolution as *endogenous* change contradicts the essential fact that Darwinian evolution works essentially in *open* systems. As Jack Cohen and Ian Stewart (1994, p. 367) wrote: 'evolution is *the* central area where both content and context combine to provide scientific insight.' Although Schumpeter discussed economic

---

[8] Despite the error being repeated by many others elsewhere, it is notable that Nelson and Winter have since rectified this omission. Nelson (1995) and Winter (1986b, 1987b, 1990a) have both referred approvingly to Veblen. And Nelson (1996) has gone so far as to write: '[I now] understand fully that I am part of the old institutional economics'.

inertia and conservatism, and competitive selection, these do not form part of any developed analogy with Darwinism.

As argued in a preceding chapter, it was Veblen who was the first to apply the three Darwinian principles of variation, heredity and selection. Hence Nelson and Winter's idea of the 'natural selection' and quasi-genetic quality of institutions and routines has a much stronger resonance in the earlier evolutionary economic theory of Veblen than the work of Schumpeter. Veblen is a unique precedent for the application of the principles of evolutionary change which Nelson and Winter themselves explicate. Although Nelson and Winter failed to acknowledge his influence, a much more appropriate precedent than Schumpeter for their rediscovery and development of the biological analogy was Veblen, as pointed out by Curtis Eaton (1984) in his review of their book. For these reasons, the work of Nelson and Winter is as much 'Veblenian' as 'Schumpeterian' in character.

Two important questions are raised. First, why did Nelson and Winter place so much emphasis on the inspiration of Schumpeter, but none at all on Veblen? Second, can any indirect traces of the influence of Veblen and the 'old' institutionalist tradition be found in Nelson and Winter's work?

In answer to the first question, it is obvious that in developing their ideas Nelson and Winter consulted Schumpeter's works much more often than Veblen's. But this answer is not sufficient, especially in two authors so careful about intellectual precedents and relatively knowledgeable about the intellectual evolution of their own discipline. Clearly, something relating to the 'sociology' of the economics profession is relevant here. Perhaps it is in part due to the fact that the 'Schumpeterian' label is more acceptable to the orthodox economist? In contrast, Veblen and his followers are widely seen as discredited, defunct and anti-neoclassical. The precise answer is not clear. But if scientific geniuses such as Sir Isaac Newton can misconceive of their own intellectual history it is no great disrespect even to innovative and intellectually courageous authors such as Nelson and Winter to suggest here that they may have committed the same error.

The second question, concerning an unacknowledged link between Nelson and Winter and the 'old' institutionalists, is equally complex. We have noted the failure of Nelson and Winter to note the direct influence of known members of the institutional school other than J. M. Clark and J. K. Galbraith. Part of the problem is that the influence of the 'old' institutionalists in the United States in the interwar period was so pervasive that an entire generation of economists were strongly influenced by this school without necessarily declaring a formal or tribal allegiance to institutionalism.

Robert Gordon is a classic example. He seemed reluctant to declare himself to be an institutionalist, but in his first major monograph, on large corporations, Gordon (1945) made erudite references to the work of Veblen and cited extensively the seminal and institutionalist-inspired study of Adolf Berle and Gardiner Means (1932). Veblenian themes are also present in his famous critique of the maximization hypothesis (Gordon, 1948). Gordon (1963) recognized the importance of institutions in economic life, and believed that since Veblen's time mainstream economics had partially absorbed some of the insights of the 'old' institutionalists, while the core theoretical idea of 'rational economic man' was unchanged and the predilection for mathematical formalism had become much stronger. As is again clear in his presidential address to the American Economic Association, Gordon (1976) was deeply sympathetic to institutionalism, yet he seemed to believe in reforming mainstream economics from within.

It is this same Robert Gordon who Nelson and Winter (1982, p. 16n.) cited as a precursor; one who emphasized that 'many of the decisions with which economic theory is concerned . . . are made by routinized procedures'. Likewise, Gordon's work shares with Nelson and Winter a strong and now unfashionable concern with 'big questions' in economics including 'where is the economic system going?' (Gordon, 1976, p. 10). Gordon – who died in 1978 – was at Berkeley from 1938 to 1976: the same university at which Winter taught for three years in the 1960s.

Gordon is not being singled out here as the only influence, nor even a major one, nor as a definitive demonstration that Nelson and Winter's work bore the hidden hallmarks of the 'old' institutionalism. Such a brief discussion does not close the matter. Nothing approaching a definitive history of the intellectual and institutional development of twentieth-century economics has yet been written. When it is, it will have to attempt to explain the all-too-hasty predilection of many leading mainstream US economists to write off and disregard such an important, influential and quite recent episode in their own intellectual history.

7.4. OTHER CONTRIBUTIONS IN THE 1980s AND 1990s

The challenge to mainstream economic theory in the works of Nelson and Winter is clearly manifest in several additional works. We shall confine ourselves to a few illustrative examples.

Neoclassical economics has a tendency to treat information and knowledge as resources which are scarce. They are regarded as 'out there' and obtainable by individuals like any other commodity, and at a price. In a series of works Nelson and Winter have argued against this view, rejecting the 'blueprint' view of knowledge and seeing the acquisition of knowledge as a contextual, social process, deeply embedded in groups and institutions. Clearly this very different view of information and knowledge is related to their rejection of the rationality postulate of neoclassical theory, where agents choose the 'best' option from a number of *known* alternatives. By replacing the central concepts of optimization and equilibrium by an evolutionary picture of ceaseless change, Nelson and Winter have focused on the complex processes of learning, and on the generation and transmission of knowledge.

In an important article, Nelson (1980) criticized the orthodox treatment of information and knowledge – including technological knowledge – as codifiable and cumulative. He rejected the common idea that 'technological knowledge is in the form of codified how-to-do-it knowledge which provides sufficient guidance so that if one had access to the book one would be able to do it' (p. 63). Also discarded is the notion that such knowledge is easily or directly expanded by expenditure on research and development: 'If the salient elements of techniques involve special personal skills, or a personalized pattern of interaction and cooperation among a group of individuals in an important way, then one cannot easily infer how it would work from an experiment conducted elsewhere' (p. 67).

This conceptualization of human knowledge has important implications. It involves, so to speak, a unity of knowing and doing. Furthermore, knowledge may relate to the shared practices of the group, and not simply individuals. Winter has also insisted on the proposition that the knowledge within a corporation relates essentially to the organization and the group, rather than to the individuals composing them. This theme is explored further in Chapter 11 below. Clearly, the radical reconceptualization of the notion of knowledge by both Nelson and Winter is of enormous significance, as well as being a major departure from the treatment of knowledge and information problems in neoclassical theory.

Notably, these ideas also have strong and earlier precedents in the writings of the American pragmatists who influenced early American institutional economists such as Thorstein Veblen and John Commons. Furthermore, Veblen (1919a, p. 186) himself argued that the 'great body of commonplace knowledge made use of in an industry is the product and heritage of the group'. 'These immaterial industrial expedients are necessarily a product of the community, the immaterial residue of the community's experience, past and present; which has no existence apart from the community's life, and can be transmitted only in the keeping of the community at large' (Veblen, 1919a, p. 348).

Nelson and Winter's arguments also have precursors in the classic book *The Theory of the Growth of the Firm* by Edith Penrose (1959) and in the philosophy of Michael Polanyi (1958, 1967). Contrary to the treatment of 'information problems' by neoclassical theorists, 'tacit' or 'unteachable' knowledge cannot be reduced simply to 'information' because it is partly embodied in habits and routines, and it cannot be reduced to, or transmitted in, a codified form.

In other articles, Nelson drew out a number of the implications of this general view. Because knowledge relates to the structures and routines of the firm, and is often in a non-codifiable form, 'management cannot effectively "choose" what is to be done in any detailed way, and has only broad control over what is done, and how well. Only a small portion of what people actually do on a job can be monitored in detail' (Nelson, 1981b, p. 1038).

This important view of the role and distribution of knowledge in corporate organizations is a clear rival both to Frederick Winslow Taylor's *Scientific Management* (1911) and to Harry Braverman's Marxist analysis in *Labor and Monopoly Capital* (1974). Both involve the untenable idea that the worker has become 'an appendage to the machine'. The supposed 'separation of conception and execution' which is stressed by these theorists, where managers conceive and give orders, and workers carry them out, is implicitly denied by Nelson. He argued that the firm is a 'social system' and not 'a machine'.

In another paper, Nelson (1981a, p. 109) aimed to hammer 'on the point that the analysis contained in contemporary welfare economics provides an extremely shaky intellectual basis for the favorable views that most Western-trained economists apparently have for private enterprise.' It is not that private enterprise is without its virtues, but Nelson showed that the evaluation of the merits of private enterprise is far more complex than the mask of orthodox theorising would suggest. Typically, the aim here was both to avoid all simplistic policy conclusions and to suggest a programme for major renovation or even replacement of orthodox theory.

More recently, Nelson (1991) has extended his evolutionary analysis of the firm, arguing that the differences between real-world firms must be recognized by economic theory. Orthodox theory often ignores intra-industry firm differences, or denies that they are of any economic significance. In contrast, within an evolutionary approach, both the generation and function of corporate diversity is explicable.

Nelson (1993, 1998) has also contributed to the analysis of 'national systems of innovation' and to the modern theory of economic growth. As in all his studies, the aim was to help develop economics as an operational and empirically-enriched science, which can engage with real-world problems and avoid the dogmatic and simplistic policy pronouncements with which we are unfortunately all too familiar.

Winter's continuing willingness to expose the limitations of orthodox economics is evidenced in a forceful critique of neoclassical rationality (Winter, 1986a), demonstrating a tireless attack on this key proposition over several decades. He rejected the characterisation of human agents as 'superoptimizers', asserting the need for 'a fruitful relationship between theory and empiricism in economics' (p. S432). 'There is an important role for inquiry into the learning and adaptive processes of boundedly rational economic actors who are forced to act in a changing world they do not understand' (p. S433).

Against the prevailing individualism and mechanistic reductionism of mainstream economics, Nelson and Winter have both pioneered a new route of enquiry that promises to develop into the most significant challenge to the foundations of neoclassical orthodoxy for many years. Their work does not exhibit formalism for its own sake, but is a genuine attempt to rebuild economics as an operational and empirically enriched science.

It remains to be seen if and how this battle will be won: whether mainstream economics itself will change, or that the key developments will occur in business schools and elsewhere, and outside the economics departments which are generally increasingly dominated by a relatively closed and formalistic orthodoxy. Time will tell.

8. Optimization and Evolution: Winter's Critique of Friedman Revisited

Despite many challenges in the past, the assumption that firms are maximizing their profits remains prominent in economic theory.[1] Furthermore, whenever a defence of this particular assumption is offered, the famous argument offered by Milton Friedman (1953) is often favoured. Friedman gives other reasons, including the instrumentalist proposition that all that matters is predictive success. However, Friedman also justified the maximization hypothesis with the notion that the process of economic evolution or 'natural selection' will ensure that the firms that maximize 'expected returns' will have a much better chance of survival, whereas other firms are more likely to fail. Consequently, he argued, the real-world population of firms is likely to be dominated by such maximizes.

The invocation of such an argument is understandable, as Darwinian and other evolutionary ideas have had an enormous influence on modern thought. However, certain prevalent conceptions of the evolutionary process should not be taken for granted. Many of these have been inherited from nineteenth-century biology, and do not have universal or even widespread support amongst biologists today.

For instance, it is widely assumed outside biology that an evolutionary process necessarily involves the selection of individual units that are in some sense superior or relatively efficient. However, such notions have been more displaced by various developments in theoretical biology, and despite many

---

[1] This is a revised version of Hodgson (1994a).

differences of opinion amongst biologists, they are now rejected by the consensus.[2] Furthermore, of course, even if evolution selects the efficient or the fittest, such results are not necessarily desirable; outcomes of evolutionary selection and matters of welfare are not automatically the same.

Over a quarter of a century ago, Sidney Winter (1964) developed a powerful critique of Friedman's argument, but it has not had a major impact and its central propositions are rarely discussed.[3] The purpose of this chapter is to examine the viability of the crucial elements of Winter's critique, especially in the light of modern biological theory. The scope will be narrowed to consider supposed optimization and efficiency in regard to atomistic units, i.e. firms only; not in regard to the socio-economic system as a whole. Modern evolutionary theory has produced many cases where optimizing behaviour has not produced optimal global outcomes, but it is beyond the compass of this chapter to consider the question of global optimality.[4]

Despite this limitation, a re-evaluation of Winter's argument raises important and topical questions concerning the very nature of rationality in economic theory. One result of this re-evaluation is to show that the very specification of such concepts is far from straightforward. As Winter (1986a) has later emphasized, there is a huge difference between, on the one hand, just assuming and examining an equilibrium, and on the other,

---

[2] For instance, the possibility of adaptations which are immediately favourable for individuals being unfavourable for the group to which they belong is a major theme of modern sociobiology. See, for example, Clutton-Brock and Harvey (1978), Maynard Smith (1976, 1980, 1982), Wilson (1975). In addition, Dawkins (1976), Ghiselin (1974) and Williams (1966) attack the notion that the survival of an attribute can be explained in terms of its contribution to the good of the whole. Notions such as that evolution necessarily leads to optimality or progress, and that individual adaptations are necessarily functional, are favourite targets in Gould (1978, 1980, 1989) and Gould and Lewontin (1979). See also Oster and Wilson (1978, ch. 8), Sober (1981) and Dupré (1987).

[3] In sections of his later works (Winter, 1971, 1975, 1987b) some of the arguments are repeated. But in these cases the presentation is shorter than in the original, and some key points are left out. Note that the issue discussed here is quite separate from the dispute over Winter's 'fundamental selection theorem' (Winter, 1971, 1990b; Moss 1990).

[4] Day (1975, p. 26) argued convincingly that adaptive optimizing strategies, 'though perhaps based on "globally optimal" and "consistent" plans . . . will not necessarily lead to globally optimal or consistent behaviour.'

investigating the procedures and behavioural rules involved in the attainment of such an equilibrium state.

Even if rationality can be readily defined, the nature of the (unintended) outcomes that flow therefrom is itself a complex and worthy question. Here, however, we must focus simply on the question of whether or not, in some meaningful sense, rational or maximizing agents can be selected in an evolutionary process. The unintended consequences of any supposedly maximizing behaviour are relevant here, but only insofar as they impinge upon these mechanisms.

Although controversial and equally problematic, the question of what is the unit of selection will not be explored in this chapter.[5] It will be assumed that firms are selected on the basis of their profit performance, and that in some cases this may reflect characteristics which are 'genetically encoded' in the firm's structure.

The chapter has the following sections. 8.1 surveys the background and substance to Friedman's argument and presents Winter's critique. 8.2 identifies the restrictive conditions under which evolution may favour the maximizers. 8.3 considers a more radical extension of Winter's argument: the deconstruction of rationality. 8.4 concludes the chapter.

8.1. EVOLUTIONARY SELECTION IN ECONOMICS: FROM ALCHIAN TO WINTER

8.1.1. Alchian, Enke and Friedman: Evolution as a Maximizer

Armen Alchian (1950, 1953) proposed that the assumption of maximizing behaviour by individual firms is not necessary for the scientific purposes of prediction. If firms never actually attempted to maximize profits, 'evolutionary' processes of selection would ensure the survival of the more profitable enterprises. Thus Alchian saw the idea of evolutionary selection less as a buttress and more as an alternative to the assumption that individual firms are actually attempting to maximize their profits.

---

[5] On this issue in the economic context, see Hodgson (1991a; 1993b, ch. 12). It relates to the question of methodological individualism discussed in Sober (1981) and Hodgson (1988).

Stephen Enke (1951) shifted the emphasis somewhat, first by arguing that with sufficient intensity of competition and 'in the long run', conditions of intense competition mean that only the optimizers will remain viable. Friedman (1953) developed the argument. He saw 'natural selection' as grounds for assuming that agents act 'as if' they maximize, whether or not firms and individuals actually do so. His evolutionary defence of the maximization hypothesis is as follows:

> Let the apparent immediate determinant of business behaviour be anything at all – habitual reaction, random chance, or whatnot. Whenever this determinant happens to lead to behaviour consistent with rational and informed maximization of returns, the business will prosper and acquire resources with which to expand; whenever it does not, the business will tend to lose resources and can be kept in existence only by the addition of resources from outside. The process of 'natural selection' thus helps to validate the hypothesis – or, rather, given natural selection, acceptance of the hypothesis can be based largely on the judgement that it summarizes appropriately the conditions for survival. (Friedman, 1953, p. 22)

However, like Alchian (1950, 1953) and others, Friedman was vague about the mechanisms of selection and the nature of the evolutionary process. Edith Penrose (1952, 1953) had already raised serious concerns about this type of thinking, noting in particular the lack of attention in such 'evolutionary' analogies to the fact of deliberative human behaviour. The transplanted evolutionary analogy had no clear model of individual behaviour and was thus incoherent in its own terms. Competition played an explicit role in these theories but: 'Competition cannot reasonably be expected to exist if men are presumed to act randomly' (Penrose, 1953, p. 605). This put on the agenda the need for a behavioural model within an evolutionary, or any other, economic theory.

8.1.2. Winter's Reformulation and Critique: Heritable Traits

Likewise, Winter (1964) saw several difficulties and ambiguities in Friedman's argument. His major line of attack is to point out that for selection to work there must be some sustaining feature that ensures that the maximizers or near-maximizers that are 'selected' through competition will continue for some time in that mode of behaviour. For instance, if firm behaviour is random, as Friedman conjectured, then there is no reason to assume that a firm that happens to be maximizing will continue to do so in the next period. Further, such randomness could mean that a firm on the brink of bankruptcy at one instant could by chance be a good profit maximizer in the next. As we shall see below, even if 'habitual reaction' is the actual determinant of firm behaviour, then the selection of maximizers is not guaranteed.

For natural selection to work there must be heritable variation in fitness and this is missing from Friedman's account. He correctly presumed that the evolutionary selection process discriminates between firms on the basis of their manifest behaviour, or – to use the corresponding biological term – the phenotype. However, for selection to work consistently in favour of some characteristics rather than others, this behaviour cannot be predominantly accidental. There has to be some equivalent to the genetic constitution or genotype, such as the routines or culture of the firm, which fixes or constrains the phenotype. To presume that maximization emerges from an evolutionary process means that routines giving rise to such behaviour are being selected through their superior capacity for survival. What is required is a degree of inertia in such routines so that selection can operate effectively (Matthews, 1985; Hannan and Freeman, 1977). Although they are not nearly as permanent as the gene, organizations create and sustain structures and patterns of thought and action which have self-reinforcing and durable qualities (Itami, 1987; Hrebeniak and Joyce, 1985; Metcalfe and Gibbons, 1989; Powell and DiMaggio, 1991).

Further, the more the relation between genotype and phenotype is determined and fixed then the more effective the evolutionary process will be in selecting particular characteristics through time. In these circumstances, by working on phenotypes, and causing the extinction of some and the prosperity and replication of others, the selection process can then be successful in indirectly altering the characteristics of the 'gene pool' of the group of firms. However, the phenotype is never determined by the genotype alone, and the phenotype is likely to be a function of the environment as well as of the genotype.[6]

The genotype-phenotype distinction in biology suggested to Winter an analogous and important distinction in the socio-economic sphere: between rules of action and action itself. Richard Nelson and Sidney Winter (1982) develop the idea that habits or routines act as the economic analogue of the gene in biology, although this notion has earlier origins in the work of Thorstein Veblen (1919a).[7] Routines in the firm have a relatively durable

---

[6] Some biological theorists have recognized the difficulties thus created for the explanation of the nature of evolutionary selection (Brandon and Burian, 1984; Sober, 1984a; Waddington, 1972).

[7] See Hodgson (1992a, 1993b).

quality through time. They may help to retain skills and knowledge, and to some extent they have the capacity to replicate through imitation, personal mobility, takeovers, and so on. There is also the possibility of 'mutation'. As Winter (1971, p. 247) wrote: 'The assumption that firms have decision rules, and retain or replace them according to the satisficing principle, provides both genetic stability and an endogenous mutation mechanism'.

8.1.3. Winter and Frequency Dependence

However, in identifying an economic analogue to the mechanism of heredity provided by the gene in biology, Nelson and Winter argue that such an evolutionary process does not always result in a preponderance of profit-maximizing firms. As Winter (1964, p. 240) put it:

> If the habitual reactions of some firms at a particular time are consistent with profit maximization, and if as a consequence these firms expand relative to other firms in the economy, this very fact will tend to alter the market price environment facing all firms. It is not clear why, in this altered environment, the same firms should continue to have the good fortune to be closer to maximizing behavior than their competitors . . . the environment is changed by the dynamic process itself.

Here Winter has exposed a central problem with Friedman's argument which can be illuminated with use of evolutionary concepts from modern biology. Indeed, Winter's suggestion that the 'environment is changed by the dynamic process itself' and that 'no theory of long-run evolutionary change can logically take the environment of the individual . . . as exogenous' (Winter, 1971, p. 258) have their analogue in biology in feedback effects between organisms and their environment.

The significance of these 'frequency dependence effects' has been recognized by biologists in later years. While a favourable adaptation may occur in relation to a given environmental situation, and the first few adaptations may be favourable for the units concerned, the accumulation of such adaptations may alter the environment itself, and the eventual result may be that the same adaptation no longer yields beneficial results for any individual unit.[8]

---

[8] For discussions see Kauffman (1988), Lewontin (1974), Sober (1985) in biology, and Hodgson (1993b, ch. 13) and Witt (1991) in economics.

This idea has an obvious application to economics. A firm may find a market niche involving the manufacture of a new product. Although the firm may initially make large profits from the venture, a large number of other firms grasp the same opportunity and the market may then become flooded and the product may no longer be profitable. What was profitable for one or a few alone may not be profitable for many together.

The changing topography of the fitness (or profits) surface resulting from such frequency dependence effects may inhibit the selection of maximizers. A group of maximizers having climbed a sometime global maximum might find themselves overshadowed by a new and unobtainable global peak, or even plunged into a new depression. A group of sluggish non-maximizers might find themselves lunged upwards by earth movements in their favour. With such a shifting fitness surface we often have no reason for asserting that one local optimum will prove to be lastingly better than another.

8.1.4. The Problem of New Entrants

In addition to frequency dependence, Winter suggested that the question of the characteristics of new entrants to the industry has to be considered. There is a brief suggestion that problems may arise if selection is thwarted by a 'disruptive entry of non-maximizers' (Winter, 1964, p. 242). This is related to an argument in modern biology. Stephen Jay Gould and Richard Lewontin (1979) undermine the idea of natural selection as a universally optimizing agent. One of their arguments is that the natural selection of optimally adapted forms can be thwarted by less efficient organisms with a greater birth or immigration rate.

This clearly applies to the economic sphere. If the industry is subjected to a rapid flow of new entrants which are relatively unadaptable and non-maximizing then they may swamp the maximizers even if selection processes are working in favour of the latter. In general, the rate of immigration, the characteristics of the entrants, and the relationship of these characteristics to the selected population, will affect the chances of maximizers being selected. This conclusion is important because it shows that the particular kind of mechanism governing the creation of new entrants is as significant as the selection process *per se*.

8.1.5. Winter's Discussion of Returns to Scale

Winter (1964) went on to consider the question of returns to scale. He presumed a population of firms, including some maximizers and some non-maximizers, which have identical production functions and all work at full capacity, but differ in terms of their initial levels of scale. Consider first the case of increasing returns:[9]

> it could happen that a non-maximizer has an initial scale advantage over all the maximizers. Provided this departure from maximization is not too severe, the scale advantage may more than compensate for it. If the greater profitability of the non-maximizer then induces a higher growth rate, the scale advantage of the non-maximizer will become still larger, and none of the assumptions made thus far provide any reason to think that the maximizers will ever catch up. Alternatively, suppose that returns to scale are diminishing. Then the maximizer will run into less favourable production conditions as it expands relative to the non-maximizers . . . the possibility arises that maximizers and non-maximizers may coexist indefinitely simply because the maximizers cannot expand enough to put lethal market pressure on the non maximizers. (Winter, 1964, p. 243)

Winter argued that an adequate selection process depends, at least, on the assumption of constant returns to scale, and he has continued to repeat this assertion (Winter, 1987b, p. 545). It is argued below that this proposition is false.[10]

The discussion of problems of scale exemplifies a more general argument made by Winter. He attempted to show that even if a unique maximum exists, under plausible conditions the maximizing firms may not be able actually to reach the maximum. The adjustment process may be either too slow relative to offsetting factors such as the immigration rate of other firms, or the process may even itself undermine the topography being climbed.

8.1.6. Addressing Friedman's 'As If' Argument

Given the number of significant points raised by Winter, it is worth considering where the main critical thrust lies. Arguably, the first aim of Winter's critique is to first identify the (restrictive) set of conditions under which the selection of maximizers could work. This set is then compared with plausible conditions in the real world, to examine the degree of

---

[9] Winter (1964) does not distinguish between cases of increasing returns related to learning phenomena, and those related to a given cost function. In either case his argument concerning the possible non-selection of maximizers carries weight, even if the particular consequences may be different.

[10] Winter's (1975) discussion of the issues of scale is very brief, and does not restate the propositions concerning decreasing, constant, or increasing returns.

restrictiveness, and to compare with perceived 'behavioral realism'. This interpretation of Winter's (1964) article is confirmed more clearly by later works such as Winter (1971) and Nelson and Winter (1982).

Clearly this particular type of argument must (initially) take the cases most favourable to Friedman, and could not rely upon anomalies such as 'multiple adaptive peaks' (see below). Neither could it rest upon Winter's nevertheless important idea (noted above) that there may be economically feasible processes which do not lead to the selection of maximizers, due to frequency dependence effects.

One major difficulty, however, is that Friedman does not make his underlying assumptions clear, neither does Winter attempt to spell all of them out in detail. In particular, Winter seems to assume without further discussion that Friedman implies a rather simplistic 'hill-climbing' notion of maximization.

The 'restrictive conditions' critique leads Winter (1964) to attempt to demonstrate that the selection of maximizers will not occur in the normally-assumed case of decreasing returns, but only in the rather special case of constant returns. This would imply that Friedman has to assume constant returns to make his argument work. It is shown below, however, that Winter's argument is fallacious, and that the selection of maximizers works best in the case of decreasing returns. An aim of this present chapter is to attempt to discover the valid cases and to correct this error. However, a search for valid cases must consider a fairly broad canvas of alternatives. It is shown that the more plausible conditions under which maximization is most likely to occur are not actually identified in Winter's (1964) paper.

A second theme taken up here is to show that a thread of Winter's argument leads to an even more penetrating critique of Friedman's defence of maximization. This thread starts at the point of Winter's distinction between rules of action and action itself. It is suggested below that the pressing problem of the specification of the precise rules of action that could be appropriately associated with maximizing behaviour is highly problematic. Consequently, a fundamental criticism of Friedman's argument is that it is incompletely specified; it assumes that the substance and procedures of maximizing behaviour are self-evident when in fact they are not. This argument ties up with recent critical reflections on the nature of rationality, coming from game theory and elsewhere.

8.2. UNDER WHAT CONDITIONS DOES EVOLUTION FAVOUR THE SELECTION OF HILL-CLIMBING MAXIMIZERS?

8.2.1. The General Question of Returns to Scale

We have already noted that Friedman (1953) is very vague about how maximizers are selected in an evolutionary process. Neither does Winter give a clear explanation of what 'maximizing behaviour' means. In this context it seems reasonable to start with the simplest possible assumption and take agents as naive 'hill-climbing' maximizers. In other words, if they are on a slope they go up it, without any anticipation of where it may lead, or of what may be the effect of such an action. Such agents make no broader examination of the topography or anticipate its movements: there is no question of rational expectations or of intelligent foresight. This is a highly limited assumption, but our first concern is to examine the internal logic of Friedman's argument and Winter's critique and for that reason it is initially adopted here. The assumption is relaxed in the following section of this chapter.

Discussion shall also be postponed of how agents 'know' the slope of the hill, given that they do not necessarily have information even about their immediate environs. This raises more general questions about access to information and the nature of rational behaviour which are also discussed later.

In conventional theory, it is the absolute profit level, not the profit rate or any other profit ratio, that is maximized. Winter (1964, p. 243) likewise considered this 'profit maximizing competitive firm of traditional theory.' As Winter was attempting an internal critique of neoclassical theory, then this was a reasonable assumption. The heights of the landscape in which hills are being climbed is thus assumed to correspond to the absolute levels of profit.

Note also that a 'maximizing firm' is not necessarily one which has attained a maximum, but one which is behaving according to the strict and naive hill-climbing rule. Non-maximizing firms are simply firms which do not obey this rule, even if they are in a superior situation, or have 'better' behavioural rules. However, equilibrium thinking is so ingrained that economists persistently confuse a behaviourally maximizing firm with one that has attained a maximum. Consequently, we shall use the term 'hill-climbing' to describe this kind of naive 'maximizing' behaviour.

There are no barriers to entry. However, in the discussions of evolutionary selection in this section, it shall be assumed that some firms 'die' and new ones enter or are 'born', but that neither their characteristics nor the overall population change sufficiently to give rise to the special evolutionary anomalies discussed in the preceding section. Such anomalies are excluded in order to attempt to identify the (limited) circumstances in which Friedman's 'natural selection' argument could actually work.

Initially, we consider cases involving monotonic returns to scale, and with 'well behaved' production functions. For simplicity of exposition, we shall also assume that market competition is such to produce a linear marginal revenue curve for each firm.

8.2.2. Constant Returns to Scale

Consider first the case of constant returns to scale with fixed proportions. In this instance, of course, marginal and average costs are identical. Cost and revenue functions are both described in scale space by upward-sloping straight lines through the origin. However, market conditions will determine whether the cost line is above or below the one describing revenue. The profits function will thus also be linear and pass through the origin, but it may be of positive, negative or zero slope. Accordingly, profits will always be in direct proportion to the scale of the firm.

If revenue exceeds cost then the larger firms will reap a greater total profit, and in these circumstances a group of smaller hill-climbers may be less successful than larger firms which behave differently. Conversely, if cost exceeds price then all firms will have an incentive to contract in order to minimise losses, and smaller firms may be able to hang on while larger and furiously contracting hill-climbers – with their bigger losses – may go bankrupt. Clearly, it is not guaranteed that the hill-climbers will be favoured.

What happens if equilibrium is reached before the population of firms comes to consist of hill-climbers alone? Being a competitive equilibrium, this means that prices and quantities have adjusted to the point where profits are zero for every surviving firm, whatever its level of output. Given constant returns, the profits function will necessarily be flat and zero profits will be obtained for all levels of scale. No group or type of firms will be better or worse off than any others. Clearly, the equilibrium will be stable, no adjustment will take place, and there will be no further evolutionary selection of hill-climbers. Winter's proposition that hill-climbers will be selected with constant returns is thus invalid, under both disequilibrium and equilibrium conditions.

Now consider random or other exogenously determined slight variations in revenue or cost. One limitation of Winter's (1964) presentation was that he simply considered static rather than variable functions of revenue and cost. In fact, these may vary because of perturbations in overall demand or in the conditions of production facing a firm or group of firms. Generally, such variations are important in an evolutionary paradigm.

Such perturbations may cause the line describing the relationship between profits and scale to shift from a positive to a negative slope, or vice-versa. Even if this shift is small, the scale at which profits are maximized (or losses minimised) will switch from one extreme end of the feasible range to another. In these particular circumstances, hill-climbers chasing optimal conditions will have to expand or contract rapidly in scale. Under such variable conditions there is no obvious reason why the violently fluctuating hill-climber should be at an advantage compared with an inertia-driven firm of an intermediate and more-or-less-fixed scale, even if the costs of expansion or contraction are ignored.

There is another important conclusion that follows from consideration of such fluctuating conditions. If there are advantages from large-scale production then hill-climbers will rapidly expand in size. The market could then become flooded and the price forced down to cost. If there is some inertia or adjustment delay in the system then the price may fall below costs and all firms will make a loss and the larger losses must be associated with the larger-sized firms. (Recollect that under the constant returns assumption the profits function with respect to scale is always a straight line passing through the origin.) Hence the relative advantage will then shift to small scale production because the losses will be smaller in absolute terms. The rush of hill-climbers to contract will eventually starve the market, and the consequent increase in prices and revenue could cause the advantage to shift back to large scale production once again.

As the textbook analysis of the cobweb cycle makes clear, the damping and stabilization of such fluctuations is not inevitable. Furthermore, studies of the behaviour of such systems show that random disturbances could perpetually upset such a gravitation towards stability even if it existed (Allen, 1988; Crutchfield *et al*, 1982). Too zealous searching and maximization may be destructive for the population as a whole. Of course, such problems can arise in more complicated cases, and without constant returns.

Consider the existence of a significant proportion of habit-ridden and slow-to-adjust firms that do not hill-climb. The greater the significance of such a stabilising subset, the less violent the overall fluctuations in output quantity and price. Although such fluctuations could accelerate the selection of hill-climbers, the general conditions for each individual hill-climber may be improved if surrounded by a significant number of sluggish firms. We reach the important conclusion that the evolutionary selection of hill-climbers may be aided or enabled by the existence of a number of firms which are not so responsive to their circumstances.[11]

8.2.3. Non-Constant Returns to Scale

We now turn to the case of decreasing returns to scale. Here also Winter's argument is fallacious. Hill-climbers will search for the level of output at which overall profit is greatest, and by chance they may inhabit this peak with others. However, changing cost and revenue conditions will cause shifts in the position of this optimum, creating conditions where the hill-climbers respond and the others can be weeded out. The effectiveness of this weeding process will depend upon the degree of variation in the cost and profit conditions faced by firms. With this caveat, and contrary to Winter, the selection of hill-climbers in standard models is less problematic under decreasing returns to scale.

However, in the case of increasing returns Winter's argument is valid. For completeness, we may go further than both Nelson and Winter and consider the implications of non-monotonic returns. Clearly, under such conditions the profit function may have several maxima. In biological jargon there is the possibility of a 'multiplicity of adaptive peaks on a fitness surface', as noted by the biologist Sewall Wright (1956) long ago. In these circumstances the selection process may lead to the congregation of units around a local, rather than the global, maximum. With a multiplicity of adaptive peaks the path followed and thus the peak obtained is path

---

[11] This is reminiscent of the fisheries model of Allen and McGlade (1987) in which individual fishing boats are divided into maximizing 'Cartesians' who move to places which are most likely to yield fish on the basis of information available, and 'Stochasts' who take risks and search randomly. Given that a fleet composed entirely of Cartesians would over-fish specific locations and be unlikely to find new ones without the help of some wandering Stochasts, Allen and McGlade conclude that a mixture of Cartesians and Stochasts is overall more productive than a pure population of maximizers. A similar case is the model developed by Conlisk (1980). After assuming that optimizing behaviour is relatively costly, he finds that a mixed population of rational optimizers and slavish imitators can evolve to an equilibrium still involving a mixture of both types. Allen and McGlade's analysis, however, does not depend on such relative costs, but on the assumption of limited resources with an unknown spatial distribution.

dependent: a result of history. It is thus possible, for example, for a group of non-climbers to be congregated around the global maximum, while the hill-climbers are busy climbing an inferior peak, unaware of greater heights elsewhere.[12]

The above discussion yields eight cases pertaining to the nature of returns to scale. These may be represented as follows:

	Stochastic Perturbations of Cost or Revenue Functions?	
	No	Yes
Decreasing Returns	(1)	(2)
Constant Returns	(3)	(4)
Increasing Returns	(5)	(6)
Non-Monotonic Returns	(7)	(8)

Winter discussed cases (1), (3) and (5) only. He concluded that the selection of hill-climbers is favoured simply in case (3). In contrast, it has been argued here that there are strong reasons – relating to the scale conditions – why the selection of hill-climbers may be confounded in all cases except (2).

8.2.4. Another Restrictive Condition and a Reprise

In economics, the case of perfect competition excludes frequency dependence, because each new entrant to the market by definition has no significant effect on prices. More realistically, however, firms or economic agents have market power, as the case of oligopoly. Schaffer (1989) considered a situation where firms have the choice of either maximizing profits or behaving 'spitefully' by using their market power. In the latter case the firm is not profit maximizing but is hurting the profit maximizing firms more than it hurts itself.

---

[12] Analogous problems of multiple equilibria are now familiar in general equilibrium and game theory.

With these assumptions it can be shown that profit maximization is not an evolutionary stable strategy (Maynard Smith, 1982), and can be driven out by the spiteful firms. Schaffer's argument suggested that either perfect competition, or restrictive cases of imperfect competition which exclude 'spite', must be added to the list of conditions which must apply before the evolutionary selection of maximizers is likely.

The result is that the set of assumptions under which the selection of 'hill-climbing' maximizers is likely is highly restrictive. Something like perfect competition must prevail. Selection works best under decreasing returns, but only if there are sufficient perturbations of the cost or revenue functions to 'shake out' the non-climbers. However, the perturbations must not be so great as the process of selection is violently disrupted. Other disruptive effects must also be avoided: for instance the number of new miscellaneous entrants must be limited so that the selection of hill-climbers is not swamped. In sum, the Friedmanite assumption of 'natural selection' of hill-climbing maximizers is hazardous, and in general untenable.

8.3. THE DECONSTRUCTION OF RATIONALITY

We may now discuss some ostensibly more sophisticated notions of maximizing behaviour. Given that mere hill-climbing behaviour does not necessarily lead to optimal or lasting results, the possibility of more complex search and optimization routines and rational expectations should be considered.

There are some models in which rational, optimizing behaviour is selected in an evolutionary process. Hansson and Stuart (1990) see preferences arising out of evolutionary selection and Ursprung (1988) relates standard assumptions of economic rationality to genetic fitness. However, both these approaches rely on a conception of evolution which excludes the regeneration of novelty or variety. Furthermore, the constructed preference functions eliminate radical uncertainty in the sense of Knight or Keynes (concerning events to which no calculable probability may be attributed).

Without the regeneration of novelty or variety, a modelled selection process may often find some line of finality or equilibrium as an asymptote. Although equilibrium is possible in an evolutionary process, it could always be disrupted by sufficient disturbances and sources of renewed variety. The attainment of equilibrium means that the knowledge held by (simulated or real) agents leads to mutually consistent behaviours. In other words, an evolutionary learning algorithm produces equilibrium only when all agents act as if they have nothing more to learn.

Goldberg (1975) drew similar conclusions. He argued that optimizing approaches to decisions cannot succeed in the longer run because the assumption of an (eventually) constant decision environment does not hold up. Hence there is always an argument for a diversity of responses, and the keeping of options open. Similarly, Cooper (1989) argued that the classical theory of rational choice relies on static assumptions, the notion of an eventually constant decision environment, and the idea of global rationality, all of which are challenged by evolutionary theory.

8.2.5. Search Routines and Rational Expectations

We now consider some particular cases, such as the possibility of the 'natural selection' of firms which have rational expectations. To presume a process involving their evolutionary selection, rational expectations must be assumed on behalf of a subset of firms only. However, this creates problems, because those with rational expectations must have some notion of how all agents are going to behave, including non-maximizers or those without rational expectations. This is the issue – examined extensively in game theory – of the existence or non-existence of 'common knowledge of rationality'.

As Haltiwanger and Waldman (1985, 1991) demonstrate, if agents are heterogeneous in regard to behavioural algorithms or computational capacities then the behaviour of the more 'rational' can be confounded. It is possible for either 'sophisticated' or 'naive' information processors to have disproportionate effects on the system as a whole. Their argument not only undermines the standard conclusions of the rational expectations model, but also rehabilitates adaptive or other 'less rational' processes of expectations formation (Heiner, 1989).

Second, in such a world of complex topography the basic functions are bound to be non-linear. As Grandmont and Malgrange (1986) and others have argued, this confounds the rational expectations model still further by introducing the possibility of chaotic behaviour. Even if agents are aware of the basic underlying model of the economy, chaotic systems are so vulnerable to any slight error or perturbations that extended prediction or reliable expectations-formation is impossible.

8.2.6. Imitation, Strategy and the Question of the Maximand

As noted above, for evolutionary selection to work behaviour must be related to the genotypical aspect, i.e. relatively ingrained routine. Although selection works directly on phenotypes, evolutionary development must relate to underlying genotypical forms. Thus the key question is not 'will maximizing behaviour be selected?' but 'will routines giving rise to maximization become dominant through repeated selection?' It is necessary to examine the routines giving rise to such behaviour and not simply the behaviour itself. As Simon (1959, p. 255) argued: 'to predict the short run behaviour of an adaptive organism, or its behaviour in a complex and rapidly changing environment, it is not enough to know its goals. We must also know a great deal about its internal structure and particularly its mechanisms of adaptation'.[13]

It has often been observed that firms cannot know any cost or revenue curves directly. Such information must either be obtained from data divulged by other firms, or by imitation and trial and error. To search for higher profits, a firm must either develop a strategy that takes account of expectations of changing market conditions in the future, or it must take a sample of other firms, obtain data concerning their characteristics and performance, and imitate those that are expected to perform better in the future. To some extent, of course, imitative and strategic behaviour can be combined.

Strict maximization could plausibly involve a high degree of imitative behaviour, searching through a sample of close competitors in order to obtain information that could lead to incremental improvements in performance. However, a problem with slavish imitation of others is that it may lead to a situation of market overcrowding and frequency dependence effects.

Furthermore, by definition, imitative behaviour is reactive, depending upon information and perceptions which relate to the past. Additionally, time is required before a firm can adjust. What seems profitable now may not be so in the future. Imitative behaviour does not embody anticipatory moves, unless an anticipatory algorithm is part of the repertoire of the firm being imitated. Although some elements of imitation are useful and inevitable, as Schumpeter (1934, 1976) argued the most successful firms are

---

[13] Responding to this, Winter (1971) proposed a theoretical model of firm behaviour, dominated by routinised decision rules, that is apparently consistent with empirical evidence.

often those that are pro-active and entrepreneurial, and by luck or careful strategy occupy a profitable niche in time to reap the benefits.

In sum, it is not altogether obvious what 'maximizing behaviour' means in this context. Out-of-equilibrium maximization remains an ill-defined concept. Friedman's loose definition is far from adequate, and with hindsight Winter's discussion of the attributes of maximization seems over-restrictive. What is established, is that with all the notions of maximization discussed so far in this chapter, there are good reasons to doubt that evolutionary processes of selection will generally favour such 'maximizing' firms.

In the simple optimization models of standard theory, information concerning payoffs is obtainable without cost. However, with imperfect and costly information, full optimization is not possible. Winter (1964, p. 264) had began to reveal some of the problems, writing: 'at some levels of analysis, all goal seeking behavior is satisficing behavior. There must be limits to the range of possibilities explored, and those limits must be arbitrary in the sense that the decision maker cannot *know* that they are optimal.' Furthermore, 'an optimization whose scope covers all considerations including its own costs . . . sounds like it may involve the logical difficulties of self-reference' (Winter, 1975, p. 83). These problems have subsequently been explored by John Conlisk (1980, 1996) and others. The literature on costly optimization produces a crucial anomaly: 'The paradoxical difficulty facing the consumer when optimizing is costly is that it is not possible to make an optimal choice and know that the choice made is optimal' (Pingle, 1992, p. 8).

When we move from a static and known world to a dynamic and uncertain one then a Pandora's Box of anomalies and difficulties for the standard conception of rationality is opened. The fact that the precise meaning of 'maximizing behaviour' is unclear in an evolutionary context becomes obvious if an attempt is made to simulate the phenomena discussed here on a computer. Do such optimizers maximize their search range, and/or their flexibility and adaptability, and/or their propensity to divulge information? If a combination of these attributes is involved, what is the precise mixture? Can maximizing behaviour be captured by a genetic algorithm (Goldberg, 1989; Holland, 1986)? Or does maximization mean strategic or pro-active behaviour of some type, and/or entrepreneurial flair and eccentricity?

A clearer and more adequate definition of maximization in such a context is yet to be found in the literature. Evidently, there should be alternatives to the super-optimizer of neoclassical theory and the aimless wanderer of some evolutionary simulations. Perhaps the recent literature on artificial intelligence (Cohen, 1985; Davis and Lenat, 1982; Michalski *et al*, 1986; Tanimoto, 1987) and its application to economic modelling will provide some insights here.

The key point, however, is that the above investigations move us from equilibrium, and involve considerations of learning by agents. Crucially, what is meant by 'rational learning' is not at all clear or self-evident. There may be attempted answers to this question, such as Bayesian learning, but none is uncontentious or without its own problems.[14] Pushed to the limits, in the kind of disequilibrium situations investigated by Winter, the erstwhile consensus over the meaning of 'rationality' disappears.

8.4. CONCLUDING OBSERVATIONS

For the reasons given here it would be rash to assume that 'natural selection' will generally lead to maximizing firms, as Friedman and others have presumed. It has been pointed out above that such propositions often flow from an incomplete specification of evolutionary mechanisms and processes, or from now discredited versions of evolutionary theory.

Winter (1964) focused on several types of selection 'anomaly'.[15] For example, new entrants to the industry may confound the assumed selection process. If there are strong feedback effects between units and their environment, the selection of maximizers may be further disrupted. In such cases, Winter's critique is supported by recent theoretical work in biology.

Winter (1975, p. 99) conceded that the 'natural selection argument does provide some support for the "as if" optimization approach', but under limited assumptions. It has been shown here, however, that the plausible basis for this approach is in the case of decreasing returns with random perturbations, and not constant returns as Winter asserted. Orthodox theory is quite happy with decreasing returns, but it remains to be seen whether persistent 'random perturbations' may prove disruptive for that theory, for the normal focus is on smooth transitions to equilibria.

---

[14] As Hey (1981) demonstrates, a process of Bayesian learning in search of an optimum depends upon the assumption of correct prior knowledge. Accordingly such search models may break down if such an assumption does not apply.

[15] For a discussion of several kinds of selection anomaly see Hodgson (1991b; 1993b, ch. 13).

It has been shown that in an evolutionary context the very idea of 'maximizing behaviour' is highly problematic. If the rational agent has full information about the world and the future and its opportunities, then the notion of maximization is relatively straightforward. However, out of equilibrium, in a processional or evolutionary context, and with true uncertainty and much ignorance, the idea of maximization is difficult to specify, at least in a single and indisputable sense. As George Shackle (1967, p. 295) put it: 'Perfect rationality belongs only to the timeless equilibrium in which all actions conform to a general simultaneous solution of the pooled statements of the tastes and resources of all participants.'

It is no accident that similar concerns about the very specification of rationality have arisen in game theory, especially in repeated games and when attempting to theorise the behaviour of a rational agent dealing with a population of other agents amongst which some (small number) may be irrational (Binmore, 1987; 1988; Varoufakis, 1990). Further, as Sugden (1990, p. 89) argued, 'game theory may rest on a concept of rationality that is ultimately little more than a convention'. He wrote elsewhere:

> There was a time, not long ago, when the foundations of rational-choice theory appeared firm, and when the job of the economic theorist seemed to be one of drawing out the often complex implications of a fairly simple and uncontroversial system of axioms. But it is increasingly becoming clear that these foundations are less secure than we thought, and that they need to be examined and perhaps rebuilt. Economic theorists may have to become as much philosophers as mathematicians. (Sugden, 1991, p. 783)

Likewise, as Giovanni Dosi and Massimo Egidi (1991, p. 151) show, with changing and uncertain environments 'the very notion of "optimality" becomes an ambiguous theoretical notion.' Indeed, much earlier, Alchian (1950, p. 211) had pointed out that 'where foresight is uncertain, "profit maximization" is *meaningless* as a guide to specifiable action.' Given the problems raised with both the definition and operationalization of notions such as 'rationality' and 'maximizing behaviour', it appears that the onus is now on the supporters of the 'natural selection' argument to provide a more precise idea of the meaning of such behaviour in such circumstances.

We ought to be reminded that several decades ago, the management theorist Peter Drucker (1955, p. 59) warned that any formal set of rules aimed at profit maximization for the firm would almost certainly be defective. We may be able to identify a range of factors which contribute to long-run profits, but because of the complexity of firm–environment interactions these cannot be modelled with any precision.

The present chapter underscores the importance of agent–environment interactions, the need to be specific about behavioural and selection mechanisms, and the sensitivity of selection to initial conditions. Notably, evolutionary theory in economics is paying much heed to developments in catastrophe and chaos theory, and promises to further our understanding of complex socio-economic systems. This does not mean that prediction or analysis in economics is necessarily obsolete, but that more attention must be given to the generative structures and mechanisms that govern economic transformation and change.

Strangely, the invocation of the 'natural selection' argument by Friedman and others is not used to bolster an evolutionary approach to the understanding of economic problems, but profit maximization along traditional lines. As well as the obvious problem of mixing the biological and the mechanical metaphors, the procedure itself is open to question. As Koopmans (1957, pp. 140–41) remarked, if evolutionary selection is the basis for a belief in profit maximization, 'then we should postulate that basis itself and not the profit maximization which it implies in certain circumstances.' Usefully, modern evolutionary theory immediately suggests a variety of circumstances in which the validity of the maximization idea is under strain. Only further detailed theoretical investigation can tell us more.

PART FOUR

Evolutionary Theories of the Firm

9. Transaction Costs and the Evolution of the Firm

The classic article on 'the nature of the firm' by Nobel Laureate Ronald Coase (1937, p. 386) opens with the following sentence: 'Economic theory has suffered in the past from a failure to state clearly its assumptions.' This present chapter is not only a plea for precision of language in the theory of the firm. It is also argued that there are conceptual problems with the 'new institutionalist' theory of the firm advanced by Oliver Williamson (1975, 1985), relating to its individualist mode of analysis and its implicit but still underdeveloped evolutionism.[1]

After some general remarks about the transaction cost theories of Coase and Williamson, the argument in this chapter proceeds in the following steps:

1) Following earlier work by Carl Dahlman (1979), Richard Langlois (1984) and myself (Hodgson, 1988, ch. 9), it is reiterated here that the concept of transaction costs must refer in the main to problems of radical uncertainty and lack of knowledge.
2) It is argued that the informational substance of transaction costs implies that the concept cannot be simultaneously combined with both the notion of omniscient calculation and Herbert Simon's idea of bounded rationality.
3) Hence, given transaction costs, retaining the concept of bounded rationality means the rejection of the idea of omniscient calculation. But this then means that we are in want of an explanation as to why a

---

[1] This chapter is a revised version of Hodgson (1993c).

governance structure associated with lower transaction costs should generally predominate over another.

4) Accordingly, a comparative statics analysis is ruled out, and exponents of exclusively transaction cost explanations would seem forced to rely on the only alternative mode of explanation: the supposed evolutionary selection of the cost-minimising firms.

5) However, an evolutionary analysis poses a problem as to whether the individual or the firm is the unit of selection, and this is related to the 'appropriability critique' of Gregory Dow (1987).

6) To protect against the appropriability critique, the firm itself must be regarded as a unit of selection, rather than the individuals within it.

7) The most viable arguments for regarding the firm as such a collective entity bring us closer to the propositions of the 'old' rather than the 'new' institutionalism.

8) Furthermore, the evolutionary framework of analysis does not give support to some key propositions concerning hierarchy and efficiency advanced by Williamson.

The conclusion is that it might be more fruitful to examine the firm with some of the presuppositions of the 'old' institutionalist tradition, emanating in particular from the work of Thorstein Veblen and John Commons, in which the assumption of the given, hedonistic individual is abandoned.

9.1. TRANSACTION COSTS AND FIRMS

9.1.1. The Coasean Argument

The famous work of Coase (1937) did not only include an explanation of why firms exist, but it also (and necessarily) made a conceptual distinction between the firm and the market. For Coase the key feature of the firm is its internal 'supersession of the price mechanism' (p. 389) and the allocation of resources by command rather than through price. The question as to why firms exist then becomes the question as to why it is that the price mechanism is not used to allocate resources within the area of production taken over by the firm. For instance, why is it not normally the case that each worker, or group of workers, trades the semi-finished product with colleagues, until it reaches completion? Instead, the firm supplants such a mechanism by organizing relations differently, without such exchanges. As Coase (1937, p. 388) put it:

Within a firm, these market transactions are eliminated and in place of the complicated market structure with exchange transactions is substituted the entrepreneur-co-ordinator, who directs production.

Coase (1937, pp. 390–1) then argued that:

The main reason why it is profitable to establish a firm would seem to be that there is a cost of using the price mechanism. . . . It is true that contracts are not eliminated when there is a firm but they are greatly reduced. A factor of production (or the owner thereof) does not have to make a series of contracts with the factors with whom he is co-operating within the firm, as would be necessary, of course, if this co-operation were as a direct result of the working of the price mechanism.

Following on from this approach, Williamson (1985, p. 1) has developed his central thesis that economic institutions such as the firm 'have the main purpose and effect of economizing on transaction costs'. Thus Williamson's explanation of the existence of non-market institutions is that they arise because they are less costly than continuous recourse to the market or exchange. Thus he too endorses a conceptual difference between the market itself and the non-market institution of the firm.

9.1.2. The Concept of the Firm

All the foregoing is familiar, but even at this preliminary level there are some possibilities of misinterpretation. Consider the argument raised by Frederick Fourie (1989, p. 145):

Although there is no consensus on exactly what a firm is, the management of some *production* or distribution process appears to be central to the firm. Consider, however, that a market, unlike a firm, cannot produce. . . . If this is true, markets and firms are not alternative modes of production, but are inherently and essentially dissimilar.

Unfortunately, this is a misreading of Coase's argument. Note first, that by a 'firm', Coase and Fourie mean different things. Coase himself is partly responsible for this confusion, as shown in the following chapter. While towards the end of his essay Coase (1937, pp. 403–4) does talk specifically about the employment relationship, fifty years later Coase (1988) negated this emphasis and saw the essence of the firm in terms of organizational coordination.

Contrary to Fourie, while the management of production is central to the firm, production does not always involve firms in Coase's sense. For Coase, the firm involves the organization and coordination of multiple agents; the firm is essentially a multiple-person agency. In contrast, it is possible to conceive of ways of organizing production other than under the rubric of the firm. The obvious case is the market-coordinated community of self-employed producers, in which individual producers also trade their products directly on the market.

Nowhere does Coase (or Williamson) suggest or imply that the self-employed producer can constitute a firm; clearly, by the firm, he has multiple-person entities in mind. Fourie, contrary to Coase, saw the self-employed producer as an example of a 'firm', and as a result their argument is at cross purposes. For Fourie, production *always* involves firms. In contrast, Coase conceives of the firm in terms of an organization encompassing at least one person. Hence it is quite reasonable for Coase to advance the proposition that the market is an *alternative* way of organizing production to the firm. At least two alternatives are possible: there can be a community of self-employed producers organized by the market, or there can be a capitalist firm organizing the same segment of productive activity through an employment relationship. Essentially, Fourie's 'criticism' stems from a different definition of 'the firm'. To avoid confusion, we must adopt either Fourie's or Coase's terminology: we cannot have both.[2]

For clarity, when we refer to the firm it should always be in terms of an enduring productive organization of two or more persons. With this definition of the firm, it is evident that all active firms engage in production, but not all production need involve firms.

A special case is 'the capitalist firm'. In *Capital,* Karl Marx saw this as an institution involving an employment relationship between a capitalist and his employees. Marx, like Coase, contrasted the capitalist firm with the world of self-employed producers. When using concrete examples, Coase

---

[2] Pitelis (1991, p. 52) correctly identifies the contentious question here as being 'whether single producers qualify as firms', this depending crucially on the definition of the firm 'one is willing to adopt'. However, Fourie's criticism has found its supporters, including Dietrich (1991, pp. 41–2) who wrote that: 'to assert that firms *replace* markets, as Coase does . . . suggests that trading can take place without production and distribution (i.e. without firms), which is clearly impossible.' Dietrich, like Fourie, saw production as inextricably linked to 'the firm', ignoring the fact that by 'the firm' Coase means a multiple-person organization, and disregarding the possibility of (non-firm) productive units consisting of single persons.

and Williamson wrote mainly about capitalist firms, but their analysis would seemingly apply to *any* firm involving *multiple* agents, organized together in some manner – hierarchical, cooperative, participatory, or whatever – but not through the market. In its most general form, the Coase–Williamson transaction costs analysis addresses all such (multiple-agent) firms, but not the single, self-employed producer.

It is also clear that Coase (1937) is comparing the capitalist firm as a system for organizing production with a system of market-coordinated, self-employed producers. Consequently, the Coasean explanation of the nature of the firm points to the higher transaction costs involved in the market-coordinated mode.

This leads to another issue in the post-Coasean literature. Coase made a straightforward comparison between the organization of production through a series of market contracts and the organization of production under the rubric of the firm.[3] Inspired by Coase, Williamson went further by comparing different kinds of firm 'governance structures' in terms of their supposed relative efficiency. For Williamson and others, the transaction costs idea is not used simply to compare a market-coordinated system of production with a firm-coordinated one, but to compare different types of firm, be they hierarchical, participatory, U-form, M-form, or whatever. This would not be so problematic if the concept of transaction costs was clearly defined. But unfortunately, as discussed in the next section, it is not.

9.1.3. The Concept of Transaction Costs

The concept of transaction costs seems to elude clear definition. As such, the term does not actually appear in Ronald Coase's original (1937) article. Robert Clower (1969) argued that the reduction of 'bargaining costs' is the main factor determining the relative efficiency of a monetary over a barter economy. The first use of the term 'transaction cost' was apparently by H. B. Malmgren (1961, p. 401). Another early appearance was in an article by Kenneth Arrow (1969, p. 48) where he referred to transactions costs as the 'costs of running the economic system'. Yet the term was not clearly explicated or defined.

Despite using the term extensively, Williamson has still failed to provide an adequate definition of transaction costs. It is not that he ignores the

---

[3] Coase (1988, p. 47) made it clear that his 1937 article was intended to compare the firm with the market, rather than firms with firms: 'I did not investigate the factors that would make the costs of organizing lower for some firms than for others.'

problem. In one article it is noted that 'the concept wants for definition' (Williamson, 1979, p. 233) but he then proceeds not to define the term, but to list a set of 'factors' which relate to this mode of analysis. These 'factors' include sundry observations such that 'opportunism is especially important for economic activity that involves transaction-specific investments', and that 'the assessment of transaction costs is a comparative institutional undertaking'. He then went on to note: 'Beyond these general propositions, a consensus on transaction costs is lacking.' But Williamson does not help to generate such a consensus under the illumination of a clear definition. Given this lack of clarity with regard to a core concept, it is not surprising that Stanley Fischer (1977, p. 322 n.) wrote:

> Transaction costs have a well-deserved bad name as a theoretical device, because solutions to problems involving transaction costs are often sensitive to the assumed form of the costs, and because there is a suspicion that almost anything can be rationalized by invoking suitably specified transaction costs.

Similarly, Dahlman (1979, p. 144) notes that the idea of transaction costs 'has become a catch-all phrase for unspecified interferences with the price mechanism'. Furthermore, as Dahlman pointed out, the typical formal representation of transaction costs among mathematical economists, as a proportion of the value of the goods that are exchanged, differs in no significant way from a regular transportation cost. This hardly seems to be a sound innovation upon which an economic theory of institutions can be based.

9.1.4. Transaction Costs and Lack of Information

Overall, Dahlman offered us a useful lead into the further analysis of transaction costs. He suggested that three types of cost are involved, corresponding to three different, sequential phases of the exchange process, namely: 'search and information costs, bargaining and decision costs, policing and enforcement costs.' However, 'this functional taxonomy of different transaction costs is unnecessarily elaborate: fundamentally, the three classes reduce to a single one – for they all have in common that they represent resource losses due to lack of information' (Dahlman, 1979, p. 148).

It can be accepted that for purposes of theoretical clarification, Dahlman's argument is an important step forward; but many problems still remain and it is not entirely clear what a complete reduction of costs to those of information could mean. Indeed it could be fitted neatly into a neoclassical framework. Following the lead of George Stigler's classic (1961) article, search and information costs could be accommodated alongside, and treated similarly to, other costs in a probabilistic framework. In this approach information is treated just like any other commodity, and subject to the marginalist rule that its consumption is optimal when the marginal cost of information search and acquisition is equal to its expected marginal return.

On reflection, however, the very idea of a rational calculus of information costs is open to objection. As Arrow (1962) and others have pointed out, if we lack a piece of relevant information then how can we have any firm expectation of its marginal return? The very fact that the information is lacking means at most that such expectations are hazy and ill-defined. Clearly there is a problem of circularity here.

Furthermore, with such a treatment of information it is not clear why, for informational reasons, market contracting is superseded by the organization of the firm. After all, if information is simply a commodity like any other, there is no apparent special rationale for the firm to act as the minimiser of these information-related, transaction costs. Seemingly it would be possible to deal with such information problems through the due process of contract and trade.

Consider a model of productive organization of individual contractors all trading semi-finished products with each other, and each making marginal adjustments to deal with information costs along the lines proposed by Stigler. What has to be shown in this case is that some kind of economy of information costs can be obtained by organizing the agents together under an institutional umbrella. But it is still not clear why such an institution should be a firm, and not merely an association of producer-traders who pool relevant information.

More specifically, 'search and information costs' could be reduced substantially by a market research agency under contract from the producer-trader association, 'bargaining and decision costs' could be reduced by a team of consultants, and 'policing and enforcement costs' could be brought down by pooling information regarding the credit, performance and other reliability ratings of the agents involved. If informational economies of scale are substantial, why is it that such syndicates of independent producers should not arise to minimise the information costs that they would each face on their own, and thus obviate the need for the firm?

It is not immediately clear that such a syndicate would be more or less efficient than the firm in reducing such costs, but it is clearly more efficient than a mere aggregation of producer-traders. Thus the 'information costs' version of the transaction costs argument still fails to supply a convincing reason for the existence of the firm and for the relative rarity of alternative arrangements, such as the syndicate, in real life.

Not only is the above type of argument ineffective in providing a rationale for the firm, the treatment of information is itself unsatisfactory. There is no distinction given between sense-data, i.e. the jumble of neurological stimuli which reach the brain, and information or knowledge, which involve the imposition of a conceptual framework. There is no regard made to the processes of assessment or computation with given information, which can lead to different conclusions depending on the method of calculation and the cognitive framework. It is well known, for example, that the firm's balance sheet is capable of different interpretations and even different 'bottom line' statements of profit and loss, depending on the interpretations and methodology of the accountant. These examples raise the problem, as Jim Tomlinson (1986, p. 239) pointed out, of treating 'information in a "positivist" manner, i.e. as a set of facts, indifferent to any problems of the conceptual frameworks which are necessarily involved'.

The 'information costs' version of the transaction costs argument does not appear to supply a convincing reason for the existence of the firm and for the relative rarity of alternative arrangements in real life. As Brian Loasby (1976) has argued, there is no need in theory for non-market forms of organization in the general equilibrium model. Even the probabilistic version of general equilibrium theory, which implies information problems of a stylised and limited kind, provides no reason why firms, as such, should exist.

Langlois's (1984) solution to this problem is to make a distinction between different kinds of information problem which parallels Frank Knight's (1921) famous distinction between risk and uncertainty. The essence of the argument is that 'parametric uncertainty' (akin to Knight's 'risk') cannot be used to find the source of transaction costs which are relevant to the explanation of the relative efficiency of organizations such as a firm. A similar argument has been offered by Neil Kay (1984, chs 2–4) who has shown that, in a neoclassical world of perfect knowledge, the firm is stripped of most of its familiar structures and functions. The outcome is the same if problems of probabilistic risk (or 'parametric uncertainty') are introduced, because there 'is a close affinity between perfect knowledge and risk in terms of homogeneity and replicability of associated events.' The argument leads inexorably to the consideration of true or radical uncertainty as an essential concept to understand economic institutions such as the firm.

By emphasising true uncertainty (as opposed to risk), but with different features and qualifications, Loasby, Kay and Langlois are all returning to Knight's *Risk, Uncertainty and Profit* and a core idea in its discussion of the firm that its 'existence in the world is the direct result of the fact of uncertainty' (Knight, 1921, p. 271). An answer to Coase's question as to why firms exist has re-emerged in terms of a non-probabilistic concept of uncertainty. Transaction costs may or may not remain an intermediate category in the argument. But it is clear that transaction costs as a category are not meaningful without some concept of true or radical uncertainty. Following Knight, there is a *prima facie* case for seeing the concept of uncertainty as a necessary – but not sufficient – concept to explain the existence of any kind of firm.

9.1.5. Evolution or Comparative Statics?

If the concept of transaction costs is tied up with the existence of real uncertainty then there are important implications for the type of analysis involved. We may reach the same conclusion by noting Williamson's apparent reliance on Herbert Simon's (1957, 1959) concept of 'bounded rationality'. Williamson (e.g. 1985, p. 32) wrote repeatedly in the following terms: 'Economizing on transaction costs essentially reduces to economizing on bounded rationality'.

Simon's argument, of course, is that a complete or global rational calculation is ruled out, and thus rationality is 'bounded'; agents do not maximize but attempt to attain acceptable minima instead. But it is important to note that this 'satisficing' behaviour does not arise simply because of inadequate information, but also because it would be too difficult to perform the calculations even if the relevant information was available.

Given this point, a prevailing orthodox interpretation of Simon's work, following William Baumol and Richard Quandt (1964), can be faulted. Contrary to this 'cost minimizing' interpretation, bounded rationality refers primarily to the matter of computational capacity and not to additional 'costs'. Simon's concept of 'satisficing' does not amount to cost-minimizing behaviour. Clearly, the latter is just the dual of the standard assumption of maximization; if 'satisficing' was essentially a matter of minimising costs then it would amount to maximizing behaviour of the orthodox type.[4]

---

[4] Thus Jensen and Meckling (1976, p. 307 n.) were in error when they wrote that 'Simon's work has often been misinterpreted as a denial of maximizing behavior . . . His later use of the term "satisficing" . . . has undoubtedly contributed to this confusion because it suggests rejection of maximizing behavior rather than maximization subject to costs of information and decision making.' Indeed, the misinterpretation of Simon's work is Jensen and Meckling's. The term 'satisficing' is employed by Simon precisely to distance his conception from

Hence the term 'economizing on bounded rationality' is misleading and rather incongruous. The word 'economizing' suggests rational, optimizing behaviour that would be inconsistent with 'bounded rationality' in Simon's sense of the term.

Essentially, the Coase–Williamson type of transaction costs analysis involves comparative static comparisons of different types of governance structure.[5] Coase compares the market, viewed as a kind of disorganized governance structure, with the firm. Williamson compares different types of firm structure as well. In each case the reference is to a comparison of transaction costs across two or more equilibrium situations.[6]

It is important to emphasize, however, that if governance structure X is associated with lower transaction costs than governance structure Y this does not itself explain why more X-type governance structures should exist in the real world. Apart from the logical problems with such an argument (Ullmann-Margalit, 1978), there are no omniscient agents doing comprehensive cost calculations. Indeed, given the considerations of bounded rationality, it is impossible for any entrepreneurial agent to perform the cost calculations to identify the lower transaction costs involved with X. Both uncertainty and limited computational capacity prevent such an assessment.

Williamson has a choice. He can either accept or reject the assumption that transaction cost minimisation is assumed to be performed by a deliberative, rational agent within the firm. However, if he accepts this

---

'substantive' rationality and maximizing behaviour. It is symptomatic that Williamson, for example, used the term 'bounded rationality' much more often than 'satisficing'.

5 Nutzinger (1982) points out that the transaction costs associated with each governance structure are not independent of co-existing institutions. Hence the relative efficiency of difference institutions is compared only by making strong *ceteris paribus* assumptions, and in a partial equilibrium framework. Such efficiency comparisons do not have the greater generality of a general equilibrium analysis.

6 Dietrich (1991) argued that the 'transaction benefits' of each governance structure must be taken into account as well as the 'costs'. While this point is valid, it points to another ambiguity in the definition of transaction costs. The term could be defined net (by deducting transaction benefits from costs), or gross (exclusive of transaction benefits). Clearly, the net definition of transaction costs is the one that is relevant to the Coase–Williamson theory of the firm. On the contrary, Dietrich implies that Williamson has a gross definition in mind, but this is not demonstrated by reference to Williamson's work.

assumption he cannot simultaneously embrace the concept of bounded rationality. If 'economizing on transaction costs' is cost-minimising behaviour by a calculating agent, then this is inconsistent with Simon's concept.

In practice, Williamson seems to incline to rationality rather than behaviouralism, at least when it comes to 'choosing' the more efficient governance structure. As Brian Loasby (1990, p. 227) remarks: 'Transactions cost analysis appears to make the choice of administratively rational procedures itself a substantively rational choice.'

It has been argued, however, that the concept of transaction costs is tied up with information problems and uncertainty. Consequently, we cannot dispense with bounded rationality: it is the omniscient, calculating agent that has to go. This creates a further problem. Without anyone knowing the full comparative costs of two governance structures, we lack an explanation of why the governance structure associated with lower transaction costs should predominate over the other. We have comparative statics, but without the means of explaining any real-world process of comparison.

One ostensible means of overcoming this difficulty is to drop the assumption of a fully deliberative agent and situate the analysis in an evolutionary rather than a comparative statics framework. In fact, although Williamson's work is mainly in terms of comparative statics, he alluded to an evolutionary explanation in several passages.[7] However, the invocation of the analogy with natural selection is not accompanied by a detailed explanation of the evolutionary processes and causal linkages involved.

9.2. EVOLUTIONARY SELECTION AND THE FIRM

9.2.1. Are Firms the Units of Evolutionary Selection?

One of the first issues that must be addressed in an evolutionary framework is that of identifying the unit of selection. Clearly, in this context it must be assumed that governance structures are the entities being sifted and selected in the evolutionary process. But this assumption is problematic. Indeed, it

---

[7] For example, Williamson (1985, p. 22–23, 394). Nevertheless, there are adjoining appeals for the development of a 'fully developed theory of the selection process' (1985, p. 23) and statements of the need to assess such propositions 'more carefully' (1985, p. 394 n.).

raises the whole controversial question of the viability of group selection. In biology, 'genetic reductionists' such as Richard Dawkins (1976) argue, along with methodological individualists from the social sciences such as Viktor Vanberg (1986), that the notion of group selection is incoherent.

The prominent biological argument against group selection – endorsed by Dawkins, Vanberg and many others – is that there is no clear mechanism to ensure that an advantageous pattern of behaviour for the group will for some reason be replicated by the actions of the individuals concerned. In particular, such a mechanism must ensure that 'free-riders' do not become dominant in the more productive groups. Free riders would have the benefits of being members of a group whose other members together worked in a more productive manner, but bear no personal costs or risks in terms of self-sacrificial behaviour themselves. Consequently, in the absence of any compensating mechanism, it is likely that free-riders within the group will expand in numbers, crowd out the others, and alter the typical behaviour of the group as a whole. Thus, despite the possible benefits to the group of self-sacrificial behaviour, it appears that there is no mechanism to ensure that groups with these characteristics will prosper above others. What seems crucial is the selection of the constituent individuals and not the groups as a whole.

This is essentially a problem that Gregory Dow raises in his 'appropriability critique' of transaction costs analysis. He wrote:

> A central dogma of transaction cost economics is that only the aggregate cost of a governance structure, and *not* the incidence of those costs among agents, affects the likelihood that the structure will be adopted. . . . Before the efficiency postulate of transaction cost economics can be justified in selection terms, one must come to terms with the fact that selection forces do not act on the costs or benefits experienced by arbitrary social aggregates. These forces operate only through the private payoffs of the entities selected upon, just as natural selection acts only upon individual organisms, rather than for the good of the species or the ecosystem. (Dow, 1987, p. 32–3)

However, the statement that 'natural selection acts only upon individual organisms' is not universally accepted within biology. Indeed, some biologists, such as Dawkins, argue that the gene, not the individual, is the unit of selection. Conversely, many biologists and philosophers of biology argue that several different levels of selection, including group selection, are viable.[8]

Biologists who argue the case for the possibility of group selection do not suggest that group selection will always operate; it depends upon the processes and structures involved. Essentially, group selection is seen to act if all organisms in the same group are 'bound together by a common fate' (Sober, 1981, p. 107). A population of (diverse) units is so interlinked – with externalities and spillover effects between its members – that it is selected upon as an entity.[9]

What if the behaviour of this interlinked group could somehow be explained in terms of the individuals involved? Philosophers of biology such as Elliott Sober (1981) point out that a reductionist explanation in terms of genes – if one were possible – leaves open the question of what causes the gene frequencies themselves to alter. Although all information about ostensible group selection may be reduced to and represented by selection coefficients of organisms or genes, such a formal reduction to the genic or individual level leaves the question unanswered as to what causes the frequency of genes in the gene pool to change. Likewise, we may remark, methodological individualist explanations leave open the questions of the origin or moulding or composition of a population of individuals with their preferences and purposes.

Given the possibility of group selection in biology, it can be conjectured that the same phenomenon might occur in the socio-economic sphere. Considerations of institutions, rules, norms and culture are apposite. Assume that a particular characteristic affects all members of a group to a similar degree, such as the enforcement of different modes of diet, dress or

---

[8] These arguments are reviewed more extensively in Hodgson (1993b).

[9] Accordingly, the process of *competition between firms* may be *endangered* by excessive labour mobility from firm to firm. If competition is to weed out the more efficient firms then this requires stability of the firm as a unit. Movements of individuals from firm to firm confound the competitive selection of firms with higher levels of skill and competence. This is true *a fortiori* if the processes of group and individual learning take a substantial amount of time, or depend on the stability of employment of the personnel in the work groups. The policy conclusion is diametrically opposed to the proposal that labour markets should have to be made more free to improve labour mobility. Instead, the emphasis is on the stability and longevity of the employment relationship, the enhancement of trust and learning, and the promotion of organizational integration to facilitate dynamic growth. This important but neglected argument was put forward by Campbell (1994).

behaviour. Assume further that this characteristic affects the future growth and prosperity of the group. Then there may be grounds for considering that group selection is at work.

9.2.2. Group Selection and the Firm

For the firm to be considered as a unit of selection, similarly appropriate considerations must be involved. There must be something going on within the firm which 'binds its members together by a common fate', as Sober put it. Clearly, all employers and employees within a firm have a stake in its prosperity and survival. However, the appropriability critique is still relevant if the owners of capital or labour power can desert the ailing firm for a more profitable alternative. The viability of these 'exit' options depends upon the state of the labour and capital markets. Their attraction may depend, in part, on asset specificity (Pagano, 1991). Especially with the textbook assumptions of self-seeking individuals and competitive environments, there is little adhesive to bind the members of the firm together. One option, of course, is to abandon the textbook assumptions and examine the firm in a more realistic light.

There are additional reasons why the firm can be considered as a collective or systemic entity. Consider the question of the skills embodied in the firm's routines. As elaborated in Chapter 11 below, Sidney Winter (1982) argued that the capabilities of an organization such as a firm are not generally reducible to the capabilities of individual members.

Clearly, there is an important question here concerning the possibility of collective knowledge. This is a matter of controversy within social theory. For instance, Ward Goodenough (1981, p. 54) wrote that: 'People learn as individuals. Therefore, if culture is learned, its ultimate locus must be in individuals rather than in groups.' In contrast, there is the 'collectivist' position of anthropologists such as Marvin Harris (1971, p. 136), more in accord with that of Winter:

> Cultures are patterns of behavior, thought and feeling that are acquired or influenced through learning and that are characteristic of groups of people rather than of individuals.

Winter and others have argued that although tacit or other knowledge must reside in the nerve or brain cells of a set of human beings, its enactment depends crucially on the existence of a structured context in which individuals interact with each other. Otherwise, no such knowledge can become manifest. Furthermore, because organizational knowledge is tacit knowledge, no individual can express it in a codified form. The knowledge becomes manifest only through the interactive practice of the members of the group.

There are many cases where the organizational knowledge is maintained within a structure, perhaps even for long periods of time, despite the turnover of its individual members. Just as our personal memory of past events is retained, despite the loss and renewal of our brain cells, organizational knowledge may survive the gradual but complete replacement of the individuals comprising the organization.

Clearly both individual and organizational outcomes depend upon the nature of any such organizational knowledge. Here is a clear case of the fates of a number of individuals being bound together in a single group. Such organizational learning is thus feasibly associated with group selection. Organizational knowledge can relate to a subset of the workers within a firm. If the knowledge relates to all the workers in a firm, or crucial aspects of its management, then the organization in which that particular organizational knowledge resides is the firm as a whole.

Consideration of organizational learning has raised the question of culture within the firm. Arguably, an important feature of the firm is the 'trust dynamic' (Fox, 1974) that it engenders between its members. In contrast, in the sphere of the competitive market trust and long-term cooperation, while present to some degree, are undermined by competition between the many different and transient agents. In the market there is a changing and volatile population, where each individual is pursuing his or her objectives largely in accord with the overt calculus of profit and loss. In distinction, opportunistic and self-seeking behaviour is certainly present and significant within the firm, but, contrary to Williamson, it is diminished and kept under check within its boundaries. The firm, by engendering loyalty and trust to some degree, encourages people to act differently. By trust or compulsion, that is by the use of social power, the managers of the firm may succeed in imposing their will on the employees. Without this ability to generate more cohesive and less atomistic behaviour the firm would not be able to function.

Given that capitalism is not a system of slavery, workers, unlike machines, may be hired but not bought. This means that capitalists face the ongoing problem of losing workers with acquired skills. In part, this may explain a relatively greater inclination for firms to invest in machines rather than people (Pagano, 1991, pp. 324–5). In addition, capitalists have an incentive both to provide incentives for workers to remain with the firm, and to engender loyalty and greater social cohesion within the institution.

Hence a key to understanding the nature of the firm is its ability to mould human preferences and actions so that a higher degree of loyalty and trust are engendered. In contrast, following the tradition of individualistic social scientists, Williamson put forward a model of individual human nature (i.e. 'opportunism') and recklessly assumes that this applies equally to quite different forms of institutional arrangement, and that in particular it applies equally and universally to the market and all types of firm (Moschandreas, 1997). No recognition is made of the effect of the institutional environment in moulding actions and beliefs.

Samuel Bowles (1985) has appropriately described the view of the human agent in this individualistic tradition as one of 'malfeasance', with its obsessions with self-seeking behaviour and with derivative phenomena such as 'shirking' at work. In contrast, as Bowles pointed out, the work performance function should not be regarded as exogenously given or as a consequence of immutable 'human nature'. Instead, it is partly a function of the changeable institutions, cultures and power structures involved.

If the firm has the effect of moulding the preference functions of the actors within it, by engendering loyalty and the like, then we cannot explain the firm by an individualistic framework where all preference functions are taken as given whatever the institutional context. Furthermore, the effect of culture on perceptions and preferences may act to bind agents together to some extent in a common group. Even if there are subcultures, involving antagonisms within the firm, the common culture binds the members together as a selectable group. In sum, there are reasons to suggest that the firm may be a (group) unit of selection, but many involve abandoning individualistic theoretical premises.

With endogenous preferences, and in an evolutionary context, the role of the concept of transaction costs is marginalised somewhat.[10] Instead, much more emphasis is put on the role of the firm as a durable social institution, incorporating its own culture, and acting as a protective enclave from market forces (Dore, 1983; Hodgson, 1988; Nelson, 1981b; Teece and Pisano, 1994).

---

[10] Note also Rotemberg's (1991) argument that under certain conditions the internal organization of the firm may be suboptimal, even if the firm is profit maximizing. This also challenges the view that the reason for the existence of the firm is its capacity to reduce transaction costs.

9.2.3. Context Dependence and Suboptimality

Given that an evolutionary framework of analysis is more promising than comparative statics, we may re-examine Williamson's own invocation of evolutionism in his work. Along with his theoretical argument that hierarchy should be more efficient, Williamson frequently appealed to the empirical evidence of the preponderance of hierarchical firms in the real world to support his claim that such firms are more efficient than other types of organization, such as participatory or cooperative firms. He argued that the competitive process has led to the selection of hierarchical firms and for this reason they must be assumed to be more efficient than their rivals.

However, a closer inspection of evolutionary theory undermines Williamson's claim.[11] Even if the 'selected' characteristics of firms were the 'fittest' then they would be so in regard to a particular economic, political and cultural environment only; they might not be the 'fittest' for all circumstances and times. Consider the following illustrative example of a type of context dependence where the chief effect is of the frequency of the population on fitness, called 'frequency dependence' in biology (Lewontin, 1974). Assume two types of firm, Type A and Type B. The population as a whole is a mix of Type A and Type B firms, with the associated culture and inter-firm relations. Given that a new entrant can be of either type, their profits can be given by one of the following formulae:

Profit of Type A entrant firm = 50 + (% of Type B Firms)

Profit of Type B entrant firm = (% of Type B Firms)

Such illustrative profit values can be justified in terms of the different types of organization form and inter-firm relations. For instance, Type B firms can be associated with more open and participatory structures and more cooperative inter-firm behaviour including, for instance, the informal exchange of technical know-how (von Hippel, 1987, 1988). Accordingly, there could be positive externalities associated with firm of such a type.[12]

---

[11] For more extensive discussions of the issue of suboptimality in evolution, with references to both biology and economics, see Hodgson, (1991b, 1993b). For the flavour of the argument from biology see Gould (1978, 1980, 1989), Gould and Lewontin (1979), Oster and Wilson (1978, ch. 8) or Dupré (1987).

[12] In a study of Italian cooperatives, Gherardi and Masiero (1990) argued that the development of a close-knit system of intra-organizational trust relations and networking activities has been crucial to their success.

Assume, first, that the initial (large) population is composed entirely of Type *A* firms. In this case the profit for each Type *A* new entrant will be 50, and for each Type *B* new entrant will be 0. Clearly, Type *B* firms are unlikely to become established if Type *A* firms are dominant. However, if the initial population is composed entirely of Type *B* firms then the profit for each Type *A* new entrant will be 150, and for each Type *B* new entrant will be 100. Consequently, in this case, Type *A* firms can successfully invade the Type *B* population. In sum, Type *A* firms are likely to become or remain dominant, whatever the starting position. This will happen even if average profits are greater in an industry composed entirely of Type *B* firms than one composed entirely of Type *A*. Assume that the above equations apply to all firms, and not simply new entrants. Then the average profits of a Type *A* population will be 50 and of a Type *B* population will be 100. Yet Type *B* firms are always at a relative disadvantage.

Furthermore, if the industry was dominated by Type *B* firms then the situation might not last because new entrants of Type *A* would be at a great advantage in those circumstances. Unless corrective action was taken – such as some arrangement for formal or informal regulation of the industry by the state or by an industrial association – the greater overall benefits related to Type *B* dominance would be eventually undermined and destroyed by incoming Type *A* firms.

This hypothetical example illustrates a number of general points. First, given that pay-offs are dependent on the nature of the industry as a whole, then the selected characteristics likewise depend on the overall environment. Indeed, research on worker cooperatives suggests that their success is highly dependent on the type of financial and cultural regime that prevails in the economy as a whole. (For example, Thomas and Logan, 1982.) Second, 'natural selection' does not necessarily favour the more efficient units, nor always the optimal or near-optimal outcomes. The low density of cooperative or participatory firms in the real world should not be taken to mean that either individual firms of this type, or an industry dominated by them, are necessarily less efficient.

9.2.4. Path Dependence and Suboptimality

The historical evolution of the factory system and the modern firm is not simply a question of the quasi-natural selection of the most efficient organizational forms. Issues of path dependence (Arthur, 1989), as well as context dependence, may be significant. For example, some historical research has suggested that the factory system was influenced at its origin by the military structures of the time: the hierarchical regimentation of the soldiery had its parallel in the similar organization of the workforce.[13]

Charles Sabel and Jonathan Zeitlin (1985) argue on the basis of historical evidence that in Europe there was an alternative path to industrialization based on small-scale firms and flexible specialization. Also looking at the evolution of the factory system, Maxine Berg (1991) compares explanations based on the supposed dictates of technology with the idea of such an alternative road. She concluded that industrialization could have taken many possible pathways and occurred in different sequences. Ugo Pagano (1991, p. 327) considered the two-way and cumulative interaction of technology with property rights, pointing out that: 'In this context, simple efficiency stories may well lose their meaning. Each outcome is likely to be path dependent and inefficient interactions between property rights and technology are likely to characterise the history of economic systems.'

In the context of modern industrial structures, Richard Langlois (1988) argued explicitly that path dependence may be relevant in the evolution of organizational form. Likewise, and contrary to his earlier view, Douglass North (1990) now accepts that path dependent processes also apply to institutions, and therefore the surviving arrangements are not necessarily the most efficient. The issue of path dependence is raised explicitly by Michael Everett and Alanson Minkler (1993) in their study of the legal and financial impediments to the formation of labour-managed firms in the earlier phases of the industrial revolution.

The Williamsonian hypothesis that existence implies greater relative efficiency would deem the military-industrial parallel to be irrelevant: whatever the original circumstances the more efficient forms would prosper and survive. The alternative industrial roads of flexible specialization or labour-management would be deemed to have been avoided because of their inefficiencies. On the contrary, the possibility of path dependence suggests that alternative, less-hierarchical or less-regimented forms of organization could have been just as viable. Only painstaking historical research, rather than bold evolutionary generalizations based on a limited appreciation of biology, can adjudicate on this and related questions.

Above all, in the present context, much further examination of the performance characteristics of various types of hierarchic and less-hierarchic firm is necessary before generalizations concerning the efficiency of one organizational form rather than another can be made.

---

[13] With variations, this idea is proposed in McNeill (1980), Mumford (1934), Nef (1950), M. R. Smith (1985) and J. M. Winter (1975) amongst others.

9.3. IN CONCLUSION: THE 'OLD' AND THE 'NEW' INSTITUTIONALISM

It has been suggested here that there are questions of clarity, theoretical problems and dilemmas, involved in the Coase–Williamson type of explanation of the nature of the firm in terms of transaction costs.[14] It has been indicated that the inclusion of endogenous preference functions, in which individuals are moulded by the internal culture of the firm, may be necessary for a viable theoretical explanation of the nature of that institution. It is precisely on points such as these that the 'old' institutionalism differs from the 'new'.

It is often insinuated, however, that Williamson's work is close to that of the 'old' institutionalist John Commons. Note Williamson's (1975, pp. 3, 254) repeated and often cited suggestion that he was following the work of Commons in taking the transaction as the 'ultimate unit of analysis'. For Commons (1934, p. 55), however, the transaction was typically a *'unit of economic activity'* (emphasis in original), forming others, such as the 'larger unit of economic activity, a Going Concern'. Although there is a very superficial resemblance of terminology, Williamson's mode of analysis differs profoundly from that of Commons. For Williamson the unit of *analysis* is the given, abstract, atomistic and 'opportunistic' individual, whereas Commons stresses the organic and collective quality of institutions.

Commons's reason for describing the transaction and the 'going concern' as units of economic *activity*, is to break from the classical idea that the units in economics should be the *'commodities owned* and the *individuals* who owned the commodities, while the "energy" was human labour' (ibid., p. 56). Commons made an analogy to quantum theory in support of his view that it is not mechanistically-related entities or 'particles' but processes and events that should be the stuff of economics. Furthermore, in stressing the notion of activity, Commons is attempting to break from an atomistic mode of thought: 'These going concerns and transactions are to economics what Whitehead's "organic mechanism" and "event" are to physics, or the physiologists "organisms" and "metabolism" are to biology' (ibid,. p. 96). It should be clear that Commons's organicism bears no significant resemblance to Williamson's atomistic and individualistic line of thought.

---

[14] Pagano (1991, p. 318 n.) provides a division of labour argument why the hierarchy in the firm may be advantageous even in a situation of zero transaction costs, because of the advantages resulting from putting those with management skills in charge of the coordination of production.

Ironically for Williamson, it was Veblen, rather than Commons, who prefigured the transaction cost idea. In his *Theory of Business Enterprise*, Veblen (1904, pp. 46–8) wrote:

> The amount of 'business' that has to be transacted per unit of product is much greater when the various related industrial processes are managed in severalty than where several of them are brought under one business management. A pecuniary discretion has to be exercised at every point of contact or transition, where the process or its product touches or passes the boundary between different spheres of ownership. . . . [B]usiness consolidation . . . [eliminates] the pecuniary element from the interstices of the system as far as may be . . . the work of pecuniary management previously involved is in large part dispensed with, with the result that there is a saving of work and an avoidance of that systematic mutual hindrance that characterizes the competitive management of industry.

This is arguably a clearer precursor of the transaction cost idea, and pre-dating Commons's (1924, 1934) work on the transaction as a 'unit of economic activity'.

Furthermore, while both Williamson and some 'old' institutionalists appealed to an evolutionary analogy in their work, Veblen and Commons did not support the kind of Panglossian interpretation to be found in the work of Williamson and many others. In contrast to much 'new' institutionalist writing, the work of Veblen and Commons does not involve the notion that evolution always works towards progressive or optimal outcomes.

In sum, while the work of Coase and Williamson has had an enormous positive effect in stimulating our thinking about the firm, the transaction costs theory, as it stands, is nevertheless still in want of further clarification and subject to theoretical criticism. It is again to Williamson's credit that by acting as a founder of the 'new' institutionalism he has, perhaps unwittingly, directed renewed attention to the 'old'. Unfortunately, however, we do not discover an adequate theory of the firm in the work of Veblen and Commons. Nevertheless, there are enough methodological and theoretical indications to suggest that further work may be productive using 'old' institutionalist tools.

10. The Coasean Tangle: The Nature of the Firm and the Problem of Historical Specificity

This chapter addresses an issue that is overlooked in most of the literature on the nature of the firm, including classic contributions such as those of Frank Knight (1921) and Ronald Coase (1937).[1] It concerns the definition and historical specificity of the firm itself. Most writers in this area seem to assume that 'the firm' is essentially *any* organization devoted to the production of goods or services. With such a broad and general definition of the firm it is necessary to regard the slave estates of classical antiquity, along with medieval guilds, feudal manors, monasteries, hospitals, worker cooperatives, state bureaux, cottage industries, nationalised industries and modern households *all* as 'firms'. Typically, in all of these past and present organizations, production – defined as the intentional creation by human beings of a good or service, using appropriate knowledge, tools, machines and materials – takes place. The firm is thus seemingly ubiquitous and pre-eminent throughout all civilised human history. The firm embraces all productive activity, from the slave sweating under the whip, to the contract knitter of scarves by the fireside, and to the loving husband preparing breakfast in bed for his spouse.

There is nothing wrong, in principle, with having such a broad definition. But while the majority of authors writing in the area fail to provide a narrower definition of the firm, they seem to assume that their general

---

[1] This chapter is a revised version of Hodgson (1998a). The author is very grateful to S. Masten for comments leading to revisions and responses in the present version.

pronouncements on 'the nature of the firm' apply principally or specifically to the modern capitalist corporation. Exceptions are economic historians such as Douglass North (1990) and others, such as Robert Pollak (1985), who apply standard theories of the firm – such as transaction cost analysis – explicitly to other types of organization. This, in turn, raises the question of the limits of such theories: can they be applied to every organizational form? Do, for instance, the precepts of transaction cost analysis advanced by Coase (1937) and Oliver Williamson (1975, 1985) and others apply in every organizational case? Are they founded upon eternal and universal features of human nature?[2] For example, considering the core Williamsonian concept of 'opportunism', are monks in monasteries and loving partners in a household inclined to 'self-interest seeking with guile' as much as corporate managers or recalcitrant industrial workers?

Most of the literature ignores these questions of universality and historical applicability, and simultaneously retains a vague and imprecise notion of 'the firm'. At the same time this literature presumed that it is of direct and primary relevance to the understanding of a specific form of productive organization in the modern era. In fact this organizational form has been prominent only for a few hundred years and for much of that time it has directly involved a small minority of the world's human population.

The plan of this chapter is as follows. Section 10.1 considers the seminal contribution of Coase (1937) on the theory of the firm. It is argued that the problem of historical specificity is alluded to by Coase but dealt with in an unsatisfactory manner. Section 10.2 considers the problem of historical specificity in economics in general terms: the dangers in over-extensive and ahistorical assumptions and abstractions are outlined. Section 10.3 provides a definition of the capitalist firm. It is suggested, however, that to confine the firm to its capitalist manifestation is too narrow a definition. Indeed, there are reasons for defining the firm quite widely. Accordingly, in Section 10.4 a plausible boundary between 'the firm', broadly defined, and other forms of productive organization is considered. In this manner a definition of the firm is provided that includes the capitalist firm as a subset. Section 10.5 considers the perceived modern problem of the blurring of the boundaries between the firm and the market and argues that the distinction between firms and (market) exchange is still necessary and valid. Section 10.6 considers the implications of the argument for further theoretical and empirical work on the nature of the firm.

---

[2] For instance, Magill and Quinzii (1996, p. 11 n.) remark that 'the transaction costs arguments are derived from basic (universal) attributes of human beings'.

10.1. THE COASEAN TANGLE

Coase's work is ambiguous on the question of historical specificity. In his classic 1937 paper he saw the employment contract – involving both an employer and employee – as central to the firm. Implicitly, therefore, Coase's notion of the firm excludes the self-employed worker: a Coasean firm must have a minimum of two persons. He described the 'entrepreneur-co-ordinator, who directs production' (p. 388) and employs factors of production. Without mentioning labour specifically, these 'factors' agree in return 'for a certain remuneration . . . to obey the directions of an entrepreneur *within certain limits*' (p. 391, emphasis in original). A contract without such limits would be 'voluntary slavery' and, according to a cited authority, 'void and unenforceable' (p. 391n). Later in the same article Coase centres more specifically on the employment contract. He implies that it is central to 'the concept of a firm' and asks if his description of it 'fits in with . . . the real world' (p. 403). Although Coase began general and ahistorical notions such as 'factors of production' he drifted into language relating specifically to the modern employment contract and ends up directly addressing the legal specification of that core element of modern corporate capitalism.

Half a century later, however, Coase had slipped back into ahistorical generalities. He wrote:

> I consider that one of the main weaknesses of my [1937] article stems from the use of the employer–employee relationship as the archetype of the firm. It gives an incomplete picture of the nature of the firm. But more important, I believe it misdirects our attention. The incompleteness that comes from using the analogy of the employer–employee relationship is something of which I was very much aware in the 1930s. In the last section of my article, in which I attempt to show the realism of my concept of the firm, I compare it to the legal relationship of employer and employee. However I add in a footnote that the legal concept and the economic concept are not identical 'in that the firm may imply control over another person's property as well as over their labour.' And in my notes written around 1934, I said that the employer–employee contract approaches the firm relationship but that the full firm relationship will not come about unless 'several such contracts are made with people and for things which cooperate with one another.' Nonetheless, in the text of my article in at least one place I seem to have forgotten this necessary qualification and I write as if all that were involved is the relation of employer to employee. (Coase, 1988, p. 36)

The main suggestion here is to identify the essence of the firm in terms of organizational coordination. Such a notion of the firm is used by other authors, notably Edith Penrose (1959, p. 24) who saw the firm as 'a collection of productive resources the disposal of which between different uses and over time is determined by administrative decision.'

Despite being a genuine attempt to clarify some parts of his 1937 article, Coase's 1988 statement is confused and only partially convincing. Perhaps the nearest thing to a definition of the firm in his 1937 article is of an organization, within which, in place of 'exchange transactions is substituted the entrepreneur-co-ordinator, who directs production' (p. 388). Yet this was not clearly flagged as a definition and he quickly moved on to the quite different issues of why 'the price mechanism is superseded' and why firms exist. Defining something is not the same thing as explaining why it emerges and how it is sustained.

In 1988 it was still not clear whether he was primarily addressing the question of the definition or of the nature of the firm, or both. The definition of an entity does not necessarily identify its most important features. A mammal is defined as an animal that suckles its young, yet this definition (legitimately) ignores other important features, such as having a well-developed nervous system and warm blood. Accordingly, a (capitalist) firm could be reasonably defined (partially) in terms of an employment relationship yet this does not necessarily imply that attention will be 'misdirected' away from other important features that such organizations may possess.

In 1988 Coase had reservations about 'the use of the employer–employee relationship as the archetype of the firm'. If Coase used the word 'archetype' in its proper sense to mean 'typical specimen' then he was doing himself an injustice. No passage in his 1937 article suggests this. In that article the firm is always regarded as involving *more* than the employment relationship.

Further, in the real world today it would be quite reasonable to suggest that the firm – in the sense and context that that word is used by Coase, Williamson and others – typically involves an employment relationship as an important feature. Rarely is it excluded from modern real-world firms, and any such test of 'realism' is likely to identify it as a prominent feature, perhaps among others. This would suggest, however, an historically specific approach to the theory of the firm – one that is not developed to any great extent in Coase's 1937 article and seemingly rebutted in 1988.[3]

---

[3] In private correspondence, Coase (1996) has clarified matters somewhat. He wrote that in 1937: 'The firm I was talking about was undoubtedly what you [Hodgson]

His notion of the '*analogy* of the employer–employee relationship' (emphasis added) is equally perplexing. An analogy involves a suggestion of resemblance of function or appearance between two things which are in fact different. For example: 'that cloud looks like an elephant'. Is Coase saying that the firm is like an employment relationship but in fact involves something else instead? The answer to this question depends on the definition of the firm. If attention is confined to the capitalist firm then the statement 'the firm is like an employment relationship' would be false. Capitalist firms have employment relationships as a major feature but they are not strictly 'like' that relationship because they have other essential features as well. They contain employment relationships but they are more than employment relationships. To say: 'the employment relationship is analogous to the capitalist firm' is like saying 'the skin is analogous to the face'. Both statements are invalid.

In 1988, Coase was also critical of his earlier citation of legal doctrine on the employment relationship to support his claim of realism. In his 1937 article this legal doctrine was used to point to 'the fact of direction which is the essence of the legal concept of "employer and employee", just as it was in the economic concept which was developed above' (p. 404). Three observations are appropriate on this point. First, it is not clear what the difference is between the 'legal concept' and the 'economic concept', other than that one is framed by lawyers and the other by economists. If both are devised to address a real world phenomenon then they cannot be different and both be accurate depictions of that same whole or essential reality. They may represent different and partial views of the same phenomenon but even in this case they cannot be mutually contradictory. What is important is the essence of the phenomenon, not the disciplinary tags that we attach to the concepts that are used to describe it.

Second, if in reality – as we may reasonably presume – most contemporary firms do in fact involve employment relationships then the consideration of the legal specification of that relationship is highly relevant to the issue in hand. What is important, however, is to consider the historical generality, or otherwise, of that specification in relation to the definition of the firm that has been utilised. Coase, however, does not consider the key question of historical specificity or generality in either 1937

---

call "the capitalist firm".' Further, in 1988: 'What I had in mind is that the employer–employee relationship is a necessary but not a sufficient condition for the existence of the firm as I conceive it.' In contrast, according to the definitions proposed here, the employment relationship is neither necessary nor sufficient to define the firm. However, all relations of employment exist within firms.

or 1988. It will be suggested that this shortcoming is not confined to his work alone, and gives rise to a number of fundamental problems in the literature on the theory of the firm.

Third, Coase in 1988 misses a key element in his 1937 quotation from Francis Batt's *Law of Master and Servant*. In the quotation Batt was attempting to distinguish between an employment or 'master–servant' relationship and a contract for the services of an independent contractor. The law of master and servant applies to an employment contract where the master has 'the right to control the servant's work . . . It is this right of control or interference . . . which is the dominant characteristic in this relation and marks off the servant from an independent contractor' (Batt, 1929, p. 6; quoted in Coase, 1937, p. 404). Although Coase quoted this passage, he did not acknowledge that a distinction was made by Batt that is essential to the definition of an employment relationship.

As another legal expert put it, a servant or employee 'is any person who works for another upon the terms that he is subject to the control of that other person as to the *manner* in which he shall do his work' (James, 1966, pp. 322–3). In contrast, with a contract for services the worker is an independent contractor, without an employer to control the pattern and manner of the work.[4]

Although Coase does not spell it out, this distinction between a 'contract of service' and a 'contract for services' is in fact crucial to *his* theory of the firm. The key point is not the question of control as such; some type and degree of control is present even in the case of an independent contractor. If we hire a contractor to clean our windows we do not have control over the manner of work but we do have some control over the contractor, by requiring that the service is carried out according to the agreed contract. Some degree of control is present *both* in employment contracts and in contracts for service (sales contracts).

Herbert Simon has insisted on a similar distinction. Simon (1951, p. 294) argued that the employment contract differs 'fundamentally from a sales contract – the kind of contract that is assumed in ordinary formulations of price theory'. In a sales contract a 'completely specified commodity' is exchanged for an agreed amount. Even in cases where complete

---

[4] This is not to deny the abundance of difficult and intermediate cases. 'The difference between the contract of service and "contract for services" has taxed the ingenuity of judges' (Wedderburn, 1971, p. 53). Additional criteria are often used, particularly whether the worker owns or provides the instruments of work. The complex nature of the employment contract is explored further in Hodgson (1998e).

specification is absent, the details of the agreement are often regarded by law as implicit or 'understood'. In contrast, in the employment contract the worker agrees to perform one of a mutually agreed and limited range of patterns of work, and allows the employer to select and allocate the tasks. In addition, the worker accepts the authority of the employer, notably concerning the specification of the work to be performed. In other words, the employee does not agree to a single task and pattern of work and the employer has, within limits, the legal right to control the work of the employee. Although the above definition of an employment contract requires some further refinement it usefully serves our purposes here.

On this issue, two points are worthy of emphasis and both seem to have escaped Coase. The first is that *without such a distinction between an employment contract, on the one hand, and sales contracts or self-employment contracts, on the other, the firm itself becomes indistinguishable* – at least in Coase's terms – *from a market*. Employees become identical to self-employed workers selling their services. Without such a distinction we end up in a position similar to that of Armen Alchian and Harold Demsetz (1972, p. 777) where they argue that:

> It is common to see the firm characterized by the power to settle issues by fiat, by authority, or by disciplinary action superior to that available on the conventional market. This is a delusion. The firm has no power of fiat, no authority, no disciplinary action any different in the slightest degree from ordinary market contracting between any two people. . . . Telling an employee to type this letter rather than to file that document is like my telling a grocer to sell me this brand of tuna rather than that brand of bread.

Coase has to invoke a distinction between an employment relationship and a sales contract in order to escape this difficulty. This distinction is under- rather than over-stressed in his 1937 article. By 1988 he abandons the issue entirely.

Second, the same kind of considerations do *not* apply to other 'factors of production'. There is an important problem here. Despite the emphasis given to the employment contract in the 1937 article, Coase seemed keen to retain the neoclassical idea of a symmetry of 'factors of production', ignoring the special features that differentiate 'labour' from 'capital'. Hence the phrases, 'co-ordination of the various factors of production' (1937, p. 388) and the idea of a 'factor of production (or the owner thereof)' making contracts where 'the factor . . . agrees' (p. 391) to its terms. *The fact is that contracts are never made or agreed by 'factors'; they are always devised and concluded by people* (or by organizations of people, by legal 'persons').

The 'entrepreneur-co-ordinator' will enter into contracts with owners of capital goods and with workers selling their capacity for work. Both 'labour' and 'capital' are purchased, but they are both bought and sold by 'persons' in law.

Important distinctions between 'labour' and 'capital' emerge. As Alfred Marshall (1949, p. 471) noted: 'when a person sells his services, he has to present himself where they are delivered. It matters nothing to the seller of bricks whether they are to be used in building a palace or a sewer: but it matters a great deal to the seller of labour'. The good or service being supplied – in this case labour – remains united with its possessing agent.[5]

An important and related feature is that owners of labour power, but not typically of capital, can agree, during the period of production itself – and to use Coase's (1937, p. 391) own words – 'for a certain remuneration . . . to obey the directions of an entrepreneur *within certain limits*'. In other words, within certain bounds, there is legally enforceable control over the manner and pattern of work.

The last phrase is important. Control itself does not necessarily mean employment. There are many cases where an entrepreneur does have a degree of control over another firm and thereby its employees. Examples would include a machine maintenance contract put out to a separate firm. Consider also the many cases in modern capitalism where the firm acts as a holding company or operates a franchising system. In all these cases there may be interference in the running of the client business. However, even if this interference is extensive, it does not involve control of the client firm's employees in the same way as in a direct contract of employment. Legally, the maintenance engineers are not employees of the firm in which the machine is being maintained. Although control may be exercised, these workers are employees of the maintenance company, not of the firm owning the machine. Ultimately, they must obey the authority of the company that legally employs them. It is that company that has control over the manner of their work.

Nevertheless, as case law recognizes, distinctions between employment contracts and contracts for services (sales contracts) are sometimes blurred in reality. Nevertheless, the distinction retains validity and meaning. At one extreme is the employment contract where the employee has the right of detailed interference and control. At the other, is the case where the 'factor' sold to the firm is a well-defined good or service. This 'factor' is sold

---

[5] In an earlier work (Hodgson, 1982b) this proposition formed part of a general theory of exploitation not involving the labour theory of value.

according to contract and control and interference by the purchaser in the process of production is minimal.[6]

Production processes involving human beings depend vitally upon dispersed, uncodifiable and tacit knowledge. The complexity and inaccessibility of much of this knowledge means that neither worker nor manager can know fully what is going on. All production involves learning; and in principle we do not know now what is yet to be learned in the future. Further, production processes are generally complex to the degree that precise analysis and prediction are often confounded. In particular, they involve human actors, who are sometimes unpredictable. Finally, they are subject to uncertain shocks and disturbances from the outside world. Overall, key outcomes are uncertain, in the Keynesian and Knightian sense, and also many events and innovations are both unenvisaged and unforeseen.

For these reasons, employment contracts are imperfectly and incompletely specified. The terms of the contract cannot in practice be spelt out in full detail because of the complexity of the work process, and the degree of unpredictability of key outcomes. These problems of complexity and uncertainty are found to some degree in other contracts, but with employment contracts they are particularly severe. This is because of the degree of complexity and uncertainty involved, and the fact that the work process continuously and directly involves conscious and capricious human agents. Accordingly, we are in a strange Heisenbergian world where the use-value of labour power is not known fully until it is used.

In contrast, other 'factors' such as machines or raw materials, do not resist, make choices based on whim, become enthusiastic, take pride in their work, or work to rule. Unlike labour, when they are engaged in production their owners are typically elsewhere. The owner of labour power, unlike the owner of 'capital', necessarily accompanies his or her 'factor' to the place of work and is the very agency of its use in that sphere. It is a universal aspect of the human condition and exists even when employment contracts are absent. It applies to a slave as much as to a modern industrial worker.

Allied with the flawed notion of a symmetry between 'labour' and 'capital' is the mistaken idea that production is essentially an allocative

---

6 Even if the extremes are not found in reality, the two polar ideal types are necessary to define the continuum. See the discussion of ideal types below. Note also the fascinating extensive discussion of the employment contract in Ellerman (1992). Where Ellerman is at his weakest, however, is in failing to see that the difference between employment contracts (which in policy terms he opposes) and contracts of self-employment (which he applauds) is not so clear-cut in many real-world situations.

rather than a creative process. Although classical economists such as Smith centred their analysis on production, what has marked neoclassical economics since its inception in the 1870s is the analytical supremacy of exchange. Even production is treated as a variant of exchange. The firm is seen as a place where the 'entrepreneur-co-ordinator' allocates 'factors'. By failing to recognize the place of human agency within 'labour' and within production itself, production becomes an allocative process under the direct or indirect control of the 'entrepreneur'. Coase (1937, p. 389, emphasis added) seems to succumb to this error in his seminal paper: 'The purpose of this paper is to bridge what appears to be a gap in economic theory between the assumption . . . that resources are *allocated* by means of the price mechanism and the assumption . . . that this *allocation* is dependent on the entrepreneur-co-ordinator.'

This misconception of production as primarily an allocative rather than a creative process is a defect not only of the account of Coase but also of that of Williamson (1975, 1985). Their work is likewise vulnerable to the reproach that production is neglected in favour of allocation. This point is developed further in the following chapter.

In contrast to a contract involving the exchange of goods, production involves the use of labour and the intentional and ongoing involvement of a worker. The outcome of this process is not entirely determined by contractual agreements. To understand production we have to move beyond contracts, markets and costs (Hodgson, 1988, 1998e).

10.2. THE PROBLEM OF HISTORICAL SPECIFICITY IN ECONOMICS

Since the 1870s, economics has often been defined in universal terms, as 'the science of choice'. Especially since Lionel Robbins (1932) published his highly influential *Essay on the Nature and Significance of Economic Science* it is regarded as the study of the proper method of allocating scarce physical and human resources among competing ends. Robbins explicitly abandoned the idea that economics was defined by the study of what could be described as economic phenomena. Since the publication of his essay the prevailing practice amongst economists has been to regard this subject as being defined by a single type of method or analysis, with an associated set of core assumptions. In this view, economics involves a set of general and ahistorical assumptions that apply to all forms of organization – past and present – under scarcity.

Remarkably, however, Coase differed from this view. He has defined economics as the study of 'the working of social institutions which bind the economic system together: firms, markets for goods and services, labour markets, capital markets, the banking system, international trade, and so on' (Coase, 1977, p. 487). In this institutionalist definition, and in his equally notable rejection of the assumption of utility-maximizing individuals in favour of studying 'man as he is' (Coase, 1984, p. 231), Coase was seemingly out of step with mainstream economists. An appeal for the study 'of social institutions which bind the economic system together' suggested a concern for the analysis of specific institutions and structures, rather than an exclusive devotion to ahistorical generalities. Again there was a laudable concern for realism, but one that fitted awkwardly in the seemingly universal elements of his theoretical framework.

One of the first and most important critics of unwarranted attempts to found economics on universal and ahistorical categories was Karl Marx. In his view, ahistorical categories such as 'utility', 'choice' and 'scarcity' cannot capture the essential features of a specific socio-economic system. His recognition of processes of historical development and transformation led him to the view that particular concepts that capture the essence of particular systems have to be pre-eminent. Concepts such as 'utility', 'choice' and 'scarcity', although claimed by their employers as universal, are actually most fitting for the modern period of socio-economic development. In contrast, Marx made the claim that his core categories – 'commodities', 'money', 'exchange', 'capital' – were abstract expressions of real social relations found within the capitalist mode of production. Such categories are held to be operational as long as such social relations exist. For similar reasons the economic historian William Cunningham (1892, p. 493) criticized the rising neoclassical economics at the end of the nineteenth century:

> The underlying assumption against which I wish to protest is . . . [t]hat the same motives have been at work in all ages, and have produced similar results, and that, therefore, it is possible to formulate economic laws which describe the action of economic causes at all times and in all places.

By confining itself to allegedly universal and ahistorical concepts, mainstream economics fails to become rooted in any specific socio-economic system. Its very generality provides limited means for an understanding of capitalism or other specific systems. Instead of attempting to confront a particular economy, or *real* object, it becomes confined to a remotely abstract and artificial *idea* of an economy, the economy in general.

The accent on the analysis of historically specific institutions and structures is found in various schools of heterodox economics. The Marxian contribution has already been noted. The problem of historical specificity was central to the discourse of the German historical school from the 1840s to the 1930s. In the writings of Keynes and most Post Keynesians there is generally a degree of emphasis on specific institutions and structures and an attempt to relate the analysis to specific economies rather than ahistorical generalities.[7] Further, the emphasis on specific institutions is a hallmark of the 'old' institutional economics of Thorstein Veblen, John Commons, John Maurice Clark and Wesley Mitchell.

However, there are problems with any attempt to root economics in historically specific assumptions alone. Taking neoclassical and Marxian economics as opposite theoretical poles, each gets trapped in the obverse type of problem when it comes to assumptions about specificity or universality in economic analysis. Neoclassical economics is built on allegedly universal assumptions about choice and scarcity. We discover that they are not, in fact, universally applicable and that they reflect the dominant, but even then not all-pervasive, ideology of a particular moment of capitalist development. The analytical starting point of Marxian economics is the specific features and relations of the capitalist mode of production. Yet even Marxian theory is permeated with transhistorical concepts such as mode of production, forces of production, relations of production, and labour time. We discover that the analysis ends up relying on concepts and theories that in fact span human history. Neoclassical economics aspires to universality but ends up being specific; Marxism aspires to complete specificity but ends up relying on concepts that stretch for millennia.

Two conclusions follow. The first is that the theoretical analysis of a specific socio-economic system cannot rely entirely on concepts drawn from that system. This is because the very organization and extraction of these concepts must rely on other categories of wider applicability. To talk of capitalism we must refer to other socio-economic systems; if we speak of socio-economic systems we are using that transhistorical concept; and so on. The very meta-theoretical terms of this discourse are themselves ahistorical. While historical and institutional specificity is important, we are obliged to rely to some degree on the universal.

---

[7] The work of Pasinetti (1981) may be regarded as an exception, as he attempted to establish universal and 'pre-institutional' principles and results. Furthermore, in Sraffa (1960) there is only a partial and generally inexplicit recognition of the effects of institutional realities.

The second conclusion is that the entire analysis of any given system cannot and should not be based on universal concepts alone. The first levels of abstraction must be quite general, but if those universalist layers are extended too far – as in the case of neoclassical theory – then the danger is that we end up with conceptions that are unable to come to grips with reality. The scope of analysis of the first levels of abstraction should be highly confined. We now move on the problem of the nature of the firm with these conclusions in mind.

10.3. THE CAPITALIST FIRM

If the conclusion of the preceding section is correct, the investigation of 'the nature of the firm' must rely on both universal and historically specific concepts, articulated together in a particular way. First of all, however, we must make it clear what we are talking about when we refer to the general notion of the firm. A broader matrix must be constructed in which particular types of firm can be placed. Some definitions are proposed here that do not depart too far from prevailing practice but should help to sharpen up discussion of the issue and lead us back to a further evaluation of Coase's pioneering work.

Let us examine the issue from an historically specific point of view. For the two hundred or more years of its existence, the capitalist system has been made up with capitalist firms. The 'capitalist firm' was usefully defined by Karl Marx (1976, pp. 291–2) in *Capital*, as an institution where:

(1) 'the worker works under the control of the capitalist to whom his labour belongs' and
(2) 'the product is the property of the capitalist and not that of the worker'
(3) Further, such capitalist firms produce commodities for sale in the pursuit of profit.

Clearly, points (1) and (2) of this definition imply that a capitalist firm involves an employment relationship and excludes one-person firms. Points (2) and (3) imply the existence of private ownership of the means of production. They also are tied up with the fact that the capitalists, rather than the workers, are the 'residual claimants': they take up the profits and losses from the sale of the products, after all other costs are paid. The definition has formal and legal, as well as cultural and informal, aspects. It entails an employment relationship and excludes co-operatives and one-person firms, as Marx himself made clear on repeated occasions.

Today, however, firms are often corporate entities rather than owned and controlled by individuals. With the concept of a 'legal person' the definition can be extended to groups and institutions as well as individuals. Capitalist firms are thus owned largely by individuals or institutions that generate an income from the ownership and control of private capital assets. The capital that is locked up in the firm has an actual or potential market value and the firm itself can be sold as a capital asset.

The state does not qualify as a 'capitalist' institution because it is not itself saleable as a block of capital. The state derives its principal income not from the ownership of capital assets and the sale of commodities but from taxation. Further, the state is not typically or necessarily predisposed to search for profits, at least as a primary objective.

To drive home the importance of the employment contract, consider the real world cases where a capitalist firm ends the employment contract with its employees and asks them to be self-employed providers of services. Firms may also hire contract labour from an agency to avoid the non-wage labour costs entailed by employment legislation. If the capitalist firm took this to the limit, and retained not a single worker or manager in an employment contract, then it would cease to be capitalist. However, as long as it had at least one such employee – and no matter to what degree it relied on additional agency or self-employed labour – it would remain a capitalist firm, albeit in an attenuated form.

The capitalist mode of production is regarded by Marx as a socio-economic system in which most production takes place in capitalist firms. Commodities are defined by Marx as goods or services that are typically exchanged on the market. The products of capitalist firms are commodities. Marx (1981, p. 1019) clearly identifies a 'characteristic trait' of the capitalist mode of production as follows:

> It produces its products as commodities. The fact that it produces commodities does not in itself distinguish it from other modes of production; but that the dominant and determining character of its product is the commodity certainly does so. This means, first of all, that . . . labour generally appears as wage-labour . . . [and] the relationship of capital to wage-labour determines the whole character of the mode of production.

In short, for Marx, capitalism is generalised commodity production.[8] It is generalised in a double sense, first because under capitalism most goods and services are commodities. Second, because under capitalism the capacity to work is itself a commodity. An important feature of capitalism is the existence of labour markets and the hiring of workers by employers. In addition, the capital market performs a crucial regulatory function in allocating other resources within the economy. Capitalism is a market system but not all economies involving markets and private property are capitalist systems. A necessary feature of capitalism is the widespread use of the employment relationship, involving employer control over the manner and pattern of work.

Note that this definition of 'the capitalist firm' has the employment relationship as a necessary feature. Capitalist firms are not reducible to employment contracts alone – a possibility that seemed to worry Coase – because of the second condition: 'the product is the property of the capitalist and not that of the worker'. Accordingly, organizations can have employment contracts but not be capitalist firms. All firms with employment contracts are here termed as 'employment firms', of which capitalist firms are a subset. Examples of employment firms that are not capitalist firms are plentiful, even in the modern world. Many hospitals and schools in the public sector do not sell their services to their consumers – hence they do not produce commodities – yet they widely utilise contracts of employment. Nationalised industries and public corporations use employment contracts but they are publicly owned. Charities typically employ people but donate services and assets without sale or charge.

Considering the multitude of alternative possibilities to 'the capitalist firm', even in capitalist society, is there something to be said for Coase's (1988) position where historical specificities are seemingly abandoned? The strict answer is no, because such an abandonment would ignore the specific features of a key and pervasive institution in modern society: the capitalist firm. However, a reasonably comprehensive theory of productive institutions cannot ignore the large number of organizations that do not conform to this stereotype, violating one or both of Marx's conditions (1) and (2) above. The violators include productive organizations with employment relationships that are not strictly capitalist in nature (e.g. many charities, public hospitals and schools) and productive organizations without employment contracts

---

[8] Marx does not explicitly use this three-word definition of capitalism and some have expressed a distaste for it, for various reasons. In its defence, these three words do connote the key issues of property rights, markets, employment relations and thereby class divisions within capitalism.

that sell (e.g. self-employed producers, worker cooperatives, many slave estates) or typically do not sell (e.g. self-sufficient peasants, modern households) their products. All these could be regarded as 'firms' but they are not capitalist firms, at least according to Marx's definition.

Clearly, there is something to be said *both* for a historically specific definition that captures the key elements of 'the capitalist firm' *and* for a more general definition of 'the firm' that addresses a multitude of types of productive organization – past and present. Two definitions are required, not one – where one definition delimits a subset of the other. We now move on to construct a broad definition of the firm. Then we consider the capitalist firm as a special case.

10.4. THE FIRM AND ITS NEGATION

If it is not confined to its capitalist variant, how comprehensively should 'the firm' be defined?[9] The answer to this question is primarily a matter of analytical usefulness. As Plato put it, for 'carving reality at its joints'. In this spirit there is a case against an excessively wide definition. Is it meaningful to describe a group of primitive hunters, chasing and slaying animals, and processing their skins and meat, as a firm? Is a small team of Neolithic farmers, sowing their seed and husbanding their cattle, a firm?

In these cases at least, arguably no. A key point is that in such primitive societies – collectively regulated largely by ritual and tradition – it is not obvious what could be meant by the 'non-firm'. If the firm was defined so broadly, every productive activity in such societies would take place in a 'firm'. The concept of the firm would thus represent everything and mean nothing. Reality would not be carved at its joints. The problem here is to establish the widest possible definition of the firm that retains such a separable skeletal attribute.

Alternatively, a narrow definition of the firm could be adopted. For example, the firm could be defined as equivalent to 'the capitalist firm', or confined to the industrial era, or be restricted only to firms with employment

---

[9] Etymologically, the word derives originally from the Latin adjective *firmus*, meaning strong, powerful, durable and lasting. As a noun, the word went on to acquire the significant meaning of (legally binding) 'signature', and with this important connotation it survives today in some amended form in several Romance languages. The *Concise Oxford English Dictionary* defines the firm rather loosely as 'partners carrying on business; group of persons working together'.

contracts. Against this, however, there is a case for capturing a wide class of entities under the umbrella title of 'the firm' in order to focus on its essential attributes, and to use sub-categories such as 'the capitalist firm' to delineate specific types. The latter strategy is embraced here. Because the notion of the firm in the existing literature is both broad and vague, it seems appropriate to rectify the vagueness first. If others find the following definition too broad, it is reasonable for them to suggest further stipulations.

Accordingly, the following qualification is suggested: the notion of the firm applies only to those socio-economic systems involving well-developed individual or group ownership, and well-defined contracts and property rights. Notably, such ownership and property are necessary conditions for buying and selling to take place. Also there must be a system of law that recognizes 'legal persons' making transactions – individuals or groups that are deemed to have discretion and choice, and may enter into contracts with others. Incidentally, whenever such conditions have occurred in human history, there has always been a state with major functions including the protection of property, the regulation of contracts, and the adjudication over legal disputes concerning property. In all, such conditions are roughly equivalent to the existence of human civilization.[10]

At least by the time of the Roman Empire, a clear system of contract law had emerged, although it was not so well-formed in earlier civilizations. It was also in Italy, with its surviving legacy of Roman law, and in the twelfth century and after, that the medieval family firm spread and prospered. Surviving records show the legal basis of the medieval firm. As Avner Greif (1996, p. 476) elaborates: 'The essence of the family firm, as originally developed in Italy, was that several individuals agglomerated their capital by establishing a permanent partnership with unlimited and joint liability.'[11]

If ownership and property are essential to the firm it may be regarded as possible to define a firm in the manner of Sanford Grossman and Oliver

----

[10] Although there is no unanimously accepted definition of civilization (Daniel, 1968, ch. 1), several definitions involve the existence of trade, money or property. Notably, state bureaucracy is common to all civilizations. Accordingly, and contrary to Williamson's (1975, p. 20) famous remark that 'in the beginning there were markets', we may concur with Ingham (1996a, p. 264) 'There is a temptation to suggest that, both historically and analytically speaking, in the beginning there were bureaucracies!'

[11] As Greif (1996, p. 489) continues: 'The family firm during the 13th and early 14th centuries was a partnership (*compagnia*) among members of the founding family as well as non-family members. Each partner invested some capital in the company and each one's share in the profit was proportional to his investment.'

Hart (1986, p. 692) 'in terms of the assets it owns'. However, as David Ellerman (1992), Richard Langlois (1998, p. 16) and Louis Putterman (1988) all indicate to varying degrees, such a definition, while having the benefit of sharpness, would be unsatisfactory. Consider a consortium which owns a factory, machinery and raw materials, and hires out these assets to a team of managers who, in turn, produce and sell products in their own right. Would the owners of the assets – the consortium – be the firm? No. They would simply be the providers of the capital goods. The team of managers and their employees would constitute the firm. The management team would own that which is produced in the factory. Their contractual role as owners of the product makes this team the firm, not the owners of the capital goods. As Ellerman (1992, p. 12) puts it: 'Being the firm . . . is a contractual role, not a property right.'

It is important to emphasize that the firm is a singular legal person, in line with its etymology from *firmus,* or (legal) signature. The status of 'legal person' is conferred upon the firm by custom, by the evolution of the firm beyond its previously frequent ownership by a single individual, or in modern capitalism by the statutes of corporate law. It is important not to confuse the firm with a network of multiple legal persons, who may have separate ownership of their own products. For example, despite all the emphasis in their work on contracts and property rights, Eirik Furubotn and Rudolf Richter (1997, p. 272) wrote: '*A firm* is understood in this book as a network of relational contracts between individuals . . . with the purpose of efficiently organizing production.' This loose definition is unable to make a distinction between a firm and a network, simply because the former is defined as an example of the latter. To make such a distinction it is important to recognise the firm as a singular legal person, able to make contracts with others, via networks, markets or other arrangements.

One of the key features of a firm is that it is an organized enclave, apart from the market. It has already been argued, in Chapter 2 above, that true markets rarely, if ever, exist within firms. Many modern firms, however, have separate divisions with their own accounting procedures and profit targets. A key test is whether these divisions have separate legal status, and are recognised as 'legal persons'. If so, they themselves constitute firms, even if they are largely owned by, and subordinate to, another company.

The firm is defined here as a type of organization. Definitionally, an organization involves at least one person, a principle of sovereignty (who is in charge?) and a chain of command.[12] Organizations involve both power and control. As one-person businesses are definitionally non-organizations, the possibility of a single person acting as a firm is excluded. According to the definition adopted here, a firm is an organization always made up of two or more people. We are now in a position to posit a broad but historically limited and refined definition of the firm:

A firm is defined as an integrated and durable organization of people and other assets, acting tacitly or otherwise as a 'legal person', set up for the purpose of producing goods or services, with the capacity to sell or hire them to customers, and with associated and recognized corporate legal entitlements and liabilities. These corporate entitlements include the right of legal ownership of the goods as property before they are exchanged and the legal right to obtain contracted remuneration for the services. Corporate legal liabilities may be incurred in the production and provision of those goods or services.

This definition does not exclude the possibility that some goods or services could be donated rather than sold. Note also that the term 'legal' has a strong customary element; the phrase 'legal or customary' could just as well replace 'legal' in this definition. As suggested above, a sense in which a firm is integrated is that it is regarded as a 'legal person' owning its products and entering into contracts. Further aspects of integration are explored below. The sense in which a firm is durable is that it constitutes more than a transient contract or agreement between its core members and it incorporates structures and routines of some expected longevity.[13]

---

[12] As Khalil (1992) argued, these characteristics distinguish an organization from a spontaneous order in the sense of Hayek (1982) and others.

[13] Masten (1998) expressed some dissatisfaction with an earlier version of this definition. First, (p. 58) he suggested that phrases such as 'more than transient' and 'some expected longevity' require more precision. I agree. But I see no reason why these terms could not be sharpened, and no reason why the basic form of the definition has to be rejected at the outset.

Second, Masten (p. 61) stated: 'Also unclear is the meaning of the ownership of services. Does a firm "own" its services more than a household? Hodgson's definition begins to unravel when the sale of services rather than goods are contemplated.' I think not. A barber shop *sells* the service of a haircut. A household can sell goods or services, but only if the household is a 'legal person' capable of corporate ownership. In the present and original version (Hodgson, 1998a) of my article I indicated that the 'modern household' is typically not a firm but 'peasant family units' can qualify as firms. The reason here is nothing to do with the household 'owning' services more or less than firms. A household can

An important feature of this definition is that it applies only to socio-economic systems that are regulated to a significant degree by law and contract.[14] For a contract to be deemed meaningful the parties to it must be seen to have a choice over the matter.[15]

Furthermore, such societies are sufficiently complex to accommodate alternative productive arrangements. Accordingly, the possibility of organizing production *outside* the firm exists. Given that the above definition refers to the firm as owning its product, this rules out the individual buying and selling part-completed products within the firm itself: the firm itself cannot by definition be organized as a market, even if some internal transfers do take place. But there is nothing in principle to preclude the dissolution of the firm and its replacement by a market of self-employed producers – the celebrated thought experiment in Coase's 1937 essay.

If the firm is defined as above then the associated stipulations make possible an exchange- or market-based alternative to the firm. The existence of property and contract are necessary for such alternatives to occur in a sufficiently developed form. The limits to the notion of the firm are thus stipulated and explained.

---

qualify as a firm if, according to my definition, it is devoted to the production of saleable goods or services to which, as an organization, it has legal entitlement, as property. Most modern households do not qualify as firms because they are not set up principally to produce goods or services – meals, childcare, cleaning, sex – which are potentially and customarily saleable by the household. In contrast, households described as 'peasant family units' can qualify as firms because many of the goods and services they produce are treated as potentially saleable corporate property, some typically being exchanged or sold on the market. Contrary to Masten, the inclusion of services in this argument does nothing to 'unravel' it.

Nevertheless, I am very grateful to Masten for prompting me to refine my definition. I am also pleased to report that in subsequent email correspondence (2–5 February 1998) Masten and I have reached more agreement over the issues involved.

[14] The fact that a firm is an historically specific rather than a universal economic category accounts for the failure of a standard definition to emerge. For similar reasons there is no commonly accepted definition of the market (Hodgson, 1988). Mainstream economics shuns historically specific definitions even of such key concepts because of its mistaken belief that the core principles of economics must be ahistorical and universal.

[15] It is not necessary to go into the old philosophical dispute about 'free will' here. It is simply being suggested that such societies assume the existence of individual (or group) discretion – otherwise the notion of contract would not be meaningful.

Consider the possible ways in which the firm, as an organization of people, may become an *integrated* entity. In history, several possible such arrangements are found, including the following:

- **Slavery**. The slave is purchased as a chattel and forced to work, without legal right of exit.
- **Bondage**. Feudal serfs are bound for a lifetime to their lord and to his land by law, with few possibilities of exit.
- **Employment**. In law, employment relationships provide the right of exit by the employee, after a short period of notice is served. Without additional measures, employment relationships can be casual and not much more integrative than the hiring of self-employed contractors. However, these measures exclude legal compulsion; legal confinement in an employment contract is 'tantamount to slavery'. Workers are likely to remain with an employer for longer periods when: there is no known alternative employment or income; wages for equivalent work are perceived as higher than elsewhere; working conditions are perceived as better than elsewhere; or there is an effective culture of loyalty and commitment to the firm. Employers often have an incentive to retain employees because they have acquired specific skills during their period of employment.
- **Cooperation**. Workers may combine together and form a cooperative, in which they own the firm and its means of production in common. Typically, each worker's part-ownership of the firm's capital assets provides a major incentive for each worker to remain with the firm. Other incentives may exist, such as the lack of sufficiently attractive alternative sources of income, and an enhanced culture of loyalty to fellow-workers.

There are many additional and intermediate forms but the above four cases are clearly significant, both conceptually and historically.

The capitalist firm, as defined in Section 10.3 above, is a subset of all possible types of firm. The household is not a capitalist firm, but is it a firm? This is partly a matter of refinement of the definition of the firm given above. As the definition is framed, the modern household is not a firm because most of its services – such as child-rearing – are not owned by anyone or are owned by members of the household rather than the household as a whole. Although the household acts to sustain and reproduce the capacity to work of the wage-earner(s), it is typically the individual worker, rather than the household, who receives remuneration for that paid work. In contrast, even public hospitals and schools that donate their services provide a product that is under the tenure and management of the organization as a whole, rather than the individual doctors or teachers. Arguably a line can be drawn between the modern household – typically with one or two wage-earners – and the peasant or other family unit. In the latter case that unit typically sells its products – even if it uses the legal name of the head of the household – as a unit and acts as a corporate entity in such a sale; it thereby qualifies as a firm, according to the above definition.

The above definitions need further clarification and refinement but this is not possible because of limits of space. At this stage it is convenient simply to illustrate the above definitions, as in Figure 10.1. Features of this classification – such as the acceptance of the possibility of both organized and unorganized markets – are justified elsewhere (Hodgson, 1988).

Figure 10.1: Conceptual Distinctions Between Firms and Non-Firms

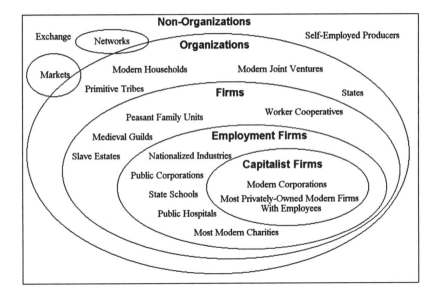

10.5. THE FIRM AND THE MARKET – ARE THE BOUNDARIES NOW BLURRED?

The wide historical limits of 'the firm' have been suggested above: firms have existed since the establishment of human civilization. Several writers suggest that in recent times the identification of a clear boundary between the firm and the rest of the economy has become increasingly problematic.

This problem is recognized by Penrose (1959, pp. 20–22) and Richardson (1972), among others. There is also the phenomenon of growing networks and increasing intermediate relations between firms (Grabher, 1993). In modern capitalism a cornucopia of hybrids, relational contracts and joint ventures is evident. Thus, against his earlier stark dichotomy between markets and hierarchies, Williamson (1985, p. 83) is 'now persuaded that transactions in the middle range are much more common' than he previously recognized. He thus proposed a continuum. Like others, he now addresses the supposed phenomenon of intermediate forms.

Two other theoretical approaches may seem, at first sight, to depict more adequately the increasingly hazy boundaries between firm and market. One is the famous article of Alchian and Demsetz (1972) in which the distinction between a firm and a market virtually dissolves. Another approach is provided by sociologists in the 'networks' tradition (Powell, 1990; Wellman and Berkowitz, 1988; White, 1992). Although of a very different theoretical genre, it can lead to a similar conclusion. The firm and the market can be regarded simply as different kinds of network and the essential distinction is again dissolved. Hence we reach an identical end result. One approach says: 'firms are markets'. The other, likewise: 'both are much the same'.

There is a problem here. Even a continuum must be defined in terms of polar ideal types: in this case, market and firm. Furthermore, even if modern networks create new kinds of relationships between firms, they do not abolish the firm. Above all it is important not to confuse conceptual model with real-world muddle. Even if in modern capitalism the boundaries between firm and market are in fact being broken down, and even if new forms of productive organization are now emerging which will eclipse the firms-markets dichotomy, the conceptual distinction between the 'firm' and the 'market' is necessary to make sense of these statements. In order to describe such a muddled reality we need clear ideal types to guide us. Without them we are conceptually blind. Clear and unmuddled concepts are necessary to penetrate a muddled world.

All empirical analysis presupposes a set of concepts and an implicit or explicit theory. Given that prior concepts are unavoidable; the question is how they are chosen. In their analysis of socio-economic systems social scientists are obliged to rely on 'ideal types'. These are abstract descriptions of phenomena that indicate the general features upon which a theorist will focus for purposes of explanation. A process of abstraction must occur where the essential structures and features of a system are identified.

The fact that a system is complex, tangled, or changing does not alter this requirement for clear concepts of analysis. As Max Weber (1949, p. 107) argued long ago:

Indeed, it is *because* the content of historical concepts is necessarily subject to change that they must be formulated precisely and clearly on all occasions. In their application, their character as ideal analytical constructs should be carefully kept in mind, and the ideal-type and historical reality should not be confused with each other.[16]

A definition of the firm has been provided above. It is important to ask: what productive contractual arrangements typically exist in a modern economy where the firm is absent? Both Coase (1937) and Williamson (1975) saw 'the market' as the antithesis of the firm and seemingly as the prior natural order. However, as Richardson (1972) argued, the characterisation of firms existing like 'islands of conscious power in this ocean of unconscious co-operation like lumps of butter coagulating in a pail of buttermilk' (Robertson, 1923, p. 85) is both misleading and descriptively false. Relations between firms are neither universally nor typically uncoordinated. The alternative to the firm is not necessarily the day-to-day rivalry of the open market. Instead, inter-firm relations are often characterised by close, ongoing contracts based on established connections, rather than open competition (Goldberg, 1980).

Given this, it is best not to characterise the pivotal dichotomy as being between the firm and the market. More generally, and accurately, the essential dichotomy is between firms, on the one hand, and the contractual *exchange* of more-or-less well specified goods or services, on the other. Exchange involves a transfer of property rights as well as goods or services (Commons, 1950, pp. 48–9). But not all exchange takes place in markets. Markets are specially developed and institutionalised groups of exchanges, involving measures to structure, organize and legitimate such transactions (Dosi, 1988a; Lowry, 1976; Hodgson, 1988).

Modern capitalism involves complex relational exchanges between firms that sometimes entail less clearly-defined transactions and relations of mutual trust and obligation (Powell, 1990; Sabel, 1993; Sako, 1992). These developments blur the actual boundaries between firms and exchange. Nevertheless, 'the ideal types of market and hierarchy serve as a useful starting point for studying the organization of industry' (Bradach and Eccles, 1989, p. 116). Recognition of the fuzzy character of the reality does not imply the abandonment of ideal types. Indeed, without clear conceptual

---

[16] On the concept of ideal types see Commons (1934, pp. 719–48), Schutz (1967) and Weber (1949, 1968).

axes to mark out the space of possibilities the fuzziness itself would be beyond our perception.

Having established the ideal types of 'firm' and 'exchange', the key questions to be addressed remain similar to those originally formulated by Coase (1937): In what circumstances will production be organized within firms rather than via combinations of exchange relations? If the existence of the firm is due to its relatively higher efficiency over such exchanges, what is the explanation for this advantage? Further, what prevents the firm growing to the extent that it replaces all exchange and market relations, or vice-versa?

The formulation of these questions by no means involves a denial of the evolving and muddled nature of modern capitalism. Indeed, modern socio-economic systems may eventually change to the extent that the 'firm' and 'exchange' are no longer the appropriate primary ideal types upon which to ground the analysis. That day has not yet come, however. We still live in capitalist society, even if many of its features are different from the Victorian capitalism of Marx. The dichotomy between firms and exchanges remains an essential feature of the modern world. In this respect Coase and Williamson are right.

10.6. THE NATURE OF THE FIRM – TOWARDS AN EXPLANATION

According to the definition formulated above, the firm has existed for thousands of years and has taken several quite different forms. In contrast, the capitalist firm has been established for only a few centuries and has been globally prominent for roughly one hundred years only. An appraisal of this historical perspective is necessary before the key questions concerning the nature of the firm are addressed.

The crucial point is this: is it possible or likely that the answers to the key questions concerning the nature of the firm will apply to all firms and types of firm, since the dawn of human civilization? Given the broad definition of the firm adopted here, it is not possible to centre explanations of the nature of the firm on historically specific features such as the employment contract. In contrast, the definition is sufficiently narrow to embrace notions of power and control, and throughout the historical range of possible circumstances.

If Coase would accept the broad but bounded definition of the firm proposed here then he would be wrong in 1937 to see the employment contract as a necessary component of the firm, but right in his 1988 self-criticism on this point. However, he would have to make the general legal character of the firm clear, and he would have to emphasize the general feature of its organizational integration and durability, in contrast to markets or exchange. This he failed to do, in part because he did not appreciate the problem of historical specificity. Furthermore, to explain the *particular form* and degree of organizational control in the *capitalist* firm he would have to acknowledge that it is then necessary to explore the employment contract and distinguish employment from self-employment. From this historically specific viewpoint the 1937 focus on employment contracts was warranted and the 1988 self-criticism misplaced. This conflict of outcomes, stemming from a tension in Coase's thought between institutional specificities and neoclassical generalities, could perhaps explain the ambivalence and lack of clarity over the theoretical status of the employment contract in his writings on the firm as a whole.

Significantly, according to the above definition of the firm, there is always the possibility of a market- or exchange-based, productive alternative to the firm itself. This is because the definition presupposes the existence of private property and exchange relations. Accordingly, 'market' forms of productive organization are possible, and the existence of the firm could possibly (but not necessarily) have something to do with lower transaction costs, as suggested by Coase and Williamson. Transaction costs explanations depend on historical circumstances where such alternatives exist. Nevertheless, such alternatives have been in existence for thousands of years. This does not show that the transaction cost argument is valid. It simply suggests that such an argument is plausible within the adopted definitional boundaries.

However, consideration of the wider historical context exposes a possible weakness as well as a strength of transaction cost explanations. This weakness derives precisely from their ubiquity and extensive applicability. An enormous variety of types of firm have existed since human civilization first became established, in southern Mesopotamia five thousand years ago. Any theory that attempts exclusively to explain the nature and existence of *all* those organizations on the basis of a *single* set of principles is bound to ignore important features of specific types of firm, such as the capitalist firm. Unlike firms in general, capitalist firms have be prevalent for only a couple of hundred years. A general theory of *all* firms will not be able to tell us very much about the specific nature and origin of the *capitalist* firm. From this aspect the potential frailty of the transaction cost theory derives from its over-extensive domain of application.

It is important to address particular types of firm as well as firms in general. A primary candidate for such special treatment is the capitalist firm, as defined above. Hence the question of the nature of the *capitalist* firm resolves into two separate sets of questions. The first concern the nature of the firm per se, and how in general can its existence be explained. The second set of questions concern the capitalistic aspects of the problem, including: why do *capitalist* firms exist? and why did the *capitalist* firm supplant other forms of productive organization? Clearly, the answers to the first set of questions need not be the same as the answers to the second.

Accordingly, in regard to specific types of firm, the possibility is thus opened up of a plurality of explanations. Further, what has explanatory power in the most general context does not necessarily identify the most important explanatory elements in the case of specific types of organization.

For instance, in the case of the capitalist firm it may be that its spread and resilience is not best explained in the general terms of reductions in transaction costs but in terms of specific features relating to durable employment contracts. The advantages of the modern capitalist firm over market- or exchange-based alternatives may lie in its capacity to develop an integrated corporate culture to facilitate learning and the acquisition of specialist skills. Accordingly, competence-based or capabilities theories of the firm (Foss, 1993; Foss and Knudsen, 1996; Grant, 1996; Montgomery, 1995; Penrose, 1959; Teece and Pisano, 1994) may have validity in the case of this specific historical form, as well as there being a possible place for an even more general theory, such as that based on transaction costs. Hybrid or plural explanations are thus plausible and legitimate, as long as they are mutually complementary and do not contradict one another.

Clearly, the debate over the relative weight given to each part of a hybrid theory cannot be resolved by theory alone. Empirical study is also required. However, all empirical tests have a finite domain. It is vital to specify the type or types of organization being considered before conclusions are drawn. Furthermore, the body of empirical work is likely to be of limited value unless it involves conjoint testing of multiple hypotheses. Finally, and perhaps most importantly, theoretical and empirical work on the firm should not provide a broad definition of that institution and simultaneously and exclusively address a limited range of historical and empirical possibilities. We need theory and evidence concerning both the firm in general, and concerning particular types of firm. Failure to distinguish adequately between the specific and the general has impaired such endeavours since the seminal works of Knight and Coase, and it continues to do so. Investigators of the firm should make it clear what species they are investigating.

11. Evolutionary and Competence-Based Theories of the Firm

This chapter explores evolutionary and competence-based theories of the firm.[1] 'Evolutionary' approaches to the theory of the firm often invoke the biological metaphor of natural selection. The classic example here is the seminal work by Richard Nelson and Sidney Winter: *An Evolutionary Theory of Economic Change* (1982). Exponents of evolutionary approaches argue that they provide better theoretical tools to understand technological and organizational change within the firm, especially when compared to the more static, equilibrium-oriented approaches of neoclassical economic theory.[2]

Evolutionary theories can be regarded as a subset of a wider class of theories, variously described as 'capabilities', 'resource-based', or 'competence-based' theories of the firm. We shall use the latter term here, although the other terms are common in the literature.[3] The competence-based perspective sees the existence, structure and boundaries of the firm as explained in some way by the associated existence of individual or team competences – such as skills and tacit knowledge – which are in some way

---

[1] This chapter makes extensive use of material from (1998c) which received a 'Citation of Excellence, Highest Quality Rating' by Anbar Electronic Intelligence.

[2] Note the definition of neoclassical economics in Chapter 2 above.

[3] Some authors prefer the term 'resource-based' because it clearly relates to *all* resources, human and nonhuman. However, the term 'competence-based' is gaining over it in popularity, and it shall thus be adopted here. Few relevant phenomena, including technology-based economies of scale, do not inextricably have human competences at their core.

fostered and maintained by that organization. Early precursors to this view include Adam Smith and Karl Marx, who saw the division and management of labour as crucial to the developments of skills and providing a key rationale for the firm. But there is a variety of twentieth century exponents, notably including Frank Knight (1921), Edith Penrose (1959), George Richardson (1972), as well as Richard Nelson and Sidney Winter (1982). The central idea of competences provides the basis for evolutionary and non-equilibrium theories of industrial competition and development. Within this group there is a diversity of views, particularly over the nature of (tacit) knowledge, the units and methodology of analysis, and the application of the evolutionary analogy. (See Chandler, 1990; Kogut, 1991; Lazonick, 1990; Nelson, 1991; Pavitt, 1988.) Nevertheless, the competences paradigm has attracted a wide and growing following and its ideas are now prominent in the literature on corporate strategy (Wernerfelt, 1984; Prahalad and Hamel, 1990; Pettigrew and Whipp, 1991; Winter, 1987a). Furthermore, the competence-based approach has links with similar approaches in a number of allied areas, including technology studies and international business (Dosi *et al*, 1988; Dosi *et al*, 1990; Cantwell, 1989; N. Rosenberg, 1994).

The competence-based or competence perspective contrasts with the other large set of theories, frequently described as contractual or contractarian theories of the firm. The focus there is not on the developing resources and skills within the firm but on explicit and implicit contracts between employers, employees and other contractors. The contractual approach emanates from the work of Ronald Coase (1937) and emphasizes the cost of making and monitoring transactions. But even within itself it includes contrasting theories. On the one hand, for instance, there is Oliver Williamson (1975, 1985) who clearly emphasizes the distinction between markets and hierarchies. On the other is Armen Alchian and Harold Demsetz (1972)[4] and 'nexus of contracts' theorists such as Eugene Fama (1980) who enforce no such distinction but see monitoring or metering costs as crucial. Another influential contractarian approach to the theory of the firm, centring on a formal analysis of incomplete contracting and the principal-agent problem, has been developed by Oliver Hart, and his associates Sanford Grossman and John Moore (Grossman and Hart, 1983, 1986; Hart, 1988, 1995; Hart and Moore, 1990). Despite their differences, all these exponents see the informational and other difficulties in formulating, monitoring and policing contracts as the crucial explanatory

---

[4] Note that Demsetz's later position (Demsetz, 1988) is different in some crucial respects from that in his classic joint article with Alchian.

elements. In particular, work in the Coase–Williamson tradition is described as 'transaction cost' economics, because of its emphasis on the costs of formulating, enforcing and monitoring contracts.

A primary distinction in theoretical analyses of the firm is thus between 'contractual' and 'competence' perspectives, with 'transaction cost' theories as a subset of the former and 'evolutionary' approaches as a subset of the latter. It should be noted, however, that while 'contractual' and 'competence' perspectives are quite different in character, several writers try to incorporate both approaches in their work. Indeed, the plausibility of hybrid explanations may stem from the complex nature of economic reality and the fact that a number of causal mechanisms are simultaneously at work. As long as they do not involve internal inconsistencies, plural rather than singular explanations may, in principle, be possible and plausible. An example of a plural position is the work of Richard Langlois (Langlois, 1992; Langlois and Robertson, 1995). Similarly, David Teece and Gary Pisano (1994) place emphasis on human learning and the enhancement of competences or 'dynamic capabilities' while paying some recognition to the role of transaction costs. They argue that the firm arises 'not only because of transaction costs . . . but also because there are many types of arrangements where injecting high powered (market-like) incentives might well be destructive of the cooperative activity and learning' (p. 539). The relationship between evolutionary, competence-based, contractarian and transaction cost theories is illustrated in Figure 11.1.

Figure 11.1:
Relationships Between Contractarian and Competence-Based Theories

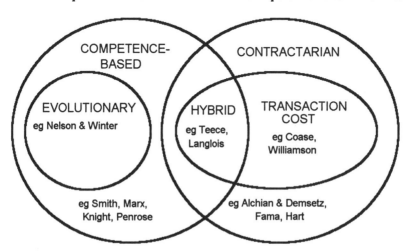

Despite efforts by some theorists to unify contractarian and competence-based approaches, some of the impetus behind the development of competence-based theories stems from dissatisfaction with exclusively transaction cost explanations or with the logic of transaction cost arguments. At first some problems with the contractarian approach are raised. This provides the point of departure for a discussion of the competence-based alternative. Its evolutionary variants are examined subsequently. The chapter concludes with a discussion of the relevance for the theory of corporate strategy.

11.1. PROBLEMS WITH CONTRACTARIAN APPROACHES

Three key features of existing contractarian approaches are identified here, and later contrasted with aspects of the competence-based analysis of the firm. The three features are:

1) Given individuals – typically with given and independent preference functions – are assumed. Transactions between these social atoms are identified as the basic starting points of analysis and it is assumed that all such transactions are evaluated by individuals in terms of uni-dimensional utility levels. Typically, this leads to a neglect of (a) the limits of contracts and exchange and the necessity of non-contractual relations, particularly loyalty and trust, and of (b) processes of radical individual transformation and development, notably an adequate concept of learning. The individualistic focus similarly excludes notions such as organizational learning and group knowledge, leading to an associated neglect of the types of skill and knowledge associated with teams.

2) The analysis of the firm is reduced to contracts between individuals, often involving the minimisation of transaction costs, but typically neglecting technology and production in the following manner. The characteristic assumption of a uniformity of technology over different governance modes implies a separability of production and technology from governance structures or transaction costs. Accordingly, the explanatory contribution of production costs and technology is ignored while governance modes are evaluated. As a result, the emphasis is not on production, accumulation and growth but on the choice of governance structures and the efficient allocation of given resources.

3) A focus on comparative static explanations, where one organizational arrangement is deemed to have lower (transaction) costs than another,

leads to inadequate treatment or neglect of dynamic aspects of the problem, notably learning, innovation and technological development. Furthermore, the focus becomes one of static, cost-minimising efficiency, rather than dynamic efficiency and long-term advantage. Comparative-static or equilibrium-based explanations also have difficulties accounting for the manifest heterogeneity of firm behaviour and performance in the real world.

We now consider these three points in more detail.

11.1.1. Given, Atomistic Individuals

Arguably, with the contractarian approaches – including the 'new' institutional economics of Williamson and others – we have no more than half of the story about institutions in general and firms in particular. The focus is on how given, cost-minimising or utility-maximizing individuals relate to each other to form and sustain institutions. The possibility of individual preference functions themselves being moulded by culture and institutions is ignored. The individuals themselves remain impenetrable atoms: they are not affected fundamentally by institutions and culture. As Roderick Martin (1993, p. 1096) observes, paradoxically 'the new institutional economics does not take institutions seriously enough: organization is reduced to the status of a means of regulating relationships in default of market relations'.

Transaction cost and other contractarian analyses reduce the interaction between individuals to the calculus of costs. Individuals act as utility-maximizing automata on the basis of given preferences. Not only do preferences arise mysteriously from within the individual; social institutions bear upon individuals simply via the costs they impose. As Mary Douglas (1990, p. 102) pointed out in an article critical of Williamson:

> He has a theory of firms, but his theory of the relationship between individuals and firms could be better. He believes firms vary, but not individuals. He has the same representative rational individual marching into one kind of contract or refusing to renew it and entering another kind for the same set of reasons, namely, the cost of transactions in a given economic environment.

On the basis of the assumption of given individuals, contractarian approaches extend concepts that pertain primarily to a market environment into a quite different sphere. In his classic critique of the contractarian tradition in social science, Emile Durkheim insists on the existence, necessity and irreducibility of non-contractual elements in all social relationships, even within the sphere of markets and exchange. He pointed out that while in general an explicit agreement is necessary for any valid contract, there are elements involved that cannot be reduced to the expressed intent of any individual: 'For in a contract not everything is contractual' (Durkheim, 1984, p. 158). Whenever a contract exists there are factors, not reducible to the intentions or agreements of individuals, that have regulatory and binding functions for the contract itself. His key argument is that for all contracts there exists a set of binding rules to which there is no explicit or detailed reference by the parties involved. All market-based and contractual systems thus rely on essentially non-contractual elements – such as trust and moral norms – to function.

This strikes at the core of contractarian theories of the firm where non-contractual relations such as trust and loyalty are neglected. Just as seriously, the conception of the given individual cannot readily incorporate notions such as learning and personal development. Instead of a mechanism by which one individual with given aims and preferences directs another, management becomes a process of learning and discovery in which new aims appear. As Brian Loasby (1995, p. 472) put it:

> it is typically assumed that the best action in any situation is known to the agent who is expected to act, and that the problem is to ensure, if possible, that this is indeed the action that the agent will take; but the primary task of managers is to discover, or (more often) to encourage other people to discover, what action is best, after first identifying what problems or opportunities should receive attention; and it is a major objective of good organization to facilitate this process of identification and discovery.

Instead of the mere input of 'facts', learning is a developmental and reconstitutive process. Typically, neoclassical economics treats learning as the cumulative discovery of pre-existing 'blueprint' information, or Bayesian updating of subjective probability estimates in the light of incoming data (Bray and Kreps, 1987). There are severe problems, however. A process of Bayesian learning in search of an optimum depends upon the existence of correct prior knowledge (Hey, 1981). Furthermore, as Giovanni Dosi and Massimo Egidi (1991), Richard Nelson (1980) and others have argued, the Bayesian approach is a very limited way of conceiving of the role of learning, which in reality is much more than a process of blueprint discovery or statistical correction.

In standard contractual analyses, agents act as if they shared the same model of the world. There may be problems of imperfect information but generally these do not emanate from interpretative ambiguity and differences of perception or cognition. Instead, obstacles to efficient coordination within the firm are typically founded on presumed clashes of individuals' goals and interests, as evidenced by Williamson's persistent emphasis on individual opportunism (Kogut and Zander, 1992; Moschandreas, 1997). Given such assumptions, attention is directed at the lack of a complete sharing of (unambiguous) information or at allegedly inappropriate incentive structures. This 'positivist' stance fails to acknowledge that for information to become knowledge it must be interpreted, and different interpretations are always possible, even with the same set of information (Hodgson, 1988; Nooteboom, 1992, 1995; Fransman, 1994). In standard contractarian explanations, key obstacles to efficiency are not located in the existence of dissimilar cognitive frameworks or different ways of seeing and understanding. This is a serious omission.

Learning depends on acquired cognitive frameworks but at the same time it is an essentially open-ended, provisional and potentially fallible process. It is not simply the progressive acquisition of unambiguous or codifiable knowledge. As well as the possibility of interpretative ambiguity, much knowledge is tacit (Polanyi, 1958, 1967) and has to be communicated by example and shared experience rather than by the written or spoken word. Furthermore, learning is a process of problem-formulation and problem-solving, rather than the acquisition and accumulation of given 'bits' of information 'out there'. This process involves conjecture and error, in which mistakes become opportunities to learn rather than mere random perturbations (Berkson and Wettersten, 1984; Popper, 1972; Rutherford, 1988).

In general, and acutely within organizations, learning involves the alteration of cognitive frames and mental models of the world (Argyris and Schön, 1978; Senge, 1990; Tomer, 1987; Cohen and Sproull, 1996). Accordingly, learning often involves the rejection of inadequate ways of seeing and doing. Learning is not the cumulative addition of knowledge upon a *tabula rasa*: it involves destruction as well as construction. Developing the capacity to unlearn, and learn anew, is itself a part of the learning process. As Kate Cartier (1994, p. 190) put it: 'The idea that knowledge is accumulated [as in the work of Arrow and others] is at variance with the theory that it is continuously reformulated.' Furthermore, problems do not themselves provide nor necessarily suggest solutions: much learning must involve intuition and creativity.

According to Argyris and Schön (1978) and others, learning is not simply information absorption. Learning begins when individuals discover that their mental models, which indicate the expected consequences of particular actions under a variety of assumed conditions, are in error. Because of discrepancies between actual and expected outcomes, people may revise their models, that is, they learn. Organizational learning involves a process of inquiry, reflection and evaluation in which the model is revised and becomes embedded in organizational memory and the regular practices of the organization (Cohen and Sproull, 1996).

There are further reasons why an enriched conception of learning is not found in the equilibrium analysis of neoclassical economics. Neoclassical economics assumes rational agents, yet it is not obvious what is meant by 'rational learning'. How can agents be said to be rational at any given moment when they are in the process of learning? The very act of learning means that not all information is possessed and global rationality is ruled out. Learning is more than the acquisition of information; it is the development of the modes and means of calculation and assessment. If the methods and criteria of 'optimization' are themselves being learned how can learning itself be optimal? By its nature, learning means creativity and the potential disruption of equilibrium. In short, the phenomenon of learning is antagonistic to the concepts of rational optimization and equilibrium.

A strange paradox exists in neoclassical economics, especially since Lionel Robbins (1932) insisted that the subject must be defined in terms of scarcity and choice. On the one hand, that which is in fact highly scarce, computational competence, is assumed to be in abundance (Pelikan, 1989). In typically assuming that all individuals can make optimal decisions in a complex environment and when faced with a large number of alternatives, it is implied that every individual has an unlimited ability to process vast amounts of information, a boundless computational capacity, and the analytical abilities of an advanced mathematician.

Otherwise, neoclassical economics generally assumes given, depletable resources. Hence, apart from the computational and analytical competences associated with the rationality assumption, other managerial or labour skills are regarded as given. Yet in reality they are not strictly confined: the skills of a manager or a worker can be enlarged. These resources are not strictly limited or given *ex ante* because of the phenomenon of 'learning by doing'. As Hirschman (1985, p. 16) pointed out: 'Use of a resource such as a skill has the immediate effect of improving the skill, of enlarging (rather than depleting) its availability.' So, while competences are genuinely scarce, they are not simply given – they have to be developed. We are thus dealing with a problem of creation and production, rather than simply the allocation of given resources.

That the knowledge within a corporation relates essentially to the organization and the group, rather than to the individuals composing them, is significantly emphasized by Winter. He wrote that: 'it is undeniable that large corporations are *as organizations* among society's most significant repositories of the productive knowledge that they exercise and not merely an economic contrivance of the individuals currently associated with them' (Winter, 1988, p. 170). As Winter (1982, p. 76) had elaborated elsewhere:

> The coordination displayed in the performance of organizational routines is, like that displayed in the exercise of individual skills, the fruit of practice. What requires emphasis is that . . . the learning experience is a shared experience of organization members . . . Thus, even if the contents of the organizational memory are stored only in the form of memory traces in the memories of individual members, it is still an organizational knowledge in the sense that the fragment stored by each individual member is not fully meaningful or effective except in the context provided by the fragments stored by other members.

Accordingly 'it is firms, not the people that work for firms, that know how to make gasoline, automobiles and computers' (ibid.). Note also that Masahiko Aoki (1990) wrote of the collective nature of employee knowledge in the firm. Since 'learning and communication of employees take place only within the organizational framework, their knowledge, as well as their capacities to communicate with each other are not individually portable' (p. 45). Similar points were stressed by Dosi and Marengo (1994, p. 162): 'organizational knowledge is neither presupposed nor derived from the available information but rather emerges as a property of the learning system and is shaped by the interaction among the various learning processes that constitute the organization.' Related points were made by William Lazonick (1994, p. 247): 'Innovation is social process that requires the conscious involvement . . . of many people with a variety of specialized skills and functions. Innovation requires collective organization because it is complex, cumulative and continuous.' Teece and Pisano (1994, pp. 544–5) elaborated a similar theme:

> While individual skills are of relevance, their value depends upon their employment, in particular organizational settings. Learning processes are intrinsically social and collective and occur not only through the imitation and emulation of individuals, as with teacher-student or master-apprentice, but also because of joint contributions to the understanding of complex problems. Learning requires common codes of communication and coordinated search procedures.

Contrary to the view of information and knowledge as portable and readily transmissible, knowledge is embedded in social structures and is not immediately transparent. This is partly because opportunities for learning within the firm are transaction and production-specific (Teece, 1988). Also learning is an instituted process of interpretation, appraisal, trial, feedback, and evaluation, involving socially-transmitted cognitive frames and routinised group practices which are often taken for granted. Organizational knowledge interacts with individual knowledge but is more than the sum of the individual parts. It is context dependent, culture-bound and institutionalised.

11.1.2. The Neglect of Production

Mainstream economics often assumes given resources, thereby neglecting production. The analytical preoccupation is with attempts to get the optimal benefit from given resources. In general, contractarian theories of the firm share this bias. In focusing on contracts and transactions, in the contractarian approach attention is shifted away from the production of more resources to the allocation of given goods and services. Furthermore, in transaction cost analysis different governance modes are compared in the context of a given technology. This implies a hermetic separation between social relations and structures on the one hand and technology on the other, enabling a clear conceptual and empirical distinction between production costs and transaction costs. As Ugo Pagano (1991) elaborated, it is also not clear why the causality between technology and organization should run predominantly in one direction. Paul Milgrom and John Roberts (1992, pp. 33–4) highlighted some of the theoretical problems involved in trying to separate the production and governance, and their corresponding costs. The transaction costs argument assumes that production costs are given and do not differ across governance or transaction modes. However, technologies are often linked to transaction modes and structures of governance. When technology is endogenously determined, its choice may be for reasons other than cost minimisation. All this is fairly obvious once we dispense with a purely 'engineering' view of production and see production costs as also affected by social relations between agents. As well as machines, tools and materials, production depends on human activity. Clearly, the ability and motivation of workers to learn will often depend on the organization of production, property rights, and so on. This reinforces the argument that production costs cannot be independent of social relations. Accordingly, an exclusive focus on the minimisation of transaction costs is misconceived.

It is a common mistake to treat production as an extension of exchange, or as an 'exchange with nature'. This error derives from the assumption of a particular kind of given individual, exclusively engaged in contract and trade, as the sole and ultimate animating force in the socio-economic system. Decisions to buy and sell are seen to impel and determine production, as expressed in the idea of 'consumer sovereignty'. Contracts and marketplace decisions are regarded as primary and active, production as consequent and passive. As a result there is no substantial distinction between production and exchange, as the former is seen as being animated by (and even taking the form of) the latter. Once the deal is struck the wheels of production are essentially predetermined. The law of contract, through appropriate penalties, ensures that the goods will appear at the appointed time and in good order. In this case all the key choices and actions take place in the determination of the contract itself. Output is assumed to flow mechanically from input. Production is merely an annex of the market; a place where agents act in accordance with the relevant clauses of the deal.

What is neglected here are key differences between production and exchange. Marx appropriately criticized those economists who continued to view matters solely from the point of view of circulation and allocation, and thereby neglected production.[5]

In contrast to a contract involving the exchange of goods, production involves the use of labour and the intentional and ongoing involvement of a worker. Production is the intentional creation by human beings of a good or service, using appropriate knowledge, tools, machines and materials. When we buy a car or a bag of potatoes they pass from the hands of the seller, and we may thus part company. On the contrary, the employment of a worker does not terminate the relationship between the buyer and seller, the employer and employee. As Alfred Marshall (1949, p. 471) observed, unlike goods or machinery, labour remains physically united with its original owner, even when it is hired out to an employer.

---

[5] Marx (1981, p. 455) argued: 'The genuine science of modern economics begins only when theoretical discussion moves from the circulation process to the production process'. Marx's point was taken up by Bukharin (1972, pp. 54–6) in the early twentieth century and developed by Robinson (1942, pp. 18, 92; 1960, pp. 92–3) in critiques of Austrian and neoclassical economics. The extent to which Marx provided an extensive analysis of the processes of production in *Capital* – as Adam Smith did in *The Wealth of Nations* – is often underestimated, and the relative and absolute importance of his contribution therein is undervalued, even by many latter-day Marxists.

The fact that the seller of labour remains involved far beyond the specification and conclusion of any employment contract means that the scope for decision and choice is extended. If choice and decision are to be real, there must always be the possibility of acting otherwise. Insofar as individuals have discretion and real choice, and may meaningfully make decisions, there is a degree of indeterminacy and uncertainty (Loasby, 1976; Shackle, 1972). As Herbert Simon (1951) and others have pointed out, labour is not a 'passive factor of production'. In modern capitalism, the fact that the worker has not been replaced by a machine may result in part from the fact that an *ex ante*, complete and mechanical specification of the tasks of work is impossible. Employment contracts are imperfectly specified. The terms of the contract cannot be spelt out in full detail because of the complexity of the work process, and the degree of unpredictability of key outcomes. These problems are found in other contracts, but with employment contracts they are particularly severe. For instance, each agent will learn during the execution of the contract, and the agent cannot in principle predict the future knowledge that is to be learned. There is also a heavy reliance on the types of tacit knowledge associated with productive skills.

The fact that a relationship between buyer and seller necessarily endures after the contract is agreed extends its social and non-contractual dimension. For example, modern industrial relations depend a great deal on the generation of trust within the firm and the development of a climate of commitment and loyalty (Fox, 1974). Attempts to specify these factors in contractual terms would not only be impossible because of the complexities and uncertainties involved, they would also be self-defeating. The whole point about such qualities as loyalty and trust is that they are not reducible to a cost calculus. As Kenneth Arrow (1974, p. 23) remarks on trust: 'If you have to buy it, you already have some doubts about what you've bought'. Trust and loyalty cannot be modelled adequately in a contractarian framework.

11.1.3. Dynamic Evolution versus Comparative Statics

Another inherent limitation of the contractarian approach must be emphasized. Notably, Williamson has repeatedly admitted that his approach is one of comparative statics. Typically, the incidence of transaction costs in equilibrium is compared in two or more governance structures, and the structure with the lowest costs is deemed to be more efficient. Williamson (1985, pp. 143–4) acknowledges that a shift from considerations of static to those of dynamic efficiency is not encompassed by his theory: 'the study of economic organization in a regime of rapid innovation poses much more difficult issues than those addressed here . . . Much more study of the relations between organization and innovation is needed.'

As Pagano (1992) explained, the 'new' institutional economics of Williamson and others has downplayed matters of disequilibrium. Analytically, the adoption of an equilibrium approach ignores the difference between *ex ante* and *ex post* forms of coordination. Firms and markets have different coordinative capabilities in dynamic, disequilibrium situations. Firms, through foresight and planning can have advantages *ex ante*: markets typically coordinate *ex post*. This possible and additional reason for the existence of firms is ignored in equilibrium and comparative static analyses.

The neglect of technological innovation and dynamic change is indeed a most serious problem for the equilibrium-oriented approach (Hodgson, 1988, pp. 212–3; Nooteboom, 1992, pp. 284–5). Accordingly, Bengt-Åke Lundvall (1993, pp. 62) concluded that the failure to incorporate innovation is a serious weakness of the static, transaction cost approach: 'one ought to supplement and correct the approach by bringing "innovation as a process of interactive learning" to the centre of analysis.' Consideration of static rather than dynamic efficiency is rooted in the comparative statics of Williamson and Coase. Yet the ability of the firm to foster human learning, technological innovation, and research and development may be a central reason for its existence. It is now widely accepted that learning and technical change cannot be adequately accommodated in a static framework.

Future knowledge is by its nature unknown and the results of research and development are uncertain, in the most radical sense. Uncertainty, in the radical sense of Knight (1921) or Keynes (1936), applies to situations where the calculation or attribution of a numeric probability is impossible: 'the price of copper and the rate of interest twenty years hence, or the obsolescence of a new invention . . . About these matters there is no scientific basis on which to form any calculable probability whatever. We simply do not know' (Keynes, 1973, pp. 113–14). Arguably, such ignorance makes the attachment even of subjective probabilities implausible. This insurmountable difficulty in the specification of outcomes makes the existence of complete futures markets for all innovations and knowledge impossible. Prediction of specific events in a complex and uncertain world is severely constrained and generally analytically irreducible to probabilistic risk. The existence of radical uncertainty in these and other areas means that the future is not reducible to the present – for instance by means of probabilities. For this reason contracts cannot cope fully with the future.

In these circumstances substantial reserves of skills and material resources are required as buffers to deal with contingencies. If these contingencies could be reduced to quantifiable probabilities then they could be readily dealt with by means of subcontracts and insurance. It is because they are not readily quantifiable in this manner that the firm comes in. It has the scale, and the material and complex human resources to cope with uncertainty. The firm may cope with uncertainties by lumping them together within a single organization, which has resources to bear many unquantifiable and unforeseeable shocks. Such arguments are traceable to Knight who argued that the existence of the firm 'is the direct result of the fact of uncertainty' (1921, p. 271). An emphasis on radical uncertainty is also found in the writings of Brian Loasby (1976), Neil Kay (1984), Richard Langlois (1984) and others. Like Knight, these authors regard the firm's capacity to cope with radical uncertainty as a central factor in the explanation of its existence. The focus on uncertainty reinstates the concept of time and further moves us from comparative statics.

With the above considerations the analysis of the firm is put on a quite different track. Recognition of the firm as a means of coping with uncertainty is crucial. Uncertainty is not only about future events themselves but also about the opportunities available. In the context of an uncertain world the analysis of human behaviour has to be centred on the development of capabilities to deal with complexity and change, and on the modes of generation and transmission of knowledge about the evolving socio-economic environment.

In a dynamic perspective the exclusive focus is no longer on equilibrium outcomes. Out of equilibrium, greater diversity of structure and performance is possible. As Jack Downie (1958), Edith Penrose (1959), Wilfred Salter (1960) and Joseph Steindl (1952) indicated – in four classic studies that have suffered unwarranted neglect – there are often enormous and sustained variations in productivity between different firms in the same industry. This contrasts with the textbook picture of firms being driven towards the same long-run equilibrium where costs (and revenues) arc typically the same across firms. A dynamic and open-ended approach challenges the relevance of a long-run equilibrium and admits an ongoing diversity of outcomes. Penrose in particular took on board the central importance of firm heterogeneity and related it to the notion of firm-specific knowledge accumulation. Along with the equilibrium framework of mainstream economics, the Marshallian hypothesis of the 'representative firm' was discarded. The emphasis on dynamics and learning in an out-of-equilibrium context enables a more satisfactory accommodation of the real world fact of firm heterogeneity (Eliasson, 1991; Metcalfe, 1988; Nelson, 1991).

11.2. THE GENESIS OF COMPETENCE-BASED THEORIES OF THE FIRM

It should not be assumed that competence-based theories of the firm are uniform or consistent. Indeed, a variety of approaches could be grouped under this heading. Furthermore, there is not yet a consensus over terminology and key concepts. Nevertheless, the outlines of this general approach are visible. This will be sketched by discussing in brief the works of three major authors who have played a crucial role in the development of the competence-based approach.

11.2.1. Adam Smith and his Critics

The genesis of the competence-based theory of the firm can be traced back to Adam Smith. In his *Wealth of Nations* (1970 [1776]) Smith argued that the division of labour within the firm meant that workers could specialise and enhance their skills through learning-by-doing. Labour productivity was thus increased. This productivity growth in turn led to more sales and the enlargement of the market. In turn, greater demand for products encouraged factory-owners to expand their activities and subdivide the labour process even further. Smith thus described a process of cumulative causation: a virtuous circle of economic growth and prosperity. This was not a story of static equilibrium, instead a tale of dynamic growth and development, in which individual skills are progressively enhanced.

However, in some respects Smith's account is incomplete. Williamson (1975) showed that Smith failed to provide an explanation of which production had to be organized within a firm. The division of labour in production could enhance productivity growth even if the workers were self-employed contractors, buying raw materials and semi-finished products and selling the items after their particular task was completed. Following Coase (1937), Williamson argued that the firm becomes an advantageous creation when the transaction costs of detailed, individual to individual trading are significantly in excess of firm-based organization and employment contracts. This transaction cost argument has proved to be powerfully persuasive for many economists. Competence-based theories of the firm must either supply an alternative explanation or incorporate the transaction cost argument as a part of a hybrid theory. The latter option is explicitly or implicitly adopted by several theorists.

In addition, while Smith recognized the benefits of the division of labour through some enhancement of skills, what is missing in his writings is an idea of corporate culture and the organization's role in the generation, transmission and protection of practical knowledge. As Edwin Cannan (1929, p. 122) pointed out, Smith tucked away the whole question of the 'increase of knowledge under the wings of his exposition of the advantages of the division of labour'. Instead of information and knowledge, Smith (1970, p. 112) wrote principally of 'the increase of dexterity in every particular workman'. Thus Smith saw the specific benefit of learning-by-doing that emanates from the division of labour as primarily one of manual dexterity. Wider notions of learning, knowledge and culture are not prominent. True, he considered in some detail the mental as well as the manual division of labour. However, his implicit separation of the processes of conception and execution in the labour process – prefiguring Frederick Taylor and 'scientific management' – robs manual labour of tacit or and other knowledge and denies the unity of knowing and doing. Furthermore, although Smith put technological change to the forefront, this is not linked explicitly and primarily to an increase in knowledge but to an increase of physical capital goods. Apart from an increase of manual dexterity, the worker's aims and conceptions remain unchanged.[6]

To a considerable degree, the critique of Smith by the German economist Friedrich List in his *National System of Political Economy,* first published in 1841, is relevant here. List (1904, pp. 182–3) criticized Smith for neglecting the importance of both non-material and unexchangeable factors in enhancing the productive potential of a nation. List (1904, p. 108) also wrote: '*The causes of wealth* are something totally different from *wealth itself.* . . . *The power of producing wealth* is therefore infinitely more important than *wealth itself*'. Furthermore, Smith 'did not recognize the difference between productive power and mere values of exchange, and did not investigate the former independently of the latter' (List, 1904, p. 120). In contrast to Smith, List put much greater emphasis on the importance of mental and educative labour. Intellectual labour was not 'unproductive' but given a central place in the analysis. List contended that considerations of productive potential and – in modern parlance – dynamic efficiency could not be reduced solely to current costs and prices. He argued that the productive powers of a nation are greater than the sum of the productive powers of the individuals within it, considered in isolation, because of the productive benefits provided by the national infrastructure and culture. List's

---

[6] Babbage (1846) modified Smith's account of the division of labour, putting emphasis on the pre-existing variety of skills and competences, as the prior basis for allocating different tasks. Like Smith, however, Babbage's conception of management is essentially Taylorist in its separation of conception and execution.

emphasis on learning and the learning environment meant that it was not possible, as in neoclassical economics, to take the individual as given, as a starting point of analysis. If we apply this thesis to organizations rather than nations then we derive a key proposition germane to the competence-based theory of the firm.

Like Smith, Marx in *Capital* also put emphasis on the dynamic processes of production. However, with the rise of neoclassical economics in the 1870s, attention was shifted away from the processes of production and towards the market. The firm became represented less as an organization and more as a set of cost and revenue curves. Although he was responsible for much of this neoclassical analysis, Marshall (1949, p. 115) also emphasized other factors:

> Capital consists in a great part of knowledge and organization . . . Knowledge is our most powerful engine of production . . . Organization aids knowledge; it has many forms . . . it seems best sometimes to reckon organization apart as a distinct agent of production.

However, this important recognition of the role of organization and knowledge was not pursued sufficiently, and was largely ignored by Marshall's neoclassical followers.

11.2.2. Frank Knight

Almost a century and a half after the appearance of *The Wealth of Nations*, another major milestone in the development of the competence-based theory of the firm was established by Frank Knight (1921). Knight gave much greater stress to the role of knowledge in his theory of the firm and emphasized the pervasiveness of uncertainty. Indeed, as noted above, it was the 'fact of uncertainty' that explained the existence of the firm. Knight (1921, p. 244) saw the firm as a means of coping with uncertainty by 'grouping' together activities in larger units of organization:

> The difference between free enterprise and mere production for a market represents the addition of specialization of uncertainty-bearing to the grouping of uncertainties, and takes place under pressure of . . . the anticipation of wants and control of production with reference to the future.

What is involved here, however, is not the mere addition of competences and activities under an organizational umbrella. To cope with uncertainty a system of 'cephalized' and hierarchic management and administration evolves:

> When uncertainty is present the task of deciding what to do and how to do it takes the ascendancy over that of execution, the internal organization of the productive groups is no longer a matter of indifference or a mechanical detail. Centralization of this deciding and controlling function is imperative, a process of 'cephalization', such as has taken place in the evolution of organic life, is inevitable, and for the same reasons as in biological evolution. (Knight, 1921, p. 268–9)

(The use of a biological metaphor should be noted.) Notably, however, uncertainty can never be eradicated and action in such a context requires judgement and other elusive entrepreneurial skills. Typically, and especially in unique cases, these skills are tacit, idiosyncratic and unmeasurable:

> The receipt of profit in a particular case may be argued to be the result of superior judgement. But it is a judgement of judgement, especially one's own judgement, and in an individual case there is no way of telling good judgement from good luck, and a succession of cases sufficient to evaluate the judgement or determine its probable value transforms the profit into a wage. (Knight, 1921, p. 311)

It is a key role of management in the firm to cope with uncertainty by exercising judgement and developing such capacity for judgement in others:

> The fundamental fact of organized activity is the tendency to transform the uncertainties of human opinion and action into measurable probabilities by forming an approximate evaluation of the judgement and capacity of the man. The ability to judge men in relation to the problems they are to deal with, and the power to 'inspire' them to efficiency in judging other men and things, are the essential characteristics of the executive. If these capacities are known, the compensation for exercising them can be competitively imputed and is a wage; only, in so far as they are unknown or known only to the possessor himself, do they give rise to a profit. (ibid.)

Knight thus implies that not all economic competences – particularly that relating to the exercising of judgement in a climate of uncertainty – can be given a market value. Knight's implicit answer to the question 'why do firms exist?' is different from that provided by Coase and Williamson. It is not fundamentally because of the higher transaction costs that the firm cannot be broken down into self-employed producers trading with each other. It is because a complete market for all entrepreneurial and managerial skills is impossible in principle.

In his classic paper on the firm, Coase (1937, pp. 400–401) attempted to rebut Knight's argument, writing: 'We can imagine a system where all advice or knowledge was bought as required.' Coase thus misses the point. Compared with goods and other services, knowledge cannot be so readily 'bought as required' (Foss, 1996). Consider first the famous problem later highlighted by Arrow (1962); we do not know the value and nature of information until after it is purchased. Even more seriously, as Knight (1921, p. 268) argued, uncertainty and ignorance create the 'necessity of acting upon opinion rather than knowledge'. Thus what is involved with managerial and entrepreneurial skills is not mere information or knowledge but sophisticated and essentially idiosyncratic judgements and conjectures in the context of uncertainty. Further, as Knight alluded with his identification of the problem of 'judgement of judgement' – and as Pavel Pelikan (1989) has later elaborated – the purchase or allocation of competence itself require competence: there is a potential problem of infinite regress. Indeed, as Knight (1921, p. 298) himself wrote: the problem 'of selecting human capacities for dealing with unforeseeable situations involves paradox and apparent theoretical impossibility of solution.'

This is a key difference between contractual and competence-based theories of the firm. Coase regards all managerial and entrepreneurial competences as potentially contractible whereas Knight denies that they all can be. Knight's emphasis on uncertainty and on the (idiosyncratic) nature of judgement required to cope with it, provides an argument for the limits of contractual exchange. Just as Durkheim insists that there are non-contractarian elements to any contract, Knight argued that in a context of uncertainty some competences cannot be usefully or readily bought or hired.

When an entrepreneur spots a new and hitherto unrecognized market opportunity he or she is exercising an idiosyncratic and peculiar skill. Accordingly, as Nicolai Foss (1993, p. 136) pointed out:

> Fundamentally, there are two different ways in which an actor may realize the rents from his own specific assets: He can sell his services through a contractual relationship, or start a firm. Because of the idiosyncrasy of entrepreneurial competence, the first option is generally blocked: There does not in the market exist a way to evaluate the entrepreneur's worth . . .

This is much more than a matter of excessive transaction costs. Concerning such competences no adequate cost calculus is possible. Similarly, Teece and Pisano (1994, p. 540) wrote:

The very essence of capabilities/competences is that they cannot be readily assembled through markets . . . the properties of internal organization cannot be replicated by a portfolio of business units amalgamated through formal contracts, as the distinctive elements of internal organization simply cannot be replicated in the market. That is, entrepreneurial activity cannot lead to the immediate replication of unique organizational skills through simply entering a market and piecing the parts together overnight.

The latter quotation, from two leading developers and exponents of the competences or capabilities approach to the theory of the firms, shows the importance of the recognition of the limits to contracts and markets within organizations. One of the major architects of this insight was Knight, although his contribution is not always recognized. Knight was primarily responsible for emphasising the role of knowledge and uncertainty in the analysis of organizations, marking a major advance on the work of earlier economists, including Smith. However, in subsequent years, Knight's path-breaking analysis of the firm had more influence on macroeconomics, through its general emphasis on uncertainty, than on the theory of the firm. Like Coase's seminal paper of 1937, Knight's 1921 book was frequently cited but little read.

11.2.3. Edith Penrose

There are a number of points of similarity between Knight's argument and another neglected classic, *The Theory of the Growth of the Firm* (1959) by Edith Penrose. This work is one of the key statements in the development of the competence-based theory of the firm. Like Knight, Penrose (1959, p. 24) saw the firm as the organized combination of competences: 'a firm is more than an administrative unit; it is also a collection of productive resources the disposal of which between different uses and over time is determined by administrative decision.' Again redolent of Knight, she wrote 'A firm needs a variety of "reserves" for its operation, whether they be financial reserves, inventory reserves, or labour reserves' (Penrose, 1959, p. 94). Implicitly, such reserves are required in order to cope with uncertainty.

Just as Knight alluded to the idiosyncratic nature of non-routine judgement, Penrose (1959, p. 53) gave stress to the tacit and elusive nature of skills. Much knowledge, she argued, cannot be formally taught, or communicated by language. It is the 'result of learning, but learning in the form of personal experience. . . . experience itself can never be transmitted; it produces a change – frequently a subtle change – in individuals and cannot be separated from them.' This learning through experience 'shows itself in two ways – changes in knowledge acquired and changes in the ability to use knowledge.' Penrose thus recognized uncertainty but her theory was also built on the tacit or unteachable nature of much of the operational knowledge within the firm.

The dynamic development of tacit knowledge and other capabilities was the centrepiece of her theory. She thus focused on the *growth* of the firm rather than equilibrium conditions, criticizing the orthodox theory of the firm because within it 'there is no notion of an *internal* process of *development* leading to cumulative movements in any one direction' (Penrose, 1959, p. 1, emphasis in original). Her theory was one of endogenous change and development rather than movements along or shifts in cost and revenue curves: 'the "firm" must be endowed with many more attributes than the "firm" in the theory of the firm, and the significance of these attributes is not conveniently represented by cost and revenue curves' (Penrose, 1959, p. 14).

A key idea in this theory of endogenous change, like that of Smith long before, was that of learning by doing: 'That the knowledge possessed by a firm's personnel tends to increase automatically with experience means, therefore, that the available productive services from a firm's resources will also tend to change' (Penrose, 1959, p. 76). Penrose thus offered a theory of the growth of the firm based on the enhancement of its competences. However, what is involved here is not mere growth by extrapolation. Typically, growth also involves change and development within the firm itself: 'both an automatic increase in knowledge and an incentive to search for new knowledge are, as it were, "built into" the very nature of firms possessing entrepreneurial resources of even average initiative' (Penrose, 1959, p. 78).

Further, competences within the firm are both context-dependent and organically related to each other:

> When men have become used to working in a particular group of other men, they become individually and as a group more valuable to the firm in that the services they can render are enhanced by their knowledge of their fellow-workers, of the methods of the firm, and the best way of doing things in the particular set of circumstances in which they are working. (Penrose, 1959, p. 52)

Another passage made a similar point:

> Businessmen commonly refer to the managerial group as a 'team' and the use of this word implies that management in some sense works as a unit. An administrative group is something more than a collection of individuals; it is a

collection of individuals who have had experience in working together, for only in this way can 'teamwork' be developed. Existing managerial personnel provide services that cannot be provided by personnel newly hired from outside the firm, not only because they make up the administrative organization which cannot be expanded except by their own actions, but also because the experience they gain from working within the firm and with each other enables them to provide services that are uniquely valuable for the operation of the particular group with which they are associated. (Penrose, 1959, p. 46)

Competences do not reside merely in individuals: they are dependent on the organizational context. Typically they have a social and organic quality, many depending on the shared experiences and interactions within the firm.

In discussing the limits to the growth of firms, Penrose (1959, p. 5) showed 'not only that the resources with which a particular firm is accustomed to working will shape the productive services its management is capable of rendering . . . but also that the experiences of management will affect the productive services that all its other resources are capable of rendering.'

In sum, Penrose saw the firm as a complex and structured combination of competences and resources. Placing emphasis on organization and managerial competences, Penrose saw the firm as undergoing a process of constrained but cumulative development. Similar ideas lay behind Alfred Chandler's (1962, 1977, 1990) magisterial studies of the historical development of the capitalist firm. These influential and detailed historical investigations further paved the way for the competence-based approach.

Citation analysis suggests that Penrose's book attracted moderate interest for twenty years after its appearance, achieving a high absolute level of citations in 1976. After a lull in the 1980s, what is remarkable is the growth in the absolute and relative number of citations since 1993, showing that the book – and the competence-based discourse around it – is enjoying a reviving popularity.[7]

Her book is a modern masterpiece in the competence-based approach. Ironically, as noted in preceding chapters, Edith Penrose (1952) had earlier provided one of the most forceful critiques of the use of biological and

---

[7] Penrose's book was reprinted in 1995. Both the annual number of citations and the annual 'citation share' (the number of citations for the work divided by total number of citations in the social sciences, in millions) have revived in the 1990s.

evolutionary analogies in economics.[8] She could not have known in 1952 that that the next major step in the development of the competence-based theory of the firm would be made by Nelson and Winter, and expressed in a book making full use of an evolutionary analogy from biology to understand the processes of economic change. This book is featured in the next section.

Figure 11.2: Citations to Penrose's *Theory of the Growth of the Firm*

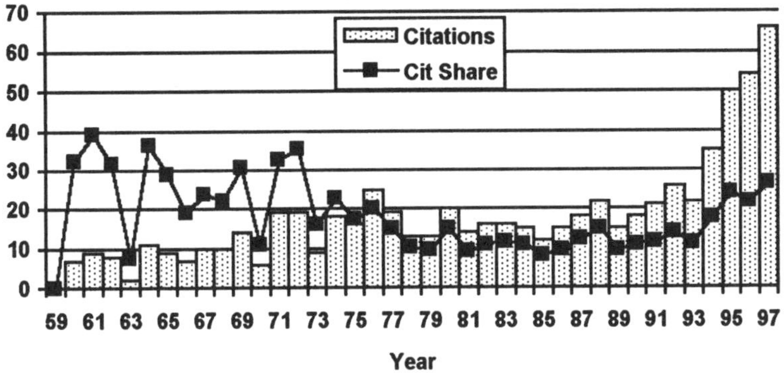

11.2.4. Richard Nelson and Sidney Winter

As elaborated in preceding chapters, in their 1982 classic book *An Evolutionary Theory of Economic Change*, Nelson and Winter developed an alternative theoretical framework to profit maximization for the analysis of the firm. Instead of such an optimizing procedure, they proposed an evolutionary model in which selection operates on the firm's internal

---

[8] In a number of verbal statements to the present author and to others prior to her death in October 1996, Penrose made it clear that she was much more sympathetic to the employment of evolutionary analogies. In conversation in 1994–96 she was still very much concerned with the very meaning of the notion of human consciousness, as she had been in 1952. However, her reading of works such as R. Penrose (1994) – who I understand is not a relative – had led her to explore the possibility of a reconciliation of the phenomenon of consciousness with evolutionary theory. Unlike many mainstream economists, she was never afraid of crossing disciplinary boundaries. Nevertheless, many of her cautionary remarks concerning the limitations of the direct and unmodified application of biological models to economics still apply.

routines. They saw these routines as a kind of DNA within the firm, storing knowledge and sustaining its identity and effectiveness.

At the same time, Nelson and Winter saw the need to explain innovation as well as organizational conservatism and replication. They assumed that if firms went below a threshold level of profitability then that would trigger a 'search' for better techniques or routines. Above this threshold, the firm would 'satisfice'. Thus inspired by the work of Herbert Simon, Nelson and Winter assume that agents attempt to gain a given 'aspiration level' rather than to optimize. Competition drives the whole process and triggers the search for new techniques or routines.

Evolutionary theories of the firm pay more attention to processes of learning and development within organizations. The agent is an explorer and creator rather than a strict maximizer. The firm is a changing organism, typified by both reactive and purposeful behaviours. Because of its radically different depiction of economic agents and processes, Nelson and Winter's theory marks an intellectual revolution in economics. However, as yet it has had only a limited impact on orthodox opinion among economists. One reason why theorists of management and business have been attracted to Nelson and Winter's work is its direct link to competence-based theories of the firm and business strategy.

Echoing Knight and Penrose as well as Veblen, Nelson (1980) had criticized the orthodox treatment of information and knowledge – including technological knowledge – as codifiable and cumulative. His idea of knowledge as largely tacit, idiosyncratic, and context dependent was incorporated in Nelson and Winter's book and forms a key part of their theory. It connects to their core theoretical concept of the routine. The idea of knowledge being embedded in routines is a particular presentation of the concept of competences or capabilities which is the defining notion in competence-based theories.

Traditional neoclassical theory had disregarded the industry-wide variety of organizations and behaviours; the equilibrium framework suggest a population of surviving and equally efficient firms. The move away from equilibrium thinking and the incorporation of a metaphor of ongoing biological selection meant thus the establishment of a theory where firm differences were possible, and mattered (Nelson, 1991). The key reasons for this divergence lay in the fact that individuals can interpret given information in a variety of ways, the fact that responses to external stimuli can be varied, and the fact that idiosyncratic and firm-specific information is the rule. As noted above, earlier exponents of a competence-based theory of the firm – particularly Penrose (1959) in her dynamic framework – had also stressed the variety of organizational and behavioural possibilities and the existence of firm heterogeneity.

Despite the abstract and theoretical nature of Nelson and Winter's 1982 treatise, subsequent work by both authors has shown direct and fruitful applications to industrial policy and strategic management. The application of this broad theoretical approach to management practice is illustrated in Nelson (1991) and a number of other works. For instance, Nelson (1993) has also developed a pioneering analysis of 'national systems of innovation'. The argument here was that innovation and technical change are not simply matters for individual entrepreneurs, but also involve cultural and institutional features at the national level. The work of Nelson and others in this area is currently one of the most fruitful policy-oriented areas of economics research (Lundvall, 1992). Broadly, this work imported and developed the idea of knowledge as largely tacit, idiosyncratic and context dependent. Competences are established and developed within an appropriate framework of institutions and culture. The metaphors of evolutionary selection and mutation can be deployed to describe the general process of development of competences within a socio-economic system. The policy focus becomes one of structuring and guiding these processes in a beneficial way.

The application to strategic management of evolutionary theories in particular and competence-based approaches in general is the subject of the next section.

11.3. APPLICATIONS TO STRATEGIC MANAGEMENT

Fundamentally, the difference of approach asserted by the competence-based perspective is ontological (in emphasising hidden capacities and powers), epistemological (in insisting on non-positivistic conceptions of learning and knowledge) and methodological (in rejecting explanations ultimately in terms of individuals alone). In contrast to much of mainstream economic theory, the emphasis is on dynamic as well as static efficiency, and on production as well as allocation.

It is the purpose of this section to address a large modern literature in which competence-based approaches have been applied to strategic management. Space prohibits an extensive survey of what is now a large literature. It is, however, possible to identify some cardinal themes. To recapitulate, key features of the modern competence-based approach are as follows:

- There is a recognition of learning-by-doing as a source of endogenous growth. This emphasis on learning and growth means that individuals themselves are in a process of development, in contrast to static and equilibrium-based approaches.
- There is a recognition of the role of radical uncertainty and other chronic problems pertaining to information and knowledge in the firm.
- There is a recognition of tacit knowledge and the way in which it is not merely bound up with individuals but with relationships within the organization and the organizational structure as a whole.
- The aforementioned emphasis on learning and the tacit, idiosyncratic and context dependent nature of knowledge leads to the conclusion that not all activities within the firm are contractible.

The key role of knowledge should be emphasized. Further, knowledge is distinguished from information because knowledge can be obtained only via processes of cognition and interpretation (Cartier, 1994). Typically, contractarian theories do not make or emphasize this distinction, the focus being on information asymmetries rather than the idiosyncratic, organization-bound character of knowledge. Martin Fransman (1994, p. 715) thus made a distinction between theories of the firm based on 'individual and organizational responses to information-related problems' and approaches which see 'the firm as a repository of knowledge.' The competence-based analyses of Chandler, Nelson, Penrose, Teece and Winter come into the latter category.

In contrast to the standard textbook theory, the firm is not understood principally through its cost and revenue curves. Instead, there is an emphasis on knowledge, learning, routines and other resources. In other words, the competence perspective understands the firm's competitive situation primarily in regard to its resources, rather than its market position. As Richard Rumelt (1984, p. 57) explained, in essence the strategy concept 'is that a firm's competitive position is defined by a bundle of unique resources and relationships, and that the task of general management is to adjust and renew these resources and relationships, as time, competition, and change erode their value.'

This notion that competitive strategy requires both the exploitation of existing internal and external firm-specific capabilities and of developing new ones was suggested by Penrose (1959) and P. Selznick (1957). It was not until the 1980s that this idea made a major impact on strategic management literature, with the contributions of Teece (1982, 1988), Birger Wernerfelt (1984), Jay Barney (1986) and others.

To some degree there is also a contrast with the approach to competitive strategy advocated by Michael Porter (1980).[9] Barney (1986) and Ingemar Dierickx and Karel Cool (1989) argue that by concentrating excessive attention on product market strategies, the Porter framework neglects the cost of developing the basis of and implementing those very strategies. Resources must be acquired or built before a product market strategy may be implemented. Again, instead of an exclusive outward orientation toward market niches and advantageous cost-revenue combinations, the competence-based perspective also puts emphasis on building up resources and organizational routines within the firm itself. Organization and production are emphasized, as well as the market. As Teece and Pisano (1994, p. 553) put it:

> We posit that the competitive advantage of firms stems from dynamic capabilities rooted in high performance routines operating inside the firm, embedded in the firm's processes, and conditioned by its history. Because of imperfect factor markets, or more precisely the non-tradability of 'soft' assets like values, culture, and organizational experience, these capabilities generally cannot be bought: they must be built. This may take years – possibly decades. . . . The capabilities approach accordingly sees definite limits on strategic options, at least in the short run. Competitive success occurs in part because of processes and structures already established and experience obtained in earlier periods.

Accordingly, strategic emphasis is put on learning and the growth of knowledge within the firm. As Ray Stata (1989, p. 64) argued: 'the rate at which individuals and organizations learn may become the most sustainable competitive advantage'. Michael Porter and Claas van der Linde (1995, p. 98) addressed the weighty evidence consistent with this conclusion:

> Detailed case studies of hundreds of industries, based in dozens of countries, reveal that internationally competitive companies are not those with the cheapest inputs or the largest scale, but those with the capacity to improve and innovate continually.

This ties in with the work of researchers concerned with 'organizational learning' such as Peter Senge (1990). He made a relevant and useful

---

[9] Note, however, that Porter (e.g. 1990, p. 73) rightly put emphasis on learning, and notes that much of modern competition involves shifting the organization's capacity to learn.

distinction between adaptive learning, where the organization copes with changes in the external world but does not make any central changes in its shared mental model, and, in contrast, generative learning is more creative and significant changes in the shared mental model are made. Obstacles to organizational learning are identified in such research, such as inaccessible and obscure mental models, defensive modes of behaviour, lack of good team work, lack of shared vision, or a lack of a system-wide view by employees.

The competence-based approach also addresses key strategic questions such as the identification in specific cases of the possible advantages of vertical integration. Again the orientation is less towards market evaluations and more towards the building of organizational resources. Rumelt (1974) and Teece *et al* (1994) argue that because capabilities cannot easily be bought and must be built, opportunities for growth from diversification are thus likely to be limited, lying 'close in' to the firm's existing lines of product.

It must be noted, however, that different protagonists of the competence-based approach put different emphases on aspects of the analysis. Seeing the dangers in a more static variant of the competence-based approach, Teece and his collaborators advocate an analysis of 'dynamic capabilities'. They argue that static variants have proved to be strategically defective:

> Well-known companies like IBM, Texas Instruments, Phillips, and others appear to have followed a 'resource-based strategy' of accumulating valuable technology assets, often guarded by an aggressive intellectual property stance. However, this strategy is often not enough to support a significant competitive advantage. (Teece and Pisano, 1994, p. 538)

Hence the dynamic aspects of strategy are emphasized:

> Winners in the global marketplace have been firms that can demonstrate timely responsiveness and rapid and flexible product innovation, coupled with the management capability to effectively coordinate and redeploy internal and external competences. Not surprisingly, industry observers have remarked that companies can accumulate a large stock of valuable technology assets and still not have many useful capabilities. We refer to this source of competitive advantage as 'dynamic capabilities' to emphasize two key aspects which were not the main focus of attention in previous strategy perspectives. The term 'dynamic' refers to the shifting character of the environment; certain strategic responses are required when time-to-market and timing is critical, the pace of innovation is accelerating, and the nature of future competition and markets is difficult to determine. The

term 'capabilities' emphasizes the key role of strategic management in appropriately adapting, integrating, and re-configuring internal and external organizational skills, resources, and functional competences toward changing environment. (ibid.)

The emphasis on the development of the 'core competences' of the corporation raises the question of the identification of that core and its boundaries (Prahalad and Hamel, 1990). Langlois and Robertson (1995, p. 7) address this issue in these terms:

firms and other types of organizations consist of two distinct but changing parts. The first part, the *intrinsic core*, comprises elements that are idiosyncratically synergistic, inimitable, and noncontestable.   . . .   The remainder of the organization consists of *ancillary capabilities* that are contestable and may not be unique.

Much of the strategic management literature is concerned with the operationalization of distinctions along these lines. The aim is to identify the strategic focus of the organization. A number of studies suggest that this has implications for such issues as the choice of the appropriate diversification strategy for the firm (Rumelt, 1974; Wernerfelt and Montgomery, 1988; Chatterjee and Wernerfelt, 1991).

Despite a long history stretching back to the birth of modern economics at the end of the eighteenth century, the competence-based approach to the theory of the firm and corporate strategy is still in its infancy. It offers, however, a crucial reorientation away from a market-based analysis and towards organization, knowledge and learning.

References

Ackerman, Frank (1997), 'Consumed in Theory: Alternative Perspectives on the Economics of Consumption', *Journal of Economic Issues,* **31**(3), September, 651–64.

Ahmad, Syed (1991), *Capital in Economic Theory: Neo-classical, Cambridge and Chaos*, Aldershot: Edward Elgar.

Alchian, Armen A. (1950), 'Uncertainty, Evolution, and Economic Theory', *Journal of Political Economy,* **58**(2), June, 211–22. Reprinted in Witt (1993b) and in Hodgson (1998f).

Alchian, Armen A. (1953), 'Comment', *American Economic Review,* **43**(3), September, 600–3.

Alchian, Armen A. (1977), *Economic Forces at Work*, Indianapolis: Liberty Press.

Alchian, Armen A. and Demsetz, Harold (1972), 'Production, Information Costs, and Economic Organization', *American Economic Review,* **62**(4), December, 777–95. Reprinted in Alchian (1977).

Alexander, Samuel (1920), *Space, Time and Deity*, 2 vols, London: Macmillan.

Alland Jr, Alexander (1967), *Evolution and Human Behavior*, New York: Natural History Press.

Allen, Peter M. (1988), 'Evolution, Innovation and Economics', in Dosi, Freeman, Nelson, Silverberg and Soete (1988, pp. 95–119).

Allen, Peter M. and Lesser, M. (1991), 'Evolutionary Human Systems: Learning, Ignorance and Subjectivity', in Saviotti and Metcalfe (1991, pp. 160–71).

Allen, Peter M. and McGlade, J. M. (1987), 'Modelling Complex Human Systems: A Fisheries Example', *European Journal of Operational Research,* **30**, 147–67.

Andersen, Esben Sloth (1994), *Evolutionary Economics: Post-Schumpeterian Contributions*, London: Pinter.

Anderson, Philip W. (1995), 'Viewpoint: The Future', *Science,* **267**, 17 March, 1617–8.

Aoki, Masahiko (1990), 'The Participatory Generation of Information Rents and the Theory of the Firm', in Aoki, Masahiko, Gustafsson, Bo and Williamson, Oliver E. (eds) (1990), *The Firm as a Nexus of Treaties*, Sage, London, pp. 26–51.

Archer, Margaret S. (1995), *Realist Social Theory: The Morphogenetic Approach*, Cambridge: Cambridge University Press.

Argyris, Chris and Schön, Donald (1978), *Organizational Learning: A Theory of Action Perspective*, Reading, MA: Addison-Wesley.

Arrow, Kenneth J. (1962), 'Economic Welfare and the Allocation of Resources to Invention', in Nelson, Richard R. (1962), *The Rate and Direction of Inventive Activity: Economic and Social Factors*, Princeton University Press, Princeton, pp. 609–25.

Arrow, Kenneth J. (1969), 'The Organization of Economic Activity: Issues Pertinent to the Choice of Market Versus Nonmarket Allocation', in *The Analysis and Evaluation of Public Expenditure: The PPB System*, vol. 1, US Joint Economic Committee, pp. 59–73, Washington DC: US Government Printing Office.

Arrow, Kenneth J. (1974), *The Limits of Organization*, New York: Norton.

Arrow, Kenneth J. (1986), 'Rationality of Self and Others in an Economic System', *Journal of Business*, **59**(4.2), October, S385–S399. Reprinted in Hogarth, R. M. and Reder, M. W. (eds) (1987), *Rational Choice: The Contrast Between Economics and Psychology*, Chicago: University of Chicago Press.

Arrow, Kenneth J. (1994), 'Methodological Individualism and Social Knowledge', *American Economic Review (Papers and Proceedings)*, **84**(2), May, 1–9.

Arrow, Kenneth J. (1995), 'Viewpoint: The Future', *Science*, **267**, 17 March, p. 1617.

Arrow, Kenneth J. and Hahn, Frank H. (1971), *General Competitive Analysis*, Edinburgh: Oliver and Boyd.

Arthur, W. Brian (1989), 'Competing Technologies, Increasing Returns, and Lock-in by Historical Events', *Economic Journal*, **99**(1), March, 116–31. Reprinted in Freeman (1990).

Ashley, William J. (1924), 'Evolutionary Economics', in *Birkbeck College Centenary Lectures: 1823–1923. A Course of Lectures Given at the College in Connection With the Celebration of the Centenary*, with a Preface by J. Ramsay McDonald MP, London: University of London Press, pp. 35–61.

Ayres, Clarence E. (1935), 'Moral Confusion in Economics', *International Journal of Ethics*, **45**, January, 170–99. Reprinted in Samuels (1988).

Ayres, Clarence E. (1944), *The Theory of Economic Progress*, 1st edn., Chapel Hill, North Carolina: University of North Carolina Press.

Ayres, Clarence E. (1952), *The Industrial Economy*, Cambridge, MA: Houghton Mifflin.

Ayres, Clarence E. (1958), 'Veblen's Theory of Instincts Reconsidered', in Dowd, Douglas F. (ed.) (1958), *Thorstein Veblen: A Critical Appraisal*, Ithica, NY: Cornell University Press, pp. 25–37.

Ayres, Clarence E. (1961), *Toward a Reasonable Society: The Values of Industrial Civilization*, Austin: University of Texas Press.

Axelrod, Robert M. (1984), *The Evolution of Cooperation*, New York: Basic Books.

Babbage, Charles (1846), *On the Economy of Machinery and Manufactures*, 4th edn. (1st edn. 1832), John Murray, London.

Baker, Wayne E. (1984), 'The Social Structure of a National Securities Market', *American Journal of Sociology*, **89**(4), 775–811. Reprinted in Swedberg (1996).

Barber, Bernard (1977), 'The Absolutization of the Market: Some Notes on How We Got from There to Here', in Dworkin, G., Bermant, G. and Brown, P. (eds) (1977), *Markets and Morals*, Washington, DC: Hemisphere, pp. 15–31.

Barber, William J. (1994), 'The Divergent Fates of Two Strands of "Institutionalist" Doctrine During the New Deal Years', *History of Political Economy*, **26**(4), Winter, 569–87.

Barber, William J. (1996) *Design Within Disorder* (Cambridge: Cambridge University Press).

Barney, Jay B. (1986), 'Strategic Factor Markets: Expectations, Luck and Business Strategy', *Management Science*, **32**, 1231–41.

Basalla, George (1989), *The Evolution of Technology*, Cambridge: Cambridge University Press.

Batt, Francis R. (1929), *The Law of Master and Servant*, New York: Pitman Publishing.

Baumol, William J. (1995), 'What's Different About European Economics?', *Kyklos*, **48**, Fasc. 2, 187–92.

Baumol, William J. and Quandt, Richard E. (1964), 'Rules of Thumb and Optimally Imperfect Decisions', *American Economic Review*, **54**(2), March, 23–46.

Becker, Gary S. (1976a), *The Economic Approach to Human Behavior*, Chicago: University of Chicago Press.

Becker, Gary S. (1976b), 'Altruism, Egoism, and Genetic Fitness: Economics and Sociobiology', *Journal of Economic Literature*, **14**(2), December, 817–26. Reprinted in Hodgson (1995a).

Becker, Gary S. (1981), *A Treatise on the Family*, 1st edn., Cambridge, MA: Harvard University Press.

Becker, Gary S. (1996), *Accounting for Tastes*, Cambridge, MA: Harvard University Press.

Becker, Gary S. and Posner, Richard A. (1993), 'Cross-Cultural Differences in Family and Sexual Life: An Economic Analysis', *Rationality and Society*, **5**(4), October, 421–31.

Beed, Clive (1991), 'Philosophy of Science and Contemporary Economics: An Overview', *Journal of Post Keynesian Economics*, **13**(4), Summer, 459–94.

Bell, Daniel and Kristol, Irving (eds) (1981), *The Crisis in Economic Theory*, New York: Basic Books.

Bellerby, John R. (1927), 'The Evolution of a Wage Adjustment System', *International Labour Review*, **16**(1-3).

Bellomy, Donald C. (1984), 'Social Darwinism Revisited', *Perspectives in American History*, New Series, **1**, 1–129.

Berg, Maxine (1991), 'On the Origins of Capitalist Hierarchy', in Bo Gustafsson (ed.) (1991), *Power and Economic Institutions: Reinterpretations in Economic History*, Aldershot: Edward Elgar.

Bergson, Henri (1911), *Creative Evolution*, translated from the French edition of 1907, New York: Henry Holt.

Berkson, William and Wettersten, John (1984), *Learning from Error: Karl Popper's Psychology of Learning*, La Salle: Open Court.

Berle, Adolf A. and Means, Gardiner C. (1932), *The Modern Corporation and Private Property*, New York: Commerce Clearing House.

Bertalanffy, Ludwig von (1950), 'The Theory of Open Systems in Physics and Biology', *Science*, No. 111, 23–9.

Bhaduri, Amit (1969), 'On the Significance of Recent Controversies in Capital Theory: A Marxian View', *Economic Journal*, **79**(3), 532–9, reprinted in Harcourt and Laing (1971) and in Bhaduri (1993).

Bhaduri, Amit (1993), *Unconventional Economic Essays*, Oxford: Oxford University Press.

Bhaduri, Amit and Robinson, Joan (1980), 'Accumulation and Exploitation: An Analysis in the Tradition of Marx, Sraffa and Kalecki', *Cambridge Journal of Economics*, **4**(2), June, 103–15. Reprinted in Bhaduri (1993).

Bhaskar, Roy (1975), *A Realist Theory of Science*, Leeds: Leeds Books. 2nd edn. 1978, Brighton: Harvester.

Bhaskar, Roy (1979), *The Possibility of Naturalism: A Philosophic Critique of the Contemporary Human Sciences*, Brighton: Harvester.

Bicchieri, Cristina (1994), *Rationality and Coordination*, Cambridge and New York: Cambridge University Press.

Biddle, Jeffrey E. (1990), 'Purpose and Evolution in Commons's Institutionalism', *History of Political Economy*, **22**(1), Spring, 19–47. Reprinted in Hodgson (1998f).

Biddle, Jeffrey E. (1996), 'A Citation Analysis of the Sources and Extent of Wesley Mitchell's Reputation', *History of Political Economy*, **28**(2), Summer, 137–69.

Binmore, Kenneth (1987), 'Modelling Rational Players, I', *Economics and Philosophy*, **3**, 179–214.

Binmore, Kenneth (1988), 'Modelling Rational Players, II', *Economics and Philosophy*, **3**, 9–55.

Blaas, Wolfgang and Foster, John (eds) (1992), *Mixed Economies in Europe: An Evolutionary Perspective on their Emergence, Transition and Regulation*, Aldershot: Edward Elgar.

Black, Max (1962), *Models and Metaphors: Studies in Language and Philosophy*, Ithaca: Cornell University Press.

Blaug, Mark (1968), *Economic Theory in Retrospect*, 2nd edn., Cambridge: Cambridge University Press.

Blaug, Mark (ed.) (1986), *Who's Who in Economics: A Biographical Dictionary of Major Economists 1700–1986*, 2nd edn., Brighton: Wheatsheaf.

Blinder, Alan (1990), 'Discussion', *American Economic Review*, **80**, May, 445–7.

Boettke, Peter J. (1989), 'Evolution and Economics: Austrians as Institutionalists', *Research in the History of Economic Thought and Methodology*, **6**, 73–89.

Boggio, Luciano (1985), 'On the Stability of Production Prices', *Metroeconomica*, **37**(3), October, 241–67.

Bohm, David (1980), *Wholeness and the Implicate Order*, London: Routledge and Kegan Paul.

Böhm, Stephan (1989), 'Hayek on Knowledge, Equilibrium and Prices: Context and Impact', *Wirtschaftspolitische Blatter*, **36**(2), 201–13.

Bonaccorsi, Andrea, Pammolli, Fabio and Tani, Simone (1995), 'On R&D and the Nature of the Firm', University of Pisa, mimeo.

Boulding, Kenneth E. (1950), *A Reconstruction of Economics*, New York: Wiley.

Boulding, Kenneth E. (1978), *Ecodynamics: A New Theory of Societal Evolution*, Beverly Hills: Sage.

Boulding, Kenneth E. (1981), *Evolutionary Economics*, Beverly Hills, CA: Sage Publications.

Boulding, Kenneth E. (1991), 'What is Evolutionary Economics?', *Journal of Evolutionary Economics*, 1(1), January, 9–17.

Bowler, Peter J. (1983), *The Eclipse of Darwinism: Anti-Darwinian Evolution Theories in the Decades around 1900*, Baltimore: Johns Hopkins University Press.

Bowles, Samuel (1985), 'The Production Process in a Competitive Economy: Walrasian, Neo-Hobbesian, and Marxian Models', *American Economic Review*, 75(1), March, 16–36.

Boyd, Robert and Richerson, Peter J. (1980), 'Sociobiology, Culture and Economic Theory', *Journal of Economic Behavior and Organization*, 1(1), March, 97–121. Reprinted in Witt (1993b).

Bradach, J. L. and Eccles, R. G. (1989), 'Price, Authority and Trust: From Ideal Types to Plural Forms', *Annual Review of Sociology*, 15, 87–118.

Brandon, Robert N. and Burian, Richard M. (eds) (1984), *Genes, Organisms, Populations: Controversies Over the Units of Selection*, Cambridge, MA: MIT Press.

Braverman, Harry (1974), *Labor and Monopoly Capital: The Degradation of Work in the Twentieth Century*, New York: Monthly Review Press.

Bray, Margaret and Kreps, David M. (1987), 'Rational Learning and Rational Expectations', in George R. Feiwel (ed.) (1987), *Arrow and the Ascent of Modern Economic Theory*, Macmillan, London, pp. 597–625.

Buchanan, James M. (1969), 'Is Economics the Science of Choice?', in Erich Streissler (ed.) (1969), *Roads to Freedom: Essays in Honour of Friedrich A. von Hayek*, London: Routledge and Kegan Paul, pp. 47–64.

Bucher, Carl (1901), *Industrial Evolution*, New York: Henry Holt.

Bukharin, Nikolai (1972), *The Economic Theory of the Leisure Class*, translated from the Russian edition of 1917, New York: Monthly Review Press.

Burns, Arthur R. (1936), *The Decline of Competition: A Study of the Evolution of American Industry*, New York: McGraw-Hill.

Burrow, John W. (1966), *Evolution and Society: A Study of Victorian Social Theory*, Cambridge: Cambridge University Press.

Burt, Cyril (1962), 'The Concept of Consciousness', *British Journal of Psychology*, 53, 229–42.

Burton, M. P. and Phimister, E. (1995), 'Core Journals: A Reappraisal of the Diamond List', *Economic Journal*, 105(2), March, 361–73.

Bush, Paul Dale (1993), 'The Methodology of Institutional Economics: A Pragmatic Instrumentalist Perspective' in Marc R. Tool (ed.) (1993),

Institutional Economics: Theory, Method, Policy, Kluwer, Boston, pp. 59–107.

Caldwell, Bruce J. (1982), *Beyond Positivism: Economic Methodology in the Twentieth Century*, London: Allen and Unwin.

Camic, Charles (1986), 'The Matter of Habit', *American Journal of Sociology*, **91**(5), 1039–87.

Campbell, Donald T. (1965), 'Variation, Selection and Retention in Sociocultural Evolution', in Barringer, H. R., Blanksten, G. I. and Mack, R. W. (eds) (1965), *Social Change in Developing Areas: A Reinterpretation of Evolutionary Theory*, Cambridge, MA: Schenkman, pp. 19–49. Reprinted in *General Systems*, **14**, 69–85; and Hodgson (1998f).

Campbell, Donald T. (1974), '"Downward Causation" in Hierarchically Organized Biological Systems', in Ayala, Francisco J. and Dobzhansky, T. (eds) (1974), *Studies in the Philosophy of Biology*, Berkeley and Los Angeles: University of California Press, pp. 179–86.

Campbell, Donald T. (1994), 'How Individual and Face-to-Face-Group Selection Undermine Firm Selection in Organizational Evolution', in Baum, Joel A. and Singh, Jitendra V. (eds) (1994), *Evolutionary Dynamics of Organizations*, Oxford: Oxford University Press, pp. 23–38.

Cannan, Edwin (1929), *A Review of Economic Theory*, New York: Augustus Kelley.

Cantwell, John (1989), *Technological Innovation and Multinational Corporations*, Oxford: Basil Blackwell.

Carlson, Mathieu J. (1997), 'Mirowski's Thesis and the "Integrability Problem" in Neoclassical Economics', *Journal of Economic Issues*, **31**(3), September, 741–60.

Cartier, Kate (1994), 'The Transaction Costs and Benefits of the Incomplete Contract of Employment', *Cambridge Journal of Economics*, **18**(2), April, 181–96.

Chamberlain, Neil W. (1963), 'The Institutional Economics of John R. Commons', in Dorfman, Joseph, Ayres, Clarence W., Chamberlain, Neil W., Kuznets, Simon, and Gordon, Robert A. (1963), *Institutional Economics: Veblen, Commons, and Mitchell Reconsidered*, Berkeley, CA: University of California Press, pp. 63–94.

Chandler, Alfred D. Jr (1962), *Strategy and Structure: Chapters in the History of the Industrial Enterprise*, New York: Doubleday.

Chandler, Alfred D. Jr (1977), *The Visible Hand: The Managerial Revolution in American Business*, Cambridge, MA: Harvard University Press.

Chandler, Alfred D. Jr (1990), *Scale and Scope: The Dynamics of Industrial Capitalism*, Cambridge, MA: Harvard University Press.

Chatterjee, Sayan and Wernerfelt, Birger (1991), 'The Link Between Resources and Types of Diversification', *Strategic Management Journal*, **12**, 33–48.

Chomsky, Noam (1959), 'Review of *Verbal Behavior* by B. F. Skinner', *Language*, **35**, 26–58.

Clark, John Bates (1885), *The Philosophy of Wealth: Economic Principles Newly Formulated*, London and New York: Macmillan.

Clark, John Maurice (1935), 'Aggregate Spending by Public Works', *American Economic Review*, **25**(1), March, 14–20. Reprinted in Clark, John Maurice (1967), *Preface to Social Economics*, New York: Augustus Kelley.

Clark, Norman G. and Juma, Calestous (1987), *Long-Run Economics: An Evolutionary Approach to Economic Growth*, London: Pinter.

Clower, Robert W. (1969), 'Introduction', in Robert W. Clower (ed.) (1969), *Monetary Theory*, Harmondsworth: Penguin, pp. 7–21.

Clutton-Brock, T. H. and Harvey, P. H., (eds) (1978), *Readings in Sociobiology*, Reading: W. H. Freeman.

Coase, Ronald H. (1937), 'The Nature of the Firm', *Economica*, **4**, November, 386–405. Reprinted in Williamson and Winter (1991).

Coase, Ronald H. (1977), 'Economics and Contiguous Disciplines', in Mark Perlman (ed.) (1977), *The Organization and Retrieval of Economic Knowledge*, Boulder, CO: Westview Press.

Coase, Ronald H. (1984), 'The New Institutional Economics', *Journal of Institutional and Theoretical Economics*, **140**, 229–31.

Coase, Ronald H. (1988), 'The Nature of the Firm: Origin, Meaning, Influence', *Journal of Law, Economics, and Organization*, **4**(1), Spring, 3–47. Reprinted in Williamson and Winter (1991).

Coase, Ronald H. (1996), Personal communication to G. Hodgson, dated 15 February.

Cobb, John C. (1926), 'Quantitative Analysis and the Evolution of Economic Science', *American Economic Review*, **16**(3), 426–33.

Cohen, Jack and Stewart, Ian (1994), *The Collapse of Chaos: Discovering Simplicity in a Complex World*, London and New York: Viking.

Cohen, Michael D. and Sproull, Lee S. (eds) (1996), *Organizational Learning*, London: Sage.

Cohen, Paul R. (1985), *Heuristic Reasoning: An Artificial Intelligence Approach*, Boston: Pitman Advanced Publishing.

Colander, David C. and Coats, A. W. (1989), *The Spread of Economic Ideas*, Cambridge: Cambridge University Press.

Colander, David C. and Landreth, Harry (eds) (1996), *The Coming of Keynesianism to America: Conversations with the Founders of Keynesian Economics*, Cheltenham, UK and Brookfield, US: Edward Elgar.

Coleman, James S. (1990), *Foundations of Social Theory*, Cambridge, MA: Harvard University Press.

Coleman, James S. and Fararo, Thomas (eds) (1990), *Rational Choice Theory: Advocacy and Critique*, Newbury Park: Sage.

Commons, John R. (1897), 'Natural Selection, Social Selection, and Heredity', *The Arena*, **18**, July, 90–7. Reprinted in Hodgson (1998f).

Commons, John R. (1924), *The Legal Foundations of Capitalism*, New York: Macmillan. Reprinted 1968 (Madison: University of Wisconsin Press) and 1974, New York: Augustus Kelley.

Commons, John R. (1934), *Institutional Economics – Its Place in Political Economy*, New York: Macmillan. Reprinted 1990 with a new introduction by M. Rutherford, New Brunswick, NJ: Transaction.

Commons, John R. (1950), *The Economics of Collective Action*, edited by K. H. Parsons, New York: Macmillan.

Conlisk, John R. (1980), 'Costly Optimizers versus Cheap Imitators', *Journal of Economic Behavior and Organization*, **1**, 275–93.

Conlisk, John R. (1996), 'Why Bounded Rationality?', *Journal of Economic Literature*, **34**(2), June, 669–700.

Cooper, W. S. (1989), 'How Evolutionary Biology Challenges the Classical Theory of Rational Choice', *Biology and Philosophy*, **4**(4), October, 457–81.

Copeland, Morris A. (1931), 'Economic Theory and the Natural Science Point of View', *American Economic Review*, **21**(1), March, 67–79. Reprinted in Samuels (1988) and Hodgson (1998f).

Copeland, Morris A. (1936), 'Commons's Institutionalism in Relation to the Problem of Social Evolution and Economic Planning', *Quarterly Journal of Economics*, **50**(2), 333–46.

Copeland, Morris A. (1958), 'On the Scope and Method of Economics' in Dowd, Douglas F. (ed.) (1958), *Thorstein Veblen: A Critical Appraisal*, Ithica, NY: Cornell University Press, pp. 57–75. Reprinted in Hodgson (1995a).

Coricelli, Fabrizio and Dosi, Giovanni (1988), 'Coordination and Order in Economic Change and the Interpretative Power of Economic Theory', in Dosi *et al* (1988, pp. 124–47). Reprinted in Hodgson (1993d).

Crozier, John Beattie (1906), *The Wheel of Wealth: Being a Reconstruction of the Science and Art of Political Economy on the Lines of Modern Evolution*, London: Longmans Green.

Crutchfield, James P., Farmer, J. Doyne and Huberman, B. A. (1982), 'Fluctuations and Simple Chaotic Dynamics', *Physics Reports*, **92**, 45–82.

Crutchfield, James P., Farmer, J. Doyne, Packard, Norman H., Shaw, Robert S. (1986), 'Chaos', *Scientific American*, **255**(6), December, 38–49.

Cunningham, William (1892), 'The Perversion of Economic History', *Economic Journal*, **2**, 491–506.

Currie, Martin and Steedman, Ian (1990), *Wrestling With Time: Problems in Economic Theory*, Manchester: Manchester University Press.

Cyert, Richard M. and March, James G. (1963), *A Behavioral Theory of the Firm*, Engelwood Cliffs, NJ: Prentice-Hall.

Dahlman, Carl J. (1979), 'The Problem of Externality', *Journal of Law and Economics*, **22**(1), April, 141–62.

Daniel, Glyn (1968), *The First Civilizations: The Archaeology of their Origins*, London: Thames and Hudson.

Darwin, Charles (1872), *On the Origin of Species by Means of Natural Selection*, last edn., London: John Murray.

David, Paul A. (1985), 'Clio and the Economics of QWERTY', *American Economic Review (Papers and Proceedings)*, **75**(2), May, 332–7. Reprinted in Freeman (1990) and Witt (1993b).

Davidson, Paul (1972), *Money and the Real World*, 1st. edn., London: Macmillan.

Davis, Randall and Lenat, Douglas B. (1982), *Knowledge-Based Systems in Artificial Intelligence*, New York: McGraw-Hill.

Dawkins, Richard (1976), *The Selfish Gene*, Oxford: Oxford University Press.

Day, Richard H. (1975), 'Adaptive Processes and Economic Theory', in Richard H. Day and T. Groves (eds) (1975), *Adaptive Economic Models*, New York: Academic Press, pp. 1–38.

Day, Richard H. and Chen, Ping (eds) (1993), *Nonlinear Dynamics and Evolutionary Economics*, New York: Oxford University Press.

Debreu, Gerard (1959), *Theory of Value: An Axiomatic Analysis of Economic Equilibrium*, New Haven: Yale University Press.

Debreu, Gerard (1974), 'Excess Demand Functions', *Journal of Mathematical Economics*, **1**(1), March, 15–21.

Degler, Carl N. (1991), *In Search of Human Nature: The Decline and Revival of Darwinism in American Social Thought*, Oxford and New York: Oxford University Press.

Delorme, Robert and Dopfer, Kurt (eds) (1994), *The Political Economy of Diversity: Evolutionary Perspectives on Economic Order and Disorder*, Aldershot: Edward Elgar.

Demsetz, Harold (1988), 'The Theory of the Firm Revisited', *Journal of Law, Economics, and Organization*, **4**(1), Spring, 141–62. Reprinted in Williamson and Winter (1991).

Depew, David J. and Weber, Bruce H. (eds) (1985), *Evolution at a Crossroads: The New Biology and the New Philosophy of Science*, Cambridge, MA: MIT Press.

Dewey, John (1939) *Theory of Valuation* (Chicago: University of Chicago Press).

Diamond, Arthur M. Jr (1989), 'The Core Journals of Economics', *Current Contents*, (1), January 2, 4–11.

Dierickx, Ingemar and Cool, Karel (1989), 'Asset Stock Accumulation and Sustainability of Competitive Advantage', *Management Science*, **35**, 1504–11.

Dietrich, Michael (1991), 'Firms, Markets and Transaction Cost Economics', *Scottish Journal of Political Economy*, **38**(1), February, 41–57.

Dillard, Dudley (1948), *The Economics of John Maynard Keynes: The Theory of a Monetary Economy*, London: Crosby Lockwood.

Dobzhansky, Theodosius (1955), *Evolution, Genetics and Man*, London: Wiley.

Dobzhansky, Theodosius (1968), 'On Some Fundamental Concepts of Darwinian Biology', in Theodosius Dobzhansky, M. K. Hecht, M. K. and W. C. Steere (eds) (1968), *Evolutionary Biology*, Amsterdam: North Holland, pp. 1–34.

Doeringer, Peter B. and Piore, Michael J. (1971), *Internal Labor Markets and Manpower Analysis,* Lexington, MA: Heath.

Dore, Ronald (1983), 'Goodwill and the Spirit of Market Capitalism', *British Journal of Sociology*, **34**(4), December, 459–82.

Dorfman, Joseph (1955), 'The Role of the German Historical School in American Economic Thought', *American Economic Review (Papers and Proceedings)*, **45**(2), May, 17–28.

Dosi, Giovanni (1988a), 'Institutions and Markets in a Dynamic World', *The Manchester School*, **56**(2), June, 119–46.

Dosi, Giovanni (1988b), 'The Sources, Procedures, and Microeconomic Effects of Innovation', *Journal of Economic Literature*, **26**(3), September, 1120–71. Reprinted in Freeman (1990).

Dosi, Giovanni and Egidi, Massimo (1991), 'Substantive and Procedural Uncertainty: An Exploration of Economic Behaviours in Complex and Changing Environments', *Journal of Evolutionary Economics*, **1**(2), April, 145–68.

Dosi, Giovanni and Marengo, Luigi (1994), 'Some Elements of an Evolutionary Theory of Organizational Competences', in England (1994, pp. 157–78).

Dosi, Giovanni and Metcalfe, J. Stanley (1991), 'On Some Notions of Irreversibility in Economics', in Saviotti and Metcalfe (1991, pp. 133–59).

Dosi, Giovanni, Freeman, Christopher, Nelson, Richard, Silverberg, Gerald and Soete, Luc (eds) (1988), *Technical Change and Economic Theory*, London: Pinter.

Dosi, Giovanni, Pavitt, Keith and Soete, Luc (1990), *The Economics of Technical Change and International Trade*, Hemel Hempstead: Harvester Wheatsheaf.

Douglas, Mary (1990), 'Converging on Autonomy: Anthropology and Institutional Economics', in Williamson (1990, pp. 98–115).

Dow, Gregory K. (1987), 'The Function of Authority in Transaction Cost Economics', *Journal of Economic Behavior and Organization*, **8**(1), March, 13–38.

Dow, Sheila C. (1997), 'Methodological Pluralism and Pluralism of Method', in Salanti and Screpanti (1997, pp. 89–99).

Downie, Jack (1958), *The Competitive Process*, London: Duckworth.

Drucker, Peter (1955), *The Practice of Management*, London: Heinemann.

Duffie, Darrell and Sonnenschein, Hugo (1989), 'Arrow and General Equilibrium Theory', *Journal of Economic Literature*, **27**, 565–98.

Duménil, Gérard and Lévy, Dominique (1987), 'The Dynamics of Competition: A Restoration of the Classical Analysis', *Cambridge Journal of Economics*, **11**(2), June, 133–64.

Dupré, John A. (ed.) (1987), *The Latest on the Best: Essays on Evolution and Optimality*, Cambridge, MA: MIT Press.

Durkheim, Emile (1984), *The Division of Labour in Society*, translated from the French edition of 1893 by W. D. Halls with an introduction by Lewis Coser, London: Macmillan.

Dyke, C. (1985), 'Complexity and Closure', in Depew and Weber (1985, pp. 97–131).

Eaton, B. Curtis (1984), Review of *An Evolutionary Theory of Economic Change* by R. R. Nelson and S. G. Winter, *Canadian Journal of Economics*, **17**(4), November, 868–71.

Eatwell, John (1979), *Theories of Value and Employment*, London: Thames Papers in Political Economy. Reprinted in Eatwell and Milgate (1983).

Eatwell, John (1983), 'The Long-Period Theory of Employment', *Cambridge Journal of Economics*, **7**(3/4), September-December, 269–285.

Eatwell, John and Milgate, Murray (eds) (1983), *Keynes' Economics and the Theory of Value and Distribution*, London: Duckworth.

Edwards, George W. (1938), *The Evolution of Finance Capitalism*, London: Longmans, Green.

Eldredge, Niles (1985), *Unfinished Synthesis: Biological Hierarchies and Modern Evolutionary Thought*, Oxford: Oxford University Press.

Eliasson, Gunnar (1991), 'Deregulation, Innovative Entry and Structural Diversity as a Source of Stable and Rapid Economic Growth', *Journal of Evolutionary Economics*, 1(1), January, 49–63.

Ellerman, David P. (1982), *Economics, Accounting and Property Theory*, Lexington, MA: D. C. Heath.

Ellerman, David P. (1992), *Property and Contract in Economics: The Case for Economic Democracy*, Oxford: Blackwell.

Elster, Jon (1982), 'Marxism, Functionalism and Game Theory', *Theory and Society*, 11(4), 453–82. Reprinted in Roemer, John E. (ed.) (1986), *Analytical Marxism*, Cambridge: Cambridge University Press.

Elster, Jon (1983), *Explaining Technical Change*, Cambridge: Cambridge University Press.

Ely, Richard T. (1903), *Studies in the Evolution of Industrial Society*, New York: Macmillan.

England, Richard W. (ed.) (1994), *Evolutionary Concepts in Contemporary Economics*, University of Michigan Press, Ann Arbor, MI.

Enke, Stephen (1951), 'On Maximizing Profits: A Distinction Between Chamberlin and Robinson', *American Economic Review*, 41(3), September, 566–78.

Etzioni, Amitai (1988), *The Moral Dimension: Toward a New Economics*, New York: Free Press.

Everett, Michael J. and Minkler, Alanson P. (1993), 'Evolution and Organizational Choice in 19th Century Britain', *Cambridge Journal of Economics*, 17(1), March, 51–62.

Faber, Malte and Proops, John L. R. (1990), *Evolution, Time, Production and the Environment*, Berlin: Springer.

Fama, Eugene F. (1980), 'Agency Problems and the Theory of the Firm', *Journal of Political Economy*, 88(2), April, 288–307.

Farrell, Michael J. (1970), 'Some Elementary Selection Processes in Economics', *Review of Economic Studies*, 37, 305–19.

Fischer, Stanley (1977), 'Long-Term Contracting, Sticky Prices, and Monetary Policy: A Comment', *Journal of Monetary Economics*, 3, 317–23.

Fleetwood, Steven (1995), *Hayek's Political Economy: The Socio-Economics of Order*, London: Routledge.

Ford, Henry Jones (1915), *The Natural History of the State*, Princeton: Princeton University Press.

Foss, Nicolai Juul (1991), 'The Suppression of Evolutionary Approaches in Economics: The Case of Marshall and Monopolistic Competition', *Methodus*, **3**(2), December, 65–72. Reprinted in Hodgson (1995a).

Foss, Nicolai Juul (1993), 'Theories of the Firm: Contractual and Competence Perspectives', *Journal of Evolutionary Economics*, **3**(2), May, 127–44.

Foss, Nicolai Juul (1994a), 'Realism and Evolutionary Economics', *Journal of Social and Evolutionary Systems*, **17**(1), 21–40.

Foss, Nicolai Juul (1994b), 'The Biological Analogy and the Theory of the Firm: Marshall and Monopolistic Competition', *Journal of Economic Issues*, **28**(4), December, 1115–36. Reprinted in Hodgson (1998f).

Foss, Nicolai Juul (1996), 'The "Alternative" Theories of Knight and Coase, and the Modern Theory of the Firm', *Journal of the History of Economic Thought*, **18**(1), Spring, 76–95.

Foss, Nicolai Juul and Knudsen, Christian (eds) (1996), *Towards a Competence Theory of the Firm*, London: Routledge.

Foster, John (1987), *Evolutionary Macroeconomics*, London: George Allen and Unwin.

Fourie, Frederick C. v. N. (1989), 'The Nature of Firms and Markets: Do Transactions Approaches Help?', *South African Journal of Economics*, **57**(2), 142–60.

Fox, Alan (1974), *Beyond Contract: Work, Power and Trust Relations*, London: Faber and Faber.

Fransman, Martin (1994), 'Information, Knowledge, Vision and Theories of the Firm', *Industrial and Corporate Change*, **3**(3), 713–57.

Freeden, Michael (ed.) (1988), *J. A. Hobson: A Reader*, London and Boston: Unwin Hyman.

Freeman, Christopher (ed.) (1990), *The Economics of Innovation*, Aldershot: Edward Elgar.

Freeman, Christopher and Soete, Luc L. G. (1997), *The Economics of Industrial Innovation*, 3rd edn., London: Pinter.

Frey, Bruno S. and Eichenberger, Reiner (1993), 'American and European Economics and Economists', *Journal of Economic Perspectives*, **7**(4), Fall, 185–93.

Friedman, Jeffrey (ed.) (1995), *The Rational Choice Controversy: Economic Models of Politics Reconsidered*, New Haven: Yale University Press.

Friedman, Milton (1953), 'The Methodology of Positive Economics', in M. Friedman, *Essays in Positive Economics*, Chicago: University of Chicago Press. Reprinted in B. J. Caldwell (ed.) (1984), *Appraisal and*

Criticism In Economics: A Book of Readings, Boston: Allen and Unwin.

Friedman, Milton (1991), 'Old Wine in New Bottles', *Economic Journal*, **101**(1), January, 33–40.

Furubotn, Eirik G. and Richter, Rudolph (1997) *Institutions in Economic Theory: The Contribution of the New Institutional Economics*, Ann Arbor: University of Michigan Press.

Garegnani, Piero (1966), 'Switching of Techniques', *Quarterly Journal of Economics*, **80**, 554–67.

Garegnani, Piero (1970), 'Heterogeneous Capital, the Production Function and the Theory of Distribution', *Review of Economic Studies*, **37**, 407–36. Reprinted in Hunt and Schwartz (1972).

Garegnani, Piero (1978), 'Notes on Consumption, Investment and Effective Demand: I', *Cambridge Journal of Economics*, **2**(4), December, 335–53. Reprinted in Eatwell and Milgate (1983).

Garegnani, Piero (1979a), 'Notes on Consumption, Investment and Effective Demand: II', *Cambridge Journal of Economics*, **3**(1), March, 63–82. Reprinted in Eatwell and Milgate (1983).

Garegnani, Piero (1979b), 'Notes on Consumption, Investment and Effective Demand: A Reply to Joan Robinson', *Cambridge Journal of Economics*, **3**(2), June, 181–7. Reprinted in Eatwell and Milgate (1983).

Georgescu-Roegen, Nicholas (1971), *The Entropy Law and the Economic Process*, Cambridge, MA: Harvard University Press.

Gherardi, S. and Masiero, A. (1990), 'Solidarity as a Networking Skill and a Trust Relation: Its Implications for Cooperative Development', *Economic and Industrial Democracy*, **11**(4), November, 553–74.

Ghiselin, Michael T. (1974), *The Economy of Nature and the Evolution of Sex*, Berkeley: University of California Press.

Giddens, Anthony (1984), *The Constitution of Society: Outline of the Theory of Structuration*, Cambridge: Polity Press.

Giddings, Franklin A. (1896), *The Principles of Sociology*, New York: Macmillan.

Gleick, James (1988), *Chaos: Making a New Science*, London: Heinemann.

Goldberg, David E. (1989), *Genetic Algorithms in Search, Optimization, and Machine Learning*, Reading, MA: Addison-Wesley.

Goldberg, M. A. (1975), 'On the Inefficiency of Being Efficient', *Environment and Planning*, **7**(8), 921–39.

Goldberg, Victor P. (1980), 'Relational Exchange: Economics and Complex Contracts', *American Behavioral Scientist*, **23**(3), 337–52.

Goodenough, Ward H. (1981), *Culture; Language and Society*, Menlo Park, CA: Benjamin/Cummings.

Goodwin, Richard M. (1990), *Chaotic Economic Dynamics*, Oxford: Oxford University Press.

Gordon, Robert A. (1945), *Business Leadership in the Large Corporation*, Washington, DC: Brookings Institution.

Gordon, Robert A. (1948), 'Short-Period Price Determination in Theory and Practice', *American Economic Review*, **38**, June, 265–88.

Gordon, Robert A. (1963), 'Institutional Elements in Contemporary Economics', in Dorfman, Joseph, Ayres, Clarence W., Chamberlain, Neil W., Kuznets, Simon, and Gordon, Robert A. (1963), *Institutional Economics: Veblen, Commons, and Mitchell Reconsidered*, Berkeley, CA: University of California Press, pp. 123–47.

Gordon, Robert A. (1976), 'Rigor and Relevance in a Changing Institutional Setting', *American Economic Review*, **66**(1), March, 1–14. Reprinted in Samuels (1988).

Gordon, Wendell and Adams, John (1989), *Economics as a Social Science: An Evolutionary Approach*, Riverdale, MD: Riverdale.

Gould, Stephen Jay (1978), *Ever Since Darwin: Reflections in Natural History*, London: Burnett Books.

Gould, Stephen Jay (1980), *The Panda's Thumb*, New York: Norton.

Gould, Stephen Jay (1982), 'The Meaning of Punctuated Equilibrium and its Role in Validating a Hierarchical Approach to Macroevolution', in Milkman, Roger (ed.) (1982), *Perspectives on Evolution*, Sunderland, MA: Sinauer Associates, pp. 83–104.

Gould, Stephen Jay (1989), *Wonderful Life: The Burgess Shale and the Nature of History*, London: Hutchinson Radius.

Gould, Stephen Jay and Lewontin, Richard C. (1979), 'The Spandrels of San Marco and the Panglossian Paradigm: A Critique of the Adaptationist Programme', *Proceedings of the Royal Society of London*, Series B, **205**, pp. 581–98. Reprinted in Sober (1984b).

Gowdy, John M. (1985), 'Evolutionary Theory and Economic Theory: Some Methodological Issues', *Review of Social Economy*, **43**, 316–24.

Gowdy, John M. (1987), 'Bio-economics: Social Economy Versus the Chicago School', *International Journal of Social Economics*, **14**(1), 32–42. Reprinted in Hodgson (1995a).

Grabher, Gernot (ed.) (1993), *The Embedded Firm: On the Socioeconomics of Industrial Networks*, London: Routledge.

Grandmont, Jean-Michel (1986), 'Stabilizing Competitive Business Cycles', *Journal of Economic Theory*, **40**(1), October, 57–76. Reprinted in

Grandmont, Jean-Michel (ed.) (1987), *Nonlinear Economic Dynamics*, New York: Academic Press.

Grandmont, Jean-Michel and Malgrange, Pierre (1986), 'Nonlinear Economic Dynamics: Introduction', *Journal of Economic Theory*, **40**, 3–12.

Grant, Robert M. (1996), 'Toward a Knowledge-Based Theory of the Firm', *Strategic Management Journal*, **17**, Special Issue, pp. 109–22.

Green, Donald and Shapiro, Ian (1994), *Pathologies of Rational Choice Theory: A Critique of Applications in Political Science*, New Haven, CT: Yale University Press.

Greif, Avner (1996), 'The Study of Organizations and Evolving Organizational Forms Through History: Reflections from the Late Medieval Family Firm', *Industrial and Corporate Change*, **5**(2), 473–501.

Grossman, Sanford J. and Hart, Oliver D. (1983), ' An Analysis of the Principal-Agent Problem', *Econometrica*, **51**(1), 7–45.

Grossman, Sanford J. and Hart, Oliver D. (1986), 'The Costs and Benefits of Ownership: A Theory of Vertical and Lateral Integration', *Journal of Political Economy*, **94**(4), August, 691–719.

Gruchy, Allan G. (1948), 'The Philosophical Basis of the New Keynesian Economics', *International Journal of Ethics*, **58**(4), July, 235–44.

Gruchy, Allan G. (1972), *Contemporary Economic Thought: The Contribution of Neo-Institutional Economics*, London and New York: Macmillan.

Gulbenkian Commission on the Restructuring of the Social Sciences (1996), *Open the Social Sciences*, Stanford: Stanford University Press.

Haavelmo, Trygve (1954), *A Study in the Theory of Economic Evolution*, Amsterdam: North-Holland.

Hahn, Frank H. (1975), 'Revival of Political Economy: The Wrong Issues and the Wrong Arguments', *Economic Record*, **51**, September, 360–4.

Hahn, Frank H. (1980), 'General Equilibrium Theory', *The Public Interest*, Special Issue, 123–138. Reprinted in Bell and Kristol (1981) and in Hahn (1984).

Hahn, Frank H. (1982), 'The Neo-Ricardians', *Cambridge Journal of Economics*, **6**(4), December, 353–74.

Hahn, Frank H. (1984), *Equilibrium and Macroeconomics*, Oxford: Blackwell.

Hahn, Frank H. (1988), 'On Monetary Theory', *The Economic Journal*, **98** (December): 957–73.

Hahn, Frank H. (1991), 'The Next Hundred Years', *Economic Journal*, **101**(1), January, 47–50.

Hall, Robert L. and Hitch, Charles J. (1939), 'Price Theory and Business Behaviour', *Oxford Economic Papers*, **2**, 12–45. Reprinted in T. Wilson and Philip W. S. Andrews (eds) (1951), *Oxford Studies in the Price Mechanism*, Oxford: Clarendon Press.

Haltiwanger, John and Waldman, Michael (1985), 'Rational Expectations and the Limits of Rationality: An Analysis of Heterogeneity', *American Economic Review*, **75**, 159–73.

Haltiwanger, John and Waldman, Michael (1991), 'Responders Versus Non-Responders: A New Perspective on Heterogeneity', *The Economic Journal*, **101**, 1085–102.

Hamilton, David B. (1991), *Evolutionary Economics: A Study in Change in Economic Thought*, 3rd edn., New Brunswick, NJ: Transaction.

Hammermesh, Daniel S. and Soss, Neal M. (1974), 'An Economic Theory of Suicide', *Journal of Political Economy*, **82**(1), January–February, 83–98.

Hannan, Michael T. and Freeman, John (1977), 'The Population Ecology of Organizations', *American Journal of Sociology*, **82**, 929–64.

Hannan, Michael T. and Freeman, John (1989), *Organizational Ecology*, Cambridge, MA: Harvard University Press.

Hansson, Ingemar and Stuart, Charles (1990), 'Malthusian Selection of Preferences', *American Economic Review*, **80**, 529–44.

Hanusch, Horst (ed.) (1988), *Evolutionary Economics: Applications of Schumpeter's Ideas*, Cambridge: Cambridge University Press.

Harcourt, Geoffrey C. (1969), 'Some Cambridge Controversies in the Theory of Capital', *Journal of Economic Literature*, **7**, 369–405.

Harcourt, Geoffrey C. (1972), *Some Cambridge Controversies in the Theory of Capital*, Cambridge, Cambridge University Press.

Harcourt, Geoffrey C. (ed.) (1977), *The Microeconomic Foundations of Macroeconomics*, Boulder, CO: Westview Press.

Harcourt, Geoffrey C. (1982a), 'The Sraffian Contribution: An Evaluation', in Bradley, Ian and Howard, Michael (eds) (1982), *Classical and Marxian Political Economy: Essays in Honour of Ronald L. Meek*, London: Macmillan, pp. 255–75.

Harcourt, Geoffrey C. (1982b), *The Social Science Imperialists: Selected Essays*, ed. Prue Kerr, London: Routledge and Kegan Paul.

Harcourt, Geoffrey C. (1985), 'On the Influence of Piero Sraffa on the Contributions of Joan Robinson to Economic Theory', *Economic Journal (Conference Papers)*, **96**, 96–108.

Harcourt, Geoffrey C. (1994), 'Capital Theory Controversies', in Arestis, Philip and Sawyer, Malcolm (eds) (1994), *The Elgar Companion to Radical Political Economy*, Aldershot: Edward Elgar, pp. 29–34.

Reprinted in Harcourt, Geoffrey C. (1995), *Capitalism, Socialism and Post-Keynesianism: Selected Essays*, Aldershot: Edward Elgar.

Harcourt, Geoffrey C. and Laing, N. F. (eds) (1971), *Capital and Growth*, Harmondsworth: Penguin.

Harcourt, Geoffrey C. and Massaro, Vincent G. (1964), 'Mr Sraffa's *Production of Commodities by Means of Commodities*', *Economic Record*, **40**, 442–54. Reprinted in Harcourt (1972, pp. 177–204).

Harcourt, Geoffrey C. and O'Shaughnessy, T. J. (1985), 'Keynes Unemployment Equilibrium: Some Insights from Joan Robinson, Piero Sraffa and Richard Kahn', in Geoffrey C. Harcourt (ed.) (1985), *Keynes and his Contemporaries*, London: Macmillan.

Hargreaves Heap, Shaun P. and Varoufakis, Yanis (1995), *Game Theory: A Critical Introduction*, London: Routledge.

Harris, Abram L. (1934), 'Economic Evolution: Dialectical and Darwinian', *Journal of Political Economy*, **42**(1), February, 34–79. Reprinted in Hodgson (1998f).

Harris, Abram L. (1942), 'Sombart and German (National) Socialism', *Journal of Political Economy*, **50**(6), December, 805–35. Reprinted in Mark Blaug (ed.) (1992), *Gustav Schmoller (1838–1917) and Werner Sombart (1863–1941)*, Aldershot: Edward Elgar.

Harris, Marvin (1971), *Culture, Man and Nature*, New York: Crowell.

Hart, Oliver D. (1988), 'Incomplete Contracts and the Theory of the Firm', *Journal of Law, Economics, and Organization*, **4**(1), Spring, 119–39.

Hart, Oliver D. (1995), *Firms, Contracts, and Financial Structures*, Oxford: Oxford University Press.

Hart, Oliver D. and Moore, John (1990), 'Property Rights and the Nature of the Firm', *Journal of Political Economy*, **98**(6), 1119–58.

Hayek, Friedrich A. (1948), *Individualism and Economic Order*, Chicago: University of Chicago Press.

Hayek, Friedrich A. (1952a), *The Sensory Order: An Inquiry into the Foundations of Theoretical Psychology*, London: Routledge and Kegan Paul.

Hayek, Friedrich A. (1952b), *The Counter-Revolution of Science: Studies on the Abuse of Reason*, 1st edn., Glencoe, IL: Free Press.

Hayek, Friedrich A. (1967a), 'Notes on the Evolution of Systems of Rules of Conduct', from Hayek (1967b, pp. 66–81). Reprinted in Witt (1993b) and in Hodgson (1998f).

Hayek, Friedrich A. (1967b), *Studies in Philosophy, Politics and Economics*, London: Routledge and Kegan Paul.

Hayek, Friedrich A. (1982), *Law, Legislation and Liberty*, 3-volume combined edn., London: Routledge and Kegan Paul.

Hayek, Friedrich A. (1988), *The Fatal Conceit: The Errors of Socialism. The Collected Works of Friedrich August Hayek, Vol. 1*, ed. William W. Bartley III, London: Routledge.

Heertje, Arnold (1994), 'Neo-Schumpeterians and Economic Theory', in Magnusson (1994, pp. 265–76).

Heertje, Arnold and Perlman, Mark (eds) (1990), *Evolving Technology and Market Structure: Studies in Schumpeterian Economics*, Ann Arbor, MI: University of Michigan Press.

Heiner, Ronald A. (1989), 'The Origin of Predictable Dynamic Behaviour', *Journal of Economic Behaviour and Organization*, **12**, 233–57.

Hejl, Peter M. (1995), 'The Importance of the Concepts of "Organism" and "Evolution" in Emile Durkheim's *Division of Social Labor* and the Influence of Herbert Spencer', in Maasen, *et al* (1995, pp. 155–91).

Hennis, Wilhelm (1988), *Max Weber, Essays in Reconstruction*, London: George Allen and Unwin.

Herbst, Jurgen (1965), *The German Historical School in American Scholarship: A Study in the Transfer of Culture*, Ithaca, NY: Cornell University Press.

Hesse, Mary B. (1955), *Science and the Human Imagination*, New York: Philosophical Library.

Hesse, Mary B. (1966), *Models and Analogies in Science*, Notre Dame: University of Notre Dame Press.

Hesse, Mary B. (1980), *Revolutions and Reconstructions in the Philosophy of Science*, Brighton: Harvester Press.

Hey, John D. (1981), 'Are Optimal Search Rules Reasonable? And Vice Versa?', *Journal of Economic Behavior and Organization*, **2**(1), March, 47–70.

Hippel, Eric von (1987), 'Cooperation Between Rivals: Informal Know-How Trading', *Research Policy*, **16**, 291–302.

Hippel, Eric von (1988), *The Sources of Innovation*, Oxford: Oxford University Press.

Hirsch, Paul M. (1990), 'Rational Choice Models for Sociology – Pro and Con: Introduction', *Rationality and Society*, **2**(2), April, 137–41.

Hirschman, Albert O. (1985), 'Against Parsimony: Three Ways of Complicating Some Categories of Economic Discourse', *Economics and Philosophy*, **1**(1), March, 7–21.

Hirshleifer, Jack (1977), 'Economics from a Biological Viewpoint', *Journal of Law and Economics*, **20**(1), April, 1–52. Reprinted in Hodgson (1995a).

Hirshleifer, Jack (1978), 'Natural Economy versus Political Economy', *Journal of Social and Biological Structures*, **1**, 319–37.

Hirshleifer, Jack (1982), 'Evolutionary Models in Economics and Law: Cooperation versus Conflict Strategies', in R. O. Zerbe Jr and P. H. Rubin (eds) (1982), *Research in Law and Economics*, **4**, pp. 1–60. Reprinted in Witt (1993b).

Hirst, Paul Q. and Woolley, Penny (1982), *Social Relations and Human Attributes*, London: Tavistock.

Hobson, John A. (1894), *The Evolution of Modern Capitalism: A Study of Machine Production*, 1st edn., London: Walter Scott, and New York: Charles Scribner's.

Hobson, John A. (1914), *Work and Wealth: A Human Valuation*, London: Macmillan.

Hobson, John A. (1929), *Wealth and Life: A Study in Values*, London: Macmillan.

Hobson, John A. (1936), *Veblen*, London: Chapman and Hall. Reprinted 1991 by Augustus Kelley.

Hodgson, Geoffrey M. (1982a), 'Marx Without the Labour Theory of Value', *Review of Radical Political Economics*, **14**(2), Summer, 59–67. Reprinted in J. C. Wood (ed.) (1987), *Karl Marx's Economics: Critical Assessments*, Croom Helm, Beckenham, and in Hodgson (1991c).

Hodgson, Geoffrey M. (1982b), *Capitalism, Value and Exploitation: A Radical Theory*, Oxford: Martin Robertson.

Hodgson, Geoffrey M. (1984), *The Democratic Economy: A New Look at Planning, Markets and Power*, Harmondsworth: Penguin.

Hodgson, Geoffrey M. (1988), *Economics and Institutions: A Manifesto for a Modern Institutional Economics*, Cambridge and Philadelphia: Polity Press and University of Pennsylvania Press.

Hodgson, Geoffrey M. (1989), 'Post-Keynesianism and Institutionalism: The Missing Link', in Pheby, John (ed.) (1989), *New Directions in Post Keynesian Economics*, Aldershot: Edward Elgar, pp. 94–123. Reprinted in Hodgson (1991c).

Hodgson, Geoffrey M. (1991a), 'Hayek's Theory of Cultural Evolution: An Evaluation in the Light of Vanberg's Critique', *Economics and Philosophy*, **7**, 67–82.

Hodgson, Geoffrey M. (1991b), 'Economic Evolution: Intervention Contra Pangloss', *Journal of Economic Issues*, **25**(2), June, 519–33.

Hodgson, Geoffrey M. (1991c), *After Marx and Sraffa*, Basingstoke: Macmillan.

Hodgson, Geoffrey M. (1992a), 'Thorstein Veblen and Post-Darwinian Economics', *Cambridge Journal of Economics*, **16**(3), September, 285–301. Reprinted in Hodgson (1998f).

Hodgson, Geoffrey M. (1992b), 'The Reconstruction of Economics: Is There Still a Place for Neoclassical Theory?', *Journal of Economic Issues*, **26**(3), September, 749–67.

Hodgson, Geoffrey M. (1993a), 'The Mecca of Alfred Marshall', *Economic Journal*, **103**(2), March, 406–15. Reprinted in Hodgson (1998f).

Hodgson, Geoffrey M. (1993b), *Economics and Evolution: Bringing Life Back Into Economics*, Cambridge, UK and Ann Arbor, MI: Polity Press and University of Michigan Press.

Hodgson, Geoffrey M. (1993c), 'Transaction Costs and the Evolution of the Firm', in Christos Pitelis (ed.) (1993), *Transaction Costs, Markets and Hierarchies: Critical Assessments*, Oxford: Basil Blackwell, 77–100.

Hodgson, Geoffrey M. (ed.) (1993d), *The Economics of Institutions*, Aldershot: Edward Elgar.

Hodgson, Geoffrey M. (1993e), 'Commentary' [on the 'Pragmatic Instrumentalist Perspective' of Paul Dale Bush] in Marc R. Tool (ed.) (1993), *Institutional Economics: Theory, Method, Policy*, Kluwer, Boston, pp. 108–18.

Hodgson, Geoffrey M. (1994a), 'Optimisation and Evolution: Winter's Critique of Friedman Revisited', *Cambridge Journal of Economics*, **18**(4), August, 413–30. Reprinted in Hodgson (1998f).

Hodgson, Geoffrey M. (1994b), 'Capital Theory', in Hodgson *et al* (1994, vol. 1, pp. 33–8).

Hodgson, Geoffrey M. (ed.) (1995a), *Economics and Biology*, Aldershot: Edward Elgar.

Hodgson, Geoffrey M. (1995b), 'The Evolution of Evolutionary Economics', *Scottish Journal of Political Economy*, **42**(4), November, 469–88.

Hodgson, Geoffrey M. (1996a), 'Varieties of Capitalism and Varieties of Economic Theory', *Review of Political Economy*, **3**(3), Autumn, 381–434.

Hodgson, Geoffrey M. (1996b), 'Richard Nelson and Sidney Winter', in Warren J. Samuels (ed.) (1996), *American Economists of the Late Twentieth Century*, Aldershot: Edward Elgar, pp. 194–215.

Hodgson, Geoffrey M. (1997a), 'Metaphor and Pluralism in Economics: Mechanics and Biology', in Salanti and Screpanti (1997, pp. 131–54).

Hodgson, Geoffrey M. (1997b), 'The Fate of the Cambridge Capital Controversy', in Philip Arestis and Malcolm C. Sawyer (eds) (1997), *Capital Controversy, Post Keynesian Economics and the History of Economic Theory: Essays in Honour of Geoff Harcourt*, London: Routledge, pp. 95–110.

Hodgson, Geoffrey M. (1997c), 'The Evolutionary and Non-Darwinian Economics of Joseph Schumpeter', *Journal of Evolutionary Economics*, 7(2), June, 131–45.

Hodgson, Geoffrey M. (1997d), 'The Ubiquity of Habits and Rules', *Cambridge Journal of Economics*, 21(6), November, 663–84.

Hodgson, Geoffrey M. (1997e), 'Economics and Evolution and the Evolution of Economics', in Reijnders (1997, pp. 9–40).

Hodgson, Geoffrey M. (1998a), 'The Coasean Tangle: The Nature of the Firm and the Problem of Historical Specificity', in Steven G. Medema (ed.) (1998), *Coasean Economics: Law and Economics and the New Institutional Economics*, Boston: Kluwer, pp. 23–49.

Hodgson, Geoffrey M. (1998b), 'The Approach of Evolutionary Economics', *Journal of Economic Literature*, 36(1), March, 166–92.

Hodgson, Geoffrey M. (1998c), 'Evolutionary and Competence-Based Theories of the Firm', *Journal of Economic Studies*, 25(1), 25–56.

Hodgson, Geoffrey M. (1998d), 'On the Evolution of Thorstein Veblen's Evolutionary Economics', *Cambridge Journal of Economics*, 22(3), July, 415–31.

Hodgson, Geoffrey M. (1998e), *Economics and Utopia: Why the Learning Economy is not the End of History*, London: Routledge.

Hodgson, Geoffrey M. (ed.) (1998f), *The Foundations of Evolutionary Economics: 1890–1973*, Cheltenham, UK and Lyme, US: Edward Elgar.

Hodgson, Geoffrey M. (forthcoming), 'Biological Metaphors in Economics from the 1880s to the 1980s', in Kurt Dopfer (ed.), *Evolutionary Principles of Economics*, Cambridge: Cambridge University Press (forthcoming).

Hodgson, Geoffrey M. and Rothman, Harry (1999), 'The Editors and Authors of Economic Journals: A Case of Institutional Oligopoly?', *Economic Journal*, February (forthcoming).

Hodgson, Geoffrey M. and Screpanti, Ernesto (eds) (1991), *Rethinking Economics: Markets, Technology and Economic Evolution*, Aldershot: Edward Elgar.

Hodgson, Geoffrey M., Samuels, Warren J. and Tool, Marc R. (eds) (1994), *The Elgar Companion to Institutional and Evolutionary Economics*, Aldershot: Edward Elgar.

Hofstadter, Richard (1959), *Social Darwinism in American Thought*, revised edn., New York: Braziller.

Holland, John H. (1986), 'Escaping Brittleness: The Possibilities of General-Purpose Learning Algorithms Applied to Parallel Rule-Based Systems', in R. S. Michalski *et al*, 1986, ch. 20.

Hoover, Kevin D. (1995), 'Why Does Methodology Matter for Economics?', *Economic Journal*, **105**(3), May, 715–34.

Horwitz, Steven (1992), *Monetary Evolution, Free Banking, and Economic Order*, Boulder, CO: Westview Press.

Hrebeniak, Lawrence G. and Joyce, William F. (1985), 'Organizational Adaptation, Strategic Choice and Environmental Determinism', *Administrative Science Quarterly*, 36–49.

Hull, David L. (1973), *Darwin and His Critics: The Reception of Darwin's Theory of Evolution by the Scientific Community*, Cambridge, MA: Harvard University Press.

Hunt, E. K. and Schwartz, Jesse G. (eds) (1972), *A Critique of Economic Theory*, Harmondsworth: Penguin.

Hutchison, Terence W. (1992), *Changing Aims in Economics*, Oxford: Basil Blackwell.

Hutter, Michael (1994), 'Organism as a Metaphor in German Economic Thought', in Mirowski (1994, pp. 289–321). Reprinted in Hodgson (1998f).

Ingham, Geoffrey (1996a), 'Some Recent Changes in the Relationship Between Economics and Sociology', *Cambridge Journal of Economics*, **20**(2), March, 243–75.

Ingham, Geoffrey (1996b), 'Money is a Social Relation', *Review of Social Economy*, **54**(4), Winter, pp. 507–29.

Ingrao, Bruna and Israel, Giorgio (1990), *The Invisible Hand: Economic Equilibrium in the History of Science*, Cambridge, MA: MIT Press.

Itami, H. (1987), *Mobilizing Invisible Assets*, Cambridge, MA: Harvard University Press.

Jackson, William A. (1995), 'Naturalism in Economics', *Journal of Economic Issues*, **29**(3), September, 761–80.

James, Philip S. (1966), *Introduction to English Law*, 6th edn., London: Butterworths.

James, William (1890), *The Principles of Psychology*, New York: Holt.

Jensen, Michael C. and Meckling, William H. (1976), 'Theory of the Firm: Managerial Behavior, Agency Costs and Ownership Structure', *Journal of Financial Economics*, **3**(4), October, 305–60.

Jolink, Albert (1996), *The Evolutionist Economics of Léon Walras*, London and New York: Routledge.

Joravsky, D. (1970), *The Lysenko Affair*, Cambridge, MA: Harvard University Press.

Kapp, K. William (1976), 'The Nature and Significance of Institutional Economics', *Kyklos*, **29**, Fasc. 2, 209–32. Reprinted in Samuels (1988).

Kauffman, Stuart A. (1988), 'The Evolution of Economic Webs', in P. Anderson, K. J. Arrow and D. Pines (eds) (1988), *The Economy as an Evolving Complex System*, Reading, MA: Addison-Wesley, pp. 125–46.

Kaufman, W. (ed.) (1982), *The Portable Nietzsche*, Harmondsworth: Penguin

Kay, Neil M. (1982), *The Evolving Firm: Strategy and Structure in Industrial Organization*, London: Macmillan.

Kay, Neil M. (1984), *The Emergent Firm: Knowledge, Ignorance and Surprise in Economic Organization*, London: Macmillan.

Kay, Neil M. (1995), 'Alchian and "The Alchian Thesis"', *Journal of Economic Methodology*, 2(2), December, 281–6.

Keizer, W. (1989), 'Recent Reinterpretations of the Socialist Calculation Debate', *Journal of Economic Studies*, 16: 63–83.

Kelm, Matthias (1997), 'Schumpeter's Theory of Economic Evolution: A Darwinian Interpretation', *Journal of Evolutionary Economics*, 7(2), June, 97–130.

Keppler, Jan Horst (1998), 'The Genesis of "Positive Economics" and the Rejection of Monopolistic Competition Theory: A Methodological Debate', *Cambridge Journal of Economics*, 22(3), May, 261–76.

Keynes, John Maynard (1913), *Indian Currency and Finance*, London: Macmillan.

Keynes, John Maynard (1922), *A Revision of the Treaty*, London: Macmillan.

Keynes, John Maynard (1936), *The General Theory of Employment, Interest and Money*, London: Macmillan.

Keynes, John Maynard (1973), *The Collected Writings of John Maynard Keynes, Vol. XIV, 'The General Theory and After: Defence and Development'*, London: Macmillan.

Khalil, Elias L. (1992), 'Hayek's Spontaneous Order and Varela's Autopoiesis: A Comment', *Human Systems Management*, 11(2), 49–114.

Khalil, Elias L. (1993), 'Neo-classical Economics and Neo-Darwinism: Clearing the Way for Historical Thinking', in Ron Blackwell, Jaspal Chatha and Edward J. Nell (eds) *Economics as Worldly Philosophy: Essays in Political and Historical Economics in Honour of Robert L. Heilbroner*, London: Macmillan, pp. 22–72. Reprinted in Hodgson (1995a).

Kingsland, Sharon E. (1994), 'Economics and Evolution: Alfred James Lotka and the Economy of Nature', in Mirowski (1994, pp. 231–46). Reprinted in Hodgson (1998f).

Kirman, Alan P. (1989), 'The Intrinsic Limits of Modern Economic Theory: The Emperor Has No Clothes', *Economic Journal (Conference Papers)*, **99**, 126–139.

Kirman, Alan P. (1992), 'Whom or What Does the Representative Individual Represent?', *Journal of Economic Perspectives*, **6**(2), Spring, 117–36.

Kirman, Alan P. (1994), 'Economic Research in Europe: Inputs and Outputs', *Royal Economic Society Newsletter*, no. 85, April, 11–13.

Klamer, Arjo and Colander, David (1990), *The Making of an Economist*, Boulder: Westview Press.

Klamer, Arjo and Leonard, Thomas C. (1994), 'So What's an Economic Metaphor?', in Mirowski (1994, pp. 20–51).

Knies, Karl (1853), *Politische Ökonomie vom Standpunkt der geshichtlichen Methode* (Political Economy from the Perspective of the Historical Method), Braunschweig: Schwetschke.

Knight, Frank H. (1921), *Risk, Uncertainty and Profit*, New York: Houghton Mifflin.

Knight, Frank H. (1924), 'The Limitations of Scientific Method in Economics', in Tugwell (1924, pp. 229–67). Reprinted in Knight, Frank H. (1935), *The Ethics of Competition and Other Essays*, New York: Harper.

Knight, Frank H. (1952), 'Institutionalism and Empiricism in Economics', *American Economic Review (Papers and Proceedings)*, **42**, May, 45–55.

Knight, Frank H. *et al* (1957), 'A New Look at Institutionalism: Discussion', *American Economic Review (Supplement)*, **47**(2), May, 13–27.

Koestler, Arthur (1959), *The Sleepwalkers: A History of Man's Changing Vision of the Universe*, London: Hutchinson.

Koestler, Arthur (1964), *The Act of Creation*, London: Hutchinson.

Koestler, Arthur (1967), *The Ghost in the Machine*, London: Hutchinson.

Kogut, Bruce (1991), 'Country Capabilities and the Permeability of Borders', *Strategic Management Journal*, **12**, Summer, 33–47.

Kogut, Bruce and Zander, Ugo (1992), 'Knowledge of the Firm, Combinative Capabilities, and the Replication of Technology', *Organization Science*, **3**, 383–97.

Kontopoulos, Kyriakos M. (1993), *The Logics of Social Structure*, Cambridge: Cambridge University Press.

Koopmans, Tjalling C. (1947), 'Measurement Without Theory', *Review of Economics and Statistics*, **29**, August, 161–72.

Koopmans, Tjalling C. (1957), *Three Essays on the State of Economic Science*, New York: McGraw Hill.

Koutsoyiannis, A. (1979), *Modern Microeconomics*, London: Macmillan.

Krueger, Anne O. *et al* (1991), 'Report on the Commission on Graduate Education in Economics', *Journal of Economic Literature*, **29**(3), September, 1035–53.

Kuhn, Thomas S. (1970), *The Structure of Scientific Revolutions*, 2nd edn., Chicago: University of Chicago Press.

Kwasnicki, Witold (1996), *Knowledge, Innovation and Economy: An Evolutionary Exploration*, Cheltenham, UK and Brookfield, US: Edward Elgar.

La Vergata, Antonello (1995), 'Herbert Spencer: Biology, Sociology, and Cosmic Evolution', in Maasen *et al* (1995, pp. 193–229). Reprinted in Hodgson (1998f).

Lachmann, Ludwig M. (1969), 'Methodological Individualism and the Market Economy', in Streissler, E. W. (ed.) (1969), *Roads to Freedom: Essays in Honour of Friedrich A. von Hayek*, London: Routledge and Kegan Paul, pp. 89–103. Reprinted in Lachmann (1977).

Lachmann, Ludwig M. (1977), *Capital, Expectations and the Market Process*, edited with an introduction by W. E. Grinder, Kansas City: Sheed Andrews and McMeel.

Lamberton, Donald M. (ed.) (1996), *The Economics of Communication and Information*, Cheltenham, UK and Brookfield, US: Edward Elgar.

Lane, David A. (1993), 'Artificial Worlds and Economics', Parts I and II, *Journal of Evolutionary Economics*, **3**(2), May, 89–107, and **3**(3), August, 177–97.

Lane, Robert E. (1991), *The Market Experience*, Cambridge: Cambridge University Press.

Lange, Oskar R. and Taylor, Frederick M. (1938), *On the Economic Theory of Socialism*, ed. Benjamin E. Lippincot, Minneapolis: University of Minnesota Press.

Langlois, Richard N. (1984), 'Internal Organization in a Dynamic Context: Some Theoretical Considerations', in M. Jussawalla and H. Ebenfield (eds) (1984), *Communication and Information Economics: New Perspectives*, Amsterdam: North-Holland, pp. 23–49.

Langlois, Richard N. (ed.) (1986), *Economics as a Process: Essays in the New Institutional Economics*, Cambridge: Cambridge University Press.

Langlois, Richard N. (1988), 'Economic Change and the Boundaries of the Firm', *Journal of Institutional and Theoretical Economics*, **144**(4), September, 635–57.

Langlois, Richard N. (1989), 'What Was Wrong With the Old Institutional Economics (and What is Still Wrong With the New)?', *Review of Political Economy*, 1(3), November, 270–98.

Langlois, Richard N. (1992), 'Transaction Cost Economics in Real Time', *Industrial and Corporate Change*, 1(1), 99–127.

Langlois, Richard N. (1998), 'Transaction Costs, Production Costs, and the Passage of Time', in Steven G. Medema (ed.) (1998), *Coasean Economics: Law and Economics and the New Institutional Economics*, Boston: Kluwer, 1–21.

Langlois, Richard N. and Everett, Michael J. (1994), 'What is Evolutionary Economics?' in Magnusson (1994, pp. 11–47).

Langlois, Richard N. and Robertson, Paul L. (1995), *Firms, Markets and Economic Change: A Dynamic Theory of Business Institutions*, Routledge, London and New York.

Laudan, Larry (1977), *Progress and its Problems: Towards a Theory of Scientific Growth*, London: Routledge and Kegan Paul.

Laurent, John (1997), 'Keynes and Darwin', Griffith University Working Papers in Economics, No. 18, August.

Lavoie, Donald (1985), *Rivalry and Central Planning: The Socialist Calculation Debate Reconsidered*, Cambridge: Cambridge University Press.

Lavoie, Marc (1992), *Foundations of Post-Keynesian Economic Analysis*, Aldershot: Edward Elgar.

Lawson, Clive (1996), 'Holism and Collectivism in the Work of J. R. Commons', *Journal of Economic Issues*, 30(4), December, 967–84.

Lawson, Tony (1985), 'Uncertainty and Economic Analysis', *Economic Journal*, 95(4), December, 909–27.

Lawson, Tony (1989a), 'Abstraction, Tendencies and Stylised Facts: A Realist Approach to Economic Analysis', *Cambridge Journal of Economics*, 13(1), March, 59–78. Reprinted in Lawson, Tony, Palma, J. G. and Sender, J. (eds) (1989), *Kaldor's Political Economy* London: Academic Press.

Lawson, Tony (1989b), 'Realism and Instrumentalism in the Development of Econometrics', *Oxford Economic Papers*, 41(1), 236–58. Reprinted in De Marchi, Neil and Gilbert, C. (eds) (1990), *The History and Methodology of Econometrics*, Oxford: Oxford University Press.

Lawson, Tony (1994a), 'Hayek and Realism: A Case of Continuous Transformation', in Colonna, Marina, Hagemann, Harald and Hamouda, Omar F. (eds) (1994), *Capitalism, Socialism and Knowledge: The Economics of F. A. Hayek, Volume 2*, Aldershot: Edward Elgar, pp. 131–59.

Lawson, Tony (1994b), 'Realism, Philosophical', in Hodgson *et al* (1994, vol. 2, pp. 219–25).

Lawson, Tony (1996), 'Developments in Hayek's Social Theorising', in Stephen Frowen (ed.) (1996), *Hayek, the Economist and Social Philosopher: A Critical Retrospect*, London: Macmillan.

Lawson, Tony (1997), *Economics and Reality*, London: Routledge.

Lazonick, William (1990), *Competitive Advantage on the Shop Floor*, Harvard University Press, Cambridge, MA.

Lazonick, William (1994), 'The Integration of Theory and History: Methodology and Ideology in Schumpeter's Economics', in Magnusson (1994, pp. 245–63).

Leathers, Charles G. (1990), 'Veblen and Hayek on Instincts and Evolution', *Journal of the History of Economic Thought*, **12**(2), June, 162–78. Reprinted in Hodgson (1998f).

Lee, Frederick S. and Harley, Sandra (1997) 'Research Selectivity, Managerialism and the Academic Labor Process: The Future of Nonmainstream Economics in U.K. Universities', *Human Relations*, **50**(11), November, pp. 1427–60.

Leontief, Wassily (1982), Letter in *Science*, No. 217, 9 July, 104, 107.

Levhari, David and Samuelson, Paul A. (1966), 'The Nonswitching Theorem is False', *Quarterly Journal of Economics*, **80**(4), November, 503–17.

Levine, David P. (1977), *Contributions to the Critique of Economic Theory*, London: Routledge and Kegan Paul.

Levine, David P. (1978), *Economic Theory: Volume One: The Elementary Relations of Economic Life*, London: Routledge and Kegan Paul.

Lewin, Roger (1993), *Complexity*, Phoenix: Orion Books.

Lewin, Shira B. (1996), 'Economics and Psychology: Lessons for Our Own Day From the Early Twentieth Century', *Journal of Economic Literature*, **34**(3), September, 1293–323.

Lewis, Paul A. (1996), 'Metaphor and Critical Realism', *Review of Social Economy*, **54**(4), Winter, 487–506.

Lewontin, Richard C. (1974), *The Genetic Basis of Evolutionary Change*, New York: Columbia University Press.

Lilienfeld, Paul von (1873–81), *Gedanken über zur Sozialwissenshaft der Zukunft* (Thoughts on the Social Science of the Future), Hamburg.

List, Friedrich (1904), *The National System of Political Economy*, translated from the German edition of 1841 by Sampson S. Lloyd, with an introduction by J. Sheild Nicholson, Longmans Green, London.

Littleboy, Bruce (1990), *On Interpreting Keynes: A Study in Reconciliation*, London: Routledge.

Lloyd, Seth (1990), 'The Calculus of Intricacy', *The Sciences*, 38–44.

Loasby, Brian J. (1976), *Choice, Complexity and Ignorance: An Enquiry into Economic Theory and the Practice of Decision Making*, Cambridge: Cambridge University Press.

Loasby, Brian J. (1989), *The Mind and Method of the Economist: A Critical Appraisal of Major Economists in the Twentieth Century*, Aldershot: Edward Elgar.

Loasby, Brian J. (1990), 'The Firm', in John Creedy (ed.) (1990), *Foundations of Economic Thought*, Oxford: Basil Blackwell, pp. 212–33.

Loasby, Brian J. (1991), *Equilibrium and Evolution: An Exploration of Connecting Principles in Economics*, Manchester: Manchester University Press.

Loasby, Brian J. (1995), 'Running a Business: An Appraisal of *Economics, Organization and Management* by Paul Milgrom and John Roberts', *Industrial and Corporate Change*, 4(2), 471–89.

Lotka, Alfred James (1925), *Elements of Physical Biology*, New York: Dover.

LouçA, Francisco (1997), *Turbulence in Economics: An Evolutionary Appraisal of Cycles and Complexity in Historical Processes*, Aldershot: Edward Elgar.

Lowry, S. Todd (1976), 'Bargain and Contract Theory in Law and Economics', *Journal of Economic Issues*, 10(1), March, 1–22.

Lucas, Robert E., Jr (1988), 'On the Mechanics of Economic Development', *Journal of Monetary Economics*, 22, 3–42.

Lundvall, Bengt-Åke (ed.) (1992), *National Systems of Innovation: Towards a Theory of Innovation and Interactive Learning*, London: Pinter.

Lundvall, Bengt-Åke (1993), 'Explaining Interfirm Cooperation and Innovation: Limits of the Transaction-Cost Approach', in Grabher (1993, pp. 52–64).

Maasen, Sabine (1995), 'Who is Afraid of Metaphors?' in Maasen *et al* (1995, pp. 11–35).

Maasen, Sabine, Mendelsohn, Everett and Weingart, Peter (eds) (1995), *Biology as Society, Society as Biology: Metaphors*, Sociology of the Sciences Yearbook, 18, 1994, Boston: Kluwer.

Machlup, Fritz (1946), 'Marginal Analysis and Empirical Research', *American Economic Review*, 36(3), September, 519–54.

MacDonald, George (1916), *The Evolution of Coinage*, Cambridge: Cambridge University Press.

MacGregor, David H. (1910), *The Evolution of Industry*, London: Williams and Norgate.

Magill, Michael and Quinzii, Martine (1996), *Theory of Incomplete Markets,* 2 vols, Cambridge, MA: MIT Press.

Magnusson, Lars (ed.) (1994), *Evolutionary and Neo-Schumpeterian Approaches to Economics,* Kluwer, Boston.

Mäki, Uskali (1997), 'The One World and Many Theories', in Salanti and Screpanti (1997, pp. 37–47).

Malmgren, H. B. (1961), 'Information, Expectations, and the Theory of the Firm', *Quarterly Journal of Economics,* **75**, 399–421.

Mani, G. S. (1991), 'Is There a General Theory of Biological Evolution?' in Saviotti and Metcalfe (1991, pp. 31–57).

Manier, Edward (1978), *The Young Darwin and his Cultural Circle: A Study of Influences which helped Shape the Language and Logic of the First Drafts of the Theory of Natural Selection,* Dordrecht: Reidel.

Mantel, Rolf R. (1974), 'On the Characterization of Aggregate Excess Demand', *Journal of Economic Theory,* **12**(2), pp. 348–53.

Marsden, David (1986), *The End of Economic Man? Custom and Competition in Labour Markets,* Brighton: Wheatsheaf Books.

Marshall, Alfred (1890), *Principles of Economics: An Introductory Volume,* 1st edn., London: Macmillan.

Marshall, Alfred (1949), *The Principles of Economics,* 8th (reset) edn. (1st edn. 1890), Macmillan, London.

Martin, Roderick (1993), 'The New Behaviorism: A Critique of Economics and Organization', *Human Relations,* **46**(9), 1085–101.

Marx, Karl (1976), *Capital,* vol. 1, translated by B. Fowkes from the fourth German edition of 1890, Harmondsworth: Pelican.

Marx, Karl (1981), *Capital,* vol. 3, translated by David Fernbach from the German edition of 1894, Harmondsworth: Pelican.

Masten, Scott E. (1998), 'The Three Great Puzzles of the Firm', in Steven G. Medema (ed.) (1998), *Coasean Economics: Law and Economics and the New Institutional Economics,* Boston: Kluwer, pp. 50–63.

Matson, Floyd W. (1964), *The Broken Image,* New York: Doubleday.

Matthews, Robin C. O. (1985), 'Darwinism and Economic Change', in Collard, David *et al,* (eds) (1985), *Economic Theory and Hicksian Themes,* Oxford: Oxford University Press, pp. 91–117. Reprinted in Witt (1993b).

Mayer, Thomas (1993), *Truth versus Precision in Economics,* Aldershot: Edward Elgar.

Mayhew, Anne (1987), 'The Beginnings of Institutionalism', *Journal of Economic Issues,* **21**(3), September, 971–98.

Mayhew, Anne (1989), 'Contrasting Origins of the Two Institutionalisms: The Social Science Context', *Review of Political Economy*, **1**(3), November, 319–33.

Maynard Smith, John (1976), 'Group Selection', *Quarterly Review of Biology*, **51**, 277–83. Reprinted in Clutton-Brock and Harvey (1978), and Brandon and Burian (1984).

Maynard Smith, John (1978), *The Evolution of Sex*, London: Cambridge University Press.

Maynard Smith, John (1980), 'The Concepts of Sociobiology', in G. S. Stent (ed.) (1980), *Morality as a Biological Phenomenon*, Berkeley: University of California Press.

Maynard Smith, John (1982), *Evolutionary Game Theory*, Cambridge: Cambridge University Press.

Mayntz, Renate (1992), 'The Influence of Natural Science Theories on Contemporary Social Science' in Dierkes, Meinolf, Bievert, Bernd (eds) (1992), *European Social Science in Transition: Assessment and Outlook* (Frankfurt am Main and Boulder, CO: Campus Verlag and Westview Press, pp. 27–79.

Mayr, Ernst (1960), 'The Emergence of Evolutionary Novelties', in Tax, Sol (ed.) (1960), *Evolution After Darwin (I): The Evolution of Life*, Chicago: University of Chicago Press.

Mayr, Ernst (1980), 'Prologue: Some Thoughts on the History of the Evolutionary Synthesis', in Mayr, Ernst and Provine, William B. (eds) (1980), *The Evolutionary Synthesis: Perspectives on the Unification of Biology*, Cambridge, MA: Harvard University Press, pp. 1–48.

Mayr, Ernst (1985a), 'How Biology Differs from the Physical Sciences', in Depew and Weber (1985, pp. 43–63).

Mayr, Ernst (1985b), 'Darwin's Five Theories of Evolution', in D. Kohn (ed.), *The Darwinian Heritage*, Princeton: Princeton University Press, pp. 755–72.

McCloskey, Donald N. (1985), *The Rhetoric of Economics*, Madison: University of Wisconsin Press.

McCloskey, Donald N. (1991), 'Economic Science: A Search Through the Hyperspace of Assumptions?', *Methodus*, **3**(1), June, 6–16.

McDougall, William (1908), *An Introduction to Social Psychology*, London: Methuen.

McDougall, William (1921), 'The Use and Abuse of Instinct in Social Psychology', *Journal of Abnormal Psychology and Social Psychology*, **16**, December.

McDougall, William (1929), *Modern Materialism and Emergent Evolution*, London: Methuen.

McFarland, Floyd B. (1985), 'Thorstein Veblen Versus the Institutionalists', *Review of Radical Political Economics*, **17**(4), Winter, 95–105.

McFarland, Floyd B. (1986), 'Clarence Ayres and his Gospel of Technology', *History of Political Economy*, **18**(4), Winter, 593–613.

McKelvey, Maureen (1996), *Evolutionary Innovations: The Business of Biotechnology*, Oxford: Oxford University Press.

McKelvey, William (1982), *Organizational Systematics: Taxonomy, Evolution, Classification*, Berkeley, CA: University of California Press.

McNeill, W. H. (1980), *The Pursuit of Power: Technology, Armed Force, and Society Since A.D. 1000*, Chicago: University of Chicago Press.

Meade, James E. (1971), *The Controlled Economy*, London: Macmillan.

Medvedev, Zhores (1969), *The Rise and Fall of T. D. Lysenko*, New York: Columbia University Press.

Meek, Ronald (1961), 'Mr Sraffa's Rehabilitation of Classical Economics', published simultaneously in *Science and Society*, **25**, Spring, 139–56 and *Scottish Journal of Political Economy*, **8**, June, 119–36. Revised and reprinted in Meek, Ronald (1967), *Economics and Ideology and Other Essays*, London: Chapman and Hall.

Ménard, Claude (1990), 'The Lausanne Tradition: Walras and Pareto', in Klaus Hennings and Warren Samuels (eds) (1990), *Neoclassical Economic Theory, 1870 to 1930*, Boston: Kluwer, pp. 95–136.

Menger, Carl (1981), *Principles of Economics*, edited by J. Dingwall and translated by B. F. Hoselitz from the German edition of 1871, New York: New York University Press.

Menger, Carl (1985), *Investigations into the Method of the Social Sciences with Special Reference to Economics,* (published in 1963 as *Problems of Economics and Sociology*) translated by F. J. Nock from the German edition of 1883 with an 1963 introduction by Louis Schneider and a 1985 introduction by Lawrence H. White, New York: New York University Press.

Metcalfe, J. Stanley (1988), 'Evolution and Economic Change', in Silberston, Aubrey (ed.) (1988), *Technology and Economic Progress*, Macmillan, Basingstoke, pp. 54–85. Reprinted in Witt (1993b).

Metcalfe, J. Stanley (1994), 'Evolutionary Economics and Technology Policy', *Economic Journal*, **104**(4), July, 931–44.

Metcalfe, J. Stanley (1995), 'Technology Systems and Technology Policy in an Evolutionary Framework', *Cambridge Journal of Economics*, **19**(1), February, 25–46.

Metcalfe, J. Stanley (1998), *Evolutionary Economics and Creative Destruction*, London: Routledge.

Metcalfe, J. Stanley and Gibbons, Michael (1989), 'Technology, Variety and Organization: A Systematic Perspective on the Competitive Process', in Rosenbloom, R. S. and Burgelman, R. (eds) (1988), *Research on Technological Innovation, Management and Policy*, Vol. 4, Greenwich, CO: JAI Press.

Michalski, R. S., Carbonell, J. G. and Mitchell, T. M. (eds) (1986), *Machine Learning II*, Los Altos, CA: Morgan Kaufman.

Milgrom, Paul and Roberts, John (1992), *Economics, Organization, and Management*, Englewood Cliffs and London: Prentice-Hall.

Minsky, Hyman P. (1976), *John Maynard Keynes*, London: Macmillan.

Mirowski, Philip (1983), 'An Evolutionary Theory of Economic Change: A Review Article', *Journal of Economic Issues*, 17(3), September, 757–68. Reprinted in Philip Mirowski (1988), *Against Mechanism: Protecting Economics from Science*, Totowa, NJ: Rowman and Littlefield.

Mirowski, Philip (ed.) (1986), *The Reconstruction of Economic Theory*, Boston: Kluwer-Nijhoff.

Mirowski, Philip (1987), 'The Philosophical Bases of Institutional Economics', *Journal of Economic Issues*, 21(3), September, 1001–38. Reprinted in Mirowski, Philip (1988), *Against Mechanism: Protecting Economics from Science*, Totowa, NJ: Rowman and Littlefield.

Mirowski, Philip (1989a), 'The Probabilistic Counter-Revolution, or How Stochastic Concepts Came to Neoclassical Theory', *Oxford Economic Papers*, 41(2), April, 217–35.

Mirowski, Philip (1989b), *More Heat Than Light: Economics as Social Physics, Physics as Nature's Economics*, Cambridge: Cambridge University Press.

Mirowski, Philip (1990), 'From Mandelbrot to Chaos in Economic Theory', *Southern Economic Journal*, 57(2), October, 289–307.

Mirowski, Philip (1991), 'The When, the How and the Why of Mathematical Expression in the History of Economic Analysis', *Journal of Economic Perspectives*, 5(1), Winter, 145–57.

Mirowski, Philip (ed.) (1994), *Natural Images in Economic Thought: Markets Read in Tooth and Claw*, Cambridge: Cambridge University Press.

Mises, Ludwig von (1920), 'Die Wirtshaftsrechnung im sozialistischen Gemeinwesen', *Archiv für Sozialwissenschaften und Sozialpolitik*, 47(1), April. Translated and reprinted in Hayek, Friedrich A. (ed.) (1935), *Collectivist Economic Planning*, London: George Routledge, pp. 87–130. (Reprinted 1975 by Augustus Kelley.)

Mises, Ludwig von (1957), *Theory and History: An Interpretation of Social and Economic Evolution*, New Haven: Yale University Press.

Mitchell, Wesley C. (1910), 'The Rationality of Economic Activity', *Journal of Political Economy*, **18**(2-3), parts I and II, February–March, 97–113; 197–216.

Mitchell, Wesley C. (1937), *The Backward Art of Spending Money and Other Essays*, New York: McGraw-Hill.

Moggridge, Donald E. (1992), *Maynard Keynes: An Economist's Biography*, London: Routledge.

Mokyr, Joel (1990), *The Lever of Riches: Technological Creativity and Economic Progress*, Oxford: Oxford University Press.

Mokyr, Joel (1991), 'Evolutionary Biology, Technical Change and Economic History', *Bulletin of Economic Research*, **43**(2), April, 127–49. Reprinted in Hodgson (1995a).

Mongiovi, Gary (1992), 'Piero Sraffa', in Arestis, Philip and Sawyer, Malcolm (eds) (1992), *A Biographical Dictionary of Dissenting Economists*, Aldershot: Edward Elgar, pp. 536–45.

Montgomery, Cynthia A. (ed.) (1995), *Resource-Based and Evolutionary Theories of the Firm: Towards a Synthesis*, Boston: Kluwer.

Morgan, C. Lloyd (1896), *Habit and Instinct*, London and New York: Edward Arnold.

Morgan, C. Lloyd (1927), *Emergent Evolution*, 2nd edn. (1st edn. 1923), London: Williams and Norgate.

Morgan, C. Lloyd (1933), *The Emergence of Novelty*, London: Williams and Norgate.

Morgan, Lewis H. (1877), *Ancient Society*, Chicago: Charles Kerr. Reprinted 1964 with an introduction by Leslie A. White, Cambridge, MA: Harvard University Press.

Morgan, Mary (1995), 'Evolutionary Metaphors in Explanations of American Industrial Competition', in Maasen *et al* (1995, pp. 311–37).

Morishima, Michio (1966), 'Refutation of the Nonswitching Theorem', *Quarterly Journal of Economics*, **80**, 520–5.

Morroni, Mario (1992), *Production Process and Technical Change*, Cambridge: Cambridge University Press.

Moschandreas, Maria (1997), 'The Role of Opportunism in Transaction Cost Economics', *Journal of Economic Issues*, **31**(1), March, 39–57.

Moss, Scott J. (1984), 'The History of the Theory of the Firm from Marshall to Robinson and Chamberlin: The Source of Positivism in Economics', *Economica*, **51**, August, 307–18.

Moss, Scott J. (1990), 'Winter's Fundamental Selection Theorem: A Disproof', *Quarterly Journal of Economics*, **105**, 1071–74.

Mumford, Lewis (1934), *Technics and Civilization*, New York: Harcourt, Brace and World.

Murphy, James Bernard (1994), 'The Kinds of Order in Society', in Mirowski (1994, pp. 536–82).

Murrell, Peter (1983), 'Did the Theory of Market Socialism Answer the Challenge of Ludwig von Mises? A Reinterpretation of the Socialist Controversy', *History of Political Economy*, **15** (Spring): 92–105.

Murrell, Peter (1991), 'Can Neoclassical Economics Underpin the Reform of Centrally Planned Economies?', *Journal of Economic Perspectives*, **5**(4), Fall, 59–76.

Myrdal, Gunnar (1958), *Value in Social Theory*, New York: Harper.

Myrdal, Gunnar (1972), *Against the Stream: Critical Essays in Economics*, New York: Pantheon Books.

Nef, J. U. (1950), *War and Human Progress: An Essay on the Rise of Industrial Civilization*, Cambridge, MA: Harvard University Press.

Nelson, Julie A. (1996), *Feminism, Objectivity and Economics*, London: Routledge.

Nelson, Richard R. (1980), 'Production Sets, Technological Knowledge and R&D: Fragile and Overworked Constructs for Analysis of Productivity Growth?', *American Economic Review (Papers and Proceedings)*, **70**(2), May, 62–67.

Nelson, Richard R. (1981a), 'Assessing Private Enterprise: An Exegesis of Tangled Doctrine', *Bell Journal of Economics*, **12**(1), 93–111.

Nelson, Richard R. (1981b), 'Research on Productivity Growth and Productivity Differences: Dead Ends and New Departures', *Journal of Economic Literature*, **29**(3), September, 1029–64.

Nelson, Richard R. (1991), 'Why Do Firms Differ, and How Does it Matter?', *Strategic Management Journal*, **12**, Special Issue, Winter, 61–74.

Nelson, Richard R. (ed.) (1993), *National Innovation Systems: A Comparative Analysis*, Oxford: Oxford University Press.

Nelson, Richard R. (1994a), 'The Coevolution of Technologies and Institutions', in England, Richard W. (ed.) (1994), *Evolutionary Concepts in Contemporary Economics*, Ann Arbor: University of Michigan Press, pp. 139–56.

Nelson, Richard R. (1994b), 'The Role of Firm Difference in an Evolutionary Theory of Technical Advance', in Magnusson (1994, pp. 231–42).

Nelson, Richard R. (1994c), Personal communication to G. Hodgson, dated September 21, 1994.

Nelson, Richard R. (1995), 'Recent Evolutionary Theorizing About Economic Change', *Journal of Economic Literature*, **33**(1), March, 48–90.

Nelson, Richard R. (1996), Personal communication to G. Hodgson, dated March 6, 1996.

Nelson, Richard R. (1998), 'The Agenda for Growth Theory: A Different Point of View', *Cambridge Journal of Economics,* **22**(4), July, 497–520.

Nelson, Richard R. and Winter, Sidney G. (1973), 'Towards an Evolutionary Theory of Economic Capabilities', *American Economic Review (Papers and Proceedings)*, **63**(2), May, 440–9.

Nelson, Richard R. and Winter, Sidney G. (1974), 'Neoclassical vs. Evolutionary Theories of Economic Growth: Critique and Prospectus', *Economic Journal*, **84**(4), December, 886–905. Reprinted in Freeman (1990).

Nelson, Richard R. and Winter, Sidney G. (1982), *An Evolutionary Theory of Economic Change*, Cambridge MA: Harvard University Press.

Neumann, John von and Morgenstern, Oskar (1953), *Theory of Games and Economic Behavior*, Princeton: Princeton University Press.

Nightingale, John (1993), 'Solving Marshall's Problem With the Biological Analogy: Jack Downie's Competitive Process', *History of Economics Review*, **20**, Summer, 75–94. Reprinted in Hodgson (1995a).

Niman, Neil B. (1991), 'Biological Analogies in Marshall's Work', *Journal of the History of Economic Thought*, **13**(1), Spring, 19–36. Reprinted in Hodgson (1995a).

Nooteboom, Bart (1992), 'Towards a Dynamic Theory of Transactions', *Journal of Evolutionary Economics*, **2**(4), December, 281–99.

Nooteboom, Bart (1995), 'Towards a Cognitive Theory of the Firm', School of Management and Organisation, University of Groningen, mimeo.

Norgaard, Richard B. (1989), 'The Case for Methodological Pluralism', *Ecological Economics*, **1**(1), February, 37–57.

North, Douglass C. (1981), *Structure and Change in Economic History*, New York: Norton.

North, Douglass C. (1990), *Institutions, Institutional Change and Economic Performance*, Cambridge: Cambridge University Press.

Nove, Alexander (1983), *The Economics of Feasible Socialism*, London: George Allen and Unwin.

Nozick, Robert (1977), 'On Austrian Methodology', *Synthese*, **36**, 353–92.

Nutzinger, Hans (1982), 'The Economics of Property Rights – A New Paradigm in Social Science?', in W. Stegmuller, W. Balzer and W.

Spohn (eds) (1982), *Philosophy and Economics*, Berlin: Springer-Verlag, pp. 169–90.

Olson, Mancur, Jr. (1965), *The Logic of Collective Action*, Cambridge, MA: Harvard University Press.

Olson, Mancur, Jr. (1982), *The Rise and Decline of Nations*, New Haven: Yale University Press.

Orchard, Lionel and Stretton, Hugh (1997), 'Public Choice', *Cambridge Journal of Economics*, **21**(3), May, 409–30.

Ormerod, Paul (1994), *The Death of Economics*, London: Faber and Faber.

Oster, George F. and Wilson, Edward O. (1978), *Caste and Ecology in the Social Insects*, Princeton: Princeton University Press.

Pagano, Ugo (1991), 'Property Rights, Asset Specificity, and the Division of Labour Under Alternative Capitalist Relations', *Cambridge Journal of Economics*, **15**(3), September, 315–42. Reprinted in Hodgson (1993d).

Pagano, Ugo (1992), 'Authority, Co-ordination and Disequilibrium: An Explanation of the Co-Existence of Markets and Firms', *Structural Change and Economic Dynamics*, **3**(1), 53–77. Reprinted in Hodgson (1993d).

Pantzar, Mika (1991), *A Replicative Perspective on Evolutionary Dynamics*, Helsinki: Labour Institute for Economic Research, Research Report 37.

Pasinetti, Luigi L. (1966), 'Changes in the Rate of Profit and Switches of Techniques', *Quarterly Journal of Economics*, **80**(4), November, 503–17.

Pasinetti, Luigi L. (1969), 'Switches of Technique and the "Rate of Return" in Capital Theory', *Economic Journal*, **79**, 508–25. Reprinted in Harcourt and Laing (1971).

Pasinetti, Luigi L. (1981), *Structural Change and Economic Growth: A Theoretical Essay on the Dynamics of the Wealth of Nations*, Cambridge: Cambridge University Press.

Pavitt, Keith (1988), 'International Patterns of Technological Accumulation', in N. Hood and J. Vahine (eds) (1988), *Strategies in Global Competition*, Croom Helm, London.

Peirce, Charles Sanders (1934), *Collected Papers of Charles Sanders Peirce, Volume V, Pragmatism and Pragmaticism*, edited by C. Hartshorne and P. Weiss, Cambridge, MA: Harvard University Press.

Peirce, Charles Sanders (1958), *Collected Papers of Charles Sanders Peirce, Volume VII, Science and Philosophy*, edited by A. W. Burks, Cambridge, MA: Harvard University Press.

Pelikan, Pavel (1989), 'Evolution, Economic Competence, and Corporate Control', *Journal of Economic Behavior and Organization*, **12**, 279–303.

Pencavel, John (1991), 'Prospects for Economics', *Economic Journal*, 101(1), January, 81–7.

Penrose, Edith T. (1952), 'Biological Analogies in the Theory of the Firm', *American Economic Review*, 42(4), December, 804–19. Reprinted in Hodgson (1995a, 1998f).

Penrose, Edith T. (1953), 'Rejoinder', *American Economic Review*, 43(3), September, 603–7.

Penrose, Edith T. (1959), *The Theory of the Growth of the Firm*, Oxford: Basil Blackwell. Reprinted 1995, Oxford: Oxford University Press.

Penrose, Roger (1994), *Shadows of the Mind: A Search for the Missing Science of Consciousness*, Oxford: Oxford University Press.

Persons, S. (ed.) (1950), *Evolutionary Thought in America*, New Haven: Yale University Press.

Pettigrew, Andrew and Whipp, Richard (1991), *Managing Change for Corporate Success*, Oxford: Blackwell.

Pigou, Arthur C. (1922), 'Empty Economic Boxes: A Reply', *Economic Journal*, 32(4), December, 458–65.

Pigou, Arthur C. (ed.) (1925), *Memorials of Alfred Marshall*, London: Macmillan.

Pigou, Arthur C. (1928), 'An Analysis of Supply', *Economic Journal*, 38(3), September, 238–57.

Pingle, Mark (1992), 'Costly Optimization: An Experiment', *Journal of Economic Behavior and Organization*, 17(1), January, 3–30.

Pinker, Steven (1994), *The Language Instinct: The New Science of Language and Mind*, London and New York: Allen Lane and Morrow.

Pitelis, Christos (1991), *Market and Non-Market Hierarchies: Theory of Institutional Failure*, Oxford: Basil Blackwell.

Plotkin, Henry C. (1994), *Darwin Machines and the Nature of Knowledge: Concerning Adaptations, Instinct and the Evolution of Intelligence*, Harmondsworth: Penguin.

Polanyi, Michael (1958), *Personal Knowledge: Towards a Post-Critical Philosophy*, London: Routledge and Kegan Paul.

Polanyi, Michael (1967), *The Tacit Dimension*, London: Routledge and Kegan Paul.

Pollak, Robert A. (1985), 'A Transaction Cost Approach to Families and Households', *Journal of Economic Literature*, 23, 581–608.

Popper, Sir Karl R. (1972), *Objective Knowledge: An Evolutionary Approach*, Oxford: Oxford University Press.

Popper, Sir Karl R. (1982), *The Open Universe: An Argument for Indeterminism*, from the *Postscript to the Logic of Scientific Discovery*, edited by W. W. Bartley, III, London: Hutchinson.

Popper, Sir Karl R. and Eccles, John C. (1977), *The Self and Its Brain*, Berlin: Springer International.

Porter, Michael E. (1980), *Competitive Strategy: Techniques for Analyzing Industries and Competitors*, New York: Free Press.

Porter, Michael E. (1990), 'The Competitive Advantage of Nations', *Harvard Business Review*, **68**, 73–93.

Porter, Michael E. and Linde, Claas van der (1995) 'Towards a New Conception of the Environment-Competitiveness Relationship', *Journal of Economic Perspectives*, **9**(4), Fall, pp. 97–118.

Posner, Richard A. (1973), *Economic Analysis of Law*, Boston: Little, Brown.

Powell, Walter W. (1990), 'Neither Market nor Hierarchy: Network Forms of Organization', *Research in Organizational Behavior*, **12**, 295–336.

Powell, Walter W, and DiMaggio, Paul (eds) (1991), *The New Institutionalism in Organizational Analysis*, Chicago: University of Chicago Press.

Prahalad, C. K. and Hamel, Gary (1990), 'The Core Competences of the Corporation', *Harvard Business Review*, May-June, 79–91.

Proctor, R. N. (1991), *Value-Free Science? Purity and Power in Modern Knowledge*, Cambridge, MA: Harvard University Press.

Putterman, Louis (1988), 'The Firm as Association vs. Firm as Commodity: Efficiency, Rights, and Ownership', *Economics and Philosophy*, **4**(2), 243–66.

Quine, Willard van Orman (1953), *From a Logical Point of View*, Cambridge, MA: Harvard University Press.

Radner, Roy (1968), 'Competitive Equilibrium Under Uncertainty', *Econometrica*, **36**(1), January, 31–58.

Ramstad, Yngve (1990), 'The Institutionalism of John R. Commons: Theoretical Foundations of a Volitional Economics', *Research in the History of Economic Thought and Methodology*, **8**, 53–104.

Rapport, David J. and Turner, James E. (1977), 'Economic Models in Ecology', *Science*, **195**, 367–73. Reprinted in Hodgson (1995a).

Reijnders, Jan (ed.) (1997), *Economics and Evolution*, Cheltenham, UK and Lyme, US: Edward Elgar.

Reinheimer, Herman (1913), *Evolution by Co-operation: A Study in Bioeconomics*, London: Kegan, Paul, Trench, Trubner.

Reynolds, Lloyd G. and Taft, Cynthia H. (1956), *The Evolution of Wage Structure*, Oxford: Oxford University Press.

Richardson, George B. (1972), 'The Organisation of Industry', *Economic Journal*, **82**, 883–96.

Rizvi, S. Abu Turab (1994a), 'The Microfoundations Project in General Equilibrium Theory', *Cambridge Journal of Economics*, **18**(4), August, 357–77.

Rizvi, S. Abu Turab (1994b), 'Game Theory to the Rescue?', *Contributions to Political Economy*, **13**, 1–28.

Robbins, Lionel (1932), *An Essay on the Nature and Significance of Economic Science*, 1st edn., London: Macmillan.

Robertson, Dennis H. (1923), *The Control of Industry*, London: Nisbet.

Robinson, Joan (1942), *An Essay on Marxian Economics*, London: Macmillan.

Robinson, Joan (1953), 'The Production Function and the Theory of Capital', *Review of Economic Studies*, **21**(1), 81–106. Reprinted in Robinson (1960), and Harcourt and Laing (1971).

Robinson, Joan (1960), *Collected Economic Papers – Volume Two*, Oxford: Basil Blackwell.

Robinson, Joan (1961), 'Prelude to a Critique of Economic Theory', *Oxford Economic Papers*, **13**, 7–14. Reprinted in Robinson (1975) and Hunt and Schwartz (1972).

Robinson, Joan (1973a), 'Ideology and Analysis', in *Sozialismus Geschichte und Wirtschaft. Festschrift für Eduard Marz*, Wien: Europaverlags AG. Reprinted in Robinson (1979a).

Robinson, Joan (1973b), *Collected Economic Papers – Volume Four*, Oxford: Basil Blackwell.

Robinson, Joan (1974), *History Versus Equilibrium*, London: Thames Papers in Political Economy.

Robinson, Joan (1975), *Collected Economic Papers – Volume Three*, 2nd. edn., Oxford: Basil Blackwell.

Robinson, Joan (1979a), *Collected Economic Papers – Volume Five*, Oxford: Basil Blackwell.

Robinson, Joan (1979b), 'Garegnani on Effective Demand', *Cambridge Journal of Economics*, **3**(2), June, 179–80. Reprinted in Eatwell and Milgate (1983).

Robinson, Joan (1980), *Further Contributions to Modern Economics*, Oxford: Basil Blackwell.

Robinson, Joan and Naqvi, Khaleeq A. (1967), 'The Badly Behaved Production Function', *Quarterly Journal of Economics*, **81**, 579–91.

Romer, Paul M. (1986), 'Increasing Returns and Long-Run Growth', *Journal of Political Economy*, **94**(5), October, 1002–37.

Roncaglia, Alessandro (1991), 'The Sraffa Schools', *Review of Political Economy*, **3**(2), April, 187–219.

Roscher, Wilhelm (1854), *Das System der Volkswirtschaft* (System of the Folk-Economy), Stuttgart: Cotta.

Rose, Steven, Kamin, Leon J. and Lewontin, Richard C. (1984), *Not in Our Genes: Biology, Ideology and Human Nature*, Harmondsworth: Penguin.

Rosenberg, Alexander (1994), 'Does Evolutionary Theory Give Comfort or Inspiration to Economics?', in Mirowski (1994, pp. 384–407).

Rosenberg, Nathan (1994), *Exploring the Black Box: Technology, Economics, and History*, Cambridge and New York: Cambridge University Press.

Ross, Dorothy (1991), *The Origins of American Social Science*, Cambridge: Cambridge University Press.

Rotemberg, Julio J. (1991), 'A Theory of Inefficient Intrafirm Transactions', *American Economic Review*, **81**(1), March, 191–209.

Roughgarden, Jonathan (1979), *Theory of Population Genetics and Evolutionary Ecology: An Introduction*, New York: Macmillan.

Roy, Subroto (1989), *Philosophy of Economics: On the Scope of Reason in Economic Enquiry*, London: Routledge.

Rumelt, Richard P. (1974), *Strategy, Structure, and Economic Performance*, Cambridge, MA: Harvard University Press.

Rumelt, Richard P. (1984), 'Towards a Strategic Theory of the Firm', in Lamb, R. B. (ed.) (1984), *Competitive Strategic Management*, Englewood Cliffs, NJ: Prentice-Hall, pp. 56–70.

Rutherford, Malcolm C. (1983), 'J. R. Commons's Institutional Economics', *Journal of Economic Issues*, **17**(3), September, 721–44. Reprinted in Samuels (1988).

Rutherford, Malcolm C. (1984), 'Thorstein Veblen and the Processes of Institutional Change', *History of Political Economy*, **16**(3), Fall, 331–48. Reprinted in M. Blaug (ed.) (1992), *Thorstein Veblen (1857–1929)*, Aldershot: Edward Elgar. Reprinted in Hodgson (1998f).

Rutherford, Malcolm C. (1988), 'Learning and Decision-Making in Economics and Psychology: A Methodological Perspective', in Earl, Peter E. (ed.) (1988), *Psychological Economics: Development, Tensions, Prospects*, Boston: Kluwer, pp. 35–54.

Rutherford, Malcolm C. (1989), 'Some Issues in the Comparison of Austrian and Institutional Economics', *Research in the History of Economic Thought and Methodology*, Vol. 6, pp. 159–71.

Rutherford, Malcolm C. (1994), *Institutions in Economics: The Old and the New Institutionalism*, Cambridge: Cambridge University Press.

Sabel, Charles F. and Zeitlin, Jonathan (1985), 'Historical Alternatives to Mass Production: Politics, Markets and Technology in Nineteenth Century Industrialization', *Past and Present*, No. 108, August, 132–76.

Sabel, Charles F. (1993), 'Studied Trust: Building New Forms of Cooperation in a Volatile Economy', *Human Relations*, **46**(9), 1133–70.

Sako, Mari (1992), *Prices, Quality and Trust: Inter-Firm Relations in Britain and Japan*, Cambridge: Cambridge University Press.

Salanti, Andrea and Screpanti, Ernesto (eds) (1997), *Pluralism in Economics: New Perspectives in History and Methodology*, Aldershot: Edward Elgar.

Salter, Wilfred E. G. (1960), *Productivity and Technical Change*, 1st edn., Cambridge University Press, Cambridge.

Samuels, Warren J. (1977), 'The Knight–Ayres Correspondence: The Grounds of Knowledge and Social Action', *Journal of Economic Issues*, **11**(3), September, 485–525. Reprinted in Blaug, Mark (ed.) (1992), *Wesley Mitchell (1874–1948), John Commons (1862–1945), Clarence Ayres (1891–1972)*, Aldershot: Edward Elgar.

Samuels, Warren J. (ed.) (1988), *Institutional Economics*, Aldershot: Edward Elgar.

Samuels, Warren J. (1989), 'Austrian and Institutional Economics: Some Common Elements', *Research in the History of Economic Thought and Methodology*, Vol. 6, 53–71.

Samuels, Warren J. (ed.) (1990), *Economics as Discourse: An Analysis of the Language of Economists*, Boston: Kluwer.

Samuels, Warren J. (1997), 'The Case for Methodological Pluralism' in Salanti and Screpanti (1997, pp. 67–79).

Samuelson, Paul A. (1938), 'A Note on the Pure Theory of Consumer's Behavior', *Economica*, New Series, **5**(17), February, 61–71.

Samuelson, Paul A. (1947), *Foundations of Economic Analysis*, Cambridge, MA: Harvard University Press.

Samuelson, Paul A. (1962), 'Parable and Realism in Capital Theory: The Surrogate Production Function', *Review of Economic Studies*, **39**, 193–206. Reprinted in Harcourt and Laing (1971).

Samuelson, Paul A. (1966), 'A Summing Up', *Quarterly Journal of Economics*, **80**, 568–83. Reprinted in Harcourt and Laing (1971).

Samuelson, Paul A. (1989), 'Remembering Joan', in Feiwel, George R. (ed.) (1989), *Joan Robinson and Modern Economic Theory*, London: Macmillan, pp. 125–43.

Sanderson, Stephen K. (1990), *Social Evolutionism: A Critical History*, Oxford: Blackwell.

Saviotti, Pier Paolo (1996), *Technological Evolution, Variety and the Economy*, Cheltenham, UK and Brookfield, US: Edward Elgar.

Saviotti, Pier Paolo and Metcalfe, J. Stanley (eds) (1991), *Evolutionary Theories of Economic and Technological Change: Present Status and Future Prospects*, Reading: Harwood.

Schaffer, Mark E. (1989), 'Are Profit-Maximisers the Best Survivors?: A Darwinian Model of Economic Natural Selection', *Journal of Economic Behavior and Organization*, **12**(1), March, pp. 29–45. Reprinted in Hodgson (1995a).

Schäffle, Albert (1875–1881), *Bau und Leben des socialen Körpers*, 4 vols. (Anatomy and Life of the Social Body), Tübingen: Lapp.

Scheffler, Israel (1974), *Four Pragmatists: A Critical Introduction to Peirce, James, Mead, and Dewey*, London: Routledge and Kegan Paul.

Schelling, Thomas C. (1978), *Micromotives and Macrobehavior*, New York: Norton.

Schotter, Andrew R. (1981), *The Economic Theory of Social Institutions*, Cambridge: Cambridge University Press.

Schumpeter, Joseph A. (1934), *The Theory of Economic Development: An Inquiry into Profits, Capital, Credit, Interest, and the Business Cycle*, translated by Redvers Opie from the second German edition of 1926, first edition 1911, Cambridge, MA: Harvard University Press. Reprinted 1989 with a new introduction by John E. Elliott, New Brunswick, NJ: Transaction.

Schumpeter, Joseph A. (1954), *History of Economic Analysis*, New York: Oxford University Press.

Schumpeter, Joseph A. (1976), *Capitalism, Socialism and Democracy*, 5th edn., London: George Allen and Unwin.

Schutz, Alfred (1967), *The Phenomenology of the Social World*, Evanston: Northwestern University Press.

Screpanti, Ernesto and Zamagni, Stefano (1993), *An Outline of the History of Economic Thought*, Oxford: Clarendon Press.

Sebba, Gregor (1953), 'The Development of the Concepts of Mechanism and Model in Physical Science and Economic Thought', *American Economic Review (Papers and Proceedings)*, **43**(2), May, 259–68. Reprinted in Hodgson (1995a).

Seckler, David (1975), *Thorstein Veblen and the Institutionalists: A Study in the Social Philosophy of Economics*, London: Macmillan.

Selznick, P. (1957), *Leadership in Administration: A Sociological Interpretation*, New York: Harper and Row.

Sen, Amartya K. (ed.) (1970), *Growth Economics*, Harmondsworth: Penguin.

Senge, Peter M. (1990), *The Fifth Discipline: The Art and Practice of the Learning Organization*, New York: Doubleday.

Shackle, George L. S. (1955), *Uncertainty in Economics*, Cambridge: Cambridge University Press.

Shackle, George L. S. (1967), *The Years of High Theory: Invention and Tradition in Economic Thought 1926–1939*, Cambridge: Cambridge University Press.

Shackle, George L. S. (1972), *Epistemics and Economics: A Critique of Economic Doctrines*, Cambridge: Cambridge University Press.

Shackle, George L. S. (1974), *Keynesian Kaleidics: The Evolution of a General Political Economy*, Edinburgh: Edinburgh University Press.

Shackle, George L. S. (1989), 'What Did the "General Theory" Do?', in Pheby, John (ed.) (1989), *New Directions in Post Keynesian Economics*, Aldershot: Edward Elgar, pp. 48–58.

Shafer, W. and Sonnenschein, Hugo (1982), 'Market Demand and Excess Demand Functions', in Arrow, K. J. and Intriligator, M. D. (eds) (1982), *Handbook of Mathematical Economics*, **2**, Amsterdam: North-Holland.

Shove, Gerald F. (1942), 'The Place of Marshall's *Principles* in the Development of Economic Theory', *Economic Journal*, **52**(4), December, 294–329. Reprinted in John Cunningham Wood (ed.) (1982), *Alfred Marshall: Critical Assessments*, London: Croom Helm.

Simon, Herbert A. (1951), 'A Formal Theory of the Employment Relationship', *Econometrica*, **19**, July, 293–305. Reprinted in Simon (1957).

Simon, Herbert A. (1957), *Models of Man: Social and Rational*, New York: Wiley.

Simon, Herbert A. (1959), 'Theories of Decision-Making in Economic and Behavioral Sciences', *American Economic Review*, **49**(2), June, 253–83.

Simon, Herbert A. (1968), *The Sciences of the Artificial*, Cambridge MA: MIT Press.

Simon, Herbert A. (1979), 'Rational Decision Making in Business Organizations', *American Economic Review*, **69**, 493–513.

Smelser, Neil J. and Swedberg, Richard (eds) (1994), *Handbook of Economic Sociology*, Princeton: Princeton University Press.

Smith, Adam (1869), *Essays of Adam Smith*, London: John Murray.

Smith, Adam (1970), *The Wealth of Nations*, edited with an introduction by Andrew Skinner (1st edn., 1776), Penguin, Harmondsworth.

Smith, Adam (1980), 'The Principles Which Lead and Direct Philosophical Enquiries: Illustrated by the History of Astronomy', in *Essays on*

Philosophical Subjects, edited by W. P. D. Wightman, Oxford: Clarendon.

Smith, M. R. (ed.) (1985), *Military Enterprise and Technological Change*, Cambridge, MA: MIT Press.

Sober, Elliott (1981), 'Holism, Individualism and the Units of Selection', in Asquith, P. D. and Giere, R. N. (eds) (1981), *Philosophy of Science Association 1980*, Vol. 2, pp. 93–121., East Lansing, MI: Philosophy of Science Association. Reprinted in Sober (1984b) and Hodgson (1995a).

Sober, Elliott (1984a), *The Nature of Selection: Evolutionary Theory in Philosophical Focus*, Cambridge, MA: MIT Press.

Sober, Elliott (ed.) (1984b), *Conceptual Issues in Evolutionary Biology: An Anthology*, Cambridge, MA: MIT Press.

Sober, Elliott (1985), 'Darwin on Natural Selection: A Philosophical Perspective', in D. Kohn (ed.) (1985), *The Darwinian Heritage*, Princeton: Princeton University Press, pp. 867–99.

Solow, Robert M. (1956), 'A Contribution to the Theory of Economic Growth', *Quarterly Journal of Economics*, **70**(1), February, 65–94. Reprinted in Sen (1970).

Solow, Robert M. (1957), 'Technical Change and the Aggregate Production Function', *Review of Economics and Statistics*, **39**, 312–20.

Solow, Robert M. (1965), *Capital Theory and the Rate of Return*, Chicago: Rand McNally.

Sonnenschein, Hugo (1972), 'Market Excess Demand Functions', *Econometrica*, **40**(3), 549–63.

Sonnenschein, Hugo (1973a), 'Do Walras's Identity and Continuity Characterize the Class of Community Excess Demand Functions?', *Journal of Economic Theory*, **6**(4), 345–54.

Sonnenschein, Hugo (1973b), 'The Utility Hypothesis and Market Demand Theory', *Western Economic Journal*, **11**(4), 404–10.

Sperry, Roger W. (1969), 'A Modified Concept of Consciousness', *Psychological Review*, **76**, 532–36.

Sraffa, Piero (1960), *Production of Commodities by Means of Commodities: Prelude to a Critique of Economic Theory*, Cambridge: Cambridge University Press.

Stata, Ray (1989), 'Organizational Learning: The Key to Management Innovation', *Sloan Management Review*, **32**, 63–74.

Steedman, Ian (1975), 'Positive Profits With Negative Surplus Value', *Economic Journal*, **85**(1), March, 114–23.

Steedman, Ian (1977), *Marx After Sraffa*, London: NLB.

Steedman, Ian (1984), 'Natural Prices, Differential Profit Rates and the Classical Competitive Process', *Manchester School*, **52**(2), June, 123–40. Reprinted in Steedman, I. (1989), *From Exploitation to Altruism*, Cambridge: Polity Press.

Steedman, Ian, Sweezy, Paul M. *et al* (1981), *The Value Controversy*, London: NLB.

Steindl, Joseph (1952), *Maturity and Stagnation in American Capitalism*, Blackwell, Oxford.

Stent, Gunther S. (1985), 'Hermeneutics and the Analysis of Complex Biological Systems', in Depew and Weber (1985, pp. 209–25).

Stewart, Ian (1989), *Does God Play Dice? The Mathematics of Chaos*, Oxford: Basil Blackwell.

Stigler, George J. (1961), 'The Economics of Information', *Journal of Political Economy*, **69**(2), June, 213–25.

Stigler, George J., Stigler, Stephen M. and Friedland, Claire (1995), 'The Journals of Economics', *Journal of Political Economy*, **105**(2), 331–59.

Stiglitz, Joseph E. (1987), 'The Causes and Consequences of the Dependence of Quality on Price', *Journal of Economic Literature*, **25**(1), March, 1–48.

Stiglitz, Joseph E. (1994), *Whither Socialism?*, Cambridge, MA: MIT Press.

Stoneman, William (1979), *A History of the Economic Analysis of the Great Depression*, New York: Garland.

Streissler, Erich W. (1990), 'The Influence of German Economics on the Work of Menger and Marshall', *History of Political Economy*, **22**, Annual Supplement, 31–68.

Sugden, Robert (1986), *The Economics of Rights, Co-operation and Welfare*, Oxford: Blackwell.

Sugden, Robert (1990), 'Convention, Creativity and Conflict', in Y. Varoufakis and D. Young, (eds) (1990), *Conflict in Economics*, Hemel Hempstead: Harvester Wheatsheaf, 1990, pp. 68–90.

Sugden, Robert (1991), 'Rational Choice: A Survey of Contributions from Economics and Philosophy', *Economic Journal*, **101**(4), July, 751–85.

Swan, T. W. (1956), 'Economic Growth and Capital Accumulation', *Economic Record*, **32**, 334–61.

Swedberg, Richard (ed.) (1993), *Explorations in Economic Sociology*, New York: Russell Sage.

Swedberg, Richard (ed.) (1996), *Economic Sociology*, Aldershot: Edward Elgar.

Tanimoto, S. L. (1987), *The Elements of Artificial Intelligence*, Rockville, Maryland: Computer Science Press.

Taylor, Frederick Winslow (1911), *The Principles of Scientific Management*, New York: Harper.

Teece, David J. (1982), 'Towards an Economic Theory of the Multiproduct Firm', *Journal of Economic Behavior and Organization*, 3(1), 39–63.

Teece, David J. (ed.) (1987), *The Competitive Challenge*, Ballinger, Cambridge, MA.

Teece, David J. (1988), 'Technological Change and the Nature of the Firm', in Dosi *et al* (1988, pp. 256–81).

Teece, David J. and Pisano, Gary (1994), 'The Dynamic Capabilities of Firms: An Introduction', *Industrial and Corporate Change*, 3(3), 537–56.

Teece, David J., Rumelt, Richard, Dosi, Giovanni and Winter, Sidney G. (1994), 'Understanding Corporate Coherence: Theory and Evidence', *Journal of Economic Behavior and Organization*, 23, 1–30.

Teece, David J. and Winter, Sidney G. (1984), 'The Limits of Neoclassical Theory in Management Education', *American Economic Review (Papers and Proceedings)*, 74(2), May, 116–21.

Thoben, H. (1982), 'Mechanistic and Organistic Analogies in Economics Reconsidered', *Kyklos*, 35, Fasc. 2, 292–306.

Thomas, Brinley (1991), 'Alfred Marshall on Economic Biology', *Review of Political Economy*, 3(1), January, 1–14. Reprinted in Hodgson (1995a).

Thomas, Henk T. and Logan, Christopher (1982), *Mondragon: An Economic Analysis*, London: George Allen and Unwin.

Thorp, John (1980), *Free Will: A Defence Against Neurophysiological Determinism*, London: Routledge and Kegan Paul.

Tilman, Rick (1990), 'New Light on John Dewey, Clarence Ayres, and the Development of Evolutionary Economics', *Journal of Economic Issues*, 24(4), December, 963–79.

Tilman, Rick (1992), *Thorstein Veblen and His Critics, 1891–1963: Conservative, Liberal, and Radical*, Princeton: Princeton University Press.

Tobin, James (1986), 'The Future of Keynesian Economics', *Eastern Economic Journal*, 13(4).

Tomer, John F. (1987), *Organizational Capital: The Path to Higher Productivity and Well-Being*, Praeger, New York.

Tomlinson, James (1986), 'Democracy Inside the Black Box? Neo-Classical Theories of the Firm and Industrial Democracy', *Economy and Society*, 15(2), May, 220–50.

Tool, Marc (1994), 'Ayres, Clarence E.' in Hodgson *et al* (1994, vol. 1, pp. 16–22).

Tugwell, Rexford G. (ed.) (1924), *The Trend of Economics*, New York: Alfred Knopf.

Tullock, Gordon (1979), 'Sociobiology and Economics', *Atlantic Economic Journal*, September, 1–10. Reprinted in Hodgson (1995a).

Tylor, Sir Edward Burnett (1871), *Primitive Culture*, 2 vols, London. Reprinted 1958, New York: Harper.

Udéhn, Lars (1987), *Methodological Individualism: A Critical Appraisal*, Uppsala: Uppsala University Reprographics Centre.

Udéhn, Lars (1996), *The Limits of Public Choice: A Sociological Critique of the Economic Theory of Politics*, London: Routledge.

Ullmann-Margalit, Edna (1978), 'Invisible Hand Explanations', *Synthese*, 39, 282–6.

Ursprung, H. W., 1988, 'Evolution and the Economic Approach to Human Behaviour', *Journal of Social and Biological Structure*, 11, 257–79.

Van Parijs, Philippe (1981), *Evolutionary Explanations in the Social Sciences: An Emerging Paradigm*, London: Tavistock.

Vanberg, Viktor J. (1986), 'Spontaneous Market Order and Social Rules: A Critique of F. A. Hayek's Theory of Cultural Evolution', *Economics and Philosophy*, 2(1), April, 75–100. Reprinted in Witt (1993b).

Vanberg, Viktor J. (1989), 'Carl Menger's Evolutionary and John R. Commons' Collective Action Approach to Institutions: A Comparison', *Review of Political Economy*, 1(3), November, 334–60. Reprinted in Vanberg, Viktor J. (1994), *Rules and Choice in Economics*, London: Routledge.

Varoufakis, Yanis (1990), 'Conflict in Equilibrium', in Varoufakis, Y. and Young, D. (eds) (1990), *Conflict in Economics*, Hemel Hempstead: Harvester Wheatsheaf, pp. 39–67.

Vaughn, Karen I. (1980), 'Economic Calculation Under Socialism: The Austrian Contribution', *Economic Inquiry*, 18: 535–4.

Veblen, Thorstein B. (1884), 'Kant's Critique of Judgement', *Journal of Speculative Philosophy*, 43, July, 260–74. Reprinted in Veblen (1934).

Veblen, Thorstein B. (1898a), 'Why Is Economics Not an Evolutionary Science?', *Quarterly Journal of Economics*, 12(3), July, 373–97. Reprinted in Veblen (1919a) and in Hodgson (1998f).

Veblen, Thorstein B. (1898b), 'The Instinct of Workmanship and the Irksomeness of Labor', *American Journal of Sociology*, 4, September, 187–201. Reprinted in Veblen (1934).

Veblen, Thorstein B. (1899), *The Theory of the Leisure Class: An Economic Study in the Evolution of Institutions*, New York: Macmillan.

Veblen, Thorstein B. (1904), *The Theory of Business Enterprise*, New York: Charles Scribners. Reprinted 1975 by Augustus Kelley.

Veblen, Thorstein B. (1908), 'The Evolution of the Scientific Point of View', *University of California Chronicle*, **10**(4), 396–416. Reprinted in Veblen (1919a).

Veblen, Thorstein B. (1914), *The Instinct of Workmanship, and the State of the Industrial Arts*, New York: Macmillan. Reprinted 1990 with a new introduction by M. G. Murphey and a 1964 introductory note by J. Dorfman, New Brunswick: Transaction Books.

Veblen, Thorstein B. (1919a), *The Place of Science in Modern Civilisation and Other Essays*, New York: Huebsch. Reprinted 1990 with a new introduction by W. J. Samuels, New Brunswick: Transaction Books.

Veblen, Thorstein B. (1919b), *The Vested Interests and the Common Man*, New Yor: Huebsch.

Veblen, Thorstein B. (1934), *Essays on Our Changing Order*, ed. Leon Ardzrooni, New York: The Viking Press.

Verspagen, Bart (1993), *Uneven Growth Between Interdependent Economies: An Evolutionary View on Technology Gaps, Trade and Growth*, Aldershot: Avebury.

Vining, Rutledge (1939), 'Suggestions of Keynes in the Writings of Veblen', *Journal of Political Economy*, **47**(5), October, 692–704.

Vining, Rutledge (1949), 'Methological Issues in Quantitative Economics', *Review of Economics and Statistics*, **31**, May, 77–86.

Vromen, Jack J. (1995), *Economic Evolution: An Enquiry into the Foundations of New Institutional Economics*, London: Routledge.

Waddington, Conrad H. (ed.) (1972), *Towards a Theoretical Biology*, 4 vols., Edinburgh: Edinburgh University Press.

Waddington, Conrad H. (1975), *The Evolution of an Evolutionist*, Ithaca: Cornell University Press.

Waldrop, M. Mitchell (1992), *Complexity: The Emerging Science at the Edge of Order and Chaos*, New York: Simon and Schuster.

Walker, Donald A. (1996), *Walras's Market Models*, Cambridge: Cambridge University Press.

Waller, Jr, William J. (1988), 'Habit in Economic Analysis', *Journal of Economic Issues*, **22**(1), March, 113–26. Reprinted in Hodgson (1993d).

Walras, Léon (1954), *Elements of Pure Economics, or The Theory of Social Wealth*, translated from the French edition of 1926 by W. Jaffé, New York: Augustus Kelley.

Ward, Benjamin (1972), *What's Wrong With Economics*, London: Macmillan.

Ward, Lester Frank (1893), *The Psychic Factors of Civilization*, Boston.

Watson, John B. (1924), *Behaviorism*, New York: Norton.

Weber, Max (1949), *Max Weber on the Methodology of the Social Sciences,* translated and edited by Edward A. Shils and Henry A. Finch, Glencoe, IL: Free Press.

Weber, Max (1968), *Economy and Society: An Outline of Interpretive Sociology,* 2 vols, translated from the German edition of 1921–1922 by G. Roth and C. Wittich, Berkeley: University of California Press.

Wedderburn, Kenneth W. (1971), *The Worker and the Law,* 2nd edn., Harmondsworth: Penguin.

Weiner, Norbert (1954), *The Human use of Human Beings,* 2nd edn., New York: Houghton Mifflin.

Weingart, Peter, Mitchell, Sandra D, Richerson, Peter J. and Maasen, Sabine (eds) (1997), *Human By Nature: Between Biology and the Social Sciences,* Mahwah, NJ: Lawrence Erlbaum Associates.

Weintraub, E. Roy (1979), *Microfoundations,* Cambridge: Cambridge University Press.

Weintraub, E. Roy (1991), *Stabilizing Dynamics: Constructing Economic Knowledge,* Cambridge: Cambridge University Press.

Wellman, Barry and Berkowitz, S. D. (eds) (1988), *Social Structure: A Network Approach,* Cambridge, MA: Harvard University Press.

Wernerfelt, Birger (1984), 'A Resource-Based View of the Firm', *Strategic Management Journal,* **5**, 171–80.

Wernerfelt, Birger and Montgomery, Cynthia (1988), 'Tobin's Q and the Importance of Focus in Firm Performance', *American Economic Review,* **78**(1), March, 246–50.

White, Harrison C. (1981), 'Where Do Markets Come From?', *American Journal of Sociology,* **87**(3), 517–47. Reprinted in Swedberg (1996).

White, Harrison C. (1992), *Identity and Control: A Structural Theory of Social Action,* Princeton: Princeton University Press.

Whitehead, Alfred N. (1926), *Science and the Modern World,* Cambridge: Cambridge University Press.

Williams, George C. (1966), *Adaptation and Natural Selection,* Princeton, NJ; Princeton University Press.

Williamson, Oliver E. (1975), *Markets and Hierarchies: Analysis and Anti-Trust Implications: A Study in the Economics of Internal Organization,* New York: Free Press.

Williamson, Oliver E. (1979), 'Transaction-Cost Economics: The Governance of Contractual Relations', *Journal of Law and Economics,* **22**(2), October, 233–61.

Williamson, Oliver E. (1985), *The Economic Institutions of Capitalism: Firms, Markets, Relational Contracting,* London: Macmillan.

Williamson, Oliver E. (ed.) (1990), *Organization Theory: From Chester Barnard to the Present and Beyond*, Oxford: Oxford University Press.

Williamson, Oliver E. and Winter, Sidney G. (eds) (1991), *The Nature of the Firm: Origins, Evolution, and Development*, Oxford and New York: Oxford University Press.

Wilson, David Sloan and Sober, Elliott (1989), 'Reviving the Superorganism', *Journal of Theoretical Biology*, **136**, 337–56.

Wilson, Edward O. (1975), *Sociobiology*, Cambridge, MA: Harvard University Press.

Wimsatt, William C. (1980), 'Reductionist Research Strategies and Their Biases in the Units of Selection Controversy', in Nickles, T. (ed.) (1980), *Scientific Discovery, Volume II, Historical and Scientific Case Studies*, Dordrecht, Holland: Reidel, pp. 213–59. Reprinted in Sober (1984b).

Winslow, Edward A. (1989), 'Organic Interdependence, Uncertainty and Economic Analysis', *Economic Journal*, **99**(4), December, 1173–82.

Winter, J. M. (ed.) (1975), *War and Economic Development*, Cambridge, MA: Harvard University Press.

Winter Jr, Sidney G. (1964), 'Economic "Natural Selection" and the Theory of the Firm', *Yale Economic Essays*, **4**(1), 225–72. Reprinted in Hodgson (1998f).

Winter Jr, Sidney G. (1971), 'Satisficing, Selection and the Innovating Remnant', *Quarterly Journal of Economics*, **85**(2), May, 237–61. Reprinted in Witt (1993b).

Winter Jr, Sidney G. (1975), 'Optimization and Evolution in the Theory of the Firm', in Richard H. Day and T. Groves (eds) (1975), *Adaptive Economic Models*, New York: Academic Press, pp. 73–118.

Winter Jr, Sidney G. (1982), 'An Essay on the Theory of Production', in Saul H. Hymans (ed.) (1982), *Economics and the World Around It*, Ann Arbor, Michigan: University of Michigan Press, pp. 55–91.

Winter Jr, Sidney G. (1986a), 'Comments on Arrow and Lucas', *Journal of Business*, **59**(4.2), S427–34. Reprinted in C. Freeman (ed.) (1990), and in R. M. Hogarth and M. W. Reder (eds) (1987), *Rational Choice: The Contrast Between Economics and Psychology*, Chicago, University of Chicago Press.

Winter Jr, Sidney G. (1986b), 'The Research Program of the Behavioral Theory of the Firm: Orthodox Critique and Evolutionary Perspective', in B. Gilad and S. Kaish (eds) (1986), *Handbook of Behavioral Economics, Vol. A, Behavioral Microeconomics*, Greenwich, CT: JAI Press, pp. 151–88.

Winter Jr, Sidney G. (1987a), 'Knowledge and Competence as Strategic Assets', in Teece (1987, pp. 159–84).

Winter Jr, Sidney G. (1987b), 'Competition and Selection', in J. Eatwell, M. Milgate and P. Newman, (eds) (1987), *The New Palgrave Dictionary of Economics*, London: Macmillan, vol. 1, pp. 545–8.

Winter Jr, Sidney G. (1988), 'On Coase, Competence, and the Corporation', *Journal of Law, Economics, and Organization*, 4(1), Spring, 163–80. Reprinted in Williamson and Winter (1991).

Winter Jr, Sidney G. (1990a), 'Survival, Selection, and Inheritance in Evolutionary Theories of Organization', in Singh, Jitendra V. (ed.) (1990), *Organizational Evolution: New Directions*, London: Sage, pp. 269–97.

Winter Jr, Sidney G. (1990b), 'Reply' [to Moss, 1990], *Quarterly Journal of Economics*, 105, 1075–77.

Wispé, Lauren G. and Thompson, James N. (1976), 'The War Between the Words: Biological Versus Social Evolution and Some Related Issues', *American Psychologist*, 31, May.

Witt, Ulrich (1987), *Individualistiche Grundlagen der evolutorischen Ökonomie*, Tübingen: Mohr.

Witt, Ulrich (1991), 'Reflections on the Present State of Evolutionary Economic Theory', in Hodgson and Screpanti (1991, pp. 83–102).

Witt, Ulrich (ed.) (1992), *Explaining Process and Change: Approaches to Evolutionary Economics*, Ann Arbor, MI: University of Michigan Press.

Witt, Ulrich (ed.) (1993a), *Evolution in Markets and Institutions*, Heidelberg: Physica-Verlag.

Witt, Ulrich (ed.) (1993b), *Evolutionary Economics*, Aldershot: Edward Elgar.

Wolfe, Albert B. (1924), 'Functional Economics', in Tugwell (1924, pp. 443–82).

Wright, Sewall (1956), 'Modes of Selection', *American Naturalist*, 90, 5–24.

Wunderlin, Clarence E., Jr (1992), *Visions of a New Industrial Order: Social Science and Labor Theory in America's Progressive Era*, New York: Columbia University Press.

Wynarczyk, Peter (1992), 'Comparing Alleged Incommensurables: Institutional and Austrian Economics as Rivals and Possible Complements?', *Review of Political Economy*, 4(1), January, 18–36.

Yonay, Yuval P. (1997), 'The Theory of Value and the Value of Theory: The Appeals to Practical Value by Conflicting Approaches in Economics, 1918–1939', *Social Science Information*, 36(2), 311–42.

Zelizer, Viviana A. (1993), 'Making Multiple Monies', in Swedberg (1993, pp. 193–212).

Index